PENGUIN CLASSICS

SAINT IGNATIUS OF LOYOLA
PERSONAL WRITINGS

IGNATIUS LOYOLA (1491–1556), youngest son in a noble Basque family, was trained as a page at the court of Castile. He was wounded at the siege of Pamplona (1521), and while convalescing underwent a deep conversion experience. He retired for a year of reflection to Manresa, the notes jotted at that time forming the basis of the influential *Spiritual Exercises*. After a hazardous pilgrimage to Jerusalem, he undertook prolonged studies (mainly in Paris), gradually attracting like-minded students. They took vows in 1534 and shortly afterwards formed what they called the 'Society of Jesus' (popularly known as the 'Jesuits'). From 1540, when Ignatius was elected Superior General, he lived in Rome organizing, largely through a series of *Letters*, the astonishing spread of the Jesuits. He was canonized (along with his disciple, Francis Xavier, and Teresa of Avila) in 1622.

JOSEPH A. MUNITIZ was born in Cardiff in 1931 of Basque parents and educated in Wales and England, before spending three years in Spain. His years of study as a Jesuit included spells in London, Oxford, Spain and Italy. After doctoral work in Paris, he joined the staff of the *Corpus Christianorum*, Louvain, and then returned to edit the *Heythrop Journal* in London. He served as Master of Campion Hall, 1989–98, and retired to become an Honorary Research Fellow of the Centre for Byzantine Studies at the University of Birmingham. He maintains his interest in Jesuit studies as Assistant Novice Master in Harborne (Birmingham).

PHILIP ENDEAN was born in 1954. He read English at Merton College, Oxford, before entering the Society of Jesus in 1977. During his training as a Jesuit he lived in Mexico, the USA, Germany and Austria as well as in the UK. He has worked as a hospital chaplain in Manchester and as a lecturer in theology as Heythrop College, University of London. He now teaches theology at the University of Oxford, and is editor of *The Way*, a journal of Christian spirituality published by the British Jesuits.

SAINT IGNATIUS OF LOYOLA

Personal Writings

Reminiscences, Spiritual Diary, Select Letters
including the text of *The Spiritual Exercises*

Translated with Introductions and Notes by
JOSEPH A. MUNITIZ *and* PHILIP ENDEAN

PENGUIN BOOKS

PENGUIN BOOKS

Published by the Penguin Group
Penguin Books Ltd, 80 Strand, London WC2R ORL, England
Penguin Group (USA) Inc., 375 Hudson Street, New York, New York 10014, USA
Penguin Books Australia Ltd, 250 Camberwell Road, Camberwell, Victoria 3124, Australia
Penguin Books Canada Ltd, 10 Alcorn Avenue, Toronto, Ontario, Canada M4V 3B2
Penguin Books India (P) Ltd, 11 Community Centre, Panchsheel Park, New Delhi – 110 017, India
Penguin Group (NZ), cnr Airborne and Rosedale Roads, Albany, Auckland 1310, New Zealand
Penguin Books (South Africa) (Pty) Ltd, 24 Sturdee Avenue, Rosebank 2196, South Africa

Penguin Books Ltd, Registered Offices: 80 Strand, London WC2R ORL, England

www.penguin.com

First published 1996
Reprinted with updates to Bibliography 2004

037

Translations, introductions and notes copyright © Joseph A. Munitiz and Philip Endean, 1996, 2004
All rights reserved

The moral right of the translators has been asserted

Set in 9.25/11.5pt Monotype Sabon
Typeset by Datix International Limited, Bungay, Suffolk
Printed and bound in Great Britain by Clays Ltd, Elcograf S.p.A.

ISBN-13: 978-0-14-043385-2

www.greenpenguin.co.uk

Penguin Books is committed to a sustainable
future for our business, our readers and our planet.
This book is made from Forest Stewardship
Council™ certified paper.

Contents

* Numbers in square brackets are those of the letters in the MHSI edition.

THE SPIRITUAL EXERCISES

Preface

Occasionally a writer's influence is in indirect proportion to the size of his work: there can be few more decisive examples of this phenomenon than Ignatius Loyola. The only work of his to be published in his own lifetime was a Latin translation, made by a French colleague, of a very short handbook written in Spanish and bearing the title *The Spiritual Exercises*. Only 500 copies were printed and it is clear that Ignatius was extremely loath to distribute this book. Who in his day would have imagined that one day he would be included in the Penguin Classics series? To carry the paradox even further, the strongest advocate for the key importance of Ignatius as a writer has been not a member of the Society he founded, and not even a confessional believer in Christianity, but a sophisticated agnostic, the acute literary critic and pioneer in semiotics, Roland Barthes. He pointed out that Loyola shares with Sade and Fourier the distinction of being a 'logothete', one of the *fondateurs de langues*,[1] and he analyses with great finesse the levels of language, the conceptual architectonics and the sensitivity to signs to be found in the *Exercises*.

One may be excused for thinking that Barthes founded his appreciation of Loyola simply on the *Exercises*. In reality he also had access to a French translation of the *Spiritual Diary*, and he mentions in passing the 'Autobiography'.[2] This recognition of the importance of Loyola's other writings, in particular of those writings in which he was personally committed, underlies the publication of the present collection of Personal Writings, which has been conceived primarily as a first-hand introduction to a remarkable man, whose influence in the development of spiritual awareness has been unique. The texts are chosen leaving to one side his other writings that enter self-consciously into the public domain: thus Ignatius's major work, the *Constitutions*, the foundation document for the Society of Jesus, is not represented here and from his extant correspondence only a tiny proportion (as explained below), with the minimum of 'official' documents, has been included.

This collection opens with the *Reminiscences*: some may wonder if this text, preserved in the memory of a disciple serving as a human dictaphone, strictly deserves to be accepted as a 'writing' of Ignatius, but the force of his personality is certainly mirrored in these pages as Ignatius recounts his early life prior to his work as Superior General of the Society of Jesus. Next comes *The Spiritual Diary*, dating from 1544–45, with the *Pros and Cons* as a necessary preliminary. It is followed by forty *Letters*, each with its own short presentation and notes. In fourth place, and treated rather as an Appendix, the text of the *Spiritual Exercises* is printed once more.

The appeal of writings such as the last may have to remain something of an acquired taste. However, it will help if a sharp distinction is drawn between the main texts in this collection and that of the *Spiritual Exercises* (reproduced here as an indispensable background to all the other writings). The *Exercises* originated in the form of prayer notes, outlines of sequences of thoughts that had helped Ignatius as he reflected in silence before God. They take on meaning only in that sort of context. But the difficulty increases because these random notes were subsequently placed in a deliberate order, designed to foment a process (or *dialectique* as one outstanding French commentator called it[3]) within which they take on a peculiar power. When removed from their context they become as pointless as swimming instructions given to somebody who has no access to water. Fortunately this is not true of the main body of writings represented here. Although very personal, they attempt to communicate directly, or they try to pin down in words, experiences that may not be at everybody's disposal. Unlike the *Exercises* they are not attempting to initiate a dialogue between a person and the divine (*l'interlocution divine*, as Barthes termed it), though they will have a special interest for those interested in mystical phenomena as such, or in persons who claim to have experienced them. And clearly they will also have an interest for those who have heard of Loyola and the Jesuits, but have never had the opportunity to gain first-hand knowledge of either. Finally, if one compares the Personal Writings with the *Exercises* one sees how Ignatius learnt from his own rich experience of the One he called 'God', and yet at the same time could distance himself from it so as to make available what he had learned to a wide range of people. The Jesuit poet Gerard Manley Hopkins remarked that 'the effect of studying masterpieces is to make me admire and do otherwise'.[4] The Personal Writings may well present us with something to admire; the *Spiritual Exercises* aim to help us discover how we might do otherwise.

Among those to be thanked for their help with this edition, William

Hewett, the Jesuit founder of Inigo Enterprises in London, must come first in this list; it was he who encouraged, cajoled, and found the resources at the critical initial moments; this volume contains texts originally published by him, and, it is hoped, will encourage others to profit from his further publications.[5] Those who have collaborated in the production of this book are mentioned in the introductions to the various sections, but a special word of thanks is due to Michael Ivens and Philip Endean, who were the most closely involved. Paul Keegan, the Advisory Editor of Penguin Classics, Michael Campbell-Johnston, former Provincial of the British Jesuits, and my Campion Hall community have all put me very much in their debt.

Joseph A. Munitiz

NOTES

1 Roland Barthes, *Sade, Fourier, Loyola*, Editions du Seuil, Paris 1971; however, the essay on Loyola first appeared in *Tel Quel* 38, 1969 under the title 'Comment parler à Dieu?' two years after the first publication of the essay on Sade.

2 He uses the French title *Récit du Pèlerin*, published here as *Reminiscences*.

3 Gaston Fessard, *La dialectique des Exercices spirituels de saint Ignace de Loyola*, Aubier, Paris 1956.

4 *The Letters of Gerard Manley Hopkins to Robert Bridges*, ed. C. C. Abbott, Oxford University Press, London 1935, Letter 166, p. 291.

5 For information on these and other ventures, contact Inigo Enterprises, 1 Wickham Drive, Hurstpierpoint, Sussex BN6 9AP.

Chronology

1491   The date of birth remains problematic, though confirmed by (1) the testimony of Ignatius's wet-nurse, María de Garín, (2) a legal document dated 1505 only valid if Ignatius was at least fourteen years of age, combined with other testimony that he was not born before 1491. The family was distinguished in the Basque country, possessed considerable land, and had contacts with the Castilian nobility. The baptismal names were Iñigo López, the first of these being the one most used until the name 'Ignatius' began to appear.

1506   Move to Arévalo (some miles north of Avila) to serve as page in the household of Juan Velázquez de Cuéllar, Treasurer of King Ferdinand of Castile; formal courtly education.

1515   Summoned for involvement in brawl near Loyola.

1517   Financial ruin and death of his patron; Iñigo obtains post in the retinue of Antonio Manrique, Duke of Nájera and Viceroy of Navarre.

1521   Successful diplomatic mission in Guipúzcoa; then disastrous defence of Pamplona, where his right leg is shattered; operation and convalescence; conversion experience.

1522   Visits Montserrat; then moves temporarily to Manresa, where he leads a life of prayer and penance.

1523   Pilgrimage to Jerusalem, via Rome and Venice.

1524   Settles in Barcelona, starts private studies: first text of *Spiritual Exercises* (?); Letter 1.

1526   Moves (with three followers) to Alcalá for University studies; first ecclesiastical trial.

1527   Second and third trials; moves to Salamanca; interrogated by Dominicans, new trial.

1528   Moves alone to Paris, and re-starts studies.

1529–35   Arts course, with begging journeys to Flanders and England in search of funds; 'First Companions' contacted.

1532   Letters 2, 3.

1534   'Vows' at Montmartre.

1535   Travels to Spain (return visit to Loyola) and Italy.

1536   Private theology studies in Venice; Letters 4–7.

1537   First Companions regroup; ordination to priesthood, Letter 8; move to Rome, with vision at La Storta; well received by Pope Paul III.

1538   After one year's wait, proposed move to Jerusalem seen to be impossible; meets strong opposition in Rome, overcome by recourse to Pope; acquittal at trial; Letters 9–10.

1539   Deliberations about founding of new order; project arouses strong criticism.

1540   Papal Bull founding the Society of Jesus; departure of Xavier for India.

1541   Preliminary draft of *Constitutions*; election as Superior General and first formal vows.

1542–43   Growth of correspondence; active philanthropic work in Rome (with prostitutes, Jews, children).

1544–45   Discernment process recorded – *Spiritual Diary* – and begins writing of *Constitutions*.

1546   Society takes active part in Council of Trent (Letter 14); Francis Borgia joins secretly (Letter 13); opposition to episcopal dignities (Letter 15).

1547–49   Arrival of Polanco as secretary (Letter 18); alarming developments in Portugal (Letters 16, 20) and Gandía (Letters 17, 22–23); educational interests (Letter 24).

1550   Holy Year; finishes first draft of *Constitutions*; Francis Borgia in Rome announces his membership of the Society.

1551   Initial approval of *Constitutions* by all available First Companions; letter of resignation (Letter 26); founding of Roman College.

1552–54   Despite chronic ill-health (especially in 1553) active administration, with particular reflection on nature of obedience (Letters 28, 31), involvement in high political spheres (Letter 30) and education.

1553, 1555   Dictation of *Reminiscences*; continued administration (Letters 34–40).

1556   Constant ill-health, then sudden death in the morning of 31 July.

Glossary

affections/attachments (*afecciones*) Key terms in the psychological vocabulary of the *Spiritual Exercises* (Exx.); they refer to all the feelings of liking and disliking that well up in the heart and can impede objective judgement; they operate on many levels of the self, but those called in question in the Exx. are the profound influences that alter perceptions of reality; in English this sense of 'affection' has been almost lost (but cp. 'well affected' or 'disaffected').

application of the senses (*traer los sentidos*) Translated here as 'bringing the senses to bear' (Exx. 121–26), or 'prayer of the senses' (it was the Latin version that led to the now traditional title 'application of the senses'); this is a method in prayer by which one deliberately tries to imagine particular sensual details (sounds, colours, etc.) of a Gospel or other scene in order to feel part of it in a reflective, contemplative way. Ignatius seems to have been temperamentally of unusual aesthetic sensitivity, and this 'prayer of the senses' enabled him to practise a deep prayer, somewhat belied by its title, and really the culmination of a day of prayer.

coadjutors Members of the Society who are not 'professed', and therefore originally expected to be less mobile; they could be 'spiritual' coadjutors if they were priests, and 'temporal' coadjutors if they were laymen; these grades were instituted in 1546 and still exist, if in a modified form.

collateral A counsellor appointed to help certain superiors; although Ignatius was partial to the use of such officials, the post was later found to be impractical and abandoned. See **síndico** (below).

colloquy (*coloquio*) A quasi-technical term invented by Ignatius to indicate the prayer of familiar conversation that he encourages as the culmination of an exercise, and which calls for special reverence (Exx. 3); its 'normal' place comes towards the end (following the overall movement of prayer from mind to the heart), but it may occur spontaneously at any time (Exx. 53–54, 109, 199).

composition (*composición*) A preliminary to prayer, as one 'composes' oneself, by 'composing' (= recalling to mind) the locale of the scene being contemplated or by imagining a suitable setting for a topic, e.g. a happy, or a shameful, or an awesome situation (Exx. 47, 151, 232).

consolations (*consolaciones*) Exx. 316, 329–36; the complete gratuitousness of God-given consolation (consolation 'without cause') strongly impressed Ignatius and steered him clear of the Pelagian leanings that some critics have suspected in his teaching, but left him open to attack as an 'illuminist' heretic.

Constitutions Written by Ignatius (with some reluctance as he would have preferred the members to be guided by an unwritten *esprit de corps*) between his appointment as Superior General (1541) and 1550, the Holy Year proclaimed by the Pope, when they were submitted to the judgement of as many of the original group as could come to Rome. They were gradually publicized by close associates deputed by him and had not been officially promulgated at Ignatius's death.

contemplation A traditional term used by Ignatius (along with the term 'meditation') in a personal way. For him, whereas one 'contemplates' when praying about the person of Christ, one 'meditates' when praying about certain truths (mainly First Week subjects and the fourth day exercises of the Second Week). While for 'contemplation' the imagination unlocks the door, and leads to intimate, receptive prayer of the heart, for 'meditation' thought is initially required (as one ponders), even if ideally the latter will also merge into the former. But this is a far cry from the technical use of 'contemplation' to mean a form of infused mystical prayer.

desolations Exx. 317–24.

discernment (*discreción*) The Ignatian quality par excellence, and the key to the whole process of the Exercises, which are designed to facilitate a just appraisal, before God, of the movements felt in the heart and weighed by the mind (the consolations and desolations that figure so prominently, Exx. 6 and 328); Ignatius's discovery of this ability triggered his conversion, and guided him throughout his life.

examens The practice of self-correction recommended in the Exercises, Exx. 24f.

Exercises The term is explained in Annotation 1 (Exx. 1); Ignatius clearly intended his *Spiritual Exercises*, at least in their full form, for a restricted number of individuals, but the emphasis from the beginning is on openness and generosity (Exx. 5) rather than will-power.

feel The Spanish word *sentir* is a favourite of Ignatius, and to accentuate this it is usually translated here by 'feel', even if it has a wider gamut of meanings (e.g. 'to be aware').

First Companions Pierre Favre (the only priest in the group), Nicolás Bobadilla, Diego Laínez, Simão Rodrigues, Alfonso Salmerón, Francis Xavier, along with Ignatius made an initial vow at Montmartre, Paris, on 15 August 1534; the vow was repeated in 1535 and 1536, and although Ignatius was absent, the others were joined by new 'companions', viz. Jean Codure, Claude Le Jay and Paschase Broët. These men later came to a mutual decision to found the Society of Jesus as a religious order (1539).

General The overall superior of the Society in Rome.

indifference (*ser indiferente*) One of the key concepts in the Exx. (see 23, 157, 179), yet easily misunderstood if taken in a philosophical rather than a religious sense; one may 'feel' far from indifferent, but be prepared to wish to relinquish something out of love of God.

Institute The whole ethos (spirit, moral body, Constitutions) of a religious order.

meditation Cf. **contemplation**.

mortal sins In the Exx. 'mortal sins' can be either particular grave, deliberate actions (the traditional examples being homicide, adultery and apostasy), or – and in this case the translation 'capital sins' is given – the seven 'vices', habitual tendencies to evil (like pride, gluttony, avarice, etc.). But the two senses are often intertwined, and further confused by a sixteenth-century moral teaching which tended to blunt the spiritual sense of sin as the profound rejection of (and death to) God.

narrative Literally the 'history' (*historia*), a regular preamble to prayer; usually the recall of a particular Gospel passage or story, but in a wider sense any form of preliminary review of the subject-matter, with a characteristic preference for the concrete over the abstract (Exx. 2, 102, 111, 137 etc.).

ours Shorthand in the *Letters* for 'members of the Society of Jesus'.

professed (*profesos*) Priest members of the Society with final vows (included among these being a formal commitment to go to any country to which the Pope might wish to send them); initially (1540) the number was limited to sixty, but the restriction was soon lifted (1544).

Provincial The Superior with responsibility for a particular geographical area.

repetition A favourite technique of Ignatius, and easily misunderstood: an exercise is not to be simply 'repeated', but a selection is made from the material previously used, attention focusing on those insights and feelings that stand out, allowing prayer to well up, without haste or strain as the rhythm of the day moves from the head to the heart (Exx. 62, 118).

scholastics Members of the Society who are in training, either for the priesthood or for further studies; this period ends with final vows.

senses See **application of the senses**.

síndico From the Greek word meaning something like 'public prosecutor', but applied to an office customary in medieval universities; the post is mentioned several times in the *Constitutions*. Although similar to the **collateral** (*Const.* 505), he is expected to be more critical.

soul Either, in a more precise sense, the spiritual component in the body–soul dichotomy, or more in general, a human person.

spirits (*espíritus*) A classical term, dating back to the Desert Fathers at least, to refer to various psychological phenomena, roughly good and bad 'feelings' that are pictured as personified; see Exx. 8, 9, 313–36.

vows Formal promises to God to observe certain obligations. The usual religious vows cover poverty (renunciation of all rights to private possession), chastity (the practice of sexual purity), and obedience (willingness to accept orders from a legitimate superior); vows in the Society of Jesus can be 'first vows' at the end of the novitiate or 'final vows' at the end of training. On the danger of rushing (or pushing) into vows, see Exx. 15.

Bibliography

ABBREVIATIONS

AHSI   *Archivum Historicum Societatis Iesu*
BAC   Biblioteca de Autores Cristianos (cf. Complete Works)
Const.   *Constitutions* (MHSI numbering)
Dict. Sp. *Dictionnaire de Spiritualité,* ed. M. Viller and others, Beauchesne, Paris 1937–95
Epist.   *Letters* (MHSI ed.)
Exx.   *Exercises* (MHSI numbering)
FD   Fontes Documentales (MHSI)
FN   Fontes Narrativi (MHSI)
MHSI   Monumenta Historica Societatis Iesu
MI   Monumenta Ignatiana (MHSI)
MN   Monumenta Nadal (MHSI)
PG   *Patrologia Graeca,* ed. J. P. Migne, Paris 1857–66
PL   *Patrologia Latina,* ed. J. P. Migne, Paris 1844–64
Rem.   *Reminiscences* (= *Autobiography*)

I. PRIMARY SOURCES

Complete Works

MHSI provide all the standard texts
IPARRAGUIRRE, Ignacio, *Obras completas de San Ignacio de Loyola. Edición Manual,* BAC, Madrid, 1st ed. 1963 (5th ed. 1991)

Important translations:

(English trans.) GANSS, George E., and a group of English-speaking Jesuits including Parmananda Divarkar (Autobiography), *Ignatius of Loyola: The Spiritual Exercises and Selected Works,* Paulist Press, New York/Mahwah 1991
(French trans.) GIULIANI, Maurice, and a group of French Jesuits

including Antoine Lauras and Jean-Claude Dhôtel (Autobiography), Gervais Dumeige (Letters), *Ignace de Loyola: Écrits*, Collection Christus No. 76, *Textes*, Desclée de Brouwer, Bellarmin, Paris 1991

Autobiography/Reminiscences

LARRAÑAGA, Victoriano, *Obras completas de San Ignacio de Loyola*, I: *Autobiografía* (with a very full commentary), BAC, Madrid 1947

RAMBLA BLANCH, Josep María, *El Peregrino: Autobiografía de San Ignacio de Loyola*, Mensajero and Sal Terrae, Bilbao/Santander 1991 (1st ed. in Catalan 1983)

(English trans.) DIVARKAR, Parmananda, *A Pilgrim's Testament: The Memoirs of Ignatius of Loyola*, Rome 1983 (reprinted in the *Complete Works*, ed. George E. Ganss)

(English trans.) TYLENDA, Joseph N., *A Pilgrim's Journey: The Autobiography of Ignatius of Loyola*, Michael Glazier, Wilmington, DE 1985

(English trans.) YEOMANS, William, *Inigo: Original Testament, The Autobiography of St Ignatius Loyola*, Inigo Texts (William Hewett), London 1985

(French trans.) *see Complete Works*

(German trans.) SCHNEIDER, Burkhart, *Ignatius von Loyola: Der Bericht des Pilgers*, Herder, Freiburg/Basel/Vienna 1977

(German trans.) KNAUER, Peter, *Ignatius von Loyola: Der Bericht des Pilgers*, Leipzig 1990

Constitutions

(English trans.) GANSS, George E., *The Constitutions of the Society of Jesus: Translated with an Introduction and a Commentary*, The Institute of Jesuit Sources, St Louis, MO 1970

The Spiritual Diary

LARRAÑAGA, Victoriano, *Obras completas de San Ignacio de Loyola*, I, *Autobiografía* (with a very full commentary), BAC, Madrid 1947

THIO DE POL, Santiago, *La Intimidad del Paregrino* (remarkable edition of the original text with a Spanish paraphrase), Mensajero and Sal Terrae, Bilbao/Santander n.d.

(English trans.) YOUNG, William J., 'The Spiritual Journal of Saint Ignatius', *Woodstock Letters* 87 (1958), pp. 195–267 (repr. in Simon Decloux, *Commentaries on the Letters and Spiritual Diary of St Ignatius Loyola*, Rome 1980

(English trans.) MUNITIZ, Joseph A., *Inigo: Discernment Log-Book*, Inigo Enterprises, London 1987

(French trans.) GIULIANI, Maurice, *Saint Ignace. Journal spirituel*, Collection Christus, I, Desclée de Brouwer, Paris 1959 (completely revised version, in collaboration with P. A. Fabre, included in the French translation of *Complete Works* above-mentioned)

(German trans.) KNAUER, Peter (with introduction by Adolf Haas), *Ignatius von Loyola. Das Geistliche Tagebuch*, Herder, Freiburg 1961

The Spiritual Exercises

Two classical editions with commentaries:

CALVERAS, José (ed.), *Ejercicios espirituales: Directorio y Documentos de S. Ignacio de Loyola*, Editorial Balmes, Barcelona, 2nd ed. 1958

DALMASES, Cándido de, *Ejercicios Espirituales*, Sal Terrae, Santander 1987

Letters

(English trans.) YOUNG, William J., *Letters of St Ignatius of Loyola*, Loyola University Press, Chicago 1959

(French trans.) *see Complete Works*

(German and English trans.) *see* RAHNER, Hugo (SECONDARY SOURCES)

2. SECONDARY SOURCES

BERTRAND, Dominique, *La politique de Saint Ignace de Loyola: l'analyse sociale*, (first major sociological study of the letters), Cerf, Paris 1985

CARAMAN, Philip, *Ignatius Loyola* (concise, factual and pleasant introduction), Collins, London 1990

DALMASES, Cándido de, *Ignatius of Loyola; Founder of the Jesuits, His Life and Works* (dry survey by a distinguished expert), Institute of Jesuit Sources, St Louis, MO 1985 (= *El Padre Maestro Ignacio: Breve biografía Ignaciana*, BAC, Madrid 1979; 2nd ed. 1982)

ENDEAN, Philip, 'Who do you say Ignatius is? Jesuit fundamentalism and beyond' (programme article on source criticism), *Studies in the Spirituality of Jesuits*, 19 (5), 1987

LONSDALE, David, *Eyes to See, Ears to Hear: An Introduction to Ignatian Spirituality*, Darton, Longman & Todd, London 1990

MEISSNER, W. W., SJ, *Ignatius of Loyola: The Psychology of a Saint* (an important Freudian analysis of personality traits), Yale University Press, New Haven and London 1992

O'MALLEY, John W., *The First Jesuits* (masterly historical study of the nascent Society of Jesus), Harvard University Press, Cambridge, MA 1993

RAHNER, Hugo, *Saint Ignatius Loyola: Letters to Women* (pioneer exploration of Ignatius's relations with women), Herder, Freiburg; Nelson, Edinburgh–London 1960 (= *Ignatius von Loyola, Briefwechsel mit Frauen*, Herder, Freiburg 1956)

RAVIER, André, *Ignatius of Loyola and the Founding of the Society of Jesus* (original study of key administrative problems), Ignatius Press, San Francisco 1987 (= *Ignace de Loyola fonde la Compagnie de Jésus*, Desclée de Brouwer, Paris 1974)

SCHURHAMMER, Georg (trans. M. Joseph Costelloe, SJ), *Francis Xavier: His Life, His Times*, 4 vols; I: *Europe 1506–1541*, II: *India 1541–1545*, III: *Indonesia and India 1545–1549*, IV: *Japan and China 1549–1552* (encyclopedic biography of Ignatius's contemporary), The Jesuit Historical Institute, Rome 1973, 1977, 1980, 1982 (= *Franz Xaver: sein Leben und seine Zeit*, Verlag Herder, Freiburg im Breisgau 1955, 1963, 1971, 1973)

TELLECHEA IDÍGORAS, I. (tr. Cornelius Michael Buckley), *Ignatius of Loyola: The Pilgrim Saint* (original, well-researched life by Spanish scholar), Loyola University Press, Chicago 1994

ADDITIONS TO BIBLIOGRAPHY

Since 1996 the most important addition to the Bibliography is the commentary on the *Exercises* published by Michael Ivens, *Understanding the Spiritual Exercises: A Handbook for Retreat Directors* (Gracewing and

Inigo Enterprises, Leominster 1998); he has drawn on a translation of the early 'directories' to the *Exercises* also published in 1996 by Martin E. Palmer, *On Giving the Spiritual Exercises* (The Institute of Jesuit Sources, St Louis). The translation of the *Exercises* to be found in the Ivens volume has now been published separately (Gracewing and Inigo Enterprises 2004).

As Carl Jung had lectured on the *Exercises*, Kenneth L. Becker examines his comments in *Unlikely Companions: C. G. Jung on the Spiritual Exercises of Ignatius of Loyola* (Gracewing and Inigo Enterprises 2001). Feminist issues in the *Exercises* are explored in *The Spiritual Exercises Reclaimed: Uncovering Liberating Possibilities for Women* by Katherine Dyckman, Mary Garvin and Elizabeth Liebert (Paulist Press, New York 2001). The sources of the *Exercises* have been investigated in a collection of Spanish studies edited by Juan Plazaola, *Las fuentes de los Ejercicios Espirituales de San Ignacio* (Mensajero, Bilbao 1998). On Ignatius himself an ambitious work also in Spanish planned to be in two volumes has been launched: Ignacio Cacho, *Iñigo de Loyola: ese enigma* (Instituto Ignacio de Loyola, Mensajero, Bilbao 2003), and the psychoanalyst William Meissner has followed up his earlier work on Ignatius (see above) with a study of the *Exercises*, *To the Greater Glory of God: A Psychological Study of Ignatian Spirituality* (Marquette University Press 1999). David Lonsdale has also added a new chapter to a second edition (2000) of his book. Philip Endean, the co-editor of the present work, has contributed an in-depth theological study, *Karl Rahner and Ignatian Spirituality* (Oxford Theological Monographs, Oxford 2001), and the American scholar Marjorie O'Rourke Boyle studies the rhetorical aspects of the *Reminiscences* (Autobiography) in her book *Loyola's Acts: The Rhetoric of the Self* (University of California, Berkeley 1997). A contemporary account of Ignatius written by a Portuguese Jesuit, Luis Gonçalves da Câmara, is due to be published in English translation, *Remembering Iñigo* (trans. A. Eaglestone and J. A. Munitiz, S.J., Institute of Jesuit Sources, St Louis, along with Gracewing and Inigo Enterprises, Leominster 2004). Finally, the journal *The Way* (published from Campion Hall, Oxford) regularly publishes articles on Ignatian spirituality and makes a wide range of material available through its website (www.theway.org.uk).

REMINISCENCES

or Autobiography of Ignatius Loyola

as heard and written down by
LUIS GONÇALVES DA CÂMARA

translated with an introduction and notes by
PHILIP ENDEAN

Introduction

1. This particular account of Ignatius's life, written up from his own spoken narrative, seems to have arisen from initiatives taken by two of his followers: Jerónimo Nadal, who perhaps did more than anyone else to consolidate and institutionalize the Society of Jesus, and Luis Gonçalves da Câmara, the faithful, almost adoring scribe to whom Ignatius recounted his memories.

Why were these two men interested in having a text based on Ignatius's reminiscences? Nadal tells us of how he was anxious that the elderly Ignatius, having achieved his major goals, would soon die.

Since I knew that the holy Fathers, the founders of any monastic institute, normally gave those coming after, as a substitute for a bequest, such advice on which they would be able to rely as something that could be of help to them in attaining perfection of virtue, I was on the lookout for a time when I could tactfully ask Fr Ignatius for the same thing. It came in 1551 when we were together, as Fr Ignatius said, 'Just now I was higher than the sky', having undergone (I think) some ecstasy or rapture of mind, as he often used to. Reverently I asked, 'What kind of thing is this, Father?'. He diverted the talk to other things. Thinking therefore that time to be opportune, I asked and entreated Father to be pleased to expound to us how the Lord had guided him from the beginning of his conversion, so that this exposition could take for us the place of a bequest and fatherly teaching.[1]

Gonçalves da Câmara tells us of how Nadal came back to Rome from Spain in 1554, when the story-telling was in abeyance:

But when Fr Nadal came, being very pleased with what had been begun, he told me to pester Father, telling me many times that in nothing could Father do more good for the Society than in doing this, and that this was truly to found the Society.

'Truly to found the Society.' The Society of Jesus was innovative, even revolutionary, at once drawing on other traditions of religious life and radically departing from them. Many outsiders found it quite incomprehensible, and the same may well have been true of many of its second-generation recruits, particularly in Spain and Portugal. Nadal was a skilled linguist, a trained humanist and a gifted administrator. After pioneering work as founding rector of the Jesuit college in Messina, Sicily, he was commissioned by Ignatius to travel through Europe presenting his newly drafted legislation for the Society, the *Constitutions*. That meant explaining the rationale of this new foundation, in which dedication to ministry replaced traditional practices such as office in choir.

A leading theme in the rationale Nadal developed was that of a particular grace proper to the Society of Jesus, initially focused in the life of its founder, Ignatius. Hence knowledge of Ignatius's life-story was of crucial importance for those later generations who could not know him in the flesh. As Nadal put it in Alcalá in 1561, the first way for Jesuits to come to know their vocation was

talk in detail about our Father Ignatius, the beginning used by God as a means for imparting this grace, and willed to be the one to channel this vocation to others.[2]

Though the first Jesuits always acknowledged the initial inspiration of Ignatius in bringing them together, their earliest deliberations and decision-processes seem to have been corporate, with Ignatius as a kind of first among equals. It was the second generation of Jesuit leaders, notably Nadal, who stressed the image of Ignatius as solitary founder, not without resistance from some of their predecessors.[3]

2. Gonçalves da Câmara, a Portuguese, was also motivated by concern for the Society's healthy growth. He had come to Rome in 1553 in order to report on the troubled affairs of the Portuguese province (documented in a number of the Letters in the present volume), and had been a leading instigator in the removal from office of Simão Rodrigues, the first Provincial and one of Ignatius's Paris companions. He stayed in Rome until October 1555, becoming minister of the Roman house (in overall charge of the house's practical administration) in October 1554. While in this latter post, he kept a notebook (conventionally entitled the *Memoriale*) recording various things that Ignatius said and did. He tells us that one of the reasons he had long wanted to come to Rome was

the desire to have obedience of the understanding, of which I had heard so much talk in the Society. And it seemed to me that to be able to attain this virtue a good means would be to hear the teaching from the person whose ideas regarding matters of the Society are to be regarded similarly to the first principles of any science: it is neither customary nor possible to demonstrate these principles within the science.[4]

'Obedience of the understanding' is a juridical term, and may now sound degrading;[5] for Gonçalves da Câmara it must have been full of associations arising from the Portuguese conflicts. But Gonçalves da Câmara's talk of first principles here points to an insight he only half grasps, namely that a religious organization's juridical language can be properly understood only in and through a living relationship: a relationship with the persons who give the organization concerned its verve and inspiration.

Thus, whereas Nadal explained the importance of Ignatius's story in juridical and theological terms, Gonçalves da Câmara illustrates the point more personally. His account of how the *Reminiscences* originated, probably written while Ignatius was still alive, presents the narrative as emerging from a moment when the master's story enriched the disciple. And the incident seems finally to have persuaded the master himself to overcome his reticence.

In the year 1553, one Friday in the morning, 4 August, the vigil of Our Lady of the Snows, as Father was in the garden near the house or apartment which is called 'The Duke's',[6] I began to give him an account of some characteristic features of my soul, and among others I told him about vainglory. The remedy Father gave me was that I should often make an act of attributing everything in me to God, working to offer him all the good I might find in myself, acknowledging it as his and giving him thanks for it. On this he spoke to me in such a way that it greatly consoled me, in such a way that I couldn't hold back the tears. And so it was that Father told me how he had been troubled by this vice for two years, to such an extent that, when he was getting on the boat in Barcelona for Jerusalem, he didn't dare tell anyone he was going to Jerusalem, and likewise with other similar details.[7] And he added further how much peace in this regard he had later felt in his soul.

An hour or two later we went into dinner. While Master Polanco and I were eating with him, our Father said that Master Nadal and others of the Society had many times asked him to do something, and that he had never made up his mind about it, but that, having recollected himself in his room after having spoken with me, he had had such great devotion and such a great inclination to do it, and (speaking in such a way as to show that God had given him great clarity on his duty to do it) he had made his mind up completely. And the thing was to give an account of all that had passed through his soul up to that time. And he had also decided that it was to be myself to whom he would reveal these things.

Nadal can speak of how God founds the Society in Ignatius;[8] Gonçalves da Câmara illustrates what that means in the life of his followers.

3. Despite what has just been said, Ignatius still seems to have been hesitant about sharing his story. Gonçalves da Câmara's account continues as follows:

Father was then very ill, and never accustomed to promising himself a day of life. On the contrary, when someone says, 'I'll do this in two weeks' time or a week's time', Father always says, as if astounded, 'Really? And you expect to live that long?'. Nevertheless, that time he said that he expected to live three or four months in order to finish this thing.

The next day I spoke to him asking when he wanted us to begin. And he answered me that I should remind him about it each day (I can't remember how many days) until he was in a position to do it. Then, not being in such a position given his occupations, he later decided that I should remind him about it every Sunday. Then in September (I can't remember what day), Father called me and began to tell me his whole life, including his mischiefs as a lad, clearly and distinctly, with all their surrounding details. Afterwards he called me three or four times in the same month and arrived with the story at when he was in Manresa for some days, as can be seen written in a different handwriting.

Gonçalves da Câmara goes on to describe Ignatius's style of speaking and his own method of transcription. Without saying anything to Ignatius, he would go off immediately and write the narrative up in note form. Later he would make a fuller version. This process continued into September 1553, when it broke off:

From then on until Fr Nadal came, on 18 October 1554, Father was always excusing himself with various illnesses and with different matters of business that would arise, saying to me, 'When such and such a business is finished, remind me about it'. And when that business was finished, I would remind him about it, and he would say, 'Now we're in the middle of this other matter; when it's finished, remind me about it'.

As we have already seen, Nadal came back and encouraged Gonçalves da Câmara:

He spoke in the same way to Father many times, and Father told me that I should remind him about it when the business of the college's endowment was finished.

And when that was finished, 'when the matter of Prester John was finished and the post was gone'.

We began to continue the story on 9 March. Then Pope Julius III began to be dangerously ill, and died on the 23rd. Father went on deferring the matter until there was a Pope. He too, when there was one, at once fell ill and died (that was Marcellus). Father delayed until the election of Pope Paul IV.[9] And after that, with the great heat and the many occupations, he was always waylaid until 21 September, when there began to be moves to send me to Spain.[10]

On this account I put much pressure on Father to deliver what he had promised me. So he fixed it then for the 22nd in the morning, in the Rossi Tower.[11] Thus, when I had finished saying mass,[12] I went up to him to ask if it was time. He replied that I was to go and wait for him in the Rossi Tower, so that when he himself came I would be there too. I gathered that I would have to wait for a long time. And while I was delayed in one of the corridors with some brother asking me some point of business, Father came and rebuked me because, having transgressed obedience, I wasn't waiting for him in the Rossi Tower. And he was unwilling to do anything that day. Then we really insisted with him, and so he returned to the Rossi Tower, and dictated walking about, as he had always dictated.

In order to look at his face I was always coming a little closer, with Father saying to me, 'Keep the rule'.[13] And when one time I ignored this and came close, and had fallen into this two or three times, he said this to me and went away. In the end he came back again to finish dictating what has been written here, again in the tower. But since I was by now long into preparing for the journey (for the day before the departure was the last on which Father spoke to me about this material), I wasn't able to write a full version of everything in Rome. And because in Genoa I didn't have a Spanish amanuensis, I dictated in Italian what I had brought with me from Rome written in note form. I put an end to this writing in December 1555 in Genoa.

Some details in this account are problematic. In the text itself, we have clear indications that it was begun not in September 1553 but in August, and that it was finished, not on 22 October 1555, the day before Gonçalves da Câmara's departure, but two days earlier, on 20 October.[14] What is clear is that at some point in the narration there was a major break. Where that comes in the text we cannot be sure because we do not have the original manuscript to which Gonçalves da Câmara refers. The switch from Spanish to Italian occurs as Ignatius is in the middle of recounting an incident from his Paris years.

4. In the years immediately following Ignatius's death, it seems that this text was widely diffused. Gonçalves da Câmara made a number of small additions, on the basis of which the scholarly editors of the original conclude that there were at least thirteen manuscripts in circulation.[15] A Latin translation was made by Anibal du Coudray between 1559 and 1561, which was corrected by Nadal himself. In 1567, however, Francis Borgia, now Superior General of the Society, recalled all copies of the manuscript in order to leave the field clear for the first formal biography of Ignatius by Pedro de Ribadeneira.[16]

Ribadeneira and his successors drew on the *Reminiscences*, but the text itself fell into oblivion. The Bollandists included the Latin translation in the *Acta Sanctorum* for July, published in 1731, but the original Spanish and Italian remained unedited until the first edition of Ignatian biographical material in the *Monumenta Historica Societatis Jesu* appeared in 1904. A more critical text was produced in the same series in 1943. This has formed the basis of very many further versions. The *Reminiscences* are now widely used in the training of Jesuits and more generally in conjunction with the giving of the Exercises, while Ribadeneira's polished life has been largely forgotten. But this development is a comparatively recent one.

5. 'Reminiscences' is one of many titles that have been given to this text. Nadal called it 'Things done by Fr Ignatius (*Acta P. Ignatii*) as Fr Luis Gonçalves first wrote them, taking them from the mouth of the Father himself', and 'Some things done by Rev Fr Ignatius, first founder under God of the Society of Jesus'. Modern convention has tended to use the word 'autobiography' while remaining uneasy about it. Many versions take up the term by which Ignatius refers to himself, and offer a title such as 'The pilgrim's story'. The variations indicate the difficulty in determining the nature of the text.

Except on one point there seems little reason to question the accuracy of Gonçalves da Câmara's transcription. He himself tells us:

I made efforts not to put in any word other than those I had heard from Father.

His *Notebook* shows a scrupulous concern to distinguish what Ignatius actually said from his own paraphrases;[17] here in the *Reminiscences*, the use of the third person pronoun in the narrative seems designed to leave Gonçalves da Câmara free to use 'I' for details of which he is unsure; Nadal's preface speaks of Gonçalves da Câmara's excellent memory. However, the latter's preface does tell us how Ignatius recounted all his 'mischiefs as a lad'. By contrast the written text begins by dismissing these in a sentence. Moreover, the sentence in question is almost certainly wrong, in that it describes Ignatius as being twenty-six at the time of the Battle of Pamplona, whereas other sources indicate he was twenty-nine or thirty. It could well be a fabrication, substituting for a more explicit beginning.[18]

The title *Reminiscences*, which follows the lead of an earlier German translation, is meant to suggest the selectiveness of the account: we have what Ignatius chooses or happens to remember, and no more. The narrative effectively starts in 1521 and breaks off in 1538. We hear nothing of Ignatius's formative years in Castile, or of the complex adjustments and renegotiations that must have marked his years as the Society's Superior General. Further, even within its time-frame, there are important matters on which the text is silent. Ignatius and other Jesuit writers present his time at Manresa as one of intense self-absorption, and the years in Barcelona as a period of struggling to study. By contrast, the testimony collected in connection with Ignatius's beatification and canonization suggests that Ignatius was even then a much more public religious figure, well known in those towns.[19] Again, the move to Paris must have been highly significant for Ignatius's development. He became an exile dedicated to serious study; he acquired a stable, international group of companions; he seems to have taken a decision to seek ordination. The narrative, however, tells us nothing about how he reacted to the intellectual world in which he was moving. The recruiting of the companions is peripheral to the story, and Ignatius simply tells us, without warning, that he and others from the group were ordained.

The narrative we have is therefore a highly selective one, but the principles of selection remain unknown. Was Ignatius deliberately selecting only those details that he thought would help his followers? The ecclesiastical and intellectual atmosphere changed in Rome during the first decades of the Society's existence, as it became clear that all hope of reconciliation with the Lutheran movement was lost. Is Ignatius, in Rome of the 1550s, filtering out aspects of his life in Spain thirty years earlier that might now look embarrassing? Or are the gaps to be explained simply by the ups and downs of the dictation process? How do the *Reminiscences* dictated to Gonçalves da Câmara relate to other dictated reminiscences underlying other, largely untranslated, early Jesuit narratives of Ignatius's life? Our own age's overwhelming preference for Gonçalves da Câmara's text may in fact be as one-sided as an earlier age's for Ribadeneira's full-dress biography. These are unanswered questions, and most of them are unanswerable. However, no responsible interpretation of the *Reminiscences* can simply neglect them.

6. Gonçalves da Câmara notes how Ignatius's spoken language varies between the vivid and the obscure:

The way which Father has of narrating is that which is his wont in all matters, that is, with such great clarity that it seems he makes everything that happened present to the person. Given this, there was no need to ask him anything, because everything that was important to make a person get the point, Father would remember to say. [. . .] As for things where I fear I have been lacking, it is that, in order not to deviate from Father's words, I have not been able properly to explain the force of some of them.[20]

Underlying our text is a spoken narrative. To make a written text out of it, editors and translators from Gonçalves da Câmara onwards have had to use their judgement, if only on matters of punctuation. The 1731 editors of the earliest Latin translation divided the text into chapters and paragraphs. I have largely, though not entirely, followed the conventional chapter divisions, but I have introduced my own *chapter-titles* and *subheadings* within chapters. Moreover, in making my own translation, I have felt free to depart from conventional punctuation and paragraphing where the sense seemed to require this.[21]

As already noted, Gonçalves da Câmara made a number of marginal notes in various manuscripts after they had gone into circulation. Where these seem to indicate an addition to the narrative, I have placed them in the text in italic type. Where they are some kind of retrospective comment, I have reproduced them as footnotes. Where they do not seem to have any great significance, I have placed them in an end-note.

The *Reminiscences* set a translator particularly acute dilemmas as regards the balance between literalness and intelligibility. Following Gonçalves da Câmara, I believe that Ignatius's jerky style, at its best, can convey his meaning with remarkable vividness, especially if one imagines it being spoken. I have attempted, therefore, to reproduce it, not hesitating to employ non-standard usage where appropriate. Nevertheless, to produce a sensible written text a translator sometimes has to smooth over the awkwardness of the original and to simplify difficult passages. I have tried, however, to do that as little as possible.

In preparing this translation, I have found especially helpful the English version by Parmananda Divarkar, the French translation by Antoine Lauras, and the German translation by Peter Knauer. For the notes, I have drawn in particular on the MHSI edition, and the commentaries by Jean-Claude Dhôtel, Victoriano Larrañaga, Peter Knauer and Burkhart Schneider. I should also like to acknowledge occasional help from translations by Joseph N. Tylenda and Joseph F. O'Callaghan, and from the supporting material in two Spanish editions: those of Cándido de Dalmases in the fourth edition of the Ignatius volume in the *Biblioteca de Autores Cristianos*, and of Josep María Rambla Blanch. Finally, this version has benefited greatly from the careful attention of Joseph Munitiz.

NOTES

1 The so-called 'Preface of Fr Nadal' is found in a late copy of the early Latin translation. Both Nadal's and Gonçalves da Câmara's prefaces are reproduced in FN I, pp. 354–63. On internal grounds, the former's date seems to be 1567, roughly the time when, as we shall see, the text of the *Reminiscences* was being withdrawn from circulation. Some of the material from it forms part of a talk given by Nadal in Alcalá in 1561, of which both Italian and Spanish transcriptions have survived (MN V, pp. 264–67). In detail the two prefaces conflict. Though both texts are problematic, Gonçalves da Câmara's is in general to be preferred. Almost every word of the latter is quoted somewhere in this present introduction.

2 MN V, p. 262: '*el principio que tomó Dios por medio para comunicar esta gracia, y quiso que fuese ministro de esta vocación.*'

3 See James Brodrick, *The Progress of the Jesuits (1556–79)* (Loyola University Press, Chicago 1986 [first ed. 1947]), pp. 1–31; Ravier, *Ignatius of Loyola*, pp. 275–317.

4 *Notebook*, n. 3; FN I, p. 528.

5 See Letters 20.4, 31.7–19.

6 Francis Borgía, Duke of Gandía, had spent three months in Rome in 1550–51, and he and his entourage had stayed in a wing of the Jesuit house. His membership of the Society was still secret at that point.

7 See below, §36.

8 MN V, p. 287: 'in him [Ignatius] the Lord God as it were founded the Society, and one sees the first form and grace which the Lord gave to the Society'.

9 Cardinal Cervini, who was very favourable to the Society, was elected Marcellus II on 10 April 1555, and died on 1 May. Paul IV was elected on 23 May.

10 In fact he returned to Portugal.

11 An additional building adjoining Ignatius's house in Rome, bought in 1553, and named after the previous owner: see FN III, p. 179.

12 In the extant manuscripts the Spanish text of Gonçalves da Câmara's preface

breaks off here. For the continuation, we are reliant on a translation made of a lost text for the 1731 Latin edition.

13 Probably the second of the so-called rules of modesty. As promulgated in 1555, this ran: 'The eyes should normally be held low, without raising them much, nor turning them much from one side to another. And when speaking with someone, especially if it is a person demanding respect, they should not generally be fixed on their face, but rather kept low' (MI Reg, p. 518).

14 §§10, 99.

15 FN I, p. 341.

16 In 1567 Ribadeneira wrote to Nadal asking him to make sure the directive was carried out. The Provincials 'are to make a good job of gathering in what Fr Luis González wrote, or any other writing about the life of our Father, and they are to keep them and not permit them to be read, or to be circulated among our people or others. For, being an imperfect thing, it is not appropriate that it cause problems for what is being written more fully, or diminish its credibility. On this there is need to use the good effort and care which Your Reverence will understand is necessary, so that there isn't a commotion etc.'. Some months later, Ribadeneira seems to be answering a query from Nadal: 'The gathering in of Fr Luis González's writings about the life of our Father didn't originate with me, but from those Fathers who remembered our Father. And it seemed a good idea to His Paternity, so that when what is being written gets published it should not appear that there be divergence or contradiction, or that the work not have as much authority as what was written almost from the mouth of our Father. This, although very faithful in substance, is short on the details of some things, and in the relating of times by then well past, his memory was failing him owing to his old age' (MN III, pp. 490, 540).

17 *Notebook*, nn. 10–12; FN I, pp. 533–34.

18 The fact that the last part of Gonçalves da Câmara's preface is lacking in all the extant Spanish/Italian manuscripts might lead one to suspect that the beginning of the text proper has also been lost, but the MHSI editors offer good arguments for discounting that possibility. See FN I, pp. 330–31.

19 The documentation can be found in the older MHSI edition of narrative sources regarding Ignatius: *Scripta de S. Ignatio*.

20 Gonçalves da Câmara makes similar observations at a number of points in his *Notebook*: nn. 99, 202, 227; FN I, pp. 585–86, 648, 659.

21 Unfortunately the critical editions of the text at present available largely neglect issues of punctuation. If we had it, Gonçalves da Câmara's punctuation would have to be taken seriously; in its absence, a translator is free to question even his original copyists, let alone his modern editors.

1. Loyola

[1] Until the age of twenty-six he was a man given up to the vanities of the world, and his chief delight used to be in the exercise of arms, with a great and vain desire to gain honour. And so, being in a stronghold which the French were attacking,[1] and with everyone being of the opinion they should give themselves up and save their lives (for they saw clearly that they could not defend themselves), he gave so many arguments to the commandant that even then he persuaded him to make a defence, though against the opinion of all the knights.

These, however, were taking heart at his spirit and vigour. And, the day having come when the attack was expected, he made his confession with one of those companions of his in arms.[2] And, after the attack had lasted a good time, a shot hit him in one leg, completely shattering it for him; and because the ball passed between both legs, the other was badly wounded too. [2] And so, with him falling, those in the stronghold then gave themselves up to the French.

These, having taken possession of the fortress, treated the wounded man very well, treating him courteously and in a friendly way.[3] And after he had been twelve or fifteen days in Pamplona, they carried him on a litter to his home country. There, with him being in a very bad state and calling doctors and surgeons from many quarters, they judged that the leg had to be pulled apart again and the bones set in their places again, saying that, because they had been badly set on the other occasion or because they had become dislocated on the journey, they were out of place and in this state it couldn't heal. And this butchery was done again, during which, just as during all the others he had previously undergone and later underwent, he never spoke a word, nor showed any sign of pain other than clenching his fists tightly.

[3] And he was still getting worse, without being able to eat, and had the other symptoms that are normally a signal of death. When the feast of St John the Baptist arrived, since the doctors had very little confidence in his health, he was advised to make his confession. And as he was receiving the sacraments on the eve of the feast of Sts Peter and Paul,[4] the

doctors said that unless he felt improvement by midnight he could be counted as dead. The said patient had a regular devotion to St Peter, and so Our Lord willed that that same midnight he should begin to find himself better.[5] And the improvement went on increasing so much that within a few days it was judged he was out of danger of death.

[4] And as the bones were at this point coming to knit one with another, he was left with one bone above his knee mounted on top of the other. Thus the leg was left shorter and the bone at that point protruded so much as to be something ugly. As he could not bear this (for he was set on following the world and he considered this would disfigure him), he found out from the surgeons whether it could be cut. They said that it certainly could be cut, but that the pain would be greater than all those he had undergone before, given it was now healed and it would need time to cut it. And still he decided to make a martyr of himself out of self-will, though his elder brother was horrified and was saying that such pain he himself wouldn't dare suffer. The injured man suffered it with his usual forbearance. [5] And once the flesh and the excess bone at that point had been cut, the concern was to use remedies whereby the leg would not be left so short, applying many ointments to it and stretching it continually with appliances, which on many days were making a martyr of him.

But Our Lord was gradually giving him health, and he was in such a good state that he was cured in all other respects except that he could not hold himself well on his leg, and thus he was forced to be in bed. And because he was much given to reading worldly and false books, which they normally call 'tales of chivalry', he asked, once he was feeling well, that they give him some of these to pass the time. But in that house none of those books which he normally read could be found, and so they gave him a life of Christ and a book of the lives of the saints in Spanish.[6]

CONVERSION ON A SICKBED

[6] Reading through these often, he was becoming rather attached to what he found written there. But, on ceasing to read them, he would stop to think: sometimes about the things he had read, at other times about the things of the world he had been accustomed to think about before. And, out of many vain things which had previously presented themselves to him, one held his heart in such deep possession that he was subsequently absorbed in thought about it for two and three and four hours without noticing it, imagining what he was to do in the

service of a certain lady: the means he would take so as to be able to reach the country where she was, the witty love poems,[7] the words he would say to her, the deeds of arms that he would do in her service. He was so carried away by all this that he had no consideration of how impossible it was to be able to attain it. For the lady was not of the ordinary nobility, nor a countess nor a duchess: rather her state was higher than any of these.

[7] Still, Our Lord was helping him, causing other thoughts, which were born of the things he was reading, to follow these. For, while reading the lives of Our Lord and the saints, he would stop to think, reasoning with himself: 'How would it be, if I did this which St Francis did, and this which St Dominic did?' And thus he used to think over many things which he was finding good, always proposing to himself difficult and laborious things. And as he was proposing these, it seemed to him he was finding in himself an ease as regards putting them into practice. But his whole way of thinking was to say to himself: 'St Francis did this, so I must do it; St Dominic did this, so I must do it'.

These thoughts too used to last a good space, and, after other things between, the thoughts of the world mentioned above would follow, and on these too he would stop for a long while. And this succession of such different kinds of thoughts lasted a considerable time for him, with him always dwelling on the thought whose turn it was, whether this was of the former worldly deeds which he wanted to do, or of these latter from God which were occurring to his imagination, until the point came when he would leave them because of tiredness and attend to other things.

[8] Still, there was this difference: that when he was thinking about that worldly stuff he would take much delight, but when he left it aside after getting tired, he would find himself dry and discontented. But when about going to Jerusalem barefoot, and about not eating except herbs, and about doing all the other rigours he was seeing the saints had done, not only used he to be consoled[8] while in such thoughts, but he would remain content and happy even after having left them aside. But he wasn't investigating this, nor stopping to ponder this difference, until one time when his eyes were opened a little, and he began to marvel at this difference in kind and to reflect on it, picking it up from experience that from some thoughts he would be left sad and from others happy, and little by little coming to know the difference in kind of spirits that were stirring: the one from the devil, and the other from God.*

* This was the first reflection he made on the things of God; and later, when he produced the Exercises, it was from here that he began to get clarity regarding the matter of the difference in kind of spirits.

[9] And having received no small clarity from this reading, he began to think more in earnest about his past life, and about how much need he had to do penance for it.

And here the desires to imitate the saints were occurring to him, not considering details beyond promising himself, with the grace of God, to 'do it as they had done it'. All he wanted to do, once he was better, was the journey to Jerusalem as mentioned above, with all the acts of discipline and all the acts of self-denial that a generous spirit, fired with God, generally wants to do. [10] And now he was coming to forget his past thoughts with these holy desires he was having.

These desires were confirmed for him by a visitation as follows: being awake one night, he saw clearly a likeness of Our Lady with the Holy Child Jesus, at the sight of which, for an appreciable time, he received a very extraordinary consolation. He was left so sickened at his whole past life, and especially at matters of the flesh, that it seemed to him that there had been removed from his soul all the likenesses that he had previously had painted in it.[9] Thus, from that hour until August 1553, when this is being written, he never again had even the slightest complicity in matters of the flesh. On the basis of this effect one can judge that the thing has been of God, although he himself did not venture to define it, nor was he saying more than to affirm the abovesaid. But as a result his brother, like everyone else in the house, gradually realized from the outside the change that had been made inwardly in his soul.

[11] He, not troubling himself with anything, was persevering in his reading and his good intentions, and the whole time he spoke with those in the house he used to spend on things of God, with which he did their souls good. And, liking those books a lot, he had the idea of extracting certain things, briefly and in their essentials, from the lives of Christ and the saints. And so he set to writing a book with great industry (*this had about 300 leaves, all written in quarto*) for now he was beginning to get up a bit around the house. The words of Christ were in red ink; those of Our Lady in blue ink. The paper was glazed and ruled, and it was with good lettering, because he was a very good scribe. Part of the time he would spend in writing, part in prayer. And the greatest consolation he used to receive was to look at the sky and the stars, which he did often and for a long time, because with this he used to feel in himself a great impetus towards serving Our Lord.[10]

He often used to think about his intention, wishing he was already completely well so as to begin on his way. [12] And taking stock as to what he would do after he came back from Jerusalem so as always to live in penance, it occurred to him to go into the Charterhouse in Seville, without saying who he was so that they would take less notice of him, and there never to eat anything except herbs. But whenever he returned once more to thinking about the penances he wanted to do while wandering through the world, the desire for the Charterhouse would go cold on him: he was afraid he wouldn't be able to practise the hatred he had conceived against himself. Still, he instructed a house-servant, who was going to Burgos, to find out about the Rule of the Charterhouse, and the information he got about it seemed to him good.[11] But, for the reason stated above, and because he was completely absorbed in the journey he was thinking of making immediately whereas that matter didn't have to be dealt with until after his return, he wasn't looking into it all that much. Instead, finding himself now with some strength, it seemed to him it was time to take his leave, and he said to his brother: 'Sir, the Duke of Nájera,[12] as you know, now knows that I am well. It will be good for me to go to Navarrete' (the Duke was there at the time).

His brother took him to one room and then to another, and with many warnings began to beg him not to throw himself away: he should have regard for all the hopes people had of him and how much he could count for, and similar words, all with the purpose of detaching him from the good desire he had. *His brother, and some of those in the house, suspected that he wanted to make some kind of major change.* But the reply was in such a style that, without departing from the truth (because now he had a great scruple about that), he slipped away from his brother.

2. To Manresa via Montserrat

[13] And as he was thus mounting his mule, another brother of his wanted to go with him as far as Oñate. On the way he persuaded this brother that they might like to keep a vigil at Our Lady of Aránzazu.[13] Praying there that night so as to draw new strength for his journey,[14] he left his brother in Oñate, at the house of a sister whom he was going to visit, and himself went off to Navarrete. *From the day he left his homeland he would always take the discipline each night.*

And remembering a few ducats they owed him at the Duke's house, it seemed to him it would be good to claim them and he wrote a formal note to the treasurer to this effect. When the treasurer said they had no money and the Duke came to know of this, he said that they could default on everything but they wouldn't default on Loyola: he wanted to give him a good lieutenancy, were he willing to accept it, in recognition of the credit he had earned in the past.

He received the money, sending it to be distributed among certain people to whom he felt himself obliged, and a part of it to an image of Our Lady, which was in bad repair, so that it could be repaired and very finely adorned. And with that, dismissing the two servants who had been travelling with him, he went off alone on his mule from Navarrete to Montserrat. [14] And on this journey something happened to him which it will be good to have written, so that people can understand how Our Lord used to deal with this soul: a soul that was still blind, though with great desires to serve him as far as its knowledge went.

He was resolved, as has been said, to do great penances, with an eye at this point not so much to making satisfaction for his sins as to pleasing and being agreeable to God.* And so, when he would make up his mind to do some penance that the saints did, his aim was to do the same, and more besides. And in these thoughts he had all his consolation,

---

*He had such great loathing of his past sins, and so lively a desire to do great things for the love of God that, without making the judgement that his sins were forgiven, nevertheless in the penances he undertook to perform he did not pay much attention to them.

not considering anything within himself, nor knowing what humility was, or charity, or patience, or discernment in regulating and balancing these virtues. Rather, his whole purpose was to do these great exterior deeds because so the saints had done them for the glory of God, without considering any other more individual circumstances.[15]

[15] So then, as he was going on his way a Moor caught up with him, a rider on his mule; and as the two of them were going along in conversation, they came to talk about Our Lady. And the Moor was saying that he could well accept that the Virgin had conceived in the absence of a man, but he couldn't believe in her having given birth while remaining a virgin, offering for this the natural reasons that were occurring to him. Despite the many arguments which the pilgrim[16] gave him, he couldn't dislodge this opinion. At that the Moor went ahead, with such great speed that he lost sight of him as he remained thinking about what had passed with the Moor.

And at this there came upon him some impulses creating disturbance in his soul; it seemed to him he had not done his duty. And these caused him anger also against the Moor; it seemed to him he had done wrong in allowing that a Moor should say such things of Our Lady, and he was obliged to stand up for her honour. And thus there were coming upon him desires to go and find the Moor, and stab him for what he'd said.

Carrying on a long time with the conflict aroused by these desires, in the end he remained doubtful, not knowing what his duty was. The Moor, who had gone on ahead, had told him that he was going to a place which was a little further along his own route, very near the main road, but the main road did not go through the place. [16] So, having tired of analysing what it would be good to do, and not finding anything definite on which to decide, he decided on this: namely, to let the mule go on a loose rein up to the point where the roads divided. And if the mule went along the town road, he would look for the Moor and stab him; and if it didn't go towards the town but went along the main road, he'd leave him be. He acted in accord with this thought, and Our Lord willed that, though the town was little more than thirty or forty paces away, and the road leading to it very broad and very good, the mule took the main road, and left the one for the town behind.

And arriving at a large town before Montserrat, there he wanted to buy the clothes he was resolved to wear, the clothes in which he was to go to Jerusalem. And so he bought cloth, of the kind from which they normally make sacks: a kind which is not very closely woven and which has many prickles. Then he ordered a broad garment going down to his feet to be made from this, buying a staff and a small gourd,[17] and put it all in front of the mule's saddle-bow. *And he also bought some canvas sandals, of which he wore just one. And this not for decorum's sake but because he had one of his legs all tied up in a bandage and in a rather bad state: so much so that, although he was travelling on horseback, each night he found it swollen. This foot he felt he had to have shod.*

BEFORE THE BLACK MADONNA

[17] And he went on his way to Montserrat, thinking, as was always his habit, of the exploits he was to do for love of God. And because he had his whole mind full of those things from *Amadis of Gaul* and books of that sort, he was getting some thoughts in his head of a similar kind. Thus he decided to keep a vigil of arms for a whole night, without sitting or lying down, but sometimes standing up, sometimes on his knees, before the altar of Our Lady of Montserrat, where he had resolved to abandon his clothes and clothe himself in the armour of Christ.[18]

So having left that place he went along, as was his custom, thinking about his intentions. After his arrival at Montserrat, having said a prayer and come to an arrangement with the confessor, he made a general confession in writing, and the confession lasted three days.[19] He also arranged with the confessor that he should give orders to have the mule collected, and that his sword and dagger should hang in the Church at the altar of Our Lady. And this was the first person to whom he revealed what he had resolved, because up till then he had not revealed it to any confessor.

[18] At night on the eve of the feast of the Annunciation, in the year 1522, he went as secretly as he could to a poor man, and, stripping himself of all his clothes, he gave them to this poor man and clothed himself in the attire he wished for. And he went to kneel before the altar of Our Lady. And sometimes in this posture, at other times standing, he spent the whole night with his staff in his hand. And as dawn was breaking he left so as not to be recognized,[20] and he went off, not on the road straight to Barcelona, where he would have found many who would have recognized him and done him honour, but took a detour to a town called Manresa, where he was set on staying a few days in an alms-house,[21] and also to note down some things in his book. He was carrying this with much care, and thanks to it he was travelling along in great consolation.

And as he was now walking along, three miles from Montserrat a man caught up with him – this man had been coming after him in great haste – and asked him if it was he who had given some clothes to a poor man as the poor man was saying. And as he replied 'yes', the tears poured from his eyes, tears of compassion for the poor man to whom he had given his clothes: compassion, because he realized that they were making things difficult for him, thinking he had stolen them.

But however much he would try to avoid admiration, he couldn't be much around Manresa without people saying great things: the report had got about as a result of the Montserrat business. Later the rumours grew to the point of saying more than was the case: that he had left behind such a great income, etc.[22]

FIRST DISTURBANCES

[19] He used to ask for alms in Manresa each day. He wouldn't eat meat or drink wine even if they gave it to him. On Sundays he didn't fast, and if they gave him a little wine he would drink it. And because he had been very careful about keeping his hair as was the fashion at the time (and he had it nice), he decided to let it grow just anyhow as nature took it, without combing it or cutting it, nor covering it with anything by night or by day. For the same reason he was letting the nails on his toes and fingers grow, because on this point too he had been careful.

While he was in this almshouse something happened to him, many times: in full daylight he would see clearly something in the air alongside him, which would give him much consolation, because it was very beautiful, enormously so. He couldn't properly make out what it was an image of, but somehow it seemed to him that it had the shape of a serpent, and it had many things which shone like eyes, though they weren't eyes. He used to take much delight and be consoled by seeing this thing, and the more times he saw it, the more his consolation would increase. And when that thing used to disappear from his sight he would feel sad about it.[23]

[20] Up to this time he had always persisted almost in one identical interior state, with largely unvarying happiness, without having any acquaintance with spiritual things within the self. In those days, while that vision was continuing, or some short time before it began (because it went on for many days), there came to him a harsh thought which troubled him. The difficulty of his way of life would present itself to

him, as if it was being said to him inside his soul: 'And how are *you* going to be able to stand this life the seventy years you're meant to live?'[24] But to this he responded, also interiorly with great force (sensing that it was from the enemy): 'You wretch! Can you promise me one hour of life?' And in that way he overcame the temptation and was left calm. This was the first temptation that came to him after what has been recounted above. It was while he was entering a church where he used to hear the main mass each day, as well as vespers and compline, all sung, feeling great consolation at this. And he would normally read the Passion during mass, always going along in a state of serenity.

ENSNAREMENT BY SCRUPLES

[21] But then, after the temptation just spoken of, he began to undergo great variations in his soul, finding himself sometimes so much without relish that he found no savour either in praying or in hearing mass or in any other prayer he made, and at other times something coming over him pulling him towards so much the opposite, and so suddenly, that it seemed someone had taken away the sadness and the desolation from him like a person taking a cape from someone's shoulders. And at this point he began to be frightened at these variations, which he had never previously experienced, and to say to himself: 'what new life is this we're beginning now?'

At this time he still used to talk sometimes with spiritual people, who thought he was genuine and wanted to talk to him, because, although he had no knowledge of spiritual things, still in his speaking he showed much fervour and a great will to go forward in the service of God. There was in Manresa at that time a woman advanced in years, and moreover a very long-standing servant of God, known as such too in many parts of Spain, so much so that King Ferdinand had once summoned her in order to share some matters with her.[25] This woman, in conversation one day with the new soldier of Christ, said to him: 'O, may it please my Lord Jesus Christ that he will to appear one day to you.' But he became frightened at this, understanding the matter in this crude way: 'How is Jesus Christ meant to appear to *me*?'

He was still persisting with his normal confessions and communions every Sunday, [22] but here he came to have many problems from scruples.[26] For, although the general confession he had made at Montserrat had been suitably careful, and the whole thing in writing as has been said, still it seemed to him sometimes that there were some things he had not confessed. And this was causing him great pain, because, although he would confess this, he didn't end up satisfied. And so he began to seek out some spiritual men to cure him of these scruples. But nothing was of any help to him. Finally a learned man from the Cathedral, a very spiritual man who used to preach there, told him one day in confession to write down everything he could remember. So he did, but, after he had confessed, still the scruples came back, with things getting more pernickety each time, with the result that he was in a very troubled state. And although he was almost aware that those scruples were doing him a great deal of harm and that it would be good to get rid of them, still he couldn't accomplish this on his own.

He sometimes thought it would cure him were his confessor to command him in the name of Jesus Christ not to confess any of the things from the past. He therefore wanted the confessor to command this of him, but he didn't have the courage to tell the confessor this. [23] But without his telling him this, the confessor did get to the point of commanding him not to confess anything from the past unless it was sufficiently clear. But since he had all those things very clear in his mind, this directive was of no use, and so he was still left disturbed.

At this time, the said person was in a little room which the Dominicans had given him in their monastery, and he was persisting in his seven hours of prayer on his knees, getting up at midnight continually, together with all the other practices already mentioned. But in none of these was he finding any cure for his scruples, and many months had passed with them tormenting him. Once, from a state of great distress caused by them, he set himself to prayer. And in the heat of this prayer he began to shout out loud to God, saying, 'Help me, Lord: I can find no cure in human beings nor in any creature. If I thought I could find it, no struggle would be hard for me. You, Lord, show me where I am to find it. Even if I have to follow a little dog so that it can give me the cure, I'll do it.'

[24] While he was in these thoughts there often used to come over him, with great impetus, temptations to throw himself out of a large opening which the room he was in had, and which was beside the place where he used to pray.[27] But, mindful that it was a sin to kill oneself, he would revert to shouting again, 'Lord, I won't do anything that would offend you', repeating these words, like the first ones, many times.

And so there came into his thoughts the story of a saint, who, in order to obtain from God something he greatly desired, went without food for many days until he obtained it.[28] And thinking about this for a good while, in the end he decided to do it, saying to himself that he would neither eat nor drink till God did something for him or death seemed as near as could be. For if it should happen that he felt he had reached the limit – the kind of situation where, if he didn't eat, he'd inevitably die soon – then he was decided to ask for bread and to eat (as if, in that extremity, he would have been able in fact to ask or to eat).

[25] This happened one Sunday after he had been to communion. And he persisted the whole week without putting a single thing into his mouth, while not ceasing from his normal religious practices (also going to the divine offices), nor from making his prayer on his knees (and at midnight too), etc.[29] But when the following Sunday came with the need for confession, since he was accustomed to tell his confessor what he was doing in great detail, he told him also about how he had not eaten anything during that week. The confessor directed him to break that fast, and, though he still had some strength, he obeyed the confessor. And he discovered he was free of scruples that day and the next. But the third day, i.e. the Tuesday, while in prayer, he began to remember his sins. And thus, like something unravelling itself, he went on thinking about sin after sin from times previous, and it seemed to him he was duty-bound to confess them again.

But at the end of these thoughts there came to him some feelings of disgust for the life he was leading, and some impulses to cease from it; and with this the Lord willed that he woke up as if from sleep. And since he now had some experience of the difference in kind of spirits through the lessons God had given him, he began to mull over the means through which that spirit had come. As a result he decided, with great clarity, not to confess anything from the past any more. Thus from that day onward he remained free of those scruples, holding it for certain that Our Lord in his mercy had willed to liberate him.[30]

FURTHER DISCERNINGS

[26] Besides his seven hours of prayer, he was occupying himself in helping some souls[31] who would come and find him there in spiritual matters, and all the rest of the day remaining to him he would give to thinking about things of God, based on what he had meditated on or read that day. But when he went to bed, often great ideas would come to him, great spiritual consolations, in such a way that they were making him lose a lot of the time that he had allocated for sleep, which was not

much. And mulling this over a few times, he came round to thinking to himself that he had a certain amount of time set aside for dealing with God, and all the rest of the day afterwards. That led him to begin to doubt if these ideas were coming from the good spirit, and he came to the conclusion that it was better to leave them aside and to sleep for the allotted time; and so he did.[32]

[27] He was continuing in his abstinence from meat, and was firm on that – in no way was he thinking of making a change – when one day, in the morning when he had got up, there appeared to him meat for the eating, as if he could see it with his bodily eyes, without any desire for it having been there before. And together with this there also came upon him a great assent of the will that, from then on, he should eat meat. And although he could still remember his intention from earlier, he was incapable of being doubtful about this: rather he could not but make up his mind that he had to eat meat. And when he recounted this after-wards to his confessor, the confessor's line was that he should consider whether perhaps this was a temptation. But he, examining the matter well, was incapable of ever being doubtful about it.[33]

GOD'S TEACHING[34]

At this time God was dealing with him in the same way as a school-teacher deals with a child, teaching him. Now, whether this was because of his ignorance and obtuse mind, or because he didn't have anyone to teach him, or because of the resolute will that same God had given him to serve him, it was his clear judgement then, and has always been his judgement, that God was dealing with him in this way. On the contrary, were he to doubt this, he would think he was offending his Divine Majesty.

Something of this can be seen in the following five points.

[28] 1. He used to have great devotion to the Most Holy Trinity, and so used to pray each day to the three persons separately. And as he was also praying to the Most Holy Trinity as such, a thought used to occur to him: how was he making four prayers to the Trinity? But this thought troubled him little or not at all, as something of little importance. And, one day, while praying the office of Our Lady on the steps of the above-mentioned monastery, his understanding began to be raised up, in that he was seeing the Most Holy Trinity in the form of three keys on a keyboard,[35] and this with so many tears and so many sobs that he could

not control himself. And on walking that morning in a procession which was leaving from there, at no point could he restrain his tears until the mealtime, nor after the meal could he stop talking, only about the Most Holy Trinity, and this with many comparisons, a great variety of them, as well as much relish and consolation, in such a way that the impression has remained with him for the whole of his life, and he feels great devotion when praying to the Most Holy Trinity.

[29] 2. Once the way in which God had created the world was represented in his understanding, with great spiritual joy: it seemed to him he was seeing a white thing, from which some rays were coming out, and that God was making light out of it.[36] But he neither knew how to explain these things, nor could he fully and properly remember those spiritual ideas that God was at those times impressing on his soul. (In Manresa itself, where he was for almost a year, once he began to be consoled by God and saw the fruit he was bringing forth in souls as he dealt with them, he left aside those eccentricities he had from before. Now he cut his nails and his hair regularly.)

3.[37] Similarly, while being in that town in the church of the said monastery, and hearing mass one day, as the body of the Lord was being raised, he saw with his interior eyes some things like white rays which were coming from above. And although after so long a time he cannot properly explain this, still what he saw clearly with his understanding was to see how Jesus Christ Our Lord was present in that most holy sacrament.

4. Often, and for a long time, as he was in prayer, he used to see with his interior eyes the humanity of Christ. As for the form that used to appear to him, it was like a white body, not very big nor very small, but he did not see any distinction of limbs. He saw this often in Manresa. Were he to say twenty or forty times, he wouldn't be so bold as to judge that this was a lie. He has seen it another time when he was in Jerusalem, and again when travelling near Padua.[38] Our Lady too he has seen in a similar form, without distinguishing the parts. These things he has seen confirmed him back then, and they always gave him such great confirmation regarding the faith, that he has often thought to himself that if there weren't Scripture to teach us these matters of the faith, he would be resolved to die for them solely on the basis of what he has seen.[39]

[30] 5. Once he was going in his devotion to a church, which was a little more than a mile from Manresa (I think it is called St Paul's), and the way goes along by the river. Going along thus in his devotions, he sat

down for a little with his face towards the river, which was running deep below. And as he was seated there, the eyes of his understanding began to be opened: not that he saw some vision, but understanding and knowing many things, spiritual things just as much as matters of faith and learning, and this with an enlightenment so strong that all things seemed new to him. One cannot set out the particular things he understood then, though they were many: only that he received a great clarity in his understanding, such that in the whole course of his life, right up to the sixty-two years he has completed,[40] he does not think, gathering together all the helps he has had from God and all the things he has come to know (even if he joins them all into one), that he has ever attained so much as on that single occasion. *And this left him with the understanding enlightened in so great a way that it seemed to him as if he were a different person, and he had another mind, different from that which he had before.*[41]

[31] After this had lasted a good while, he went off to kneel at a cross which was nearby in order to give thanks to God. And there appeared to him there that vision which had often been appearing and which he had never recognized: i.e. that thing mentioned above which seemed very beautiful to him, with many eyes. But being in front of the cross he could well see that that thing of such beauty didn't have its normal colour, and he recognized very clearly, with strong backing from his will, that it was the devil. And in this form later the devil had a habit of appearing to him, often and for a long time, and he, by way of contempt, would cast it aside with a staff he used to carry in his hand.[42]

BEING NEAR DEATH

[32] Once while he was ill at Manresa, he arrived, as the result of a very violent fever, at the point of death: he clearly judged that his soul was due very soon to depart. At this a thought came to him, telling him he was just.[43] He struggled against this thought so much that he did nothing but push it back and bring his sins forward; he had more of a struggle with this thought than with the fever itself. But he couldn't conquer such a thought however much he struggled to conquer it. However, on being relieved from the fever a little, he was now no longer at the deathly extremity he was at before, and he began to shout loudly at some ladies who had come there to visit him to the effect that, when they saw him at the point of death again, they should for the love of

God shout at the top of their voices at him, calling him 'sinner!', and telling him to remember the offences he had caused to God.

[33] Another time, when he was travelling from Valencia to Italy by sea and in very stormy weather, the rudder broke on the ship, and the matter got to the point where, in his judgement and in that of many who were travelling in the ship, they couldn't escape death barring a miracle. On thoroughly examining himself at this time, and preparing himself to die, he couldn't be afraid of his sins, nor of being damned, but he felt great confusion and sadness from judging that he had not used well the gifts and graces which God Our Lord had imparted to him.

Another time in the year 1550 he was very sick as the result of a very severe illness which, in his judgement and indeed that of many, was to be regarded as his last. Thinking about death at this time he had such great joy and such great spiritual consolation at being due to die, that he was melting totally into tears. And this came to be such a recurring thing that he often used to refrain from thinking about death so as not to have so much of that consolation.

WINTER IN MANRESA

[34] As winter was coming on, he fell ill with a very severe illness, and to cure him the city put him in the house of the father of a certain Ferrer, who was later in the service of Baltasar de Faria. There he was looked after with great care, and many of the chief ladies used to come and watch over him at night out of the devotion they now had for him.[44] And when he recovered from this illness, he still remained very debilitated and with frequent pain in his stomach. So, for these reasons, and also because the winter was very cold, they made him dress properly and wear shoes and cover his head. Thus they made him take two drab doublets of very coarse cloth, and a hat from the same material, something like a beret. And at this time there were many days when he was very eager to speak about spiritual matters, and to find people who were receptive to them.

3. The Pilgrimage to Jerusalem

PREPARATIONS

The time when he had thought of leaving for Jerusalem was approaching, [35] and so at the beginning of the year 1523 he left for Barcelona in order to board ship.[45] Although some people were offering to accompany him, he didn't want to go except alone: his whole aim was to have God alone as a refuge. Thus one day, when some people were really pressing him to take a companion, on the ground he didn't know Italian or Latin, and telling him how much it would help him, and commending this to him, he told them that, even if it were the son or the brother of the Duke of Cardona,[46] he wouldn't go in his company. For he wanted to have three virtues: charity and faith and hope. And if he took a companion, whenever he was hungry, he would expect help from him, and when he fell, that he would help him get up, and thus he would be entrusting himself to him too, and attached to him, for these reasons; and he wanted to have this trust and attachment and hope with regard to God alone.

What he was thus expressing here was just how he felt it in his heart, and these thoughts were leading him to have desires to board ship, not just alone, but without any provisions. On beginning to negotiate his embarkation, he managed to get the ship's captain to take him free of charge seeing that he had no money, but with this condition: he had to put some ship's biscuit on the ship to feed himself. Otherwise, there was no way in the world they would take him.

[36] He wanted to arrange for this ship's biscuit, but great scruples came to him: 'So this is the hope and the faith you used to have in God, who wouldn't let you down?', etc. And this with such power that it was causing him great worry. Not knowing what to do, for he saw reasonable arguments on both sides, in the end he decided to put himself into the hands of his confessor, and so he told him how much he wanted to seek perfection and what might be more for the glory of God, and also of the things causing him to doubt whether he should take sustenance. The confessor decided he should beg what was necessary and that he should take it with him.

As he was begging this from a lady, she asked him where he wanted to sail for. He was a little doubtful whether to tell her, and in the end didn't dare go further than to tell her he was going to Italy and to Rome. And she, as if horrified, said, 'It's to Rome you're wanting to go? Well, those who go there come back in I don't know what state' (meaning that in Rome they didn't get much from things of the Spirit). The reason why he didn't dare say he was going to Jerusalem was for fear of vainglory. That fear used to trouble him so much that he never dared to say what region he came from nor who his family was. Finally he boarded ship with the ship's biscuit obtained. But finding himself on the shore with five or six blancas[47] remaining from those they had given him as he begged from door to door (because that was his normal way of living), he left them on a bench which he found there by the shore. [37] So he set sail, having been in Barcelona a little more than twenty days.

While he was still in Barcelona before setting sail, he looked, as was his custom, for all the spiritual people in order to talk to them, even if they were in hermitages far out of the city. But neither in Barcelona nor in Manresa, through all the time he was there, could he find people who could help him as much as he wanted. It was only in Manresa – that woman who was mentioned earlier,[48] who told him she was asking God that Jesus Christ appear to him: only she seemed to him to have more of an insight into spiritual things. Thus after having left Barcelona, he lost completely this anxious desire to look for spiritual persons.

THE OUTWARD JOURNEY

[38] They had such a strong wind at the stern that they arrived at Gaeta from Barcelona in five days and nights, though with considerable fear on everyone's part because it was very stormy. Throughout that region people were afraid of the plague; but he, once he left the ship, began to make his way to Rome. From among those who had travelled in the ship a mother joined him and accompanied him, together with her daughter, whom she was bringing along in boy's clothes, and also a young fellow. These followed his lead because they were begging too.

When they arrived at a homestead in the country they found a big fire with many soldiers beside it. These gave them something to eat, and they were also giving them a great deal of wine, encouraging them, so that it seemed their intention was to warm them up. Then they split them, putting the mother and the daughter above in a room, and the pilgrim together with the young fellow in a stable. But when midnight came he heard great shrieks being let out from above; and, on getting up to see what it was, found the mother and the daughter below very tearful, wailing that they had been wanting to rape them. At this there came over him such a powerful impulse that he began to shout, saying, 'Does one really have to put up with this?' and similar protests. These he delivered so effectively that everyone in the house was left terrified, without anyone doing him any harm.

The young fellow had already fled, and the three together began to travel by night, then and there; [39] and arriving at a town that was nearby, they found it shut up.[49] Not being able to enter, they spent that night, all three of them, in a church just there; it was raining. In the morning they wouldn't open the town to them, and outside they couldn't find alms, although they went to a castle that could be seen nearby.

Here the pilgrim found himself weak, as much as a result of the hardship at sea as of the other things etc., and not being able to walk any more, he remained there, while the mother and the daughter went off towards Rome. That day many people left the city. Learning that the Lady of the area was coming, he presented himself to her, telling her that he was ill only because of his weakness: he was asking her to let him enter the city in order to find some cure. She allowed this without any problems, and as he began to beg through the city he picked up a good bit of cash. And recuperating there for two days he took up his journey again, and arrived in Rome on Palm Sunday.

[40] Everyone who spoke to him there, once they knew that he didn't have money with him for Jerusalem, began to try and talk him out of going, assuring him on many grounds that it was impossible to find a passage without money. But he had a great conviction in his soul: he couldn't be doubtful; rather he was meant to find a way of getting to Jerusalem. And having obtained the blessing from Pope Adrian VI,[50] he then left for Venice, eight or nine days after Easter Sunday.

He still had six or seven ducats on him which they had given him for the passage from Venice to Jerusalem. He had taken them overcome to some extent by the fears they were pushing onto him, fears that he wouldn't make the passage any other way. But two days after having left Rome, he began to realize that this had been the lack of trust which he'd had, and it weighed on him greatly that he had taken the ducats, and he thought about whether it would be good to leave them somewhere. But in the end he decided to spend them generously on whoever crossed his path, who were normally poor people, and did so, with the result that when he later arrived in Venice he didn't have more than a few coppers on him, which that night he needed.

[41] On this journey to Venice, he was still sleeping under porticos on account of the precautions against the plague. Once as he was getting up in the morning he chanced upon a man who, seeing him look at him, began to run away in great terror, presumably because he must have perceived him as very pale. Going along in this way he arrived at Chioggia, and along with some companions who had attached themselves to him, learnt that they weren't going to let them enter Venice. His companions decided to go to Padua to obtain a certificate of health there, and so he went off with them. But he couldn't walk as far as they did, because they were walking very energetically, leaving him, near nightfall, in a big field. While he was there, Christ appeared to him in the way he normally appeared, the way we spoke of earlier,[51] and comforted him greatly. And with this consolation, he arrived at the gates of Padua the following day in the morning, without having forged a certificate as (I think) his companions had done. And he got in without the sentries demanding anything from him. Moreover, the same thing happened to him when he left, at which his companions were quite amazed: they had just got a certificate in order to go to Venice, and he hadn't bothered himself about it. [42] And when they arrived at Venice, the guards came to the boat to examine everybody, one by one, who was in it: only him they let be.

In Venice he supported himself by begging, and slept in St Mark's Square. But he always refused to go to the house of the Imperial Ambassador, nor did he make any special effort to find the wherewithal for his passage. He had a great conviction in his soul that God was to give him the means of going to Jerusalem; and this was giving him so great a confirmation that no arguments or fears they were putting to him could make him doubt it.

One day a rich Spanish man came across him, and asked him what he was doing and where he wanted to go. And learning of his intention, he took him to eat at his house. Subsequently he had him to stay for a few days until things were ready for the departure. Since Manresa, the pilgrim now had this custom: when he had a meal with people, he would never speak at table unless it was to reply briefly. But he would listen to what was being said, and pick up a few things from which he might take the opportunity to speak about God. And when the meal was ended, that is what he would do, [43] and this was the reason why the good man with all his household became so fond of him that they wanted to have him as a guest, and pressed him to stay on in the house. This same host took him to the Doge of Venice so that he could talk to him: i.e. he got the Doge to give him access and audience. The Doge, once he had listened to the pilgrim, ordered that they should give him passage on the ship carrying the Governors who were going to Cyprus.

Although that year many pilgrims for Jerusalem had come, the majority of them had returned to their homelands on account of the new situation that had arisen as a result of the capture of Rhodes.[52] Still, there were thirteen on the pilgrim ship, which left first, and eight or nine remained for the Governors' ship. As this was on the point of leaving, a serious feverish illness came over our pilgrim. After it had given him a rough time for a few days, it left him. The ship was due to depart on the day he had taken a purgative; the people in the house asked the doctor if he would be able to get on the ship for Jerusalem, and the doctor replied that certainly he could get on the ship if what he wanted was to be buried there. But he did get on the ship, and left that day. And he vomited so much that he was greatly relieved and really began to make a recovery.

On that ship there was some open dirty and obscene behaviour, which he would severely criticize. [44] The Spaniards who were travelling on it were warning him not to do this, because the crew were talking of leaving him behind on some island. But Our Lord willed that they arrived quickly at Cyprus, where, having left that ship, they went overland to another port called Las Salinas,[53] thirty miles away, and they boarded the pilgrim ship. Onto this ship too he brought nothing with which to feed himself beyond the hope he was placing in God, just as he had done on the other. Throughout this time Our Lord often appeared to him, which gave him great consolation and energy. Moreover, it seemed to him he repeatedly saw a large round object, apparently of gold: this began to appear to him after, having left Cyprus, they arrived at Jaffa.

THE HOLY PLACES[54]

As they were making their way to Jerusalem on their donkeys, following custom, two miles before arriving at Jerusalem, a Spaniard named Diego Manes, apparently a nobleman, said to all the pilgrims, with much devotion, that, since they were shortly to arrive at the place from where the holy city could be seen, it would be good were all to prepare their minds and hearts and to travel in silence. [45] This being agreeable to all, each one began to recollect himself. And a little before arriving at the place from which the city could be seen, they dismounted, because they saw the friars with the cross waiting for them. And on seeing the city the pilgrim had great consolation; moreover, from what the others were saying it was something they all had, with a joy that did not seem purely natural. And he always felt the same devotion during the visits to the holy places.

His firm intention was to remain in Jerusalem, forever visiting those holy places. And, as well as this matter of devotion, he also had the intention of helping souls.[55] For this purpose he was carrying letters of recommendation for the Guardian.[56] He gave him these, and told him of his intention to remain there out of devotion, but not the second part – his wish to be useful to souls – because this he wasn't telling anybody, while the first he had often made public. The Guardian replied that he couldn't see how his stay would be possible, because the house was in such great need that it couldn't support the friars, and for this reason he had decided to send some of them with the pilgrims back here.[57] The pilgrim replied that he didn't want anything from the house, with the sole exception that when on occasion he came for confession they would hear it. And at this the Guardian said that on those terms it would be feasible, but that he would have to wait until the Provincial came (I think he was the highest superior of the Order in that country), who was then at Bethlehem.[58]

[46] With this promise the pilgrim felt assured, and he began to write letters to Barcelona to spiritual persons. When he already had one written and was in the course of writing the second – this was the day before the pilgrims departed[59] – people on behalf of the Provincial and the Guardian came to summon him, because the former had arrived. And the Provincial told him, using kind words, how he had learnt of his good intention of remaining in those holy places, that he had thought a good deal about the matter, and that, from the experience that he had of others, it was his judgement that it would not be appropriate. For many people had had this desire, and then one had been taken prisoner, another had died, and then the order had been left having to ransom the prisoners. He should therefore get ready to go the following day with the other pilgrims.

To this his reply was that he was very firm in this intention, and that in his judgement on no account should he refrain from putting it into practice; politely he made it clear that, although the Provincial did not think it a good idea, he would not abandon his intention on account of any fear unless it was a matter obliging him under pain of sin. To this the Provincial said that they had authority from the Holy See to make anyone leave there or stay there whom they saw fit, and to be able to excommunicate anyone who was not willing to obey them. And in this case, it was their judgement that he mustn't remain etc. [47] When he wanted to show him the bulls on the strength of which they could excommunicate him, he told them that there was no need to see them: he believed their Reverences, and since this was their judgement, with the authority they had, he would obey them.

When this was over, there came over him as he was returning to where he was previously a great desire to go back and visit the Mount of Olives again before he left, now that it was not the will of Our Lord that he should remain in those holy places. On the Mount of Olives is a stone, from which Our Lord went up into heaven, and even now the footprints can be seen; this is what he wanted to go back to see. Thus, without saying a thing nor taking a guide (because those who move about without a Turk to guide them run great danger), he slipped away from the others and went off alone to the Mount of Olives. The sentries didn't want to let him in; he gave them a knife from the writing-things he was carrying. And after he had made his prayer with considerable consolation, the desire came to him to go to Bethphage.[60] And as he was there, he came to remember that on the Mount of Olives he hadn't taken a proper look at where the right foot was or where the left was. And on returning there, I think he gave his scissors to the sentries so that they would let him in.

[48] When they found out in the monastery that he had gone off like this without a guide, the friars took vigorous steps to look for him. So, as he was coming down from the Mount of Olives he came upon a Christian of the cincture,[61] who was a servant in the monastery. He had a big staff, and with a show of great anger was gesturing as if really to give it to him, and coming up to him he grabbed him roughly by the arm. He let himself be taken readily, but the good man never let him go. And as he went along this path in this fashion, grabbed by the Christian of the cincture, he had great consolation from Our Lord, in that it seemed to him he was seeing Christ always over him. And until he arrived at the monastery, this lasted all the time, in great abundance.

THE RETURN TO SPAIN

[49] They left the next day,[62] and, having arrived at Cyprus, the pilgrims split up into different ships. There were in the port three or four ships for Venice: one belonged to Turks, another was a very small vessel, and the third was a very rich and powerful ship belonging to a rich man from Venice. Some of the pilgrims asked the master of this ship to be so kind as to take the pilgrim. But he, when he found out he had no money, refused, although many people asked this of him, praising him etc. The master replied that if he was a saint he should cross as St James had crossed, or something like that.[63]

From the master of the little vessel these same people making the request obtained it very easily. They left on a day with a favourable wind in the morning, but in the later part of the day a storm came upon them, with the result that the ships became separated. The big ship went lost near those same islands of Cyprus and only the people were saved; while the Turks' ship was lost, and all the people with it, as a result of the same storm. The little vessel went through great difficulty, and finally came to make landfall at Pula.[64] And this in the full force of the winter: it was very cold and snowing, and the pilgrim was wearing no clothes other than some scruffy breeches of coarse cloth down to his knees (his legs were bare), with shoes and a shirt of black cloth, open, with many tears at the shoulders, and a short, threadbare doublet.

[50] He arrived at Venice in the middle of January of the year 1524, having been at sea from Cyprus the whole month of November and of December and what had passed of January. In Venice one of the two people[65] who had received him into their house before he left for Jerusalem found him, and gave him 15 or 16 giulii[66] as alms, and a piece of cloth. This he folded up many times and put over his stomach on account of the great cold.

Once the said pilgrim had understood that it was God's will he should not be in Jerusalem, he had constantly had with him thoughts about what was to be done. In the end he was inclining more towards studying for a time in order to be able to help souls, and was coming to the decision to go to Barcelona. Hence he set out from Venice for Genoa.

When he was one day in Ferrara in the main church, fulfilling his devotions, a poor person asked him for alms, and he gave him a marchetto, which is a coin worth 5 or 6 quattrini. After him another came, and he gave him another small coin that he had – a bit more. To the third, not having anything but giulii, he gave a giulio. When the poor people saw that he was giving alms, they did nothing else except to come, and so everything that he had ran out. In the end many poor people came together to ask for alms. He replied that they must forgive him for having nothing more.

[51] So he set off from Ferrara towards Genoa. He met on the road some Spanish soldiers, who treated him well for that night. They were horrified at how he was taking that road because it entailed passing between both armies as it were, French and Imperial.[67] They were pressing him to leave the main road and take another one, a safe one, which they were pointing out. But he did not take their advice. Instead, travelling straight on down his road, he came upon a village that had been burnt and destroyed, and thus found no one before night who would give him anything to eat. But when it was sunset he reached a village that was surrounded, and the sentries seized him straightaway, thinking he was a spy. And putting him in a hut near the gate, they began to interrogate him as one normally does when there is some suspicion, with him replying to all the questions that he knew nothing. And they stripped him and searched him right down to his shoes, and every part of his body, to see if he was carrying some letter. Not being able by any means to find anything out, they grabbed him so as to make him come before the captain: *he* would make him talk. When he said that they should take him wrapped in his doublet, they refused to give it to him, and so took him in the shirt and breeches mentioned above.

[52] On this journey the pilgrim had, as it were, a representation of when they took Christ, although this was not a vision like the others.[68] He was taken through three big streets, and he went with no sadness, rather with happiness and contentment. It was his custom to speak, whoever the person might be, using the word *vos*, having this as a matter of devotion, in that Christ and the apostles etc. used to speak in this way. As he went thus through these streets it occurred to his imagination that it would be good to desist from that custom at that juncture, and address the captain as Sir[69] – this together with some fears of the tortures that they could give him etc. But when he recognized it was a temptation, 'Since *that's* what it is', he said, 'I won't call him Sir, nor do him any reverence, nor doff my cap at him'.[70]

[53] They arrived at the captain's palace and they left him in a low room. A short while later the captain spoke to him. And he, without putting on any kind of courtesy, gave a few words in reply, with a perceptible

pause between one and the other. The captain took him to be crazy, and therefore said to those who had brought him, 'This man isn't in his right mind. Give him what's his, and throw him out'.

Having left the captain's palace, he then met a Spaniard who lived there. This man took him to his house and gave him something to break his fast and all the necessary for that night. Having left in the morning, he walked till the evening, when two soldiers in a tower saw him and came down to arrest him, taking him to the captain, who was French. The captain asked him, along with the other things, what part of the world he was from, and learning he was from Guipúzcoa said, 'I come from near there' – apparently from near Bayonne. And at once he said, 'Take him and give him some supper and treat him well'. He experienced many other little things on this journey from Ferrara to Genoa, and in the end he arrived at Genoa. There a Biscayan called Portundo[71] recognized him, who at another period had spoken to him while he was serving at the court of King Ferdinand. This man got him embarkation on a ship which was going to Barcelona – a ship in which he ran a great danger of being taken by Andrea Doria,[72] who gave them chase, he being then for the French.

4. Studies and Conflicts in Spain

[54] Having arrived in Barcelona, he told Isabel Roser of his inclination towards study, and also a certain Maestro Ardèvol who taught Latin language.[73] To both this seemed very good; he offered to teach him free of charge, and she to give whatever was necessary for his sustenance. Now the pilgrim had a monk in Manresa (I think a Cistercian), a very spiritual man. It was with this person that he wanted to be so as to learn, and to be able to give himself with more ease to the Spirit, and even to be of benefit to souls.[74] So he replied that he accepted the offer if he didn't find in Manresa the favourable conditions he hoped for. But on going there he found that the monk was dead.

And so having returned to Barcelona, he began to study with quite some diligence. But one thing was hindering him a lot, and this was that, when he began to commit things to memory, as is necessary at the beginning of language study, new insights into spiritual things would occur to him, and new enjoyments, and this in so powerful a way that he couldn't learn by heart, nor could he get rid of the insights however much he resisted them. [55] And so, thinking often about this, he said to himself, 'Not even when I set myself to prayer and when I am at mass do these insights which are so vivid come to me'; and thus little by little he came to recognize that it was a temptation. And after some prayer he went to the church of Santa María del Mar, near his teacher's house, having asked the latter kindly to listen to him for a short while in that church. And as they were thus seated there, he explained quite honestly all that was passing through his soul, and how little progress he had made up till then for that reason, but that now he was making a promise to this master, saying, 'I promise you that I shall never fall short in paying attention to you in these two years as long as I can find bread and water in Barcelona on which I can survive'. And after he had made this promise, it was with considerable effect: he never again had those temptations.[75]

The stomach pain that had taken hold of him at Manresa, on account of which he had taken to wearing shoes,[76] had left him, and he had been fine with his stomach ever since he had left for Jerusalem. And for this reason, while he was studying in Barcelona, the desire came to him to return to the penances he had done before. So he began to make a hole in the soles of his shoes. He continued widening these holes little by little, so that when the cold of winter came he was then wearing nothing but the uppers.

[56] When two years of study were over, during which (so they told him) he had made quite some progress, his master was telling him that he was now able to study an arts course, and that he should go to Alcalá.[77] But he still had himself examined by a doctor of theology. He advised him the same, and so he set off for Alcalá alone, although, I think, he already had some companions.[78]

ALCALÁ – SETTLING IN AND THE FIRST PROCESS

On arrival at Alcalá he began to beg and to live on alms. Then one day, after he had been living in this way for ten or twelve days, a cleric and others with him, seeing him beg for alms, began to laugh at him and to say some insulting things to him, as is often done with those who beg even though they are in good shape. At that point the man in charge of the new Antezana almshouse[79] was passing, and, showing his pain at this, called him and took him to the almshouse. There he gave him a room and everything he needed. [57] He studied in Alcalá for almost a year and a half. Since it was 1524, during Lent, that he arrived in Barcelona, where he studied for two years, it was 1526 when he arrived at Alcalá; and he studied the Logic of Soto, the Physics of Albert, and Peter Lombard.[80] While in Alcalá he was also occupied in giving spiritual exercises[81] and in explaining Christian doctrine, and through this there was fruit borne for God's glory. There were many people who came to considerable awareness and relish regarding spiritual matters, and others who were having various temptations, such as one woman who wanted to take the discipline but could not do it: it was as if her hand were being restrained. And there were other things like this which stimulated talk in the town, especially given the great crowd that used to gather wherever he was explaining doctrine.[82]

Shortly after his arrival at Alcalá he came to know Don Diego de Eguía, who was staying in the house belonging to his brother, a printer in Alcalá. He was well provided for,[83] and so he and his brother could help him with alms for supporting poor people, and he had the pilgrim's three companions in his house. Once when they came to him to ask for alms to meet some needs, Don Diego said he had no money. But he opened a chest for him in which he had various things, and thus gave him bed-coverings of various colours and some candlesticks and other similar things. The pilgrim took all of these wrapped in a sheet over his shoulder, and went to relieve the poor.

[58] As was mentioned earlier, there was a great deal of talk in the whole of that country about the things that were happening in Alcalá: some telling one version, some another. And the matter reached as far as Toledo and the inquisitors. When these came to Alcalá, the pilgrim was warned by their host, who told him that they were calling them 'the sack-wearers', and I think *alumbrados* [illuminists],[84] and that they would make mincemeat of them. So it was that they then began to investigate their way of life and to draw up a process, but finally they returned to Toledo without summoning them, having come only for that purpose.[85] They left the process to the Vicar General, Figueroa, who is now in the Emperor's service.

A few days later Figueroa summoned them and told them how an investigation had been made and a process begun by the inquisitors regarding their way of life; that no error could be found in their doctrine or in their way of life; and hence they could do just as they were doing without any hindrance. But since they weren't members of a religious order, it didn't seem a good idea for them all to have the same habit. It would be better (and he was commanding them this) that one pair (he indicated the pilgrim and Arteaga) should dye their clothes black, and that another two (Calisto and Cáceres) should dye them light brown. And Juanico, who was a French lad, could stay as he was.[86]

[59] The pilgrim replied that they would do what was commanded. 'But I don't know', he said, 'what good these inquisitions do. The other day a priest refused to give communion to someone like us on the ground he went to communion every week. And they've been making things difficult for me. We'd like to know if they've found any heresy in us.'

'No', said Figueroa, 'if they had found it, they'd have burnt you.'

'And they'll burn you too', said the pilgrim, 'if they find heresy in you.'

They dyed their clothes as was commanded them. And fifteen or twenty days later Figueroa ordered the pilgrim not to go around barefoot, but to put some shoes on. And he did so without fuss, as with all things of this kind that they commanded him.[87]

ALCALÁ – THE SECOND PROCESS

Four months later this same Figueroa again conducted an investigation into them. Apart from the normal kind of grounds, I think it was also some occasion when a well-to-do married lady had a particular devotion to the pilgrim, and, in order not to be seen, used to come to the alms-house wearing a veil, in the style customary in Alcalá de Henares, during the morning twilight. When she came in, she would uncover herself and go to the pilgrim's room. But they didn't do anything to them this time either, nor did they summon them after the process was completed, nor did they say anything.[88]

ALCALÁ – THE THIRD PROCESS

[60] A further four months later,[89] by which time he was in a little house outside the almshouse, a policeman came one day to his door, called him and said, 'Come along with me for a while'. And then leaving him in the prison, he said, 'You're not to leave here till you get another order'. This was in summertime, and he was not closely confined; thus many people came and visited him and he did the same things as when he was free, going through doctrine and giving exercises.[90] He always refused to take an advocate or lawyer, though many were offering themselves. He remembers especially Doña Teresa de Cárdenas,[91] who sent visitors to him, and many times offered to get him out of there. But he accepted nothing, always saying, 'He for whose love I came in here will get me out if this will serve his purpose'.

[61] He was seventeen days in the prison without them cross-examining him and without his knowing why he was there. At the end of that time Figueroa came to the prison, and questioned him about many things, to the point of asking him if he got people to keep the Sabbath.[92] Also, did he know a certain pair of women, mother and daughter? To this he said yes. Had he known of their departure before they left? He said no, on the oath he had taken. Then the Vicar General, putting his hand on his shoulder and showing happiness, said to him, 'That was the reason why you've come here'.

Among the many people who were the pilgrim's followers there was a mother and her daughter, both widows, and the daughter very young and very pretty. These had entered deeply into things spiritual, the daughter especially, so much so that, though noble ladies, they had gone on foot to the veil of Veronica at Jaén[93] (I don't know if they did this begging), and alone as well. This caused much talk in Alcalá, and Dr Ciruelo,[94] who had some responsibility for them, thought that the prisoner had put them up to this, and thus had him taken in. So, when the prisoner saw what the Vicar General had said, he said to him, 'Would you like me to talk a little more fully about this topic?'

'Yes', he replied.

'Well, you should be aware', said the prisoner, 'that these two women have often pestered me because they wanted to go about the world serving the poor first in one almshouse and then in another. And I have always dissuaded them from this intention, because the daughter is so young and so pretty etc.; and I have told them that if they want to visit poor people they can do it in Alcalá and accompany the Blessed Sacrament.'[95] When this conversation was finished, Figueroa went off along with his notary, having the whole thing in writing.

[62] At that time Calisto was in Segovia. Learning of his imprisonment, he came at once, though he was only newly recovered from a serious illness,[96] and put himself in the prison with him. But Calisto for his part told him it would be better to go and report to the Vicar General. The latter treated him well, and said that he would have to order him to go to the prison because he had to be there until those women came back in order to see if they bore his statement out. Calisto was in the prison for a few days, but when the pilgrim saw he was doing damage to his physical health (for he was not yet completely well), he had him taken out through the mediation of a doctor, a very good friend of his.

From the day when the pilgrim went into the prison until they took him out, forty-two days passed. At the end of these, now that the two devout women had returned, the notary went to the prison to read him the verdict: he could go free, they were to dress like the other students, and they were not to talk about matters regarding the Faith within the four years that they still had to study, because they weren't learned.[97] For, to tell the truth, it was the pilgrim who knew most, and what he knew was with little foundation. And this was the first thing he normally said when they questioned him.

[63] As a result of this verdict he was a little doubtful as to what he would do, because it seemed that they were blocking the door to him against his helping souls, not giving him any reason except that he had not studied. In the end he decided to go to the Archbishop of Toledo, Fonseca, and put the case in his hands.[98] He left Alcalá and met the

Archbishop in Valladolid. And, recounting faithfully to him what had happened, he said to him that, although he was not now within his jurisdiction nor obliged to observe the verdict, nevertheless he would do what the Archbishop ordered (using *vos* with him, as he did with everyone).[99] The Archbishop received him very well, and, on realizing that he wanted to move on to Salamanca, said that he had friends in Salamanca too, and a college, putting all this as an offer to him. And then as he was leaving he had four escudos given him.

SALAMANCA: ENCOUNTER WITH THE DOMINICANS

[64] Having arrived at Salamanca, he was praying in a church when a devout woman recognized him as one of the society,[100] for the four other companions had now been there for some days. And she asked him his name, and then took him to the companions' lodging-place. When in Alcalá it had been ruled they were to dress as students, the pilgrim had said, 'When you ordered us to dye our clothes, we did it, but this now we cannot do, because we don't have anything with which to buy the clothes'. So the Vicar General himself had provided them with uniform and caps and everything else for students, and dressed in this way they had left Alcalá.

In Salamanca he was making his confession to a Dominican friar in San Esteban. Ten or twelve days after his arrival, the confessor said to him one day, 'The Fathers in the house would like to talk to you'.

'So be it, in God's name', he replied.

'So', said the confessor, 'it will be good for you to come here for the main meal on Sunday. But I warn you of one thing: they'll want to ask you many things.' So on the Sunday he went with Calisto and, after the meal, the Subprior (the Prior being absent) together with the confessor, and I think another friar, went off with them into a chapel. And the Subprior began very cordially to say what good reports they had heard about their life and practices, and how they went about like the Apostles preaching. They would be glad to hear about these things in more detail.

So he began to ask what studies they had done, and the pilgrim replied, 'Of all of us, I am the one who has studied the most', and gave them a clear account of the little he had studied and of what little foundation he had.

[65] 'So then, what do you preach?'

'We', said the pilgrim, 'don't preach, but speak about things of God with certain people in an informal way, such as after a meal with some people who invite us.'

'But', said the friar, 'what things of God do you talk about? That's what we want to know.'

'We speak', replied the pilgrim, 'now of one virtue, now of another, in praise of it; now of this vice, now of that, and in criticism.'

'You aren't learned', said the friar, 'and you're speaking of virtues and vices. About this no one can speak except in one of two ways: either through learning or through the Holy Spirit. If it's not learning, then it's the Holy Spirit. *And this point: that it is of the Holy Spirit, is what we would like to know about.*'

Here the pilgrim was a little wary, as this way of arguing did not seem good to him. And after having been silent a while, he said that there was no need to speak more about these matters. As the friar insisted, 'Well, now that there are so many errors from Erasmus and so many others who have deceived the world, aren't you willing to explain what you're saying?', [66] the pilgrim said, 'Father, I won't say any more than what I've already said, unless it be in front of my superiors who can require it of me'.[101]

Before this he had asked why Calisto had come dressed in the way he was, wearing a short tunic and a large hat on his head, together with a staff in his hand and some boots almost half-way up his legs. And because he was very tall he seemed the more outlandish. The pilgrim recounted to him how they had been imprisoned at Alcalá, how they had ordered them to dress as students, and how this companion of his had given his academic gown to a poor cleric. At this the friar muttered, 'Charity begins at home', showing that this did not please him.

So, to carry on the story: since the Subprior couldn't get another word out of the pilgrim apart from this, he said, 'Well then, stay here: we'll make a proper job of getting you to tell everything'. And at that all the friars went off with some haste. On the pilgrim first asking if they wanted them to stay in that chapel or where did they want them to stay, the Subprior replied that they should stay in the chapel. Next, the friars had all the doors shut, and presumably began to talk to the judges. The two of them were still in the monastery three days later, with nothing having been said to them by the judiciary, eating with the friars in the refectory. Their room was almost always full of friars coming to see them, and the pilgrim always spoke on his usual topics. Consequently there was already something of a division among the friars, since there were many who were showing signs of being moved.

SALAMANCA: THE PRISON

[67] At the end of the three days a notary came and took them to the prison. He didn't put them below with the criminals but in a room above, where, because it was old and unused, there was a lot of dirt. And they tied them both to one and the same chain, each one by the foot, and the chain was attached to a post in the centre of the building; it would have been about five or six feet long. And every time one of them wanted to do anything the other would have to go with him. They were keeping vigil the whole of that night. The following day, when their being detained became known in the city, people sent bedding for them to the prison, and everything they needed in abundance. And there were always many people coming to visit them; the pilgrim continued his exercises of speaking about God etc.

Frías the bachelor[102] came to question each of them individually, and the pilgrim gave him all his papers – these were the Exercises – so that he could examine them. When he asked them if they had companions, they said yes, and told him where they were. And straightaway, by order of the bachelor, they went there and brought Cáceres and Arteaga to the prison (they left Juanico who afterwards became a friar).[103] But they didn't put them above with the first two, but below where the ordinary prisoners were. Here too he refused to have an advocate or a lawyer.

[68] Some days later he was called before four judges: the three doctors, Santisidoro, Paravinhas and Frías, and the fourth being Frías the bachelor. All had already seen the Exercises. And at this point they asked him many things, not only regarding the Exercises, but also theology: for example, about the Trinity and the Blessed Sacrament; how did he understand such and such an article? He began in his normal way,[104] and nevertheless, when commanded by the judges, spoke in such a way that they had nothing on which to criticize him. Frías the bachelor, who had always figured more prominently in these matters than the others, also asked him a canonical case, and he was obliged to answer everything, always saying first that he didn't know what the learned people said about these things. Later they asked him to explain the first commandment as he normally explained it. He began to do this, and he took so long and said so many things about the first commandment that they had no wish to ask him more.

Prior to this, when they were talking about the Exercises, they laid much stress on one single point at the beginning of them: that of when a thought is a venial sin and when it is a mortal one.[105] This was because he was defining that without being learned. His line of reply was, 'You decide from there whether this is true or not; if it's not, condemn it'. In the end they left without condemning anything.

[69] Among many who used to come and talk to him in the prison, there came once Don Francisco de Mendoza, who is now known as the Cardinal of Burgos,[106] and he came with Frías the bachelor. He asked him as a friend would how he was coping with imprisonment, and if it was hard for him to be a prisoner. His reply was, 'I shall answer you what I answered to a lady today, who spoke words of compassion at seeing me a prisoner. I said to her, "In this you are showing that you do not desire to be a prisoner for the love of God. Does imprisonment seem so bad to you then? Well, I tell you: there are not so many fetters or chains in Salamanca that I don't want more for the love of God"'.

At this time it happened that all the prisoners in the jail escaped, but the two companions who were with them did not run away. And when they were found in the morning with the doors open, on their own without anyone else, this gave much edification to everybody and caused considerable talk through the city. And so later they were given as their prison a real palace of a place which was nearby.

[70] After twenty-two days of imprisonment, they were summoned to hear the verdict, which was that no error could be found either in their way of life or in their doctrine, and that they could therefore do as they had been doing, teaching doctrine and speaking about things of God, so long as they did not adjudicate: 'this is a mortal sin' or 'this is a venial sin' before four years had passed during which they had done further study. After this verdict was read out, the judges showed great affection for them, as if they wanted it to be agreed to. The pilgrim said that he would do all that the verdict commanded, but that he would not agree with it, since, without having convicted him of anything, they were muzzling him so that he couldn't help others as far as he was capable. And however much Dr Frías, who appeared very friendly, pressed the point, the pilgrim said nothing further except that he would do what was being commanded as long as he was within the jurisdiction of Salamanca.

Then they were released from the prison, and he began to put before God the question of what he should do, and to think about it. He had great difficulty with staying in Salamanca, because it seemed to him that the door was shut on his doing good to souls with this prohibition against adjudicating mortal and venial sin. [71] So he decided to go to Paris to study.

When in Barcelona the pilgrim had been consulting as to whether he should study and how much, his whole question was whether, after he had studied, he should enter a religious order or continue to wander about the world.[107] And when thoughts of entering a religious order came to him, at once there would come the desire to enter a decadent one, little reformed: he was to enter religious life so as to be able to suffer more in it. He also thought that perhaps God would help those in that order, and God would give him a great confidence that he would be able to suffer all the insults and hurts they would inflict on him. Now, since at this time of being imprisoned in Salamanca these same desires that he had hadn't gone away – of doing good for souls, of studying first with this end in view, of gathering together some people with the same intention and of keeping those he already had – he came to an agreement with these latter, having decided to go to Paris, that they should wait behind, and that he would go so as to be able to see if he could find a means whereby they could study. [72] Many prominent people urged him strongly not to go, but they could never succeed with him in this. Instead, fifteen or twenty days after having come out of prison he went off alone, carrying some books, on a donkey. When he arrived in Barcelona, everyone who knew him advised him against the move to France because of the major wars taking place,[108] recounting to him very specific examples, to the point of telling him that they were roasting Spaniards on spits. But he never had any kind of fear.

5. Paris

[73] And so he left for Paris, alone and on foot, and he arrived in Paris for the month of February more or less. (According to what he told me, this was the year of 1528 or 1527.)[109] He settled himself in a house with some Spaniards and went to classes in humanities at Montaigu.[110] And the reason for this was that, since they had made him go forward in his studies in such a hurry, he was discovering himself to be very lacking in background. He was studying with the boys, following the structure and method of Paris.

In exchange for a draft from Barcelona a merchant gave him, on his arrival in Paris, twenty-five écus. These he gave for safe-keeping to one of the Spaniards in that lodging, who spent them within a short time and had nothing with which to pay him back.[111] Consequently, once Lent was over, the pilgrim had none of this money, either because he had spent it or for the reason just mentioned. And he was forced to go begging, and even to leave the house where he was. [74] He was taken in at the almshouse of St Jacques, beyond the Church of the Innocents. He had great inconvenience as far as study was concerned, because the almshouse was a good way from the college of Montaigu, and one needed to arrive back for the ringing of the Angelus if one was to find the door open, while one couldn't leave before daybreak. Thus he couldn't put in such a good attendance at his lessons. There was also another problem, that of asking for alms on which to survive.

For five years now he hadn't had the stomach pain that used to attack him, and so he began to give himself to greater penances and acts of self-denial. And as he spent some time in this almshouse life and in begging, and seeing that he was making little progress in his language study, he began to think about what he would do. And seeing that there were some who served certain regents in the college and had time to study, he decided to look for this kind of employer.[112] [75] And this was the line of thought and intention he had, finding consolation in it: to imagine that the master would be Christ, and to one of the students he would give the name of St Peter and to another that of St John, and so on for each one of the apostles. 'And when the master commands me, I'll think that it's Christ who's commanding me, and when someone else commands me, I'll think it's St Peter who's commanding me.' He made considerable effort to find an employer: for one thing he spoke to the bachelor Castro[113] and to a Carthusian monk, who knew many of the teachers, and also to others. But they were never able to find him an employer.

[76] And finally, since he was finding no solution, a Spanish monk told him one day that it would be better to go off to Flanders each year, and lose two months, or even less, in order to bring back the wherewithal to study the whole year. This method, once he had put it before God, seemed a good one to him. Acting on this advice he used to bring back a sum each year from Flanders on which he could somehow manage. Once he also crossed to England, and brought back more alms than he normally did in other years.[114]

CONFLICTS

[77] When he came back the first time from Flanders, he began to give himself more intensively to spiritual conversations than he normally did, and he gave exercises to three people almost at the same time, namely to Peralta, to the bachelor Castro who was in the Sorbonne, and to a Biscayan who was in Ste Barbe called Amador.[115] These made major changes in their lives, and at once gave all they had to poor people, even their books; they began to beg for alms around Paris and went to lodge in the almshouse of St Jacques (where the pilgrim had formerly been but which he had now left for the reasons spoken of earlier). This caused great commotion in the university, because the first two of these were distinguished people, and well known. At once the Spaniards began a campaign against the two masters. Not being able to overcome them with many arguments and means of persuasion to return to the university, many of them went out one day armed, and took them out of the almshouse. [78] And bringing them to the university, they arrived at the following agreement: after they had finished their studies, then they could pursue their intentions.

The bachelor Castro later went to Spain, preached for some time in Burgos and became a Carthusian monk in Valencia. Peralta set out for Jerusalem on foot as a pilgrim; as such he was caught in Italy by a captain, a relative of his, who took steps to bring him before the Pope, and had the Pope order him to return to Spain. (These things didn't happen at once, but some years later.)

There arose in Paris much negative talk, especially among Spaniards, against the pilgrim, and *Magister Noster* de Gouveia, saying that the pilgrim had driven Amador (who was in his college) crazy, decided – and said so – that the first time he came to Ste Barbe he would have him beaten as one who led students astray.[116]

LOOSE ENDS

[79] The Spaniard with whom he had been at the beginning and who had spent his money without paying him back left for Spain by way of Rouen. And while he was waiting for a ship at Rouen, he fell ill. As he was in that sick state, the pilgrim got to know of it through a letter from him. And there came to him desires to go to visit him and help him – thinking also that, in that meeting, he might win him over to leaving the world and dedicating himself fully to the service of God.[117] So as to be able to bring this about, the desire came upon him of going the eighty-four miles from Paris to Rouen on foot, without shoes, not eating or drinking. As he was praying about this, he found himself very fearful. In the end he went to St Dominique, and there he resolved to journey in the way just spoken of, and that great fear that he had of presuming upon God had now passed.

The following day, the morning when he was due to leave, he got up early, and, as he was beginning to dress himself, there came upon him a fear so great that it almost seemed to him he couldn't dress himself. Despite this repugnance, he left the house, and indeed the city, before it was fully day. However, the fear continued with him constantly, and stayed with him as far as Argenteuil, which is a walled town ten miles from Paris in the direction of Rouen, where the garment of Our Lord is said to be.[118] He passed through that walled town in this spiritual turmoil; then as he was going up a rise in the road, this thing began to pass from him, and there came to him a great consolation and spiritual élan, with so much joy that he began to shout through those fields and to speak with God etc.

He lodged with a poor beggar that night in an almshouse, having walked forty-two miles that day. The following day he got to lodge in a barn, and on the third day he arrived in Rouen, all this time without eating or drinking, and barefoot, as he had determined. In Rouen he consoled the sick man, helped to get him onto a ship in order to go to

Spain, and gave him letters introducing him to the companions who were in Salamanca, namely Calisto and Cáceres and Arteaga.

[80] So as not to say more of these companions, what happened to them was as follows. Once the pilgrim was in Paris, he used to write to them often, in accord with their agreement, about how it would be far from easy for him to bring them to study in Paris. But he managed to write to Dona Leonor de Mascarenhas,[119] so that she could help Calisto with letters to the court of the King of Portugal, through which he might be able to obtain one of the bursaries which the King of Portugal gave in Paris. Dona Leonor gave the letters to Calisto, and a mule on which to travel, and some ready money for his expenses. Calisto made his way to the court of the King of Portugal, but in the end he didn't come to Paris. Instead, returning to Spain, he went to Mexico[120] with a certain spiritual lady. And afterwards, having returned to Spain, he went once more to Mexico, and this time returned to Spain rich, and in Salamanca really surprised all those who had known him previously.

Cáceres returned to Segovia, his home territory, and there began to live in such a way as suggested he had forgotten his first intention.

Arteaga was made a *comendador*. Later, the Society now being in Rome, he was given a bishopric in Mexico.[121] He wrote to the pilgrim asking him to give it to someone from the Society. When a negative reply came to him, he went off to Mexico having become a bishop, and there died in strange circumstances, namely: he was ill and there were two bottles of water apparently for his refreshment, one of water, which the doctor had ordered for him, and the other containing water of Soliman[122] – a poison. The latter was given him in error, and it killed him.

STUDIES AND DEFINITIVE COMPANIONS

[81] The pilgrim returned from Rouen to Paris, and found that, because of the things that had happened with Castro and with Peralta, much talk had arisen about him, and the inquisitor was having a summons issued against him. But he didn't want to wait further, and went to the inquisitor, telling him that he had heard he was looking for him, and that he himself was ready for everything he wanted (this inquisitor was called *Magister Noster* Ory, a Dominican friar[123]), but that he was asking him to expedite the matter quickly, because he wanted to enter the Arts course on the following St Remigius's day:[124] he wanted these things to be over with first, so that he could better attend to his studies.

But the inquisitor didn't call him back: he just told him that it was true they had spoken to him of his doings, etc.

[82] Shortly afterwards came St Remigius's day, which is the first of October, and he began to attend the Arts course under a Master named Juan Peña. And he began with the intention of keeping those men who had the intention of serving the Lord, but not to go any further in looking for others,[125] so that he could study more easily.

As he began to attend the course lectures, the same temptations began to come over him as had come when he was studying Latin language at Barcelona: every time he attended a lecture, he could not remain attentive with the many spiritual things occurring to him. And seeing that through this means he was making little progress in his studies, he went up to his master and made him the promise never to be absent, but to attend the whole course, as long as he could find bread and water on which he could survive. And once this promise was made, all those devotions that were coming over him out of due time left him, and he went ahead with his studies calmly.

At this time he was in contact with Master Pierre Favre and Master Francis Xavier, whom he later won for the service of God by means of the Exercises.[126]

At this stage of his course he was not persecuted as before. And in this connection Dr Frago[127] once told him that he was surprised at how he was going about undisturbed, without anyone causing him trouble. And he answered him, 'The reason is because I'm not talking to anyone about the things of God. But when the course is over we'll be back to normal'.

[83] And as the two of them were speaking together, a friar came up to ask Dr Frago if he would be willing to find a house for him, since in the one where he had his room there had been many people who had died. He thought this was from the plague, because at that time in Paris the plague was beginning. Dr Frago, together with the pilgrim, elected to go and see the house, and they took with them a woman who was very well versed in these matters. She, on going in, confirmed that it was the plague. The pilgrim elected to go in too, and, finding a sick man, consoled him, touching his sore with his hand. And after having consoled him and encouraged him a little, he went out alone. And his hand began to hurt, so that he thought he had the plague; he was imagining this so vividly that he couldn't overcome it until, with great force, he put his hand into his mouth, really turning it about inside, and saying, 'If you've got the plague in your hand you can have it in your mouth too'. And

when he had done this, the fantasy left him, and the pain in his hand as well. [84] But when he returned to the college of Ste Barbe, where at the time he had his room and was following the course, those in the college who knew that he had been into the house with the plague ran away from him, and refused to let him come in. Thus he was forced to spend some days outside.

It is the custom in Paris for those who study arts to 'take a stone'[128] (as they say) in the third year in order to become bachelors. And because this costs an écu, some very poor students can't do it. The pilgrim began to doubt if it would be good for him to take it, and finding himself very hesitant and undecided, he resolved to place the matter in the hands of his teacher. When the latter advised him to take it, he took it. Nevertheless, there was no lack of critics – or at least there was a Spaniard who passed comment on it.

ILLNESS AND SEPARATION

Already by this time in Paris he was in a very bad way with his stomach, such that every fortnight he had a stomach-ache that used to last a good hour and sent his temperature up. And once his stomach-ache lasted sixteen or seventeen hours.[129] At this stage, when he had now passed the Arts course, studied some years of theology[130] and won over the companions,[131] the illness was steadily getting much worse, without his being able to find any cure, though many were tried. [85] The only other thing remaining that could possibly help him, so the doctors were saying, was his native air. The companions too were giving him the same advice, and insisting strongly on it with him.

And already at this time they were all resolved on what they were to do, namely, to go to Venice and Jerusalem and to spend their lives in what was beneficial to souls. And if permission was not given them to remain in Jerusalem, they were to return to Rome and present themselves to Christ's vicar,[132] so that he could employ them wherever he judged to be more for the glory of God and the good of souls. They had also planned to wait a year in Venice for the passage, and if there was no passage that year to the East, they would be freed from the Jerusalem vow and would go to the Pope etc.

In the end the pilgrim allowed himself to be persuaded by the companions, and also because those who were Spaniards had some matters of business to do which he could settle.[133] And the agreement was that once he felt well again he would go and do their matters of business, and then cross to Venice and wait for the companions there. [86] This was the year 1535, and the companions were to leave, according to the agreement, in the year 1537, on the feast of the conversion of St Paul,[134] though in fact they left in November 1536 because of the wars that came along.

THE INQUISITION AGAIN

As the pilgrim was on the point of leaving, he learnt that they had accused him before the inquisitor[135] and brought a case against him. Hearing this, and seeing as they were not summoning him, he went to the inquisitor and told him what he had heard. He was on the point of leaving for Spain and he had companions: his request was that he should be so kind as to give a verdict. The inquisitor said that it was true there was an accusation, but that he didn't see any matter of importance in it. He just wanted to look at his writings on the Exercises. On seeing them, he was very complimentary about them, and asked the pilgrim to leave the copy of them with him. So he did; nevertheless, he renewed his insistence that the proceedings be gone ahead with, right up to the verdict. The inquisitor was making excuses, but he went to his house with a public notary and witnesses for his case, and he got a sealed statement made on all this.

6. Interlude at Home

[87] When this was done, he mounted a pony that the companions had bought him and set off alone towards his native country, feeling much better on the road. And, arriving in the province,[136] he left the normal road and took the mountain one, which was lonelier. Travelling along this a little while, he met two armed men coming towards him (and that road has something of a bad reputation as regards murderers). These, after they had gone a little past him, turned round, following him at a great speed, and he became a little afraid. But he spoke to them, and learnt that they were servants of his brother, who had ordered him to be met, for, apparently, there had been some word of his coming from Bayonne in France, where the pilgrim had been recognized. So they went on ahead, and he followed along the same road. A little before he arrived on his own land, he met the same two[137] coming towards him. They were very insistent that they should escort him to his brother's house, but they couldn't force it on him. Thus he went off to the almshouse, and then, at a convenient time, went about the area looking for alms.

[88] In that almshouse he began to talk about the things of God with many people who came to visit him, and through God's grace quite some fruit was produced. Immediately on his arrival, he decided to teach Christian doctrine every day to the children, but his brother opposed this strongly, telling him that no one would come. He answered him that one would be enough. But after he had begun to do it, many came to listen to him regularly, even his brother. Besides the Christian doctrine, he also preached on Sundays and feast days in a way that was useful and helpful to souls, who were coming to listen from many miles away.

He also made an effort to suppress some bad practices, and, with the help of God, some things were put in order. For example, with gambling, he had it effectively forbidden through talking the administrator of justice round to the idea. There was also another bad practice there, namely this: the girls in that country always go round with their heads uncovered, and they don't cover them except when they marry. But there are many who become concubines, of priests and of other men, and remain faithful to them as if they were their wives. And this is so common that the concubines have no shame at all in saying they've covered their heads for so-and-so, and they're known to be such. [89] Through this custom much evil arises. The pilgrim persuaded the governor that he should make a law whereby all those women who covered their heads for someone without being their wives should be punished by the authorities. In this way, this bad practice began to disappear.

For the poor, he had arrangements set up for public provision, and regularly.[138] He also arranged that the Angelus be rung three times, namely in the morning, at midday and in the evening, so that the people could pray, as they do in Rome. But, although he was feeling well at the beginning, he later came to fall seriously ill.

After he recovered, he decided to leave to do the business that the companions had entrusted to him, and to leave without money. At this his brother got very annoyed, feeling ashamed that he should want to go off on foot in the evening. The pilgrim decided to yield on the following: to go on horseback with his brother and his relatives as far as the province boundary. [90] But when he was out of the province, he went on foot, without taking anything, and set off towards Pamplona.[139]

He went from there to Almazán, where Fr Laínez comes from, and then to Sigüenza and Toledo, and from Toledo to Valencia. And in all these home territories of the companions he refused to take anything, though they made him big offers and really pressed him. In Valencia he spoke with Castro, who was now a Carthusian monk.[140] He wanted to set sail in order to reach Genoa, but his admirers in Valencia begged him not to, because, they said, Barbarossa[141] was on the sea, with many galleys etc. And though they said many things to him, enough to cause him fright, nevertheless, nothing made him doubt. [91] Having boarded a big ship, he passed through the storm that was mentioned earlier when it was said that he was three times at the point of death.[142]

7. Italy

Having arrived at Genoa, he took the road towards Bologna, along which he endured a lot, especially once when he lost the route and began to walk alongside a river. The river was low beneath while the road went high above, and the further he made his way along the latter, the narrower it became. And it got to be so narrow that he could neither move further forward nor turn back. So he began to walk on all fours, and in this fashion he went on a good bit, with great trepidation because, every time he moved, he thought he would fall into the river. And this was the greatest exertion and physical effort he ever experienced, but in the end he made it.

Wishing to enter Bologna, and having to cross a little wooden bridge, he fell off the bridge, and thus, as he was picking himself up full of mud and water, he made many of those present laugh. And entering Bologna, he began to ask for alms and didn't get even one farthing, even though he searched the whole city.[143] He remained some time in Bologna sick, and then went on to Venice, always in the same way.

[92] In Venice at that time he occupied himself in giving the Exercises and in other spiritual conversations. The most notable people to whom he gave them are Master Pietro Contarini, Master Gasparo de Dotti and a Spaniard called by the name of Rozas.[144] And there was also another Spaniard there, who called himself Bachelor Hoces.[145] This man had a lot to do with the pilgrim, and also with the Bishop of Chieti,[146] and although he had a slight inclination to make the Exercises, nevertheless he didn't put it into practice. In the end he made up his mind to start making them, and after he had made them for three or four days, he told the pilgrim his state of mind, telling him that he was afraid (on account of the things so-and-so had told him) he might teach him in the Exercises some bad doctrine, and that for this reason he had brought certain books with him so as to be able to refer to them if by chance he might be wanting to lead him astray. This person made very remarkable progress during the Exercises, and at the end made up his mind to follow the pilgrim's life. This one was also the first who died. [93] In

Venice the pilgrim also had another persecution, there being many who were saying that his effigy had been burnt in Spain and Paris, and this matter went so far that a process was held. The verdict was given in favour of the pilgrim.

THE COMPANIONS REASSEMBLE

The nine companions came to Venice at the beginning of 1537.[147] There they split up and went to serve in various almshouses. After two or three months they all went off to Rome to ask for the blessing for the passage to Jerusalem. The pilgrim didn't go because of Dr Ortiz and also of the new Theatine Cardinal. The companions came back from Rome with letters of credit for 200 or 300 scudi, which had been given them as alms for the passage to Jerusalem. And they had refused to accept these except as letters of credit, which later, being unable to go to Jerusalem, they returned to those who had given them. The companions came back from Venice in the way they had gone, that is, on foot and begging, but divided into three groups, and in such a way that they were always from different nations.

There in Venice those who were not ordained were ordained for mass, and the Nuncio who was then in Venice gave them faculties: he who was later called Cardinal Verallo. They were ordained under the title of poverty, with all making vows of chastity and poverty. [94] In that year ships were not crossing to the East because the Venetians had broken with the Turks.[148] And so, seeing the hope of a passage getting further away, they split up over the Venetian territory with the intention of waiting out the year they had determined. After it was over, should there have been no passage, they would go off to Rome.

To the pilgrim it fell to go with Favre and Laínez to Vicenza. There they found outside the city area a certain house[149] which had neither doors nor windows, and in this they used to sleep on a little straw which they had brought. Two of them used always to go in search of alms in the area twice daily, and they brought in so very little that they were almost unable to sustain themselves. As a rule they would eat a little toast, when they had it, which the one who stayed in the house would take care of toasting. In this way they spent forty days, not attending to anything but prayers.

[95] When the forty days were up Master Jean Codure arrived and all four resolved to begin preaching. And with each of the four going into

different squares on the same day and at the same hour, they began their sermons, first shouting loudly and calling the people with their caps. With these sermons there arose a great deal of talk in the city, and many people were moved with devotion. And they got the necessary bodily goods in more abundance.

In that time when he was in Vicenza he had many spiritual visions, and many consolations, as if they were a matter of course (the opposite to when he was in Paris) and most of all when he began to prepare himself to be a priest in Venice and when he was preparing himself to say mass. Throughout all these journeys he had great supernatural visitations of the kind he was accustomed to having while he was in Manresa.

While he was still in Vicenza he learnt that one of the companions, who was at Bassano, was sick to the point of death.[150] He himself was also at the time ill with fever. Nevertheless he set off on the journey, and walked so vigorously that Favre, his companion, could not keep up with him. And on this journey he had an assurance from God, and told Favre so, that the companion would not die of that sickness. And on his arriving at Bassano, the sick person was greatly consoled and recovered quickly. Then they all returned to Vicenza and all ten were there for some time, with some going to look for alms in the villages around Vicenza.[151]

TO ROME

[96] Then, with the year ended and no passage to be found, they resolved to go to Rome, and the pilgrim too, because the other time that the companions had gone those two people about whom he was doubtful had shown themselves very well-disposed.[152] They went to Rome split up into three or four groups, and the pilgrim with Favre and Laínez, and on this journey he was very specially visited by God.[153]

He had resolved to remain a year, once he became a priest, without saying mass, preparing himself and praying Our Lady to be pleased to put him with her Son. And being one day in a church some miles before arrival in Rome, and making prayer, he sensed such a change in his soul, and he saw so clearly that God the Father was putting him with Christ, his Son, that he would not have the wilfulness to have any doubt about this: it could only be that God the Father was putting him with his Son.*

---

* And I, who am writing these things, said to the pilgrim, when he was narrating this to me, that Laínez used to recount this with other details, as I had understood. And he told me that

[97] Then, coming to Rome, he told his companions that he saw the windows shut, meaning that they were to have many things opposing them.

And he also said, 'We need to be very much on our guard and not take on conversation with women unless they be illustrious'. Later in Rome – to speak of this subject – Master Francis[354] used to hear a lady's confession, and visited her a few times to practise spiritual things, and this lady was later found to be pregnant. But the Lord willed that the man who had done this misdeed was discovered. The like happened to Jean Codure with one of his spiritual daughters who was caught with a man.

[98] From Rome the pilgrim went to Monte Cassino to give the Exercises to Dr Ortiz, and was there for forty days, during which he once saw Bachelor Hoces entering heaven, and at this had great tears and great spiritual consolation. And he saw this so clearly that, were he to say the contrary, it would seem to him to be telling a lie. From Monte Cassino he brought Francisco de Estrada.[355] Returning to Rome, he occupied himself in helping souls. They were still at the vineyard,[356] and he was giving spiritual exercises to different people at one and the same time. Of these one was staying at Santa Maria Maggiore and the other at Ponte Sesto.[357]

Then the persecutions began.[358] Miguel began to cause trouble and to speak ill of the pilgrim. The latter had him called before the governor, having first shown the governor a letter of Miguel's in which he greatly praised the pilgrim. The governor examined Miguel and the conclusion was to banish him from Rome. Then Mudarra and Barreda began persecuting, saying that the pilgrim and his companions were fleeing from Spain, from Paris and from Venice. In the end, in the presence of the governor and of the legate who was then the one for Rome, both of them confessed that they had nothing evil to say of them, neither about their habits, nor their doctrine. The legate ordered a silence to be drawn over the whole business but the pilgrim wouldn't accept it, saying that he wanted a final verdict. This didn't please the legate, or the governor either, nor even those who at first were favourable to the pilgrim. But in the end, after a few months, the Pope came to Rome. The pilgrim went to talk to him at Frascati and represented some arguments to him. The

---

all that Laínez said was the truth – it was because his own memory was not so detailed – but that he knew for certain that, at the time when he was narrating this, he had not said anything except the truth. He said the same as this to me on other things.

Pope was persuaded, and commanded that a verdict be given, which was given in favour etc.

There were set up in Rome with the help of the pilgrim and the companions some works of piety, like the Catechumens, Santa Martha, the orphans, etc.[159] The other things Master Nadal will be able to recount.

Epilogue

(GONÇALVES DA CÂMARA)[160]

[99] After these matters of narrative, I asked the pilgrim on 20 October[161] about the *Exercises* and the *Constitutions*, wanting to find out how he had produced them. He said to me that as for the *Exercises* he had not produced them all at one time, rather that some things which he used to observe in his soul and find useful for himself it seemed to him could also be useful for others, and so he used to put them in writing: for example, regarding the examination of conscience with that method of the lines etc.[162] As for the elections, he told me specifically that he had drawn them from that variety of spirit and thoughts which he had had when he was in Loyola, when he was still ill from his leg. And he told me that as for the *Constitutions* he would speak to me in the evening.

The same day before he had supper he called me, with a look of a person who was more recollected than normal, and he made a sort of formal declaration to me, the gist of which was to demonstrate the intention and simplicity with which he had narrated these things, saying that he was quite sure he had not overdone anything in the narrative, and that he had committed many offences against Our Lord after he had begun to serve him, but that he had never given consent to a mortal sin: on the contrary, always growing in devotion, i.e. in facility in finding God, and now more than ever in his whole life. And every time and hour he wanted to find God, he found him.

And that now too he had visions often, especially those which have been talked about above, when he saw Christ like a sun.[163] This often used to happen as he was going along talking about important things, and that would make him arrive at assurance. [100] When he was saying mass he would have many visions too, and when he was producing the *Constitutions* he had them too, very often.

And this he could now affirm more easily because every day he used to write down what passed through his soul, and could now find these things in writing. And thus he showed me quite a large bundle of written notes, from which he read me a good part. The majority were visions which he saw in confirmation of one of the *Constitutions*, seeing sometimes God the Father, at other times all the three persons of the Trinity, at other times Our Lady interceding, at other times her confirming, in particular, he told me, in the course of the decisions over which he had been forty days saying mass every day, and every day with many tears. And the question was whether the church should have any income, and if the Society could take advantage of that.[164]

[101] The method he used to observe when he was producing the *Constitutions* was to say mass every day and present the point he was dealing with to God and make prayer over that. And he always made his prayer and said mass with tears. I wanted to see those papers for all the *Constitutions* and I asked him if he would let me have them for a bit: he was unwilling.

THE SPIRITUAL DIARY

THE SPIRITUAL DIARY

Introduction

Even if someone were to express everything that is 'within him', we wouldn't necessarily understand him.
                                                                    L. WITTGENSTEIN[1]

The *Spiritual Diary* of Ignatius Loyola is one of the very few of his works that survive in their original hand-written form. One might have expected it to provide immediate access to his mind and spirituality. Instead many readers, even those who have some acquaintance with the life and work of Ignatius, find that the *Diary* remains a remote and impenetrable work. This is due partly to the style – elliptic and idiosyncratic,[2] and partly to the content – mystical experiences to which few people have access. However, some light can be thrown on these pages when they are replaced in their historical context.

These pages are clearly the work of a man devoted to God, living an intense interior life, endowed with special gifts. It is not quite so easy to believe that they were written by the man who had recently founded the Society of Jesus, at a time when he was extraordinarily active, both with personal apostolic work in Rome and with the taxing occupation of governing the young Society. Further, the impression conveyed by the *Diary* is that the writer is a man subject to more than the ordinary psychological tensions – a person tossed between 'great tranquillity' and the sort of experience recorded for 8 February:

I felt within me that I approached, or was taken before, the Father, and with this movement my hair rose and I felt what seemed a very remarkable burning in every part of my body, followed by tears and the most intense devotion.

With the opening of the year 1544 (the *Diary* begins in February of this year) it seems that the first great wave of activity that had been carrying Ignatius forward ever since his arrival in Rome suddenly diminished. The house of St Martha for the reform of prostitutes was founded in January, but then four months of extremely bad health crippled Ignatius's movements. In any case it must have been clear that a period of consolidation, and above all of intense organization and planning, was becoming increasingly necessary. The Society of Jesus was expanding rapidly in numbers and in the diverse directions of its personnel and their occupations. Attached though Ignatius was to the 'inner law of divine love',[3] as the guiding principle for himself and his subjects, mounting pressure from his companions and from the papacy, together with the evident dangers of dissipated energy, impelled him to begin the unwelcome task of composing the *Constitutions*.

The problem became crucial with the need for a decision concerning poverty: Ignatius realized that the principles involved were of radical importance. First, there was the complex question of poverty itself: he was sufficiently aware of life's reality to appreciate that absolute poverty might spell the end of the new order by any normal calculus of human probability. Secondly, his own authority would be particularly tested: for the first time he would have to exercise on a grand scale the power so gladly entrusted to him and so reluctantly accepted. And by a cruel twist of fate, the first point appeared to be one in which he would have to revoke a decision already approved by the early companions. In the spring of 1541 a commission (consisting of Ignatius himself and Codure) had examined whether the sacristies of churches should be allowed to possess income; this was normal even in orders of strict observance, like the Franciscans. Guided by the commission, all had agreed. But now Ignatius was asking if this decision should be set aside because it seemed to lessen the complete poverty to which they were committed. Only if the *Diary* is seen against this background can one understand the apparently excessive hesitation over such a relatively minor matter, one incidentally on which Ignatius would subsequently be overruled. The title given to these sheets of paper[4] is somewhat misleading: they are not a 'diary' in the normal sense of the term. Ignatius is keeping note of progress made during the process of making up his mind: he is making a choice or 'election', in the terminology of the *Spiritual Exercises*. The latter provide the best key to what is happening.

The *Spiritual Exercises* revolve around the central axis of reform. At the heart of the second week (the second of four) the exercitant is provided with a series of considerations and methods that will help a person to see what changes are required and how to choose them. Ignatius outlines three possible scenarios, which he had discovered by personal trial and error. The first is when one receives the sort of illumination that admits of no doubt (the conversion of St Paul is a good example). The second and third are much more protracted and complicated. The third, which is explained most fully, is dominated by the notion of the 'reasonable'. Here there are two possibilities: first, one can draw up a list of pros and cons that concern the matter at issue; secondly, by imagining different situations one can try to gain some distance from the problem, and thus study it more objectively (e.g. by pretending that one is making the decision on behalf of somebody else, or that one is on one's deathbed). There is clear proof that Ignatius was using the first of these techniques to help him: we have the list of *Pros and Cons* that he drew up (in this edition placed at the head of the *Diary*) and mentioned at several points in his reflections.[5]

However the second of the three scenarios mentioned is the most distinctively Ignatian. He describes it as

A time when sufficient light and knowledge is received through experience of consolations and desolations, and through experience of the discernment (*discreción*) of different spirits (Exx. 176).

It is clear that the *Spiritual Diary* is the record of such a time of 'discernment', with the 'consolations and desolations' (feelings of peace and joy as opposed to those of tension and unhappiness) duly noted: a descriptive title would be 'A Discernment Logbook'. It is an exceptional document in the fullness and in the sensitivity of its entries, and must be one of the finest accounts in the world's spiritual writings of one process of discernment.

NOTES

1 *Last Writings on the Philosophy of Psychology*, I, No. 191, Basil Blackwell, Oxford 1982, p. 28.
2 A note from a graphological study has its interest: the handwriting is said to reveal 'a need for clarity, for precision and for exactness; there is an exigence in the very form of expression. He constantly corrects himself, and starts anew. The rhythm remains full of life throughout these pages, where each trait has its particular value'. Carmen M. Affholder, 'Saint Ignace dans son écriture', AHSI, 29 (1960), p. 391.
3 As he says in the Preamble to the *Constitutions*: 'what helps most on our part towards this end must be, more than any exterior constitution, the interior law of charity and love which the Holy Spirit writes and engraves upon hearts'.
4 The twenty-eight pages that contain the *Diary* are the result of Ignatius taking four or six pages at a time and folding them down the middle; he was not working with a ready-made notebook.
5 8, 10, 11, 16 February.

Pros and Cons

Advantages and disadvantages
in having a fixed income for churches of
the Society of Jesus

THE DISADVANTAGES ARISING FROM A LACK OF ANY INCOME
ARE THE ADVANTAGES OF HAVING EITHER A COMPLETE OR
A PARTIAL INCOME

1st   If the Society were to possess a partial or a complete income, it could probably maintain itself better.

2nd   If such is possessed, members of the Society will not cause trouble and disedification by begging, especially as it would be clerics who would have to go begging.

3rd   If such is possessed, they will be less troubled and bothered by distracting worries in searching for alms.

4th   They will be able to give themselves with greater order and peace to the duties and set prayers.

5th   The time spent in asking and seeking for alms could be used for preaching, hearing confessions, and other pious works.

6th   The church will probably be kept cleaner and finer, more suited to rouse devotion; also it will be possible to rebuild it.

7th   Similarly, members of the Society will be able to devote more time to study, and so give more spiritual help to other people and take more care of their own health.

8th   On a former occasion, after two members of the Society had examined the point, the others gave their unanimous approbation.[1]

THE DISADVANTAGES ARISING FROM THE POSSESSION OF
INCOME ARE THE ADVANTAGES OF NOT HAVING ANYTHING

1st   If members of the Society could possess such an income, they would be less diligent in helping people, and less ready to travel and suffer hardships. Also it is not then so easy to win others to true poverty and self-abnegation in all things, as is explained in the advantages of not possessing anything explained below.[2]

ADVANTAGES ARISING FROM, AND REASONS IN FAVOUR OF,
HAVING NO INCOME WHATSOEVER

1st   The Society gains greater spiritual strength, and increased devotion, the more it contemplates and imitates the Son of the Blessed Virgin, our Creator and Lord, so poor and so afflicted.

2nd   The world's avarice is put to shame when one seeks no security.

2nd   Union with the Church seems to be more affectionate, if all are at one in possessing nothing, thinking of Christ poor in the Blessed Sacrament.

3rd   It is easier to put all one's trust in God Our Lord, if one is cut off from everything of the world.

4th   This causes humiliation and aids union with the One who humbled himself more than any other.

4th   The Society lives more oblivious of worldly consolations.

5th   Its hope in God is more continuous; and its work in His service, more diligent.

6th   In general, people are more impressed if they see that nothing of this world is being sought.

7th   One can speak with greater freedom of spirit, and with more efficacy, of all spiritual things that are for the greater profit of souls.

8th   The daily reception of alms helps and urges one on to give more spiritual assistance to souls.

9th   Others are more strongly persuaded to true poverty, if that poverty is practised to which Christ Our Lord urges, when he says, 'Everyone who has forsaken father, etc.' (Mt. 19:29, Mk 10:29).

10th   Members of the Society will probably be more diligent in helping others, and more ready to travel and suffer hardships.

11th   Poverty that excludes the possession of any income is more perfect than one that admits either a partial or a complete income.

12th   Jesus, the Lord of us all, chose this poverty for himself, and this was what He taught them, when He sent his apostles and beloved disciples to preach.

13th   When, with complete unanimity, all ten of us chose this poverty, we took as our head Jesus himself, our Creator and Lord, to go forward under his banner, to preach and exhort, as is our profession.

14th   It was on this understanding that we asked for and obtained the

Papal Bull; similarly after waiting one year for it to be expedited, we kept to our decision and it was confirmed by His Holiness.

15th Immutability is a characteristic of God; mutability and change are those of the enemy.[3]

The Spiritual Diary

In this translation the system of punctuation adopted by Ignatius, and his division of very long sentences into somewhat disjointed (and hence often ambiguous) phrases, have been adapted to conform with English usage. The words printed in italics were underlined or separated in some way by Ignatius (e.g. by encircling lines) and then written out on a separate sheet (cf. 19 February with note 24). Double and single asterisks (** and *) replace signs in the manuscript which 'seem to indicate that St Ignatius had some sort of vision' (MHSI, p. 87, n. 5). The system of numbering, to which he seems to have given some importance, has been reproduced, despite its imperfections, at the head of each entry. Numerous words and phrases have been crossed out (but are still legible) in the autograph, and a fair sample of these are given in the notes.

PART I

✝ Mass of Our Lady

Chapter 1st. Saturday [2 Feb. 1544] – Great devotion during mass, with tears, with increased trust in Our Lady, and more inclined both then and during the whole day to choose complete poverty.

Chapter 2nd. Sunday [3 Feb.] – The same; and more inclined both then and during the whole day to choose complete poverty.

Mass of Our Lady
Chapter 3rd. Monday [4 Feb.] – The same; also other feelings and a greater inclination to complete poverty; and at night a close drawing-near in affection to Our Lady with great confidence.

Mass of Our Lady
4th. Tuesday [5 Feb.] – Great devotion before, during and after mass, with tears so abundant that my eyes ached; I saw the Mother and Son

ready and willing to intercede with the Father*; both then and during the day I was set on poverty and still more moved to it; in the afternoon it was as if I felt or saw that Our Lady was ready and willing to intercede.

Mass of Our Lady

5th. Wednesday [6 Feb.] – Devotion, not without tears, before and during mass, and more inclined to complete poverty. Later I realized with considerable clarity, or in a way differing from the usual, that to have some income would raise complications, and to have a complete income would cause scandal and help to tarnish the poverty so praised by God Our Lord.

Mass of the Trinity

6th. Thursday [7 Feb.] – Very great devotion and tears before mass; I felt throughout the day a warmth and a remarkable devotion, remaining myself ever more convinced and moved to poverty. While celebrating mass, I seemed to have easy access and felt, with much devotion, an interior impulse to implore the Father; it seemed to me that the two mediators had made supplication and I received some impression of seeing them.

Mass of the Holy Name of Jesus

7th. Friday [8 Feb.] – After experiencing remarkable devotion and tears while I prayed, from preparing for mass and during mass very great devotion, also tears; only at times could I retain the power of speech; resolution fixed on poverty. After mass, devotion not without tears, while I considered the choices in the election for an hour and a half or more. When I came to offer what seemed to me most reasonable, and to which my will felt most impelled viz. that no fixed income should be allowed, I desired to make this offering to the Father through the mediation and prayers of the Mother and Son. Firstly I prayed her to assist me before her Son and Father. Next I implored the Son that together with the Mother He might help me before the Father. Then I felt within me that I approached, or was taken before, the Father, and with this movement my hair rose and I felt what seemed a very remarkable burning in every part of my body, followed by tears and the most intense devotion**. Later when I read over what I had written and saw that it was well written, fresh devotion, not without water in my eyes**; and later still, when I remembered the graces received, a new experience of devotion.

In the afternoon I once more weighed up the choices for another hour and a half or more, and made the choice for complete poverty. At the same time I felt devotion and a certain elation, with great tranquillity and no opposing urge to possess anything; the desire to continue with the election, to the extent considered necessary a few days before, now seemed to be fading.

8th. Saturday [9 Feb.][1] – On reconsidering the choices in great tranquillity and devotion, it seemed perfectly clear that no income, either partial or adequate, should be allowed: nor did it seem worthwhile to consider further: I thought the matter was settled, I felt great tranquillity of mind, and I continued to be resolved on complete poverty.

Mass of the day
9th. Sunday [10 Feb.] – On reconsidering the choices, and on making the offering of complete poverty, I felt great devotion, not without tears: so also earlier during my customary prayer, before, during and after mass, considerable devotion and tears, my resolve ever fixed on complete poverty, and feeling tranquil in the offering that had been made. I had noticed great clarity in my reasonings and later with reference to the mediators, feelings, not without vision**.

At night, on considering the choice of a complete, a partial or no income, I offered up complete poverty and felt great devotion, interior peace and tranquillity of soul, and a certain security or assent that the election was well made.

Mass of the Holy Spirit
10th. Monday [11 Feb.] – During my customary prayer, without reconsidering the reasons for poverty, I offered it to God Our Lord or implored Him that the offering already made might be accepted by His Divine Majesty; I felt considerable devotion and tears. A little later I made a colloquy with the Holy Spirit, in preparation for saying His mass; I experienced the same devotion and tears, and seemed to see or feel Him in a dense clarity or in the colour of burning flame – a way quite strange to me – all of which confirmed me in my election**.

Later, in preparation for considering and going into the various choices, now my mind was made up, I took out the written pros and cons to consider them. I prayed to Our Lady, then to the Son, and to the Father, that He might give me his Spirit to assist me in my reasonings and to give me clarity of mind, even though I spoke of the matter as already settled. I felt considerable devotion and certain fairly clear-sighted intuitions. Thus I sat down considering almost in general whether the income should be complete, partial or not at all. Then I began to lose the desire to look into pros and cons and at the same moment I received new insights, viz. that the Son first sent his Apostles to preach in poverty, and later the Holy Spirit, by granting his spirit and his gift of tongues, confirmed them, and thus, since both Father and Son sent the Holy Spirit, all three Persons confirmed such a mission.

Then receiving greater devotion and losing all desire to consider the question any longer, with tears and sobs I made, on my knees, the offering of complete poverty to the Father; and so many were the tears running down my face, and such the sobs that I could hardly get up, so great was the devotion and grace that I was receiving. Finally I did rise though even then the devotion and the sobs continued. They came when I had formally ratified, endorsed, etc., the offering of complete poverty.

A little later as I was walking and remembering what had happened, a new interior impulse of devotion and tears**.

A little later, just before going out to say mass, while I prayed for a short while, I felt intense devotion and wept on feeling or seeing in some way the Holy Spirit – the question of the election being now answered[2] – and I could neither see nor feel either of the other two Divine Persons in this way.

Later in chapel, before and during mass, great devotion and tears. Afterwards I felt great tranquillity and security of soul, like a tired man who takes a complete rest. I no longer sought or desired to seek for anything, considering the matter finished, except for thanksgiving, also out of devotion to the Father and to the mass of the Blessed Trinity which I had already proposed to say tomorrow, Tuesday.

ABOUT THE PERSONS WHO HID THEMSELVES[3]

Mass of the Trinity

11th. Tuesday[4] [12 Feb.] – On awakening, I prayed and did not cease to give thanks most earnestly to God Our Lord, in the midst of intuitions and tears, for the great benefit and clarity conceded me, so great as to be inexplicable. On rising, the interior warmth and devotion I had experienced continued. When I called to mind the great good I had received, I was moved by new and growing devotion and the impulse to weep; also on walking to Don Francisco,[5] and while with him; and on returning I did not lose the warmth and intense love.[6]

Mass of Our Lady

12th. Wednesday[7] [13 Feb.] – I knew that I was gravely at fault in having left the Divine Persons on the previous day during the thanksgiving: I wanted to abstain from saying the mass of the Trinity that I had thought of saying, and take as my intercessors the Mother and Son, that my fault might be forgiven me and I myself restored to my former grace; I would keep away from the Divine Persons and so not apply immediately to them for the former graces and offerings: I would not say their masses all that week, mortifying myself by thus absenting myself. Then I experienced very great devotion, and many most intense tears, not only during prayer but while I vested; I sobbed and as I could feel the Mother and Son to be interceding for me, I felt a complete security that the Eternal Father would restore me to my former state. Later, before, during and after mass, greatly increased devotion and a great abundance of tears: I saw and felt the mediators: I was most sure I would regain what was lost. During all these periods, both on Wednesday and Thursday,[8] I considered the offering as fully made and could see no objection to it.

Mass of the Holy Name of Jesus

13. Thursday[9] [14 Feb.] – During the usual prayer, great devotion and an exaltation of mind, remarkable tranquillity; I did not see the mediators in the same way. When I prepared to leave the room, not without tears and interior impulses. Then before, during and after mass, very copious tears, devotion, great sobs – so great that often I could not keep the power of speech for long before losing it again – many spiritual intuitions; finding easy access to the Father when I spoke his name, as the mass names Him, and a great security or hope that I would regain what was lost, feeling the Son very ready to intercede, and the Saints; I cannot describe how I saw them as I cannot explain anything else of what happened. No doubts about the first offering that was made, etc.

Mass of Our Lady in the Temple. Simeon[10]

14. Friday [15 Feb.] – During my first prayer, when I named the Eternal Father etc., there came a feeling of interior sweetness that continued, not without an impulse to weep: later considerable devotion, and, towards the end, much greater still; no mediators or persons revealed themselves. Next on preparing to leave for mass, as I began to pray, I could feel, and

was shown, Our Lady, also how great had been my fault the previous day: I felt moved within and wept, for I seemed to be putting Our Lady to shame in having her intercede for me so often, because of my many failings. So much so that Our Lady hid from me and I found no devotion in her or higher than her. A little later, when I sought to go higher, as I could not find Our Lady, a mighty impulse to weep and sob gripped me and I seemed to see or feel that the Heavenly Father showed Himself propitious and kind – to the point of making clear to me that he would be pleased if Our Lady, whom I could not see, would intercede. While preparing the altar, after I had vested, and during mass, I experienced great interior impulses and wept very copiously and intensely, sobbing violently. Often I could not speak. The same continued after mass. During much of this time, before, during and after mass, I felt and saw clearly that Our Lady was very propitious, pleading before the Father. Indeed during the prayers to the Father and the Son, and at His consecration, I could not but feel or see her, as though she were part or rather portal of the great grace that I could feel in my spirit. (At the consecration she showed that her own flesh was in that of her Son)[11] with so many intuitions that they could not be written. No doubts about the first offering that was made.

Mass of the Holy Name of Jesus
15th. Saturday [16 Feb.] – During the customary prayer, I had no feeling of the mediators; no coldness or tepidity; I had considerable devotion.[12] When I wanted to prepare for mass, I was doubtful to whom I should commend myself first and how to do so. Still in doubt, I knelt down wondering where I would begin: then I thought the Father was revealing Himself most and drawing me to his mercies. I felt Him more friendly towards me and myself better disposed to implore what I desired (I felt unable to adapt myself to the mediators). This feeling or vision grew; I wept most copiously, the tears streaming down my face, and felt great trust in the Father, as if the exile I had been under were being lifted. Later I went to mass, prepared the altar, vested and began the mass; all this time many intense tears. I felt drawn towards the Father, to whose honour I directed the things of the Son: I experienced insights into many notable things, that caused delight and were very spiritual. After mass I spent an hour considering one set of election reasons, paying attention to the point raised, and also to the income already granted:[13] it seemed to me that such things were so many knots and bonds contrived by the enemy: with great tranquillity and peace I made the election and the

offering to the Father of not possessing anything even for the church; I did the same in turn with the other set of election reasons – all this not without an interior impulse and tears.

At night I took out the notes to review and draw up reasons for the possible choices. I had been at fault during the day and began to hesitate if I should proceed further without delaying the election as before.[14] Finally I decided to continue as usual, though still doubtful to whom I would commend myself first. I felt a certain shame, or indefinable feeling, before the Mother. Finally, having first examined my conscience for all that day and begged pardon, etc, I felt the Father was very propitious, without my being able to adapt to the mediators; and some tears came.

Later, with this same warmth, I implored grace to reason with His spirit and to be moved by that spirit. Before I rose, it seemed to me pointless to reconsider the election – and at that the tears so overwhelm me and I feel such intense devotion, sobs and spiritual gifts, I am moved for a while to make my offering of complete poverty in our churches and no longer wish to prolong the matter, except for two days in which to give thanks and repeat the same offering, or a more formal one. I do so with an excess of tears, with warmth and interior devotion. The same state continued afterwards and I thought I could not rise: instead I wanted to stay there with that internal visitation.

A little later the thought came to me that during those other two days I could reconsider the choices, and that I did not seem to have decided against this. It upset me and diminished the intensity of my devotion: I wanted to put it aside. At last I rose from my knees and sitting down made an election on the matter: I called to mind some spiritual considerations. I began to weep a little and, judging the thought to be a temptation, I went down on my knees and offered to stop all consideration of elections on that point: but I would take the two days, viz. until Monday, saying mass in thanksgiving and repeating the offering.

While I made this offering and oblation, once more the tears were of such a kind and so copious, the sobs so violent and the spiritual gifts so great, that after I had made it – to the Father in the presence of Our Lady, the Angels, etc – as the tears etc. continued, I felt no desire to rise but on the contrary longed to continue in that state which I was experiencing so intensely. Then at last, feeling a very great satisfaction, I rose, devotion and tears continuing all the while, with firm resolve to fulfil the oblation and all that had been offered.

16. Sunday [17 Feb.] – During the customary prayer, I could feel no mediators or any other persons. I was coming to the end.[15] I felt considerable relish and warmth. From the middle onwards, the tears were very copious, accompanied by warmth and interior relish; no intuitions; I considered the matter ended and it seemed to me to be acceptable to God Our Lord. When I rose and turned to the preparation before mass, I thanked His Divine Majesty and offered Him the oblation already made. Neither devotion nor the impulse to weep was lacking. On going out to mass, preparing the altar, vesting and beginning mass, considerable tears: very intense and copious during mass, and such that very often I could not speak, especially during the whole of the long epistle of St Paul, which begins, 'Libenter suffertis insipientes';[16] I felt no flashes of understanding or of distinctions, nor was I conscious in any way of any persons; my love was most intense and accompanied by warmth and great relish in divine things; my soul's satisfaction increased greatly. After mass, in the chapel, and later while I knelt in my room, when I wished to give thanks for so many gifts and graces received, I lost all desire to remake offerings of the oblation made (although I was ever doing so, and not without devotion), considering the matter as settled; on the other hand, I felt drawn by the devotion I experienced to stay there enjoying the feeling. Later I wondered whether to go out or not and decided with great peace in the affirmative; thereupon I felt special interior impulses and I wept. Although it seemed to me that I could have spent more time in tears, I rose, still weeping and with my soul very satisfied, and set out having decided to complete the matter tomorrow, before dinner-time at the latest – with thanksgiving, petition for strength, and a repetition of the offering already made out of devotion for the Blessed Trinity, celebrating the mass in their honour.

Mass of the Trinity and End[17]

17. Monday [18 Feb.] – Last night, a little before retiring to bed, I felt some warmth, devotion and great trust that I would find the Divine Persons or grace in them now that I was coming to the end. After I had gone to bed, I had special consolation in thinking of Them, I was on fire[18] for the exultation in my soul. Later I slept. I awoke next morning a little before daybreak and then afterwards felt heavy-hearted and bereft of all spiritual things. While I made the customary prayer, I remained during the first half with little or no relish,[19] and moreover an uncertainty if I would find grace in the Blessed Trinity, until eventually I renewed my prayer once more, when I think I made it with consider-

able devotion, and towards the end with great pleasure and spiritual relish.

Later I decided to rise and thought of delaying the dinner hour and taking measures to ensure that I should not be disturbed until I had found the grace desired; I then felt new warmth and a devotion that made me weep. While dressing I thought of abstaining for three days in order to find what I desired. When the realization dawned on me that even this thought was from God, new strength, warmth and spiritual devotion filled me, impelling me ever more to weep. A little later I wondered where I should begin and it occurred to me that it might be with all the Saints, putting my cause in their hands, so that they might pray to Our Lady and her Son to be intercessors on my behalf before the Blessed Trinity. With great devotion and intensity of feeling, I felt my face streaming with tears; in this state I went for confirmation of the past offerings, including many things in my colloquy – beseeching and nominating as intercessors on my behalf the Angels, the holy Fathers,[20] the Apostles and Disciples and all the Saints etc., that they might plead to Our Lady and her Son: then I started once more to beseech and implore Our Lady and her Son with long reasonings that my concluded confirmation and my thanksgiving might rise before the throne of the Blessed Trinity. During all this and from then onwards, a great flood of tears, many impulses and interior sobs: it seemed moreover as if each vein and part of my body was making itself sensibly felt. Before their entire Heavenly Court I made the concluded confirmation of my offering to the Blessed Trinity, giving thanks with great and intense affection, first to the Divine Persons, then to Our Lady and her Son, then passing through the Angels, the holy Fathers, the Apostles, Disciples, to all the Saints, men and women, and to all persons who had helped me to do this.

Later[21] while I prepared the altar and vested, there came to me: 'Eternal Father, confirm me'; 'Eternal Son, confirm me'; 'Eternal Holy Spirit, confirm me'; 'Holy Trinity, confirm me'; 'My One Sole God, confirm me'. I repeated this many times with great force, devotion and tears, and very deeply did I feel it. And when I asked once, 'Eternal Father, will you not confirm me?' I knew He would: so also with Son and Holy Spirit. While saying mass, I was not weeping, yet not entirely without tears, feeling a certain warm devotion, ruby-red as it were; also many little gasps full of considerable devotion. At times however these things were not felt to any great extent and then the thought came to me, pricking and preventing devotion, that my tears were not so copious and abundant: moved by it I decided not to rest content seeing that confirmation had not been granted in this last mass of the Trinity. After mass I quietened down, comparing my own worth with the wisdom and greatness of God. I continued for some hours until the thought came to me that I should not trouble to say more masses – I felt angry with the Blessed Trinity; I had no desire to prolong the deliberation into the future; I considered that the decision already reached was final, although some slight doubt still occurred. I felt devotion all day: however, it was beset in some slight way, and seemed fearful of erring in anything.

18. Tuesday[22] [19 Feb.] Mass of the Trinity. No. 1. – Last night on going to bed I thought over what masses to celebrate or how. When I awoke in the morning, I began an examination of conscience; then and during prayer, I wept much, the tears streaming down my face. A very intense devotion lasted for a while, I had many intuitions or spiritual reminders of the Blessed Trinity. I was at peace and felt such great exultation that there was a pressure in my lungs[23] for the intense love I was experiencing in the Blessed Trinity. At this I gained confidence and decided to say the mass of the Blessed Trinity in order to decide later what should be done. The same thought while I dressed, and more intuitions of the Blessed Trinity. I was not without tears on rising and while I prayed for a short while. Later I felt devotion and spiritual confidence: I would say in succession six or more masses of the Blessed Trinity.

When I went to mass, I was not without tears before it; many tears, coming very peacefully, during mass. *I had very many intuitions about the Blessed Trinity, my understanding being enlightened with them to such an extent that it seemed to me that with hard study I would not have known so much. Later when I considered the matter further, I knew that what I had then understood feeling and seeing I could not have learnt in a whole life of study.*[24] While I prayed for a short while after mass, I found myself saying, 'Eternal Father, confirm me; Son, etc. confirm me'. The tears came pouring from my eyes, and I felt ever more decided to persevere with their masses (agreeing to however many in number they might order): many violent sobs: I drew much closer, more and more secure in my increased love for their Divine Majesty. In general the intuitions during and before mass were concerned with the appropriation[25] in the mass prayers when mention is made of God, of the Father, or of the Son, etc, *with the operations of the Divine Persons, and with the production of the Persons – in all this, I felt and saw rather than understood.* All these things confirmed what had been done and I felt encouraged for the future.

Today, even when walking in the city, I felt great interior joy, and on seeing three rational creatures together, or three animals, or three other things, the Blessed Trinity was brought before me: and so continuously.

Mass of the Trinity. No. 2

19. Wednesday [20 Feb.] – Before beginning my prayer I had a devout eagerness to commence. Once I had started, my devotion was very great, warm or bright and gentle. There were no intuitions but a tendency to security of soul, without reference to any of the Divine Persons. Later I felt confirmed about the past by the knowledge that the earlier spirit had been evil, the one that had wanted to make me have doubts and feel anger with the Blessed Trinity, as is described in chapter 17. On receiving the knowledge, I felt anew an interior impulse to weep: the same happened after, before and during mass. My devotion was greatly increased, quiet and tranquil; I wept and had some intuitions.

Both before and after mass I had the feeling or impression that I should proceed no further – or the urge to do so left me. Later this was more marked when I experienced such great quiet and satisfaction in my soul. It seemed to me pointless to continue with masses to the Blessed Trinity, except for the sake of thanksgiving or of fulfilment: I had no need for confirmation of what had happened.

Mass of the Trinity. No. 3

20. Thursday [21 Feb.] – Very great and quite continuous devotion throughout the period of prayer – warm clarity and spiritual enjoyment; also I felt drawn partly to rise in some way. Later when I prepared in my room, when at the altar and while I vested, I had more interior, spiritual impulses and felt moved to weep. After mass I remained in great spiritual repose. During mass the tears were more copious than the previous day and lasted continuously. Occasionally my power of speech was cut off. Once, or perhaps a few times, I felt spiritual intuitions so great that I seemed to understand that almost nothing more could be known on the subject of the Blessed Trinity. And this was due to the following: before, when I wanted to obtain devotion in the Blessed Trinity, I had not desired nor adapted myself to seek for it or find it when saying prayers to the Father, for I thought consolation and visitation in the Blessed Trinity would not occur then: *but during this mass I knew or felt*

or saw, 'God knows',[26] that on speaking to the Father and seeing that
He was One Person of the Blessed Trinity, I felt moved to love all the
Trinity, especially as the other Persons were all in the Trinity by their
very essence: the same feeling when I prayed to the Son and to the Holy
Spirit; when I felt consolation I was delighted with any one of them,
and I rejoiced in acknowledging it as coming from all three. So great an
achievement did it seem to have untied this knot or accomplished some-
thing similar, that I could not stop repeating to myself, with reference to
myself, 'Who are you? From where? etc. What did you deserve? Why
this? etc.'

Mass of the Trinity. No. 4

21. Friday [22 Feb.] – Throughout the customary prayer I was helped by
great grace – it was warm and shone in some way – and felt much
devotion. For my part I sometimes felt I should have no difficulty in
discontinuing; yet I continued to be helped by great grace. Later when I
prepared the altar, some impulses to weep: I kept repeating, 'I am not
worthy to invoke the name of the Blessed Trinity'. This thought, and the
repetition of the phrase, caused greater interior devotion. When I vested,
turning over these and other considerations, my soul opened more to
tears and sobs. I began mass and reached the Gospel[27] which I said with
considerable devotion; I was being helped by a warm grace which later
battled like fire with water against some thoughts.[28]

Mass of the Trinity. No. 5

22. Saturday [23 Feb.] – During the customary prayer, at first nothing;
from half-way through I found considerable devotion and satisfaction of
soul together with some indication of shining clarity. While I prepared
the altar, Jesus came into my thoughts and I felt impelled to follow Him,
for to my mind it seemed that since He was the head of the Society
[*Confirmation of Jesus*[29]], He was a greater argument for having complete poverty than all other human reasons, although all the other
reasons that had been used in the election seemed to me to reinforce the
same conclusion. This thought impelled devotion, tears, and the firm
certainty that even if no tears came during this mass, or during other
masses, this conviction would suffice amid temptations and tribulations
to make me stand firm. I continued walking with these thoughts and
vested: they increased ever more, appearing to be a confirmation of what
I had done, even if I received no consolations on this point. *It seemed in*
some way to be from the Blessed Trinity that Jesus was shown or felt,

and I remembered the time when the Father put me with the Son.[30] When I had finished vesting, so set was my intention that the name of Jesus impress itself on me, so encouraged was I, and such a confirmation did I seem to receive for what lay ahead, that the tears and sobs came with new force. At the beginning of mass, I was helped by great grace and devotion, and wept peacefully throughout; even when I had finished, a great devotion and new impulses to weep continued until I had unvested. During mass, there were several feelings in confirmation of what has been said: when I held the Blessed Sacrament in my hands, I was impelled to speak and felt intensely moved from within; that I would never leave Him, not for all Heaven or earth or . . . : then new impulses, devotion and spiritual joy. For my part I added the offering of what lay in my power and this last restriction referred to my companions who had signed.[31] *Later, whenever I remembered Jesus during the day or whenever I was reminded of Him, I could in a certain way feel or see with my understanding; the devotion and confirmation continued all the while.*

Mass of the day

23. Sunday [24 Feb.] – During the customary prayer, from the beginning to the end inclusive, I was helped by grace very far inside and gentle, full of devotion, warm and very sweet. While preparing the altar and vesting, the name of Jesus was shown me: I felt great love, confirmation and an increased resolve to follow Him: I wept and sobbed. Throughout mass, very great devotion and many tears so that quite often I lost the power of speech; all the devotion and feelings had Jesus as their object [*Confirmation of Jesus*[32]]. I could not turn myself to the other Persons, except in so far as the First Person was Father of such a Son: then I began to exclaim spiritually, 'How He is Father, and how He is Son!' During the prayer after mass I had the same feeling towards the Son. I had desired the confirmation by the Blessed Trinity, and now I felt it was communicated to me through Jesus. He showed Himself to me and gave me great interior strength and a sense of security that the confirmation was granted. I did not fear for the future. So it occurred to me, and I at once complied, to pray to Jesus to obtain pardon for me from the Blessed Trinity. I felt an increase of devotion, tears and sobs, and the hope of obtaining the grace – for I was quite resolute and strengthened for the future. Later, when I moved nearer to the fire,[33] I once more was shown Jesus and felt great devotion and the impulse to weep. Later when I walked in the street, I was shown Him and felt very great impulses

with tears. After I had spoken to Carpi,[34] on my way back, the same happened and I felt great devotion. After the mid-day meal, especially after I passed through the door of the Vicar Bishop,[35] *in the house of Trani,[36] I felt or saw Jesus, and experienced great interior impulses and wept much.* I begged and implored Jesus to obtain my pardon from the Blessed Trinity: I found there remained with me great confidence for the success of my prayer. *On these occasions my love was so great, I so felt and saw Jesus, that it seemed that nothing could happen in the future capable of separating me from Him or of making me doubt about the graces and confirmation that I had received.*

Mass of St Matthias

24. Monday [25 Feb.] – Quite great devotion during the first period of prayer: more later with warmth and abundant grace to assist me, although for my part, and owing to some impediments that I felt because of others, I found no difficulty in discontinuing: I asked for and sought no confirmation, but desired to be reconciled with the three Divine Persons. Later, vested to say mass, I did not know to whom I should commend myself, or how to begin: the thought comes 'While Jesus is communicating with me, I want to go forward'; and then I began the Confiteor, 'Confiteor Deo', just as Jesus, in the Gospel for the day, said 'Confiteor tibi etc.'[37] At that point, and later during the Confiteor, I felt new devotion not without the impulse to weep. I began the mass [i.e. the Proper] with great devotion, warmth and tears, at times losing the power of speech. *During the prayers to the Father, it seemed that Jesus was presenting them, or accompanied those that I was saying, before the Father: and I felt or saw in a way that cannot be explained in those terms.*

After mass, I had the desire to be reconciled with the Blessed Trinity and I implored Jesus for this, not without tears and sobs. I felt reassured and neither asked for confirmation nor felt the need for it, nor the need to say masses for this end – but only to be reconciled.

Mass of the Trinity. No. 6

25. Tuesday [26 Feb.] – During the first period of prayer I was not disturbed and did not discontinue: I had considerable devotion that became much greater half-way through. However during all this period, especially in the first part, I felt some weakness or bodily indisposition.

Once dressed, while I was in my room and made my preparation, I experienced new devotion and interior impulses to weep when I remembered Jesus: I felt great confidence in Him and He seemed ready to intercede for me. I no longer desired nor sought more or greater signs of confirmation of what was past. I felt quiet and peaceful on that score. Now I begged and implored Jesus to conform my will with that of the Blessed Trinity to follow the way that would seem to him best. Later, when I vested, I was shown increasingly the help and love of Jesus. On beginning mass, not without a great, quiet and peaceful devotion: also a very slight form of weeping – I thought that with less I was more satisfied and content: in that way I felt I was being ruled by the Divine Majesty, to whom it belongs to give and withdraw His graces as and when it is most convenient. Later when I moved near to the fire, still with this form of weeping, my contentment grew and I felt a new interior impulse and love towards Jesus. I no longer had that strife[38] that had been present in me about the Blessed Trinity. So also during mass I continued to feel considerable devotion in the Trinity.

Mass for the first day in Lent

26. Wednesday [27 Feb.] – During the customary prayer I did quite well and all was as usual until half-way through: then a marked improvement – great devotion, quiet and spiritual gentleness – until the end inclusive. Afterwards there remained in me a continuing devotion. I made my preparation in my room and commended myself to Jesus, not asking for any further confirmation, but that, before the Blessed Trinity, He might do his best service,[39] etc, on my behalf, in the way that would be most suitable; that I might find myself in their grace. At that, I received some light and strength: *I entered the chapel and while praying felt, or to put it more exactly, I saw, not by natural power, the Blessed Trinity and also Jesus who was representing me, or placing me before the Trinity or acting as mediator close to the Blessed Trinity, that I might communicate in that intellectual vision. On feeling and seeing in this way I was covered in tears and love, but with Jesus as the object; and toward the Blessed Trinity, a respect of submission more like a reverential love* than anything else. Later I felt in a similar way that Jesus was performing the same task when I thought of praying to the Father, for it seemed and I could feel within me that He was doing everything before the Father and the Blessed Trinity. Many tears when I began mass; and much devotion and more tears all through it. *Similarly at one stage I saw in a remarkable way the same vision of the Blessed Trinity as before, while my love towards the Divine Majesty grew even greater*; at times there was a tendency to lose my power of speech. After mass, during prayer, and several times later when near the fire, a great intense

devotion directed towards Jesus: some special interior impulses to weep, or still further.

When I write this, my understanding feels drawn to see the Blessed Trinity, and appears to see, although not distinctly as before, three Persons. During mass when I said the prayer that begins, 'Domine Jesu Christe, Fili Dei vivi' etc,[40] *it seemed to me in spirit that whereas before I had seen Jesus, as I said, then what I saw was white,[41] that is His humanity, on this occasion my feeling in my soul was different, i.e. I was aware not of the humanity alone, but of Jesus as being completely my God etc. with a fresh rush of tears and great devotion etc.*

Mass of the Trinity. No. 7

27. Thursday [28 Feb.] – Great devotion during the customary prayer: helped by great grace, full of warmth, light and love. On entering the chapel, new devotion: when I knelt, *Jesus was disclosed to me . . . or I saw him . . . at the foot of the Blessed Trinity: at that, new impulses and tears. This vision did not last as long, nor was it as clear as that of Wednesday although it seemed of the same type.* Later during mass, tears, considerable devotion and some helpful feelings. After mass, not without some tears.

Mass of the Five Wounds[42]

28. Friday [29 Feb.] – Very great devotion, very full of light, from the beginning to the end inclusive of the customary prayer: it covered and did not allow me to think of sins. When out of the house, in the church,[43] before mass, *I caught sight of the homeland of Heaven or the Lord of it, in so far as I understood the three Persons and how within the Father were the second and third.* During mass, I felt at times considerable devotion without intuitions or any impulses to weep. *When I had finished, another similar sight of the homeland or of the Lord of it, not in a distinct way but quite clearly, as is customary on many other occasions, now more now less.* Special devotion during the whole day.

Mass of the Feria

29. Saturday [1 Mar.] – During the customary prayer, greatly helped by grace; devotion during it. When I said mass outside, considerable quiet and devotion during mass: until midday, some impulses to weep, and great satisfaction of soul; from then onwards, pulled in both directions.[44]

Mass of the day, 1st Sunday in Lent

30. Sunday [2 Mar.] – During the customary prayer, greatly helped by grace; great devotion in which some clarity and warmth were mingled. Later, when I left my room on hearing a noise, and also when I returned, for some reason I felt put out; either I was struggling with thoughts of the noise, or impeded: so much so that, after I had vested, I thought of not celebrating mass. However, I overcame that suggestion; I had no desire to give any of the others an occasion for talking with anyone: I had some feelings of Christ tempted[45] and, taking courage, began mass with considerable devotion. And as it proceeded, I felt much helped by a certain grace that I felt I was receiving. Several times, and nearly continuously during the second part of the mass, I could feel tears within me. I finished without any new intuitions, except that towards the end, during the prayer to the Blessed Trinity[46] I felt a certain impulse, devotion, tears and a certain feeling of love that drew me towards the Trinity: no bitterness remained over what was past, but great quiet and peace.

Later, when at prayer after mass, more interior impulses, sobs and tears, all for love of Jesus: words came and I desired to die with Him rather than live with anyone else. I felt no fear but found a certain confidence in, and love for, the Blessed Trinity. When I wanted to recommend myself to their protection, as to distinct Persons, I could not find them but seemed to feel something within the Father, as if the other Persons were in Him. At this time, after mass, it seemed to me best that immediately after the masses to the Blessed Trinity, or the first time that I received a divine visitation, I should finish this part. I realized that it was not I who should stipulate the time for finishing and receive a visitation then, but either then or whenever the Divine Majesty thought fit and communicated such a visitation.

Mass of the Trinity. No. 8

31. Monday [3 Mar.] – During the customary prayer, at about 4.30 a.m.,[47] considerable devotion, not moved or troubled; but my head ached – so much so that I dared not rise to say mass until I had had another spell of sleep. Later, when I rose at about 8.30 a.m., I felt quite dull-witted, feeling neither good nor bad, and not knowing to whom I should commend myself. At length, when I began the preparatory prayer in my room, I felt more moved towards Jesus. During prayer I experienced some slight impulses of devotion and the urge to weep, my soul satisfied and very confident in Jesus; I felt drawn to have trust in the Blessed

Trinity. Thus I entered the chapel and was covered by a great devotion in the Blessed Trinity; my love was much increased and I had intense tears. Unlike the past few days I did not see distinct Persons, but had the feeling of one essence, perceived in a sort of shining clarity: it drew me wholly to love it. Later when I prepared the altar and vested, considerable devotion and tears continued, always helped by grace and with great satisfaction of soul. At the beginning of mass, such was the devotion that I could not begin and found great difficulty in saying 'In nomine Patris etc.' Throughout mass, great love and devotion, and very many tears: this devotion and love had for their object the Blessed Trinity. I had no special knowledge or separate visions of the three Persons but a simple awareness or a representation of the Blessed Trinity. Also I occasionally had the same sensations with Jesus for their object: I seemed to be under His shadow as though He were my guide – but without diminution in the grace I was receiving from the Blessed Trinity; on the contrary I seemed to be more united with the Divine Majesty. During the prayers to the Father, I was unable, and felt no desire, to find devotion, except the few times that the Persons made themselves seen in Him. In this way, everything, either mediately or immediately, transformed itself into the Blessed Trinity.

When mass was over and I had unvested, my love was very intense, accompanied by sobs and tears: Jesus was its object, and then as a consequence, the Blessed Trinity: I felt a certain reverent submission. I thought that were it not for the devotion of the masses still to be said, I felt satisfied. At the same time, I had full confidence that I would find ever increasing grace, love and greater repletion in the Divine Majesty.

Mass of the Trinity. No. 9

32. Tuesday [4 Mar.] – During the customary prayer, much helped by grace and devotion: if there was clarity, there was even more light,[48] and evidence of some warmth. For my part I found it all too easy to attend to any and every thought. I rose still helped by that grace. When dressed, I looked at the Introit[49] of the mass and felt all moved by great devotion and love directed towards the Blessed Trinity. Later, when I began the preparatory prayer before mass, I did not know to whom I should turn: first I attended to Jesus, and felt that He was not allowing Himself to be seen or felt clearly but in some sort of shadowy way difficult to see. Then as I attended, I felt that the Blessed Trinity allowed itself to be seen or felt more clearly or full of light. I began, and reasoned for a while with the Divine Majesty. Suddenly the tears streamed down

my face, I broke into sobs, and felt a love so intense that it seemed to unite me excessively close to Their own love, a thing full of light and sweetness. That intense visitation and love seemed quite remarkable and to surpass other visitations. Later when I entered the chapel, new devotion and tears, always directed to the Blessed Trinity: similarly at the altar. Once vested, a far greater flood of tears, more sobs, and the most intense love, all for love of the Blessed Trinity. When I wanted to begin the mass, I felt very great touches and intense devotion to the Blessed Trinity. Once the mass had started, the devotion was so great and the tears so numerous that, as it proceeded, I began to wonder if with more masses I should not become blind in one eye, for it was aching badly owing to the tears: and I thought it would be better to keep my sight, or etc. The tears ceased, although greatly helped by grace; later, however, during the greater part of the mass, this help grew less, and because of the talking in the room etc. Later, almost at the end, I turned to Jesus and recovered some of what had been lost. When I said in prayer: 'Placeat tibi Sancta Trinitas' etc,[50] directing it to the Divine Majesty, I felt an excess of love; intense tears streamed down my face. Thus whenever during this mass or before it I had special spiritual visitations, all had for their object the Blessed Trinity, which took and drew me to its love. After mass I unvested, and while at prayer before the altar, I broke into such sobs and flood of tears, all directed to love of the Blessed Trinity, that I seemed to have no wish to rise; so great was the love and spiritual gentleness I was feeling. Later, several times while sitting near the fire, I felt within me love for the Trinity and the impulse to weep. Later at the house of Burgos,[51] and also when in the street (I was out until about 3.30 p.m.), whenever I called to mind the Blessed Trinity, I felt an intense love, and sometimes the impulse to weep. All these visitations had for their object the name and essence of the Blessed Trinity: I did not feel clearly nor see distinct Persons, as I have described occasionally above. All these inspired greater security: I no longer wished to say more masses in order to be further reconciled, but I wanted to complete them – and hoped to find joy in the Divine Majesty.

Mass of the Trinity. No. 10

33. Wednesday [5 Mar.] – Much grace assisting me throughout the customary prayer; it came without my labouring to seek for it: also great devotion, full of light and very clear, with assisting warmth. While I dressed, I thought that the grace and help and devotion to the Blessed Trinity of the past day still continued. Later when I went to make the

preparatory prayer before mass, I wanted to gain help – and humility – by first addressing Jesus: the Blessed Trinity appeared a little more clearly and I turned to the Divine Majesty to commend myself, etc. The tears streamed down my face, I broke into sobs and such was the intensity of the love that I felt towards the Trinity that I thought I neither wished nor was capable of looking at myself, or of remembering the past in order to be reconciled with the Blessed Trinity. Later, in the chapel, praying gently and quietly it seemed that at first my devotion had for its object the Trinity, then it took me elsewhere, for example to the Father: in this way I felt within me a wanting to communicate with me from different directions – so that eventually, while arranging the altar, my feelings found voice in the prayer, 'Where do you wish to take me, Lord?' I repeated this many times: my devotion increased greatly, drawing me to weep. Later, while I prayed on vesting, I offered myself, very moved and with tears, to be guided and taken etc. through all these stages, wheresoever He might take me, being over me. After I had vested, I did not know where to begin. Then I took Jesus for my guide; I also appropriated to each Person His own prayer; in this way I said a third of the mass receiving considerable grace to assist me, a warm devotion and a great satisfaction of soul. There were no tears, nor (so I believe) any disordered desire to have them: I contented myself with the Lord's will. However I did say, turning to Jesus, 'Lord, where am I going, or where . . . etc? Following you, my Lord, I cannot be lost'. From then on, during the mass, many tears, also good heart and spiritual vigour. The greatest of the visitations had the Blessed Trinity as their principal object, then in lesser degree Jesus, and finally in much lesser degree the Father. On the other hand my confidence about my reconciliation with the Blessed Trinity increased continually – to such a pitch that after mass, while I prayed with tranquillity and rest of soul, on wanting to reconsider the matter to a certain degree, I could not; I was unable to bring myself to see or feel any past disharmony or unpleasantness. I found myself in the state of a tired man[52] who rests, his mind tranquil, devout, visited. This repose continued later while I sat by the fire, and on other occasions when I remembered. At night as I prayed to the Father, I did not find it, but there was revealed to me new devotion and impulses, all directed to the Blessed Trinity.

Mass of the Trinity. No. 11

34. Thursday [6 Mar.] – During the customary prayer I had no trouble in finding devotion, but rather the contrary: later it increased greatly,

being most gentle and clear with a clarity mixed with colour. After I had dressed I experienced new devotion and the call to even more, all directed to the Blessed Trinity. During the preparatory prayer, I drew closer to the Blessed Trinity, in greater quiet and spiritual serenity; I felt the impulse to greater devotion and almost to weep: I wanted to, but could not, see anything of the past with reference to the reconciliation. In chapel, great quiet devotion: on arranging the altar, the devotion grew with certain feelings or new impulses, as if to weep. Later and on vesting, and I think even before, during the other periods, certain thoughts and queries suggested themselves: 'What did the Blessed Trinity wish to do with me, that is, by what way would it take me?' Then as I conjectured on the manner and way they would choose, I wondered to myself and thought that perhaps the Trinity wanted to make me content without visitations of tears, with my not being avid for them nor inordinately attached.

I began mass with an interior, humble satisfaction, and proceeding as far as the 'Te igitur',[53] continued to experience a very deep and very gentle devotion which at times came most delicately: so softly in my soul as to make me weep. On pronouncing the words 'Te igitur', I felt and saw, not obscurely but brightly, in full light, the very Being or Essence of God, appearing as a sphere, a little larger than the sun appears; from this Essence the Father seemed to be going or deriving, so that when I said, 'Te', that is, 'Father', the image of the Divine Essence came to me before that of the Father. During this representation and vision of the Being of the Blessed Trinity, I could not distinguish or have sight of the other Persons; my devotion to what was being disclosed was very intense and I experienced many impulses and a flood of tears. In the same way, as the mass proceeded, if I considered or remembered or if I saw it anew, the tears flowed copiously and my love for the Being of the Blessed Trinity was greatly increased and very intense: I did not see nor could I distinguish any Persons except that, as I said, I could see the going forth or derivation from the Father.

As I was finishing mass, the tears and spiritual visitations were very abundant; I could see no obstacle to the reconciliation, even though I paid attention. I felt a great security. I could not doubt about what had been shown and seen; rather, when I turned to investigate and reconsider it, I felt new interior impulses, all taking me to love what I had been shown. Indeed I seemed to have more clarity of vision, reaching beyond the heavens, further than anything I might like to think of with my understanding on this earth; all was illuminated for me there, as I have said. After I had unvested and was praying at the altar, once more the same Being and spherical vision allowed itself to be seen: in some way I saw all three Persons as I had seen the first, viz., the Father in one part, the Son in another and the Holy Spirit in another, all three coming forth or having their derivation from the Divine Essence, without leaving the spherical vision. On feeling and seeing this, new impulses and tears. Later when I visited St Peter's and began to pray before the Blessed Sacrament, the same Divine Being showed itself in image to me, always in the same shining colour, and for my part I could not but see it. Later when I began to attend the mass said by Cardinal Santa Cruz,[54] I experienced the same manifestation and vision, accompanied by new impulses of soul. Two hours later I went down to the same chapel of the Blessed Sacrament with the desire of having the same experience as before but, though I sought it, I could not regain it. Later at night, several times while I was writing this, the same manifestation occurred; on this occasion the understanding saw something, though by far the most part was not so clear, nor so distinct, nor as big: it was like a fairly large spark; it represented something to the understanding, or was drawing it to itself, and showed that it was the same.

Mass of the Trinity. No. 12

25.[55] Friday [7 Mar.] – I began the customary prayer with considerable devotion; despite my desire I did not adapt myself to increase my devotion by looking upwards. From half-way through my prayer, the devotion was very great and continuous, full of a shining clarity, warm and very gentle; it continued the same after this prayer. Later, during the preparatory prayer, my mind was quiet and recollected: the same in chapel. Later on vesting, new impulses to weep, also to conform myself with the Divine Will that He might guide and carry me etc. 'Ego sum puer, etc.'[56] I began mass with great devotion, internal reverence and impulses to weep. So also when I said, 'Beata sit sancta Trinitas',[57] and throughout I experienced a new sensation, a fresh and greater devotion and a desire to weep: I did not raise my understanding to the Divine Persons, in so far as they are distinct or to be distinguished, neither did I lower it to the letters in the missal: yet this visitation seemed to be interior, mid-way between their seat on high and the letter.[58] Then, as I proceeded step by step with many tears all the time, it seemed to me that I had no permission to look upwards: and my not looking upwards, that is my looking mid-way, caused an increased intensity of devotion and intense tears. The submission and reverence I already possessed for the visions from on high increased. At the same time I gained some confidence that permission would be granted me or that a manifestation would be made to me at the right time. During these periods I felt the visitations in an imprecise way [*indiferenter*]: they had for their object now the Blessed Trinity, now the Father or Son; at times Our Lady and at others the saints, even individual saints; tears were abundant. Later, when half or more of the mass was said, i.e. after 'Hanc igitur oblationem',[59] the visitation ceased. At times, I was troubled by the heat of the fire[60] with the water thrown on it.

Because I could not find out during the Sacrament, as I wanted to bring the matter to a conclusion, once mass was finished I went over to the fire; for a long time I did not know what to decide, whether I should stop these masses, or when. Later it occurred to me that tomorrow I would say a mass of the Blessed Trinity to find out what I should do, or to finish once and for all. At that I experienced many impulses and tears; and from time to time, during a long period, I continued to receive great impulses, sobs and many floods of tears, all drawing me to a love of the Blessed Trinity. With many colloquies I came to see that if only I would wait, all was ready for ever greater enjoyment of these intense visitations. I humbled myself with the thought that it was not I who should determine when the end was to be; instead I should wait until it was disclosed to me and I had been visited. So I prepared myself resolutely to finish, and to enjoy the enjoyment I should find. The thought struck me, 'What if God should put me in Hell?' Two considerations occurred: on the one hand, the suffering I would endure there; on the other, how His name was blasphemed there. As to the first, I could neither feel nor see any suffering in that – and so it seemed to me that I was shown that it would cause me more pain to hear His most holy Name blasphemed. Later, when I sat down to eat, the tears stopped but balancing that a very deep and warm devotion continued throughout the day.

Mass of the Trinity. No. 13

26. Saturday [8 Mar.] – During the customary prayer I had great satisfaction of soul from the beginning to the end, with the growth of a great grace assisting me, and I felt a devotion, clear and full of light and warmth; when I began the preparatory prayer and was in the chapel I had considerable contentment. But on vesting, new impulses that continued to the end together with still greater ones and considerable tears. I was shown a great humility not yet to look up to heaven, and the more I shrank from looking upwards, humbling and lowering myself,

the more delight and spiritual visitation did I feel. I began the mass and continued throughout with greater inner devotion and spiritual warmth, not without tears. The devotion and the readiness to weep continued with me. During these periods, even though I intended not to raise the eyes of my understanding upwards and to try to be content with everything (indeed I was imploring that if it were equally to God's glory He would not visit me with tears),[61] nevertheless on the occasions when my understanding unintentionally mounted upwards, I seemed to see something of the Divine Being that at other times, even though I want to see it, is not in my power.

Mass of the day. 2nd Sunday in Lent
27. Sunday [9 Mar.] – The customary prayer was similar to the past. After I had dressed, during the preparatory prayer, new devotion and impulses to weep, directed principally to the Blessed Trinity and Jesus. On entering the chapel, greater impulses, more tears, all directed to the Blessed Trinity, and also, at times, to Jesus; at times the two were united or almost united, in such a way that my having Jesus as the object of my prayer did not diminish my devotion to the Blessed Trinity, or vice versa. This devotion continued until I vested; at times there were tears. Later, during mass, I felt an exterior warmth that was cause for devotion and light-heartedness. There were few movements or impulses to weep, yet I was more content without tears than I had been at times with many tears. I seemed to understand that although I experienced no intuitions, no visions and no tears, in some way God Our Lord wanted to show me a way or manner of proceeding. All day my soul was quite content. At night I found I was turning in devotion to the Blessed Trinity and to Jesus so that they manifested themselves to my understanding, allowing me to catch sight of them in some way. For my part I wanted to adapt myself to the Father, to the Holy Spirit and to Our Lady, but in that direction could find no devotion and no vision. The intuition or vision of the Blessed Trinity and of Jesus continued for a while.

Mass of the Holy Name of Jesus
28. Monday [10 Mar.] – During the customary prayer, considerable devotion especially from the middle onwards. Before the preparatory prayer, I experienced a new devotion: I thought or decided that I should live, or be, like an angel to perform the duty of celebrating mass: very gently some water came to my eyes. Later in the chapel and during mass, devotion for the same reason: I conformed myself to what the Lord

commanded, with the thought that His Divine Majesty would supply for my defect, turning everything to good, etc. During these periods I occasionally saw in some way now the Being of the Father, i.e. first the Being and consequently the Father, i.e. my devotion turned first to the essence and then to the Father, now it was otherwise and without such a clear distinction.

Mass of Our Lady

29. Tuesday [11 Mar.] – Throughout the customary prayer I felt great devotion – clear, shining and as though warm. I had tears in chapel, at the altar, and afterwards. My devotion had for its object Our Lady although I did not see her. Throughout mass, devotion; at times impulses to tears. Afterwards devotion once more. During these periods, I partly saw many times the Divine Being, and sometimes with the Father as object i.e. first the essence and then the Father. When in chapel before mass, I seemed to receive something like a permission to turn my glance upwards because it occurred to me that to look upwards was a remedy against my being disturbed by what was low. At that I was moved, and tears came. Later I tried to look upwards and whether I saw anything or not, I found devotion and a remedy against taking my attention too easily from what was my duty all during mass.

Mass of the Holy Spirit

30. Wednesday [12 Mar.] – During the customary prayer considerable devotion: from the middle onwards, the devotion was great, clear and shining, as though warm. In the chapel, as I had seen people coming down the stairs and doing so hurriedly, I was unable to bring myself to say mass. I returned to my room to adapt myself to say it and amid tears recovered my composure. The tears continued as I walked to the chapel and began mass: during part of it, my devotion was considerable and occasionally I felt the impulse to weep. During the other part I was very often battling about what should be done to bring the matter to an end; for I could not find what I sought. During these periods, no signs of visions or intuitions.

After mass and later in my room, I found myself completely bereft of all help, unable to find delight in the mediators, or in the Divine Persons; I felt as remote and separated from them as if I had never felt their influence in the past, or was ever to feel any of it in the future. Instead I was beset by thoughts, now against Jesus, now against another, and quite bewildered with a variety of schemes, to leave the house and hire a room to escape the noise, to fast, to begin more masses, to place an altar upstairs: nothing satisfied me and yet I wanted to put an end to the affair with my soul in a state of consolation and complete satisfaction. At last I considered if I should proceed further. On the one hand, I seemed to be wanting too many signs, and wanting them during certain periods or during masses ending in my own satisfaction; the question itself was clear; I was looking not for more certainty, but for a finishing touch that would be to my taste. On the other hand, I thought that if I were to cease entirely at this juncture, in a state of such exile, later I would not be contented etc. At last I considered whether, as the problem did not concern the election itself, it would please God Our Lord more were I to conclude now without waiting and searching for further proofs, or whether I should say more masses for them. To settle the matter I made an election and felt that to conclude would be more pleasing to God Our Lord. I felt myself wishing that the Lord would condescend to my desire i.e. that I might finish in a time of great visitation. Then as I became aware of my own inclination and, on the other hand, of the good pleasure of God Our Lord, I began to take notice and wanted to follow the good pleasure of God Our Lord.

At that the obscurity began gradually to lighten; tears came. As they increased I lost all desire to say more masses to this end; when it occurred to me to say three masses of the Trinity in thanksgiving, it seemed to me to be a suggestion of the evil spirit. I decided to say no more masses: and then my love for God increased, the tears streamed down my face and I broke into sobs with spasms. I knelt for a long time, then I walked, and once more I knelt, arguing along many, varied and different lines of thought. I felt great internal satisfaction. Although this great visitation (so great that my eyes ached painfully) lasted for about an hour, more or less, at last the tears ceased and I was uncertain if I should conclude at night with a similar flood of tears, if such occurred, or now. Although the flood of tears was over, I thought it best to conclude at once. To seek further and wait for the evening was only to want further proof, when it was not needed. And so I made my declaration before God Our Lord and all the Heavenly Court etc., thus concluding with the matter: I would not proceed further. Even as I made this last declaration, I felt interior impulses, I sobbed and wept; although this was a period of great floods of tears, I considered everything ended, and decided to await no more masses or visitations, but to finish today.

Finished.

When I sat at table, after 1.30 p.m., for a long while the Tempter did not succeed, but pretended to succeed in making me have doubts. Suddenly, yet calmly – as if to a beaten enemy – I said to him, 'Get to your place'. I was strengthened by tears and a complete sense of security about all I had decided. A quarter of an hour later, I awakened to a new fact; I realized or saw clearly that when the Tempter suggested thoughts against the Divine Persons and Mediators, he was putting, or trying to put, doubts into my mind on the subject; and on the contrary, when I experienced visitations from, and visions of, the Divine Persons and Mediators, all was firmness and confirmation on the matter. This realization was accompanied by spiritual delight, and water came to my eyes: in my soul a great sense of security. When I said grace after the meal, the Being of the Father partly disclosed itself, also the Being of the Blessed Trinity, while I felt a spiritual impulse moving to devotion and tears, such as I had not felt or seen all day, although I had often sought for it. Today's great visitations had no particular or distinct Person for their object, but in general, the Giver of graces.

PART II

I TOOK THESE FOUR DAYS TO AVOID CONSIDERING ANY POINTS IN THE CONSTITUTIONS

Mass of the day
1st. Thursday[1] [13 Mar.] – During mass I conformed my will to the Divine, to have no tears: it would be like a setting aside of my labours and a rest for me if I stopped searching and considering about possessing or not possessing.[2] During the rest of the day, my soul felt content and delight.

Mass of the Holy Spirit
2nd. a.l.d.[3] Friday [14 Mar.] – Many tears before, all during and after mass, sometimes out of devotion to the Father, at others out of devotion to the Son, at others etc.: so also with the Saints; no vision except in so far as my devotion had for its object at different times now the one, now the other. During all this time, before, during and after the mass, I was inspired by the thought, which penetrated to my very soul, of how much

reverence and submission should be shown on going to mass when I had to pronounce the name of God Our Lord, etc. Not tears were to be sought, but this submission and reverence. So convinced was I of this that when tears came, as I repeated acts of submission, before mass – in my room and in the chapel – and during mass, I at once restrained them in order to attend more to submission. As far as I could tell, this realization of the submission due to God Our Lord was not the effect of my own initiative: it always increased my devotion and tears. At length I concluded that this was the way the Lord desired to show me – for during the past days I had thought He intended to reveal something. Indeed, as I said mass, I became more convinced that I esteemed this grace and knowledge more highly for my soul's spiritual advancement than all the other past graces.

Mass of Our Lady
3rd. Saturday [15 Mar.] – During part of the mass I felt a certain interior submission and reverence; during the greater part nothing to enable me to feel within myself either submission or reverence.

Mass of the day
4th. a.l. Sunday[4] [16 Mar.] – Many tears before and throughout the mass; the devotion and tears had for their object now one Person now another, without clear or distinct visions. I prayed in my room before mass for the gifts of submission, reverence and humility; as for visitations and tears, I prayed they might not be given me, if it were equally to the service of His Divine Majesty, or, if they were given, that I might enjoy them with purity of intention – without self-interest. So, later, all my spiritual visitations brought with them this feeling of submission, not only towards the Divine Persons, as I named or remembered them, but even as I bowed to the altar or treated with reverence the other things used at the sacrifice.[5] I refused tears or visitations whenever I thought of them or felt the desire for them. In this way I paid attention to submission first – the visitations coming next – because I judged that to do the opposite, i.e. to pay more attention to the visitations than to submission, would be bad. Thus I was of the same opinion as on Friday last, and felt confirmed in it.

HERE I BEGAN MY PREPARATION AND FIRST CONSIDERATION
CONCERNING THE MISSIONS[6]

Mass of Our Lady

1. a.l. Monday [17 Mar.] – Tears before mass and during it, so many
that at times I lost the power of speech. All this visitation had for object
now one Person, now another, in the same way as the previous day, and
with the same effect. It confirmed my previous experience with regard to
the submission and reverence, viz. that I had found in these the way I
was intended to see. I considered it the best of all ways that I could be
shown and felt that I should follow it for ever. Occasionally before mass,
as I recollected myself in my room, I felt none of this submission and
reverence having any influence or producing relish within me. Indeed I
felt incapable of finding it and yet I wanted to possess or find it. Some
time later, in chapel, I thought it was God's will that I should make an
effort to search for it, and find it; I failed. And yet to have made the
effort seemed a good thing: to actually find was not in my power. Later,
the Giver of graces provided me with such abundance of knowledge,
visitation and spiritual relish – that mentioned above – tears, continuing
for so long (making me lose at times the power of speech), that every
time I mentioned God, 'Dominus' etc, I seemed to be penetrated so
deeply, with a submission and reverent humility so admirable, that they
seem to defy description.

Mass of the Holy Name of Jesus

2. a⁻ l d⁻⁷ Tuesday [18 Mar.] – Tears during mass; before and after mass
they were not lacking; all causing submission and reverence.

Mass of the Trinity

3. l.d. Wednesday [19 Mar.] – Many tears throughout mass; the same
after mass. During mass I often lost the power of speech: all causing
submission and reverence with many interior feelings.

Mass of Our Lady

4. a.l⁻ Thursday [20 Mar.] – Tears before mass, and some during it; also
different interior impulses, causing submission.

Mass of the Holy Name of Jesus

5. a⁻l⁻ Friday [21 Mar.] – Not without some tears before and during
mass, causing submission, also some interior impulses.

Mass of the Holy Spirit

6. l.d. Saturday [22 Mar.] – Throughout mass, a gentle flow of tears, very copious; the same after mass: before mass I felt the impulse to weep and felt or saw the Holy Spirit Himself; complete submission.[8]

Mass of the day

7. a.l. Sunday[9] [23 Mar.] – Many intense tears before and during mass; all causing submission.

Mass of the Trinity

8. l Monday [24 Mar.] – Tears several times during mass, causing submission.

Mass of Our Lady

9. a l d Tuesday [25 Mar.] – Tears before and after mass; very copious during it; vision of the Divine Being, with the Father as object, in the form of a circle on several occasions,[10] all causing submission.

Mass of the Holy Name of Jesus

10. a l Wednesday [26 Mar.] – Tears several times during mass; before mass, not without the impulse to tears. Until the Secret[11] of the mass, not only could I feel no interior submission, but I could not even find any aptitude that would help me. This led me to infer and recognize that I could not be of any assistance to myself in the acquisition of this submission: when I said the Secret, and after that, I experienced the spiritual visitation which caused submission.

Mass of the Holy Spirit

11. a.l. Thursday [27 Mar.] – Tears before mass; very many during mass; all causing submission; with vision of the Divine Being in the form of a sphere as on other previous occasions.[12]

Mass of the Trinity

12. a l. Friday [28 Mar.] – Tears during mass: not without them before mass.

Mass of Our Lady

13. Saturday [29 Mar.] – No tears before or during mass and no sign of them: during the customary prayer I received a special, or rather a most special grace: during the greater part of the mass, I experienced much

gentle devotion, as I thought that it was more perfect to be without tears, and to find, like the angels, internal devotion and love; during another part, I felt no less satisfaction than yesterday, or even more.

Mass of the day

14th. a. l d Sunday[13] [30 Mar.] – Many tears before mass, in my room, in the chapel and as I made my preparation; they were very abundant during mass, continuing throughout; afterwards they were very intense.[14] At this period of time it occurred to me that my humility, reverence and submission should be not of a man who fears but of a man who loves. So strongly did this impress itself on my soul that with great faith I said: 'Give me a lover's humility', and so also concerning my reverence and submission. As I said the words, I experienced new visitations. So also I tried to check the tears in order to attend solely to this loving humility, etc. Later in the day I felt great joy when I remembered this. I resolved not to stop there but afterwards to entertain the same sentiment, viz. that of loving humility, etc., towards creatures, unless, on occasions, it were for the honour of God Our Lord to conduct myself differently; as it says in today's Gospel, 'Similis ero vobis, mendax'.[15] During these periods several times I had the vision of the Divine Being in the form of a circle as before.

Mass of the day

15. .l d. Monday [31 Mar.] – Tears during and after mass, causing a loving reverence, etc.; at times I realized that neither love nor reverence, etc. were in my power.

Mass of the day

16. l. Tuesday [1 Apr.] – Many tears during mass, causing a loving humility, etc. It occurred to me that, in order to possess this humility during the sacrifice, it is necessary to profit from it all during the day allowing no distractions.

Mass of the day

17. a.l. Wednesday [2 Apr.] – Tears during the customary prayer, also later in my room, in the chapel and while I vested: very many during mass.[16] During these periods I occasionally had the vision of the Divine Being, sometimes with the Father for object by means of that representation of a circle: many intuitions and much new interior knowledge. During periods of greater knowledge, or of greater visitations, I

recognized that I ought to be equally content if not visited with tears, and to believe anything to be for the best, according to how God Our Lord acted or willed, visitation or no visitation. At times when I was not enjoying these great visitations, to act in this way seemed to require such perfection that I doubted, or feared, about being able to gain this grace. Later, on another occasion, while enjoying a great visitation, I thought I was finding satisfaction in this, viz. in believing it to be best if I were not visited by God Our Lord; because the reason for not being visited would be either a lack of disposition and preparation on my part some time during the day, or my having permitted thoughts that distracted me from the words of the sacrifice and from His Divine Majesty. In such cases, when I was at fault, I thought it would be better for me to enjoy no visitations: it is for my spiritual profit that God Our Lord (who loves me more than I love myself) arranges things in this way. Thus it was to my advantage to follow the correct course of action not only during the sacrifice, but all during the day, in order to receive visitations. All this was in accord with what had been hinted at the previous day when I had experienced these and similar intuitions, but then they had been so many and so delicate that I have neither the memory nor the understanding to explain or expose them.

Mass of the day

18. Thursday [3 Apr.] – I had no tears before, during or after mass: at the end I felt more content without them and also affection, judging that God Our Lord did this for my greater good.

Mass of the day

19. a.l. Friday [4 Apr.] – Tears before mass; very many during mass, with many intuitions and interior feelings; the same before mass. When one does not achieve a lover's reverence and submission, one must seek for the submission of one who fears, considering one's own faults, in order to gain the submission of love.

Mass of the day

20. a.l. Saturday [5 Apr.] – Tears before mass: many tears during mass.

Mass of the day

21. a.l.d. Sunday[17] [6 Apr.] – Tears before mass: during the mass, after the Passion, they were abundant and continuous: they led me to conform my will to the Divine; so also, tears after mass.

Mass of the day
22. l. Monday [7 Apr.] – Many tears throughout mass, drawing me to conform my will to the Divine.

Mass of the day
23. l. Tuesday [8 Apr.] – Tears during mass.
24. l. Wednesday [9 Apr.] – Tears during mass.
25. Thursday [10 Apr.] – No tears.

---

26. [11 Apr.][18]
27. [12 Apr.]

Mass of the day
28. l.d. Easter Sunday [13 Apr.] – Many tears during mass; and tears after it.

Mass of the day
29. Monday [14 Apr.] – I felt a great interior and exterior warmth: it seemed to be more supernatural: no tears.

Mass of the day
30. Tuesday [15 Apr.] – No great consolation, nor desolation, no tears.

Mass of the day
31. .l.d. Wednesday [16 Apr.] – Many tears during mass; and tears after it.

Mass of the day
32. a.l.d. Thursday [17 Apr.] – Tears before and after mass; many during it.

Mass of the day
33. l Friday [18 Apr.] – Tears during mass.

Mass of the day
34. a.l. Saturday [19 Apr.] – Tears during and before mass.

35. a.l. Sunday[19] [20 Apr.] – Tears during and before mass. *I began my preparation.*[20]

Mass of Our Lady
36. a.l. Monday [21 Apr.] – Tears during and before mass. *I must begin, because after a few days I left it.*

Mass of All Saints
37. a.l.d. Tuesday [22 Apr.] – Tears before and after mass: many and continuous tears during it.

38. Wednesday [23 Apr.] – No tears. *From today, inclusive, I left it.*[21]
39. Thursday [24 Apr.] – No tears.

Mass of St Mark
30.[22].a.l. Friday [25 Apr.] – Tears during mass and before it.

Mass of the Holy Spirit
31. Saturday [26 Apr.] – No tears.

Mass of the day
32. .a.l. Sunday[23] [27 Apr.] – Tears during and before mass.

Mass of the Trinity
33. .a.l. Monday [28 Apr.] – Tears during and before mass.
34. l Tuesday [29 Apr.] – Tears.
35. l Wednesday [30 Apr.] – Tears.
36. l Thursday [1 May] – Tears.
37. Friday [2 May] – No tears.
38. l Saturday [3 May] – Tears.
39. l Sunday [4 May] – Tears.
40. l Monday [5 May] ⎫
41. l Tuesday [6 May] ⎬ I think I had tears.
                     ⎭
42. Wednesday [7 May] ⎫
43. Thursday [8 May] ⎬ I think I had no tearts
44. Friday [9 May]   ⎭
45. l Saturday [10 May] – Many during mass.

46. a.l Sunday [11 May] – Tears before mass; very many and continuous tears during mass; the internal *loquela*[24] of the mass seemed even more divinely granted, as I had prayed for it this very day because during the week I had sometimes experienced the external *loquela*, and sometimes not, but the internal, more rarely, although on Saturday I found it a little more clear. So also during all the masses of the week, although I was not so visited with tears, yet I experienced greater quiet or contentment throughout mass from the pleasure of the *loquelas*, with the devotion I could feel, than at other times when during part of the mass I had tears. Those tears that came today seemed completely different from all others in the past: they came so slowly, seemed so from within, and were so gentle, without clamour or great impulses. I thought they came from deep inside though I cannot explain it. During the internal and external *loquela*, I felt wholly moved to the divine love and to the gift of *loquela* divinely granted; I felt within me a great harmony accompanying the internal *loquela*, but I cannot express it.

ON THIS SUNDAY, BEFORE MASS, I BEGAN, AND RESOLVED TO CONTINUE WITH, THE CONSTITUTIONS

Mass of All Saints

47. .l d. Monday [12 May] – Many tears during mass; tears also after mass. All these were like those of the previous day. I took great pleasure in the internal *loquela*; at the same time I found it resembling, or myself remembering, the *loquela* or music of heaven. My devotion and affection increased and I wept as I felt that when I had these feelings or when I was learning in this way, it was due to God.

Mass of St Sebastian

48. .a.l d. Tuesday [13 May] – Tears before and after mass; very many during mass together with the internal *loquela* which came in a wonderful manner and was greater than at other times.

Mass of Our Lady's Conception

49. .a.l. Wednesday [14 May] – Tears before mass and many later during it, while the same internal *loquela* continued.

Mass of the Holy Name of Jesus

50. Thursday [15 May] – No tears; some *loquela*; I was disturbed by someone whistling, but was not so greatly disquieted.

Mass of the Holy Spirit

51. a.l Friday [16 May] – Tears before mass, and many during it, together with the *loquela*.

Mass of the Trinity

52. a.l Saturday [17 May] – Tears before mass; many and continuous during it; with the wonderful internal *loquela*.

Mass of the day

53. Sunday [18 May] – No tears; some *loquela*, no bodily strength, and also no perturbation.

Mass of the Litanies[25]

54.l. Monday [19 May] – Tears and *loquela*.

Mass of All Saints

55. Tuesday [20 May] – No tears and no perturbation; some *loquela*.

Mass of Our Lady

56. Wednesday [21 May] – No tears; much *loquela*.

Mass of the Ascension

57. .a.l. Thursday [22 May] – Many tears before mass both in my room and in the chapel: no tears during the greater part of the mass: there was much *loquela*. However, I began to have doubts about the pleasure and delight caused by the *loquela* lest it were due to an evil spirit, seeing that the spiritual visitation of tears had ceased. A little later I thought I was taking excessive pleasure in the tone of the *loquela*, that is in the mere sound, without paying sufficient attention to the meaning of the words and of the *loquela*. At once the tears came, very many and very often, so that I realized that I was being instructed in the method I should follow. And I hoped for ever greater learning in the future.

Mass of the Ascension

58. .l. Friday [23 May] – Tears.

Mass of the Holy Spirit

59. Saturday [24 May] – No tears.

40. a.l. Sunday [25 May] – Many tears in my room, and tears in the

chapel, before mass: very many and continuous tears during mass, together with the two wonderful *loquelas*.

Mass of the Ascension
41. l. Monday [26 May] – Tears and the internal *loquela* during mass.

Mass of the Ascension
42. a.l. Tuesday [27 May] – Tears before mass; also many tears during mass together with the internal *loquela* which gradually increased.

Mass of the Ascension
43. .a l d. Wednesday [28 May] – Tears before and after mass; many tears and the wonderful internal *loquela* during it.

Mass of the Ascension
44. a.l.d. Thursday [29 May] – Tears before, during and after mass.

45. Friday [30 May] – No tears.
46. l Saturday [31 May] – Tears.
47. l Sunday[26] [1 June] – Tears.
48. Monday [2 June] – No tears.
49. Tuesday [3 June] – No tears.
50. .l. Wednesday [4 June] – Many and continuous tears.
51. Thursday [5 June] – No tears.
52. Friday [6 June] – No tears.
53. Saturday [7 June] – No tears.

There follow 240 similar entries, all very short, covering the period 8 June 1544 to 17 February 1545, when the *Diary* breaks off. They record the presence or absence of tears before, during and after mass, and add nothing further.

SELECT LETTERS

Introduction

The correspondence of Ignatius Loyola has been published in twelve volumes:[1] in sheer size it far outnumbers the extant correspondence of such sixteenth-century contemporaries as Calvin, Erasmus, Luther and Teresa of Avila.[2] Clearly any selection limited to a few dozen letters out of a total that approaches seven thousand can present only certain facets of Ignatius. Moreover not all the letters have the same degree of authenticity,[3] and they vary greatly in character – personal letters alongside little treatises, but also notes and memos. The present selection seeks above all to present the personality of their author.[4]

Ignatius began to write letters in a consistent way when he had settled into the life of study in Paris: his first letters home arrived some ten years after his departure, and his brother in one reply expressed his delight that Inigo seemed to have abandoned his policy of not writing to them.[5] There had been a few letters written by Ignatius before then (to his benefactresses in Barcelona, for example), but by 1532 he had discovered an inner certainty that had been lacking before this, and also a realization that his pen could be used in 'the service and praise of God Our Lord', by bringing comfort and mutual support to relatives and friends. The general pattern of these early letters (1532–47) is spacious, as of a man who writes with ease and calm, enjoying the process of ordering his thoughts and confident that he can communicate in depth. However, the evidence for these years is meagre, and may be the chance result of the correspondents' interests.

In 1547 one notices a marked change: from a trickle of letters per year we now have 300, and this number increases steadily until 1556 when some 1000 letters are sent out in his name. These rough statistics are easily explained by the arrival in Rome of one man, Juan Polanco, who was to be Secretary to the Society for over twenty-five years (1547–73). A born bureaucrat, in the best sense, he organized the offices and archives with amazing efficiency and foresight. However, it would be ingenuous to suppose that his contribution to the correspondence of Ignatius was restricted to receiving and cataloguing. Already in 1547 one is a little surprised to find copious references to St Bernard's sermons in the letter from Ignatius to the candidates for the Society in Coimbra, a wide-ranging survey of the ideals of the religious life, but also an attempt to deal with the particularly extravagant penitential practices adopted by the young men, partly at the instigation of the charismatic Simão Rodrigues.[6] In August of the same year Ignatius had such confidence in his secretary, then only thirty years of age, that he entrusted to him the writing of a letter on the ideal of poverty, and the product was an elegantly rhetorical little treatise, complete with quotations from Ovid, Lucan and Seneca.[7] It is instructive to compare this with a letter on the same subject (basically encouraging young men who were hungry and cold) written five years later by Ignatius: the rhetoric and the quotations have gone; in their place there is a reminder of the much harsher suffering borne by the Society's men in India, a permission to beg for funds, and a reminder that the sick should not be allowed to go short.[8] Even if the basic teaching is the same, the contrast in approach could not be sharper. One sees at once that Ignatius and Polanco complemented one another like a sword and its sheath. They were made of very different stuff, each needing the other at different moments. But one should beware of the protective covering Polanco places around his master's ideas.

Fortunately enough of the early letters survive for one to form an acquaintance with Ignatius the man, and this knowledge can serve as a yardstick for the later letters. Moreover, the overall responsibility for the Polanco letters remains that of Ignatius. And provided one is aware of the nature of the material being presented (applying the norms of source-criticism required in other historical studies[9]) the complete corpus of the letters provides a solid base for investigating how Ignatius saw the world around him, reacted to it and shaped the Society accordingly.[10]

Here the scope will be much more limited. Through the Letters one can see Ignatius from different angles, and recognize his various roles – as a friend, a spiritual director, an instructor, a businessman and a religious superior. Particular scope is given to those letters that refer to the *Exercises*, or that make more intelligible the experiences of the *Diary*, but inevitably his 'public' figure, as first overall superior of a new religious order, will intrude to some extent. The selection draws not only on the Spanish letters,[11] but also on those written in Italian and Latin.[12] Quite deliberately very few of the more explicitly 'public' letters (to heads of state and other officials) have been included, but a few 'instructions' directed to members of the Society are represented as they display how Ignatius's mind worked, and what ideals he made his own.[13] Space has also been given to some letters that are not strictly authentic, when their inspiration appears to be Ignatian, and there is one non-epistolary fragment (37) chosen to illustrate how Ignatius would have spoken to children when teaching them the catechism. In each case a prefatory notes and end-notes provide explanation.

To facilitate both reference and understanding many of the Letters have been divided into numbered paragraphs (frequently with key-word titles); the instructions often have their original numbering systems (also reproduced here), but these are rarely consistent. The places from which and to which letters are sent are noted, as well as the name of the correspondent and the date. The bracketed numbers (followed by volume and page numbers) are those of the MHSI edition.

NOTES

1 The letters began to be collected and published towards the end of the nineteenth century, and the first full edition appeared in MHSI between 1903 and 1911.

2 A statistical study of these different correspondences appears in Dominique Bertrand, *La politique de Saint Ignace de Loyola*, Paris 1985, the first major study of the Ignatian letters.

3 Very few autograph copies survive, and frequently one has to rely on office copies/memos.

4 The selection of letters was made with the help of Michael Ivens, SJ. A fuller collection has been published by Inigo Enterprises.

5 See Letter 2.4.

6 Letter 16.

7 Letter 18.

8 Letter 29.

9 See Philip Endean, 'Who do you say Ignatius is? Jesuit fundamentalism and beyond', *Studies in the Spirituality of Jesuits*, vol. 19 no. 5 (1987).

10 This is the thesis advanced by Dominique Bertrand (see note 2 above), part 4, chapter 3.

11 Translated with the help of Philip Endean, SJ, especially for Letters 4, 15, 16, 17, 20, 21, 23.

12 Translated with the help of Leo Arnold, SJ (Italian) and Robert Murray, SJ (Latin).

13 The *Constitutions* and similar documents would require a volume to themselves.

1. Advice to a good woman

Inés Pascual 1524

(No. 1 : I, 71–73 : Spanish)

The first letter that has survived, a note of condolence to a kindly woman, was written on Ignatius's return to Barcelona after almost two years away on his Jerusalem pilgrimage.

Inés Pascual[1]   6 December 1524[2]
in Manresa (?)   from Barcelona

✠

Jesus

[1] It seems to me a good idea to write to you – knowing how strongly you desire to serve Our Lord – because I think you are in for a tiring time. You have just lost that very saintly friend (the Lord decided to take her to Himself), and in that place there are many enemies and obstacles to the Lord's service, in addition to the constant temptations invented by the enemy of human nature.

[2] For love of God Our Lord, please press on, leaving behind you all the obstacles. If you keep clear of them, no temptation will have any power against you. That is what you should always do, preferring the Lord's praise to all other things, and all the more so given that the Lord does not command you to do things that require great labour or any bodily harm; His wish is rather that you should live joyfully, allowing your body to have what it needs. All your talking and thinking and social contacts should be occupied with Him, and the things necessary for the body to that end should be included. The commandments of the Lord should be given first place right in front: that is what he wants and commands us. Anyone who weighs all this up properly will find that in this life it is far more labour and trouble [to do anything else].[3]

[3] There is a certain pilgrim called Calisto[4] in that place. I would strongly recommend you to talk openly about your affairs with him. It is really quite likely that you will find more in him than first meets the eye.

[4] So, for love of Our Lord, let's make a great effort in Him, seeing that we owe Him so much. We are more likely to reach our limit in receiving his gifts than He will be in giving them!

[5] I pray to Our Lady to implore on our behalf between us sinners and her Son and Lord, and to gain us His grace, so that, along with our strenuous effort, our puny, sad spirits may be transformed and become strong and joyful in His praise.

Barcelona, the feast of St Nicholas,[5]

the poor pilgrim

Iñigo[6]

2. Dealings with brother and nephew

1532

(No. 3 : I, 77–83 : Spanish)

The world of sixteenth-century family relations may seem strange to later readers – the formality, the Latin tags (preserved here as typical) and the obligations – and in this case further complications arise from the influence of Ignatius's new studies in Paris, not to mention his own complex trains of thought.

Martín García de Oñaz[1]   end of June 1532
in Loyola, Azpeitia   from Paris

☩

IHS

May the grace and love of Christ Our Lord be with us always!

[1] On receiving your letter it was a great pleasure for me to hear of the kindness and love that the Divine Majesty has shown to your daughter[2] and to learn of your decision for your son. May God in His supreme goodness be pleased with all the plans we make, directed to His service and praise! May He allow you to pursue them, and always succeed in them when you choose them for that end.

[2] [*Nephew's studies*] My opinion, unless you happen to have a better idea, is that there would be no harm in directing your son more to the study of theology than of canon law. The former is a subject that is more likely and better disposed to enrich him with a wealth that will last for ever, and to ensure for you more peace in your old age. And I am convinced that to advance in that subject you will find no place in the whole of Christendom so well equipped as this university. For his maintenance, tuition and other academic needs I think that 50 ducats a year will be enough, provided they are well administered. I imagine that you would not want your son to suffer hardship in a foreign country, one that is different and cold, especially as I think that would prevent his studies. If you reckon up the cost, you will be making a profit with him in this university, as he will make more progress here in four years than in any other that I know of in six years – and if I were to increase that number, I don't think I would be telling a lie. If you do decide to send

him here, as I would certainly recommend, it will be a great advantage if
he can come about a week before the feast of St Remigius, which is the
coming 1 October. That is when the course of arts begins, and if he has
a sufficient grounding in grammar he could begin the arts course itself
on the feast of St Remigius. Otherwise, if he comes a little late, he will
have to wait till the following year, for the next St Remigius, when the
new arts course begins again.

[3] [*Keeping accounts in order*] Certainly I shall do all I can to guide him
in his literary studies, so that he sets himself to work hard and keeps
clear of bad company. However, your own words to me are as follows:
'Please write and let me know how much it would cost annually if you
decide that he can go into your lodging; and I would be very grateful if
you could take over the expenses, given the opportunity'. I think the
literal meaning of these words is clear to me, unless there has been a slip
of the pen: namely, you would like your son to study here and that for a
while I should make arrangements so that you do not have to spend
money on your son. But as for this message I am reading, *unde illud
proveniat, seu quo tendat, non satis percipio* [= what its motive may be
and what it implies, I do not fully understand]. Please explain more
fully, if you think that an explanation will help. As for what is due in
justice or appears reasonable, I don't think that God Our Lord will let
me fall short. It is only His most holy service that moves me, along with
your peace of mind because of Him and the good of your son, if you do
tell me to act in this way.

[4] [*Stages in the spiritual life*] You say that you are overjoyed as you have
the impression that I have abandoned my policy of not writing to you.[3]
But it is not really so surprising: when a serious wound has to be cured,
first they use one sort of ointment, then another in the middle of the
process, and finally another at the end. So at the beginning of my way
one *medela* [= cure] had to be used. Then a little further on, somewhat
later, a different one does me no harm; *saltem* [= at least] if I had felt
that it was hurting me, I would certainly not have looked for a second or
a third.

[5] [*Parallel with St Paul*] *Non mirum* [= It is no wonder] that this
should have been my experience when St Paul shortly after his conversion says, '*Datus est mihi stimulus carnis, angelus Sathanae, ut me co-
lafizet*' [= 'I was given a goad of the flesh, an angel of Satan, to box my
ears'[4]]; *alibi* [= elsewhere], '*Invenio aliam legem in membris meis, repug-
nantem legi mentis meae; caro concupiscit adversus spiritum, spiritus
autem adversus carnem*' [= 'I find another law in my members, that

rejects the law of my mind;[5] the flesh feels an urge contrary to the spirit, and the spirit for its part contrary to the flesh'[6]]. The rebellion he felt in his soul was such that he even says, '*Quod volo bonum, non ago; quod nolo malum, illud facio; quod operor, non intelligo*' [= 'The good I want, I don't do; the evil I don't want, I do do; I fail to understand my own actions'[7]]. Then later on, at another time, he says, '*Certus sum quia nec mors, nec vita, nec angeli, nec instantia, nec futura, nec creatura alia poterit me separare a charitate Domini nostri Iesu Christi*' [= 'I am convinced that neither life nor death, nor angels, nor the present, nor the future, nor any created thing will be able to separate me from the love of Our Lord Jesus Christ'[8]]. When I began, I had a certain similarity with Him. In the middle and end may the supreme Goodness not deny me His complete and most holy favour so that I can resemble, imitate and serve all those who are His true servants. Rather than irritate God or fall short of His holy service and praise in anything whatsoever, I would prefer Him to snatch me out of this life.

[6] [*Love for family*] But returning to the subject, for a good five or six years I have thought of writing to you *frequentius* [= more frequently] but I have been held back by two things: on the one hand there has been the difficulty of my studies and of my many social contacts (not for personal ends), and on the other there has been my lack of confidence or of adequate proof that my letters might be of any use to the service and praise of God Our Lord, or of any comfort to my acquaintances and *secundum carnem* [= family] relatives, such that they might become related to me *secundum spiritum* [= in spirit] and *simul* [= at the same time] that we might be able to help one another in those things that are to last us for ever. The truth of the matter now is that my love for anyone in this life has to be proportionate to the advance in God Our Lord's service and praise that such love can bring, *quia non ex toto corde Deum diligit, qui aliquid propter se et non propter Deum diligit* [= because one does not love God fully if there is something loved for itself and not for God's sake]. Supposing that there are two persons who serve God Our Lord to an equal degree, one of them a relative and the other not, then God Our Lord will be very happy that our links and affection for the one (who happens to be our own father) should be greater than for the other (who does not have that relationship); similarly in the case of a benefactor or a relative, as opposed to someone who is neither, or for a friend or acquaintance as against those who are not. Due to this same motivation we have more veneration, honour and affection for those selected to be apostles than for other lesser saints; the

reason is that their service was greater, and so was their love, for God Our Lord, *quia charitas, sine qua nemo vitam consequi potest, dicitur esse dilectio, qua diligimus dominum Deum nostrum propter se, et omnia alia propter ipsum: etiam Deum ipsum laudare debemus 'in sanctis eius', authore Psalmista* [= because the charity, without which nobody can attain to life, is said to be the love by which we love God Our Lord for his own sake, and everything else for his sake; it is also God himself whom we should praise 'in his saints'', on the authority of the Psalmist].

[7] [*The love of God*] My greatest desire, and even greater than greatest, if one could say such a thing, is that there should be crammed *impense* [= abundantly] into the hearts of yourself, my relations and friends this same true love and full force for the service and praise of God Our Lord, so that my love and service for you might be ever greater. My own victory and my own glory are to be gained in the service of the servants of my Lord. It is with this upright love and with a sincere and open heart that I set myself to speak, write and give advice. That is how *ex animo* [= wholeheartedly] I desire that people should give me advice, warnings and corrections, *cum quadam syncera humilitate et non gloria prophana et mundana* [= with a certain sincere humility and not out of some sentiment of vain and worldly glory].

[8] [*True wealth*] If a man chooses in this life to undergo sleepless nights, anxieties and preoccupations to set up great buildings, to build walls and increase his income and standing, so as to leave behind him on earth great fame and lofty renown, *non est meum condemnare, laudare autem nequeo* [= it is not my business to condemn him, but I cannot praise him]. As St Paul says, '*Rebus ipsis debemus uti tanquam non utentes, possidere tanquam non possidentes, adhuc uxorem habere tanquam non habentem, quoniam figura huius mundi brevissima est*' [= 'We ought to use things themselves as if we were not using them, and possess them as if we did not possess them; even those married should be as if they were not married. For this world has but a fleeting appearance.'[10]] *Forsan, et utinam forsan* [= Perhaps, and I hope this chance has occurred[11]].

[9] [*Personal advice*] If you have experienced any of this in the past or present I urge you out of reverence and love for God Our Lord to try with all your strength to win honour in heaven, with reputation and fame in the sight of the Lord who is to judge us. He has entrusted you with an abundance of earthly goods, so try to earn with them eternal

goods – giving good example and holy teaching to your children, servants and relations, employing the right words with the one, imposing a just punishment on another, *tamen* [= but] without anger or irritation, granting the use of your house to one person, and gifts of money or income to another, being very charitable to orphans who are poor and in need. A person should not be miserly when God Our Lord has been so generous with him. We shall have peace and kindness in proportion to how much of them we have given in this life. Seeing that you have such great power in the region where you are living, *iterum iterumque te oro per amorem domini nostri Iesu Christi* [= I beg you repeatedly out of love for Our Lord Jesus Christ] to make great efforts, not only to think about these things, but to set your mind on them and put them into practice, *quoniam volentibus nihil difficile, maxime in his, quae fiunt propter amorem domini nostri Iesu Christi* [= as nothing is difficult for those who set their minds to it, especially when what we undertake is done out of love for Our Lord Jesus Christ].

[10] Don Andrés de Loyola[12] has written to me. The truth is that just at present I would prefer us to see one another *facie ad faciem* [= face to face] rather than to write a long letter when *non est ad rem* [= it is not appropriate]. Please let this letter serve to excuse me from writing to all the others, and I hope they will accept it as intended for each.

[11] I wanted to write *semel* [= at least once] a long letter in answer to the detailed points raised in your letter and to keep you informed.

[12] Please ask the lady of the house,[13] with all her family and anyone else you think is likely to be pleased with a greeting from me, to pray a lot for me *in Domino qui nos iudicaturus* [= to the Lord who is to judge us]. I close imploring Him in His infinite and supreme goodness to give us grace so that we may feel His most holy will and fulfil it completely.[14]

Written in the year 1532.

Post scriptum I received your letter earlier this month on 20 June and as you insist very strongly that I should reply to you, I have written this version and two copies so that it can be sent in triplicate; I would not want anything you desire *in domino nostro Iesu Christo* [= in Our Lord Jesus Christ] to fail to materialize. If you receive this letter in time and it is possible for your son to reach here some twenty days before the feast of St Remigius, so much the better. If it could be earlier still, then send him so that he can acquire some grounding before he starts the course. That is also the plan of a nephew of the Archbishop of Seville, who has been accepted by our College of Sainte Barbe to study in the Arts Faculty beginning with the next St Remigius. The two could profit from the opportunity to get more grounding, because there is no lack of contacts and good will. May the supreme Goodness order all things for His holy service and continual praise.

Poor in goodness,

Yñigo

3. Comfort among calamities

Isabel Roser 1532

(No. 4 : I, 83–89 : Spanish)

A sample of the many letters to women that diversify the correspondence of Ignatius,[1] and an introduction to one of his most devoted friends.

Isabel Roser[2]   10 November 1532
in Barcelona   from Paris

Ihs

May the grace and love of Christ Our Lord be with us!

[1] Thanks to Dr Benet I have received three letters from you along with 20 ducats. May God Our Lord put them to your account on the day of judgement! I would certainly like to repay them myself, as I trust in God's goodness that He will do so in good solid coin; also that He will not let me fall into the penalty of ungratefulness, *si tamen* [= but rather] on occasions He will grant me to be useful in the service and praise of His Divine Majesty.

[2] [*A death*] You say in your letter that God's will has been accomplished in the exile and separation from this life of [Señora] Canillas. It is quite true that I cannot feel pain on her behalf: that is reserved rather for those of us who are left in this place of enormous labours, sorrows and calamities. When I knew her in this life she was loved and cherished by her Creator and Lord; so it is easy for me to be convinced that she will be well lodged and welcomed, with no nostalgia for the palaces, extravagances, riches and vanities of this world.

[3] [*Offers of help*] You also mention the apologies of our sisters in Christ Our Lord. But they owe me nothing; it is I who am indebted to them for ever, especially if out of devotion to God Our Lord they perform a service in some more deserving case. That is where our real joy should lie, and if they do not, or cannot, then truly my own desire would be to be rich to provide for them, so that they could do great good to the service and glory of God Our Lord. As long as I live, I shall always be in their debt. However I have a real hope that once we are out of this life, they will be well repaid by me.

[4] [*Ill health*] In your second letter you describe the long suffering and

illness you have had, and you mention the great stomach pains that you still have. Whenever I think of your poor state and the pain you endure, I really cannot help but feel anguish deep in my heart. I would wish you every well-being and prosperity imaginable that might help you in promoting the service and glory of God Our Lord. *Tamen* [= however] then I think that these illnesses and other temporal mishaps frequently come from the hand of God Our Lord, so that we may have greater self-knowledge and a diminished love for created things, along with a deepened realization of the brevity of this life of ours. In that way we can equip ourselves for the next life which is to last for ever. As I realize that through these things God is visiting those whom He greatly loves, I cannot feel sadness and pain because I am convinced that a follower of God comes out of an illness already half way to being a doctor in the skill of directing and organizing life for the glory and service of God Our Lord.

[5] [*Debt to Isabel*] You also mentioned there that I was to forgive you if you did not send me more support, as you had many obligations and your resources were limited. Truly, forgiveness for you is not required, but I am apprehensive about receiving it myself when I call to mind that God's divine and proper justice will not forgive me if I fail to do all that God Our Lord requires of me for all my benefactors. This is especially so in relation to the debt I owe you! In any case, when my own forces fail me in this repayment, my only remedy will be that the Lord Himself, having drawn up an account of whatever good I may have merited before His Divine Majesty, a good gained *tamen* through His grace, will spread this out among those to whom I am indebted, giving to each in proportion to the help given me in the Lord's service, *maxime* [= above all] to yourself, as my debt to you is greater than to anyone else that I have known in this life. As I am very aware of this debt, I hope that I shall draw help and profit in God Our Lord from this awareness. Please be assured that in the future the mere fact of your simply and sincerely wanting to help me will be welcomed by me with as great a pleasure and spiritual joy as any amount of money that you may be able to send me. God Our Lord requires us to keep in our thoughts and affection the giver rather than the gift, and constantly to hold the person before our eyes, as indeed in our innermost mind and heart.

[6] [*Further letters*] You also suggest that I could consider writing to the other ladies, who are like sisters to me and benefactresses in Christ Our Lord, asking them to help me from now on. That is a subject where I would prefer to follow your opinion rather than my own. Although

[Señora] Cepilla has offered in her letter and gives clear signs that she is willing to help me, for the time being I don't think I shall write to ask for help for my studies. The reason is that I am not sure if I shall still be here one year from now.[3] If I find that I am still here I am trusting that God Our Lord will help me to understand and decide how best to serve Him, and how always to attain to what He really wants.

[7] [*Slurs for Christ*] In your third letter you describe all the ill will, the underhand attacks and falsehoods that have been plaguing you from all sides. I am certainly not surprised by this, nor would I be if they were even worse. From the moment that anyone has deliberately chosen and is utterly resolved to engage themselves on behalf of God Our Lord's glory, honour and service, they have declared war on the world and lifted their banner against this age. They are prepared to reject what is highly regarded, and to welcome what is low. They are willing to make no distinction between high and low, honour or dishonour, riches or poverty, affection or dislike, welcome or rejection, in a word, the glory of the world or all the insults of our age. In future, no importance can be given to those affronts in this life that remain mere words and fail to hurt a hair of our heads. Insinuations, slurs and calumnies are painful or laughable in proportion to the desire we have for them; if our wish is to have absolute respect from, and glory among, our equals, then our roots cannot be very deep in God Our Lord, nor can we fail to suffer hurt when insults come our way.

[8] [*Acquiring patience*] Even so the joy I felt at first that the world was insulting you was offset by my sorrow on learning that you had been forced to look for medical remedies in face of the pain and worry brought on by these adversities. Provided that you can acquire real patience and resolution, bearing in mind the greater injuries and insults that Christ Our Lord underwent on our behalf and to stop others from sinning, I would pray to the mother of God that greater insults might come your way so that your merit might be greater and greater. On the other hand, if we do not acquire this patience, it would be better for us to blame ourselves for our own bodily sensuality, and because we are not as insensible and mortified in relation to the things of this world as we should be, rather than to blame those who are doing the insulting. They are providing us with the opportunities to win profits that no businessman of this world could ever have gained, and to heap up riches beyond those of anybody in this life. An example of such profit and wealth occurred in this city, in a monastery of St Francis, and it happened as follows.

[9] [*The maiden monk*] There was a house that was frequently visited by friars of St Francis. As they were very pious and holy in their social relations, a girl in the house, who was already nearly grown up, became very attached to that monastery or house of St Francis. It reached the point that one day she dressed up as a boy and went to the monastery of St Francis to ask the Guardian if 'he' could be given the habit, as he had a great desire to devote himself exclusively to the service not only of God Our Lord and the lord St Francis, but of all the friars in that house. He spoke so sweetly that they thereupon gave him the habit.

[10] [*The false accusation*] Then after he had been in the monastery leading a very devout and blessed life, one night he and another companion happened to spend a night in a house where they had arrived while on a journey, with the permission of the Superior. Now in that house lived a certain miss; she fell in love with the good friar, or rather the devil possessed her into deciding to accost the good friar, while he was asleep, so that he would have an affair with her. But as the good friar no sooner woke up than he threw her out, she became so furious that she hatched a foul plot to do as much harm to him as possible. A few days later this wicked girl went to talk to the Guardian and she asked him to do her justice, claiming that she was pregnant because of the good friar in his house, and adding so much else that the Guardian arrested the good friar. His judgement (seeing that the affair had become so well known in the city) was that the friar should be tied up and put on show in the street at the gates of the monastery; in this way all would see that justice had been done to this good friar. So there he was in this fashion for many days, delighted with the hostile acts, insults and foul slurs directed against him, not trying to justify himself with anybody, but talking quietly with his Creator and Lord within his soul, seeing that God was offering him the opportunity to gain so much merit in the eyes of His Divine Majesty.

[11] [*Virtue rewarded*] After he had been put on show in this way for a considerable time, all those who witnessed his great patience begged the Guardian to forgive all that was past and to allow him back into his affection and house. The Guardian, already moved to have pity on him, accepted back the good friar who spent many years in the house until God's will for him was accomplished. Once he was dead, they stripped the body for burial and then discovered that it was a woman and not a man, and also how great had been the calumny made against her. All the friars were amazed by what had happened, and they spent more time in praising the innocence and sanctity than they had done in criticizing

their opposites. But it is also true that many people now remember much more this brother or sister than they do all the others who over many years lived in that house. For my part, I would prefer to spend more time thinking about one wrong which I may commit than about all the wrongs that may be said against me.

[12] In all the adversities of this life, and in everything else where you may be able to be of service to God, may the Holy Trinity grant you as great a grace as I would desire to have for myself, and may His gifts to me not be greater than the gifts I desire for you.

Please ask Mosén[4] Roser and all those who you think would be *ex animo* [= truly] delighted to have had a greeting from me, to remember me a great deal in their prayers.

Paris, 10 November 1532,

Poor in goodness,

Iñigo

P.S. I see signs of great constancy in the service and glory of God Our Lord in the person of Arteaga[5] and many others in Alcalá and Salamanca. May God be ever thanked for this!

In accordance with your instructions, all is in order. I have written to [Señora] Gralla about making peace, and the letter is going with another to [Señora] Pascual. I have also written to [Señora] Cepilla.[6]

4. Steps in discernment

Teresa Rejadell 1536

(No. 7 : I, 99–107 : Spanish)

This fragment of a well-documented correspondence¹ allows us to over-hear another conversation as Ignatius provides counsel for a nun who is clearly well advanced in spiritual experience (and therefore liable to be misled by the good rather than tempted by the bad). The letter also provides a mise-en-scène for the rather abstract 'Rules for understanding movements in the soul' and the 'Notes on scruples' later incorporated into the Exercises.²

Teresa Rejadell³   18 June 1536
in Barcelona   from Venice

JHS

May the grace and love of Christ Our Lord be always in our favour and assist us!

[1] Over the past days, having received your letter, I have been made very glad by it, glad in the Lord whom you serve and desire to serve more, and to whom we must attribute everything good that can be seen in creation.

[2] You say in your letter that Cáceres⁴ will tell me about your situation at length. This he has done, and not just your situation, but also the suggestions or interpretations that he was giving you for each of the matters you were raising. Reading what he says to me, I cannot think of anything else that he might add, although I would have preferred to have the information in a letter from you. For no one is as well able as the actual person concerned to convey to another what she is experiencing.

[3] [*The work of spiritual direction*] You ask that for love of God Our Lord I should take personal care of you. The truth is that for many years now His Divine Majesty, without my deserving it, gives me desires to do everything I can to please all those, men and women, who are trying to move forward under His good will and approval, and likewise to be of service to those working at the service which is His due. As I have no doubt that you are one of these, I very much want to be able to give practical expression of those desires.

[4] [*Dealing with her particular case*] Again, you ask me to write to you

in full what the Lord says to me, and to explain precisely my opinion [on your case]. Very willingly will I say with full precision what I feel in the Lord, and if I seem harsh on any point, I shall be directing the harshness more against the one who is working to upset you, rather than against you as such. In two ways the enemy is making you upset, but not so that he makes you fall into the guilt of a sin separating you from your God and Lord, but rather he makes you upset in the sense of separating you from His greater service and your greater tranquillity. The first of these ways is that he insinuates a false humility, the second is that he introduces an extreme fear of God, in which you remain too long and become too occupied.

[PART I: FEAR THROUGH FALSE HUMILITY]

[5] [*Demonic arms: dread and complacency*] Regarding the first part, the general procedure of the enemy with those who love God Our Lord and are beginning to serve Him is to bring in hindrances and obstacles. This is the first of the weapons with which he tries to inflict wounds. Thus, 'How are you going to live your whole life in such great penance, deprived of relatives, friends and possessions, in such a lonely life, without even some slight respite? You can be saved in other ways without such great risks.' He has us believe that as a result of the hardships he sets before us we are to live a life longer and more drawn-out than ever a human being lived; he does not get us to think about the abundant comforts and consolations normally given by the Lord if the new servants of the Lord shatter these difficulties by choosing to desire to suffer with their Creator and Lord.

[6] Then the enemy tries with the second weapon, that is boasting or vainglory, giving a person to understand that there is much goodness or holiness within them, and setting them in a higher place than they deserve.

[7] [*False humility*] If the servants of the Lord resist these arrows by humbling and abasing themselves, refusing to agree that they are such as the enemy suggests, then he brings along the third weapon, which is that of false humility. Thus when he sees the servants of the Lord so good and so humble that they think all they do to be of no use, concentrating on their weaknesses and not on any kind of self-glorification, even while doing what the Lord commands, then he insinuates into these people's thoughts that if they disclose some gifts that God Our Lord has given

them, whether in deeds, intentions or desires, they are sinning through another sort of vainglory since they are talking to their own glory. He tries to get them not to speak of the good things received from their Lord, so that they are of no benefit to others, nor to themselves. Normally whenever one calls to mind what one has received, one is helped towards greater things, even if this way of talking must be very finely judged and motivated by the greater benefit to be gained. I am referring both to one's own benefit and to that of others, if the person finds suitable dispositions and thinks that people will be receptive and benefit from it. In this way, the devil by making us humble tries to lead us into false humility, that is into an exaggerated and perverted humility.

[8] [*Exemplified now*] In this case your words provide apt testimony. After recounting some weaknesses and fears that go well with humility, you say you are a poor religious and that, 'It seems to me that I want to serve Christ Our Lord'. You do not even dare to say, 'I want to serve Christ Our Lord' or that 'The Lord gives me desires of serving Him'. Instead you say, 'It "seems to me that" I want to.' If you look properly you will clearly understand that these desires of serving Christ Our Lord are not from you, but given by the Lord, and then you will say, 'The Lord gives me increased desires of serving Him, the Lord Himself!' By making His gift known you are giving praise to Him, and your exultation is in fact in Him and not in yourself, since you are not attributing that grace to yourself.

[9] ['*Agere contra*'[6]] So we must take great care: if the enemy is raising us up, we ought to lower ourselves, listing our sins and wretchedness; and if he is casting us down and depressing us, we must raise ourselves up in true faith and hope in the Lord, counting the benefits we have received. With how much love, with how great a will does He wait for us in order to save us, while the enemy does not care whether he is telling the truth or lying, but only wants to overcome. Remember how the martyrs, placed before the pagan judges, used to say that they were servants of Christ. So likewise you, when you are placed before the enemy of all human nature and tempted by him in this way, with him wanting to deprive you of the strength that the Lord gives you, and to make you weak and fearful with his snares and deceits, so that you are not bold enough to say, 'I want to serve God Our Lord', then above all you are to speak out fearlessly and profess that you are His servant, and will die rather than separate yourself from His service. 'When he brings up questions of justice, my appeal will be to mercy, and when he is for mercy, my talk on the contrary will be of justice.' That is how we must

proceed if we are not to be upset, and if the mocker is to be mocked. We have to remind ourselves of that authoritative saying of Sacred Scripture that goes, 'Take care not to be humble in such a way that in your humility, you land yourself in folly!'[7]

[PART II: FEAR OF BEING SEPARATED FROM GOD]

[10] [*Further fears*] Coming now to the second main point. In the first stage the enemy has placed in us a form of fear under the cover of a humility which is false, so that we do not speak even of good, holy and beneficial things. So likewise he brings after this another far worse fear, the fear that we are distant, separated and exiled from Our Lord. This largely follows on from what has happened previously, because to the extent that with the first fear the enemy was victorious, so he finds it easy to tempt us with this other sort. To spell this out in some way I will tell you about another series of suggestions that the enemy makes.

[11] [*The lax and the scrupulous*] If he finds a person whose conscience is lax, and who passes over sins without dwelling on them, he does as much as he can to make venial sin be thought nothing, mortal sin only venial, and a very serious mortal sin of little account. Thus he takes advantage of the fault he senses within us, that of having an excessively lax conscience. But if he finds another person with a sensitive conscience (and there is no fault simply in its being sensitive), and sees that the person does not shun only mortal sins and the venial ones that can be shunned (as not all of them are under our control[8]), but even tries to shun any semblance of slight sin or defect against perfection, then he works to entangle that conscience which is so fine, making a sin out of what is no sin, insinuating a fault where there is perfection, so as to be able to throw us into confusion and distress. Thus quite often where he cannot cause sin, or does not hope to succeed in it fully, at least he works to cause torment.

[12] [*Consolation*] Further to clarify in some way how the fear is caused, I shall speak, though briefly, about two lessons that the Lord is accustomed to give, or at least permit (he gives the one and permits the other). The one he gives is interior consolation, which casts out all disturbance and draws us into total love of the Lord. There are some whom the Lord lights up in such consolation, and there are others to whom he uncovers many secrets, and more later. With this divine con-

solation, all hardships are ultimately pleasure, all fatigues rest. For anyone who proceeds with this interior fervour, warmth and consolation, there is no load so great that it does not seem light to them, nor any penance or other hardship so great that it is not very sweet. This shows to us and opens the path with the direction we are to follow, and the opposite we are to avoid. This consolation is not always with us, but proceeds always at specific times as arranged. And all this is for our profit.

[13] [*Desolation*] Then as we are left without this sort of consolation, the other lesson soon comes: I mean that our old enemy places before us every possible obstacle to divert us from what has been begun, attacking us very much. He acts completely counter to the first lesson, often plunging us into sadness without our knowing why we are sad. Nor can we pray with any devotion, or contemplate, or even speak and hear of things about God Our Lord with any interior savour or relish. And not stopping there, if he finds we are weak and let ourselves be subjected to such tainted thoughts, he brings us to think that we have been completely forgotten by God, and we end up with the impression that we are completely separated from Our Lord. Everything we have done, everything we were wanting to do, none of it counts. In this way, he tries to make us lose trust in everything. But we can see from all this what is the cause of so much fear and weakness on our part: at one stage we spent too long a time with our eyes fixed on our own miseries, and subjected ourselves to his deceptive lines of thought.

[14] [*Knowing the foe*] So here the person fighting has to identify the enemy. If it is a time of consolation, we must lower and abase ourselves, and reflect that soon the trial of temptation will come. If temptation, darkness or sadness come, we must act against them without allowing any bitterness, and wait in patience for the Lord's consolation, which will evaporate all disturbances and shadows from outside.

[PART III: INTERPRETING LIGHTS IN PRAYER]

[15] It remains now to talk of what we feel as we learn from God Our Lord, how we are to understand it, and how, once it is understood, we are to take advantage of it. It often happens that Our Lord moves and forces us interiorly to one action or another by opening up our mind and heart, i.e. speaking inside us without any noise of voices, raising us entirely to His divine love, without our being able to resist His purpose,

even if we wanted. The purpose of His that we then adopt is such that of necessity we conform with the commandments, with the precepts of the Church and with obedience to our superiors, and it is full of complete humility because the same divine Spirit is in everything.

[16] [*Possible deceptions: adding*] Where quite often we can be deceived is that following on such a consolation, or as it fades away, while the inner mind remains in delight, the enemy arrives completely cloaked in joy and gladness, in order to make us add to what we have sensed from God Our Lord, to make us fall out of order and become totally unbalanced.

[17] [*Subtracting*] At other times he has us reduce the lesson received, setting before us obstacles, things out of keeping, so that we do not wholly carry out everything that has been shown to us. Here one needs more care than anywhere else, because at times one has to rein in one's great desire to tell of the things of God Our Lord, and at other times one has to speak out beyond where the desire or movement takes us, depending on the obligation one has to pay more attention to the needs of others than to our own desires. In these circumstances the enemy is working to increase or diminish the good purpose received. Therefore we have to proceed when trying to help others like a person crossing a ford: if we find a good passage, or a path or hope that some benefit will follow, we press on, but if the ford is choppy, and people will be scandalized by the good words in question, we always have to rein in, looking for the season or the hour that will be more appropriate for speaking.

[CONCLUSION]

[18] The matters that have been raised are not the sort that can be just written about, or at least not without a long matured process, and even then there must remain things that are best left to be sensed rather than stated, especially by letter. If Our Lord is so pleased, I hope that very soon we shall see each other in Spain, where we will be able to understand each other more intimately in some things. Meanwhile, since you have Castro[9] near, I think it would be good for you to be in correspondence with him (no harm can ensue and some good might come), and since you asked me to write to you all that I felt in the Lord, I say that you will be very blessed if you know how to hold on to what you have!

[19] I end by praying the most Holy Trinity to give us, through their

infinite and supreme goodness, the fullness of grace, so that we may feel their most holy will and fulfil it completely.

From Venice, 18 June 1536,

Poor in goodness,

Ignacio

5. Prayer made easy

Teresa Rejadell 1536

(*No. 8 : I, 107–09 : Spanish*)

Another snatch of conversation, filling in gaps left in the previous letter and stressing this time the gentleness of non-discursive meditation and the irrelevance of distractions to God's love.

Teresa Rejadell[1]   11 September 1536
in Barcelona   from Venice

Jhs

May the grace and love of Christ Our Lord be always in our favour and assist us!

[1] Two of your letters reached me on separate occasions. I replied to the first at some length, I think, and by my reckoning you will have already received it. In the second you said more or less the same as in the first, except for a few points to which I shall restrict myself here in a brief reply.

[2] You say that you find yourself very ignorant and with all sorts of deficiencies, and so on ... Quite a good step forward in knowledge! You add that part of the reason for this is that you are full of all sorts of opinions, none very precise. I quite agree with you in this observation; a person with imprecise ideas can understand little and be of less help to others. However it is the Lord who sees, and He is the one who can act in our favour.

[3] [*Avoiding strain*] Any meditation that puts a strain on the understanding will fatigue the body. However there are other types of meditation that have an order to them and are relaxed. These leave the understanding in peace and do not put a strain on the mind's inner workings. They can be performed without any forcing, internal or external. These do not tire the body, but rather allow it to rest, unless one of two things happens: first, they may deprive you of the natural sustenance and recreation that you should be giving to the body. When I say 'deprivation of sustenance' I mean if somebody is so intent on these sorts of meditations that this person forgets to eat properly at the right times. By 'recreation' here I mean a healthy relaxation, when the mind is given

freedom to roam at leisure over any good or indifferent subjects that keep clear of evil thoughts.

[4] [*Ensuring sleep*] Secondly, many of those who are given to prayer and contemplation experience that just before it is time for them to go to sleep, they are unable to do so because they have been busy working their minds, and later they go on thinking of the subjects that they have been contemplating and imagining. This is where the Enemy does his best to maintain good thoughts, so that the body will suffer being deprived of sleep. Something to be avoided at all costs! With a healthy body, there is much that you can do; but with the body ill, I have no idea what you will be able to do. A healthy body is a great help, to do both much evil and much good – much evil with those who are depraved of mind and accustomed to sin, much good with those who have their minds set on God Our Lord and are accustomed to good deeds.

[5] [*Confidence*] For the time being, as I lack knowledge of your type of meditations and spiritual exercises, and of the time given to them, and can only exhort you to take the advice that Cáceres[2] has given you, there is not much more of value that I can say to you in addition to what is already written. Once again I would like to reassure you. Be convinced especially that your Lord loves you – something I am quite convinced to be true – and repay Him with this same love, paying no attention to wicked thoughts, however disgusting or provocative, demeaning or dispiriting, when they are against your will. To be completely or even partly free from them is something that neither St Peter nor St Paul ever attained. The point is that much remains to be gained even when such thoughts continue to return, provided no attention is paid to them. Just as I am not due to be saved simply thanks to the good efforts of the good angels, so I am not due to be harmed by the bad thoughts and weaknesses that the wicked angels, the world and the flesh put before me. God Our Lord wants my own soul to conform herself to His Divine Majesty. Once the soul has conformed herself, she can set the body in motion, whether it wants to or not, in conformity with His divine will. That is where our great battle lies and the chance to please the eternal and supreme Goodness. May He, in His infinite kindness and grace, always lead us by the hand.

From Venice, 11 September 1536,

Poor in goodness,
Iñigo

6. In praise of *The Spiritual Exercises*

Fr Miona 1536

(*No. 10 : I, 111–12 : Spanish*)

A testimony to the key importance attached by Ignatius himself to his
Spiritual Exercises.

Rev. Manuel Miona[1]   16 November 1536
in Paris   from Venice

Ihs

   May the grace and love of Christ Our Lord be always in our favour
and assist us!

[1] I am really longing to know how you have been getting on! And
don't be surprised about this, as I owe you such an enormous debt in
spiritual things – like a son to his spiritual father. It is only reasonable
that I should want to make some return for all the love and kindness
that you have always had for me, and shown by your deeds. But at
present in this life the only way I knew of repaying you some slight
percentage[2] was by arranging for you to make a month's Spiritual Exercises with the person I mentioned to you (you had already agreed to
make them). Please do write and let me know if you have approved of
them and enjoyed them (I ask you out of a desire to serve God Our
Lord). If you haven't made them yet, then I implore you – by the love
and most cruel death that He suffered for our sake – to set yourself to
them. And should you regret it later, then please do not only impose any
penance on me that you might wish (I willingly accept it), but consider
me somebody ready to make fun of the spiritual persons to whom I owe
everything.

[2] In my other letters I have been writing to one person there in the
name of all, and that is why I have not yet written to you personally. For
any news about me that you might like to have, Favre[3] will be able to
inform you, and you will see for yourself in the letter that I am sending
him. Still, let me repeat once and twice and as many more times as I am
able: I implore you, out of a desire to serve God Our Lord, to do what I
have said to you up to now. May His Divine Majesty never ask me one

day why I did not ask you as strongly as I possibly could! The Spiritual Exercises are all the best that I have been able to think out, experience and understand in this life, both for helping somebody to make the most of themselves, as also for being able to bring advantage, help and profit to many others. So, even if you don't feel the need for the first, you will see that they are much more helpful than you might have imagined for the second.

[3] As for the rest, I close this letter begging the immense clemency of God Our Lord to grant us His grace, so that we may feel His most holy will, and may be able to fulfil it perfectly, *iuxta talentum omnibus commissum* [= in accordance with the talent entrusted to each one[4]], or at least sufficiently to avoid our hearing the words *Serue nequam, sciebas, etc.* [= Evil servant, you knew, etc.[5]].

From Venice, 16 November 1536,

Completely yours in the Lord,

Iñigo

7. Blueprint for a religious order

Mgr Carafa 1536

(No. 11 : I, 114–18 : Spanish)[1]

Two years before there was any question of starting a new 'religious order' Ignatius detected a malaise in a similar group begun only a dozen years earlier, the Theatines. The root problem was their attitude to wealth, exemplified in the lavish life-style adopted by one of their founder-leaders, the future Pope Paul IV (from whom, significantly, Ignatius expected only the noblest example) and in the dangerous lack of clear norms on poverty. Ignatius is realist enough to recognize that a new order has to steer a careful course between the Scylla of scandalous wealth and the Charybdis of grinding poverty. It seems that his apprehensions reached the ears of Mgr Carafa, who was violently opposed to Spaniards as he was to Protestants, and relations between the two men were permanently soured.

Bishop Gian Pietro Carafa[2]   1536
in Venice   from Venice

Ihus

[1] [*The common love of God*] On reflection we see that the life we so desire and our eternal happiness are identical with, based upon, and constituted by an intimate and genuine love of God, our Creator and Lord. The prospect of that life creates relations and obligations among all of us who exist to love one another with a sincere love, a love not imaginary but true in that same Lord whose wish it is to save us, unless, through our frailty, guilt and utter worthlessness persist. So I have thought of writing you this letter, avoiding the pomposity habitual to many letters (something I do not criticize if properly ordered in the Lord), because one may well presume that a person who abandons the world, rejecting dignities and other temporal honours, will not want to be addressed with honorific titles and esteem couched in sounding phrases. Surely, he will be the greater who in this life becomes the lesser![3] Therefore I leave out all those things that run the risk of provoking you, or disturbing you from true peace, the internal and eternal peace. In-

stead I would request you, out of love and reverence for Christ our Creator, Redeemer and Lord, to read this letter with the same love and good will with which it is written. This love is so genuine and sincere that I can beg and implore the infinite and supreme Goodness, with all the forces that He has given me (without my deserving it), to grant to you, on exactly the same terms as I ask for myself, whatever is good in this life and in the next, all good for both soul and body, and all else that may be required for God's most holy and due service. This is my wish for you and what I beg and implore for you.

[2] [*Tentative advice*] Now, inspired by the same good will, prompt and ready to serve, that I have for all those I feel are servants of my Lord, I intend to discuss here three topics with the simplicity and love mentioned above, rather as if I were talking to myself and not attempting to give somebody my opinion or a piece of advice – it is always better to take advice humbly than to give it proudly! My aim will be to draw attention and to set in motion, so that we may always try our best to ask God's help: He is the One from whom all healthy opinions and sound advice come.

[3] [*Danger for the Theatines*] First, there seem to me to be sufficient arguments, based on likely reasons and adequate guesses – and I write this quite peacefully, in love and charity – for me to fear or think that the religious group[4] given you by God Our Lord may not spread out at all, whereas if it were to increase in companions,[5] then it would be more likely to be of greater service and praise of the Lord. I restrict myself here to explaining only part of what I can understand. I was quite at a loss to know the cause of my feeling on this subject, and so I recommended it to God Our Lord very insistently and frequently, then decided to write the following remarks, just as youngsters usually do with their elders when they think they can warn them or help them for the service of God Our Lord, hopefully without themselves being directly or indirectly misled in the matter.[6]

[4] [*Carafa's excessive life-style*] Secondly, given a person's quality, his descent from such a noble house, his great dignity and lofty rank, added to being advanced in years,[7] then I cannot be scandalized or set a bad example if he is somewhat better turned out and dressed, and if his lodging is somewhat above the norm and rather better equipped – especially if out of consideration for the visitors he receives – than is the case for others of his religious group. One has to comply with the needs and advantages of particular periods. There is no need to hold such things as imperfections. Nevertheless, if one bears in mind how the saintly blessed

ones, like Saint Francis and Saint Dominic, and many others in the past, conducted themselves with their subordinates when they were founding and giving rules and good example, it does seem to me to be very wise and sensible for someone to have recourse to the true and supreme Wisdom, in order to request and obtain the greatest possible light and clarity so that he may be directed completely to His greater service and praise. There are many things that are licit but not expedient, as St Paul says about himself.[8] Otherwise others may use the excuse to lessen their efforts, or even follow the example beyond its limits. This is especially true of one's own household; they always pay more attention to the doings and sayings of their elders and betters.

[5] [*The scandal of religious wealth*] Thirdly, I hold as a maxim that God Our Lord has created everything in this life to satisfy human needs, and to serve and preserve the human race, so *a fortiori* those who are the best. Now given that your religious and holy foundation is a *via ad perfectionem* [= a way to perfection], and places those in it in a state[9] of perfection, I personally have no doubt, but am quite certain, that all those who practise obedience and a blameless life in your group, even though they do not preach or devote themselves to the other corporal works of mercy in any apparent way – as they are given much more to other spiritual works and those of greater importance – have a right to *victus et vestitus* [= food and clothing] according to the norms of love and Christian charity; they should be receiving these in order to grow strong in the service and praise of their true Creator and Lord. However it seems most advisable and more sure in this matter if one takes great precautions, and constantly prays for guidance to the Lord, for whose sake everything is undertaken. There will then be a hope of edifying the general public, and of preserving and increasing such a religious and holy group in its early steps.

[6] [*The weaker brethren*] Those who are weak or who are more worried about supplies of material goods, especially those necessary for life, may well object, basing their arguments on apparent truth, that it is most difficult for the above members of the group to continue for long in their religious calling because of three factors, all obvious reasons: (1) they are not able to beg for what they need, and lack the minimum to live; (2) they do not preach; (3) they do not devote themselves to any great extent to the corporal works of mercy, like preparing graves and saying masses for those who have died, etc.

[7] [*Need for a public image*] My point is that even if they did not practise begging, their works would become public knowledge if they

were to preach etc. Even supposing that they did not have the ability or the proper disposition to preach, if they were on the look-out, and asked some parishes to let them know when people had died, so that they could help to dig the graves, pray for them and celebrate masses gratis, then they would have a way of giving greater service to God Our Lord in a religious manner, and the general public would be more inspired to maintain them and would show much more charity towards them, and other clerics would try to interest more people and prick their consciences.

[8] [*Need for material provision*] As for those who want to live exclusively in the hope that they will be kept and fed, I can certainly agree that if one decides not to beg, but simply to serve God Our Lord and to hope in His infinite goodness, this is enough for one to be both kept and fed. However those who are weaker or more preoccupied, as I mentioned, with worldly matters may well object that Saint Francis and the other blessed saints are believed to have had this hope and confidence in God Our Lord, but that did not stop them establishing the means that seemed most appropriate to ensure that their houses were maintained and expanded, to the greater service and greater glory of the divine majesty. Any other form of action would have seemed to be tempting God, whom they were supposed to be serving, rather than following a path likely to lead to His service.

[9] [*Ignatian insights*] Other points can be left for a better occasion; I don't want to write them down as they are not considerations that I have developed and thought out for myself, but they have been put forward by others, or I happen to have heard them second-hand. But whatever I have weighed up and pondered I am quite happy to put down on paper and present before you, as though I were doing it on my own for my own consideration. No harm is likely to come from this, and some good may follow if we continue constantly to pray to God Our Lord, so that in His infinite and supreme Goodness He may find and disclose to us new remedies for the new tasks that face us. I implore and constantly pray that, with His usual kindness and supreme grace, He will deign to give a hand to all [your work], so that His greater service and praise may follow from it all, just as I hope will happen with my own affairs.

Wishing to be the servant of all the servants of God Our Lord,

I.

8. Early years in Italy

1536–37

(No. 2 in Appendix 2 : XII, 320–23 : Spanish)[1]

*An important autobiographical fragment that covers the crucial years
when the companions were coalescing into a group (in September 1537
they began to refer to themselves as 'Companions of Jesus') but still
thought of themselves as poor priests en route to Jerusalem.*

Rev. Juan Verdolay[2]   24 July 1537
in Barcelona   from Venice

Ihs

May the grace and love of Christ Our Lord be always in our favour
and assist us!

[1] Since my visit to those parts[3] and my letter to you, about two years
ago, I have not had any letter from you, nor indeed any news until
recently, some three months ago, when Isabel Rosel[4] informed me about
your health and about the excellence and soundness of your teaching.
She also said that you had written to me and were longing to have more
news about me.

[2] Clearly, I have no pressing duty to remain here, and if it were not for
the many commitments that I have voluntarily taken on, convinced as I
am of their great importance, I would not let the danger of sore feet
prevent me from reaching you, wherever you may happen to be. Having
considered the situation over there and weighed up matters here, if for
your part you think it would be for the greater service and glory of Our
Lord, I would very much wish us to meet here in Venice. I expect to be
staying here for about a year, more or less. After that, I have no idea
what God Our Lord will arrange for me.

[3] In order to keep you better informed about myself and the others
who are brothers to both of us in Christ Our Lord, and to answer the
questions you must have, I think I shall try to write you quite a long
letter as I'm sure you will be pleased to receive reliable information.

[4] [*Companions in Venice*] In the middle of January, nine[5] of my
friends in the Lord arrived here from Paris; they all have their MA

degrees and are quite well versed in theology. Four of them are Spaniards, two French, two from Savoy and one from Portugal. They had to cope with many threats from wars, long journeys on foot and the worst of the winter. All were lodged in two hospitals, and split up in order to care for the sick who are in poverty, doing the jobs that are most demeaning and physically repugnant.

[5] [*Companions in Rome*] After two months of this exercise they went to Rome, with some others who had come to share their aspirations, for Holy Week. They were poverty-stricken, penniless, and without the backing of any outstanding academics, or of anything else, placing all their trust and hope simply and solely in the Lord for whose sake they had come. So, they found without any difficulty all that they wanted and much more: they were granted an audience with the Pope. Afterwards many cardinals, bishops and professors came and were in discussion with them. One of those present was Dr Ortiz,[6] who has been quite exceptionally supportive to them. Several other distinguished scholars were also favourable. The upshot was that the Pope was very pleased with them, as were all those present at the discussion, and began to grant them every possible help: 1st, permission to go to Jerusalem, the Pope blessing them once and then a second time, urging them to persevere in their aims; 2nd, the Pope made a grant of about 60 ducats, and among the cardinals and others present they gave them more than 150 ducats, so that they brought here in letters of credit some 260 ducats; 3rd, those who are already priests were given faculties to hear confessions and to grant absolution in all circumstances reserved to bishops; 4th, those who were not priests were given the legal forms required for ordination, no mention being required of patrimony or benefice, so that any bishop could perform the ordination ceremonies to the priesthood on three successive feast-days or Sundays.

[6] [*Priestly ordinations in Venice*] Thus when they came back to Venice, we were all finally ordained to full orders, including the priesthood on the Feast of St John the Baptist [24 June 1537]. Those of us ordained were seven[7] in number, and we were granted every facility and help imaginable; so much so that we were asked to choose whether we wished to be priests *ad titulum voluntariae paupertatis, vel sufficientis litteraturae, vel utriusque;*[8] we chose *ad titulum utriusque*, and then took the vow of perpetual poverty in the presence of the local Papal Legate. He did not force us to do this, but we felt that this was what we wanted. When it came to the priestly ordination they offered us two bishops,

both of whom wanted to perform the ceremony, so we had quite a task not to offend⁹ one of them as it was not possible to have them both!

[7] [*Faculties*] Once all this had been settled, both in Rome and in Venice, without our having to pay anything as it was all done free of charge, the same Legate gave us full authority to preach, teach and explain Sacred Scripture, both in public and in private, throughout the Venetian territory; we can also hear confessions and absolve in all cases normally reserved to bishops, archbishops and patriarchs.

[8] [*New responsibilities*] I have mentioned all this partly to fulfil what I said above, but also to show you that our burden now is much heavier, and so also will be our shame if we fail to take advantage when God Our Lord is being so generous to us. Without our even asking or planning, everything that we could have wanted for our work is put in our hands. May the divine Goodness pour his grace upon us so that we do not hide in the ground¹⁰ the gifts and favours he is constantly giving us, and which we hope he will always give us if we for our part do not fall short. I do beg you, out of service and reverence for his divine majesty, to pray insistently for us. Please also ask the good men and women with whom you are in contact to do likewise. You can see how great is our need: those who receive more put themselves all the more in debt.¹¹

[9] [*Money for Jerusalem*] This year, despite all their hope for a passage to Jerusalem, there has been no boat, nor is there one now – all because of the armada being prepared by the Turks. We have come to a common agreement that the letters of credit for the 260 ducats collected should be sent to Rome, so that the money can be returned to the disposal of those who received these sums on their behalf. We do not want to use this money except for the journey proposed. Also we do not want anybody to think that we are hankering after those things for which people of the world are willing to give their lives.

[10] [*The coming year*] Once that job has been done (the letter has already been sent) and this letter is written, then the following day the people here will set out two by two to take up any work they can find likely to please Our Lord, for whose sake they are going. So they will be spread out over this part of Italy until next year, when they will see if they can cross over to Jerusalem. Then if it is not God Our Lord's good pleasure that they make the journey, they will not wait any longer but carry on with whatever they have begun.

[11] [*Expansion?*] Here some companions have wanted to stick on to us, and they do not lack sufficient learning. Still, our concern has been to restrict rather than to expand, for fear of fallings away.

Let me end praying God Our Lord in His infinite and supreme goodness that He may deign to grant us His full grace, so that we may feel His most holy will and accomplish it fully.

From Venice, 24 July 1537,

Poor in goodness,

Yñigo

P.S. After writing the above I received a letter from you. As far as I can judge and feel – knowing that Our Lord is to judge me one day – it seems to me that there will be more for you to do here, considerable though your present work is, and you will find the path you desire to serve the Lord more fully. Therefore do all you can so that we can see one another soon!

9. Thanks for support

Mgr Contarini 1538

(No. 17 : I, 134–36 : Latin)

This little thank-you note, one of several letters to Ignatius's Venetian friends and patrons, gives a glimpse both of the difficulties encountered and of the administrative workings brought into play. The contact with the powerful Contarini family gave decisive help in these crucial foundation years.

Pietro Contarini[1]   2 December 1538
in Venice   from Rome

Ihs

The grace of Our Lord Jesus Christ and peace be with us all.

[1] We have received your last letter to us, together with the one you sent to commend us to the Revd Lord [Cardinal Gasparo] Contarini. For both we are grateful to your friendliness and kindness. From the one we saw how well you remember us; from the other we realized how much we are indebted to you.

[2] As soon as your Revd uncle read your letter, he sent one of his servants to the Lord Governor, asking him by his favour to dismiss the case against us, which had come before him. Not many days later the matter was entirely concluded, and that in the way which we thought would be most to the honour of God and the benefit of souls: judgement was given to the effect that, after diligent inquiry, nothing had been found either in our way of life or in our teaching to deserve mistrust. If you are interested to see the terms of the judgement itself, you may like to know that the Imperial Ambassador[2] who is with you also has a copy, for some of our friends sent him one. We realize that this does not mean that no one will slander us in future; we never asked for that. We just wanted recognition of our honour, doctrine and upright way of life. With the help of God, we shall never be worried if we personally are called lacking in culture, education or eloquence, or again if we are called wicked, deceivers or unreliable; but what hurt was that the actual doctrine which we were preaching should be called unsound, and that our form of life should be called evil, for ours are

neither of these, but are of Christ and his Church. But enough of all this.

[3] All those you asked us in your letter to greet in your name send you their greetings in return through me. They are all well in body and I trust also in mind, as we hope through Jesus Christ Our Lord, who is our peace, rest, fulfilment, consolation and the sum of all the good for which we were made and born anew, and for the sake of which we are preserved so long in this world.

But for the present, best wishes in Him, and please continue your kind concern for us.

From the city of Rome, 2 December 1538,

Yours in the Lord,

Ignatius

10. Roman trials and tribulations

1538

(No. 18 : I, 137–44 : Spanish)¹

Taking up the story from Letter 8 this one brings it to the verge of the crucial decision to found the Society as a religious order.

Isabel Roser²   19 December 1538
in Barcelona   from Rome

May the grace and love of Christ Our Lord be always in our favour and assist us!

[1] There is little doubt in my mind that you will be quite anxious, and no less surprised, that I have written so few letters to you, despite all my wishes to the contrary. Really, if I were to forget all that I owe to the Lord through your hands, with such sincere love and good will, I think the Divine Majesty would no longer remember me! Out of love and reverence for Him you have always spent yourself so much on my behalf.

[2] [*1538 – a trying year*] But there was a reason for my dilatoriness in writing: from one day to the next, and then from one month to the next, we were quite confident that we would be able to liquidate one of our affairs, and we wanted to give you reliable information about our situation here. In fact, the affair has taken on such proportions that during eight whole months we have had to undergo the most violent opposition or persecution that we have ever experienced in our lives. I don't mean to say that we have been physically attacked, or formally arraigned, or anything of that sort. The system was rather to spread reports among the people and to describe us in incredible terms, so that we were an object of suspicion and hatred for all, becoming a focus of considerable scandal. It became necessary to appeal before the Papal Legate and the City Governor (as the Pope³ was absent at that moment in Nice) because of the great scandal that was being widely caused. We began by naming and summoning some of those who were actively involved against us, so that they could explain before higher authority what errors they had detected in our lives and teachings. In order to make the affair easier to understand from the beginning, I shall give some account of it.

[3] [*Arrival in Rome*] More than a year[4] ago three of our Society[5] arrived here in Rome, as I remember having written to tell you. The other two began to give lectures free of charge in the university college (the Sapienza), one in positive theology and the other in scholastic theology, acting on the instructions from the Pope. For my part, I set myself full-time to organizing and giving the Spiritual Exercises to persons both inside and outside[6] Rome. We decided on this policy in order to win some people of learning or power to our side; or, to be more precise, to the side, honour and homage of God Our Lord, for our 'side' is nothing but the praise and service of His Divine Majesty. Our aim was to prevent too much opposition among men of the world, so that later we might be freer to preach His holy word, as we could smell the soil, how arid it was in all good fruit and how overgrown with weeds.

[4] [*Coming together*] As a result of those Exercises (God Our Lord was at work) we won over some persons to help and support us, among them gifted academics and people of high standing. Then four months after our arrival, we thought of bringing all the members of the Society together in this city, and as they began to arrive,[7] we duly applied for permission to preach and hear confessions. The Legate granted these permits with ample powers, even though in his department some very negative reports about us were handed in to his Vicar, aimed at preventing the grant of the permits. Once we had them, four or five of us began to preach on feast days and Sundays in various churches. Similarly, in other churches we began to explain to young boys about the ten commandments, mortal sins, etc. All this time, the two courses continued at the Sapienza, and the hearing of confessions elsewhere. The others were all preaching in Italian; I was the only one to use Spanish.

[5] [*Preaching work*] For all the sermons there were quite large crowds, which far exceeded anything we had expected. There were three reasons for a low expectation: first, it was an unusual time – we began at the end of the Paschal season when the Lenten preachers and those for the big feasts were finishing, and in this part of the world the custom is to have sermons only in Lent and Advent; secondly, because normally, when the labours and sermons of Lent are over, most people – sinful that we are – tend to take their ease and enjoy the world's pleasures rather than to take up other similar efforts and new devotions; thirdly, because we have the impression that our sermons are not notable for turns of phrase and beautiful words and yet we are quite convinced, by a wealth of experience, that Our Lord in His infinite and supreme goodness does not forget

us, and worthless and insignificant though we may be, He gives help and assistance to very many others through us.

[6] [*First trial: no verdict*] Now once our appeal had been lodged as described, two men were officially summoned and questioned, and one of them found that his position before the judges was very different from what he had expected.[8] Then the others whom we had named to be summoned were so frightened that they had no desire or courage to make an appearance. Instead they brought pressure to bear upon us to make us carry on our case before different judges. They were persons of wealth, one with an income of one thousand ducats, another with one of six hundred, and yet another with even more power, all of them members of the curia or men of affairs. They intrigued so much with cardinals and other men of standing in the curia here that they kept us busy with this struggle for a long time. Finally, those who stood out as most important were summoned and came before the Legate and the Governor. They said that they had heard our sermons and lectures, etc, and they gave a full account of everything, as much of our teaching as of our way of life, justifying us completely. After all this, both the Legate and the Governor, who held us in very high esteem, wanted a veil of silence to be drawn over the whole matter, regarding both these accusers and any others. We for our part requested repeatedly, as we felt to be just, that a written report be drawn up on what was bad or good in our teaching, so that the public scandal might be dissipated. However we were never able to obtain this from them, despite all justice and right.

[7] [*Appeal to the Pope*] From then onwards there was such a terror of the legal authorities that no more was heard of what had previously been said against us, at least in public. But as we were never able to obtain a final sentence or declaration on our affair, one of our friends had a word with the Pope when he returned from Nice, requesting that a declaration be made on it. Although the Pope granted our request, it never took effect, and so two of our Society spoke to him about it. Later still, as the Pope left Rome to stay at a castle in the vicinity,[9] I went there and talked to His Holiness alone in his room for a good hour. As I was explaining to him at length our proposals and intentions, I gave a very clear account of all the times when I had been arraigned in Spain and in Paris; similarly the times when I had been imprisoned in Alcalá and in Salamanca. I did this partly so that nobody can give him more information than I have, partly so that he would be more inclined to set up an investigation about us. Either way, a sentence or declaration about our

teaching would be given. It was so very necessary for our future preaching and exhortation that we should be held in good repute, not only in the eyes of God Our Lord but also in the eyes of ordinary people, and that there should be no suspicions about our teaching and conduct, that in the end I implored His Holiness, in the name of us all, to order measures to be taken so that our teaching and conduct could be investigated and examined by any recognized judge that His Holiness might appoint, in order that if error were found, we might be corrected and punished, and if right, His Holiness might give us his support.

[8] [*New trial*] Seeing that there was room for doubt (on the basis of what I had told him), the Pope reacted very well, praising our talents and the way they were applied in good causes. He spoke to us for a while, encouraging us (and certainly with words suited to a real and upright pastor), then gave orders with all despatch to the Governor, who is both a bishop and the principal court in this city for both ecclesiastical and civil matters, to give audience to our suit at once. The Governor opened a new case, and set about it speedily. Then the Pope returned to Rome and very often spoke publicly in our favour, indeed in the presence of members of our Society (as they have the habit of going once a fortnight to hold a public discussion during His Holiness's mealtime). Most of our storm has now blown over, and day by day the fine weather is spreading. Thus it seems to me that things are going much as we would want – to the service and glory of God Our Lord – so that we are much in demand from both prelates and others to produce happy results in their lands (with God at work). We are staying still, hoping for the best opportunity. Very recently sentence has been passed and our case has been settled, thank God!

[9] [*The conjunction of witnesses*] In connection with this something happened here which is not exactly normal. Among the remarks about us that had been made up and passed around was one that said we were really fugitives from justice, wanted in several countries and especially in Paris, Spain and Venice. Well, just when the sentence or declaration was due to be passed on us, there happened to be in Rome, all recently arrived, Figueroa,[10] the Regent, who had arrested me once in Alcalá and had twice brought me to trial, the Vicar General[11] of the Papal Legate in Venice, who also brought a case against me (shortly after we had begun to preach in Venetian territory), Dr Ory,[12] who similarly brought me to trial in Paris, and the Bishop of Vicenza[13] where three or four of us had preached for a short time. Likewise the cities of Siena, Bologna and Ferrara sent authorized witnesses to bear testimony here, and the Duke

of Ferrara,[14] in addition to sending witnesses, took the matter so much to heart, as he felt that God Our Lord was being dishonoured by what was being done against us, that he wrote to his ambassador and also to our Society on several occasions. He considered the case a matter of personal interest as he was aware of the good that had been done in his city. Similar reactions came from the other cities where we have been (it has been no small achievement on our part to have known how to maintain our reputation and persevere in his city).

[10] [*Activity in Rome*] One thing for which we are most grateful to God Our Lord is that ever since we began up to the present moment, two or three sermons have not failed to be made on every feast, the two lectures have continued each day, some have been busy with confessions and others with spiritual exercises. Now that sentence has been given, we hope to increase the number of sermons, and also the instruction of young boys. Given that the earth here is so sterile and dry, and the opposition we have encountered so great, we cannot honestly say that we have lacked things to do, nor that God Our Lord has failed to be active to a degree that surpasses anything that our knowledge and understanding can encompass.

[11] [*A new order?*] On more particular matters I shall not write further here, so as not to make this letter too long, but in general God Our Lord is making us very happy. I will only mention that there are four or five who have made up their minds to join our Society, and they have persevered in their decisions for many days and many months now. For our part we do not dare to accept them because this was one among other matters that they brought up against us, namely that we were accepting others and establishing a congregation or religious order without apostolic authorization. Hence our present situation, and if we are not all agreed about how we are to proceed, we are all agreed in the resolve that we must come to an agreement in the future. In this matter we hope that God Our Lord will soon dispose how best He may be served and praised in all things.

[12] [*Request for prayers*] Now that you have learned where our affairs stand, please pray out of love and reverence for God Our Lord that we may be very patient, with our hearts set on what He may want to achieve through us, as best suited to His glory and praise. There can be no doubt that matters are now at a crucial juncture. I shall keep you informed more frequently about what is happening, for without any hesitation I can assure you that if I forget you, I can only expect to be forgotten by my Creator and Lord. That is why I am not too worried

about doing my duty and expressing my thanks in words. However, please feel quite certain, all that you have done on my behalf out of love and reverence for God Our Lord is present in His sight. In addition to that, as you have always helped me and given me special support in God's divine service and praise, you will have a full part as long as I live in whatever good deeds His Divine Majesty may wish to bring about through me, giving them the value of some merit through His divine grace. Please ask all those persons whom we both know, and who are so upright and so devoted to God, and so united with us in Christ Our Lord, to remember me and pray often for me.

[13] To finish, I implore God Our Lord, in his infinite goodness and supreme kindness, to grant us his full grace, so that we may feel His most holy will and accomplish it fully.

From Rome, 19 December 1538,

Poor in goodness,

Iñigo

P.S. As I was writing this letter, the Pope commanded arrangements to be made by means of the Governor so that orders are given to the city whereby when schools for young boys are amalgamated, we will undertake the instruction in Christian doctrine, as we began to do earlier on. As this is something that God Our Lord wants, may He grant us the strength to work for His greater service and glory. I am sending to Archdeacon Cazador[15] the text (as it is in Latin) of that declaration about us that was published here; he will inform you about it.

11. Benighted obedience

Fr Viola 1542

(No. 52 : I, 228–29 : Spanish)

This letter contains the earliest reflections by Ignatius on the notion of obedience, which will come to play such a major role in his thinking; already many factors, especially the importance of representation, are present.

Fr Giovanni Batista Viola[1]   August 1542 (?)
Paris   from Rome

✛

Ihus

May the supreme grace and love of Christ Our Lord be always in our favour and assist us continuously!

[1] I have received a letter from you and I cannot understand it. Indeed there are references in it on two occasions to obedience: once you say that you are ready to obey my wishes, and at another point you write, 'As I would prefer to welcome death rather than be remiss in obeying, I submit myself to your Reverence's judgement'. Now it is true that in my opinion obedience should try to be blind, where I understand 'blind' in two ways: (1) when the person obeying (in a case where there is no question of sin) ties up his understanding and does what he is told; (2) when the person obeying receives or has received from the Superior an order to do something, and then realizes that there are other aspects or problems about what has been ordered; the person respectfully informs the Superior about these aspects or problems that have occurred to him, without trying to urge the Superior one way or the other, so that he can carry out at once with a tranquil mind whatever is said or ordered.

[2] As for your notion of obedience, I am incapable of really understanding it. At one point you inform me of many good reasons that you think will persuade me in the choice of a different professor, and later you add in your letter the words, 'I considered it proper to write to your Reverence, asking you to kindly notify us if we should change professors or instead waste our time'. You can judge for yourself if you are really seeking obedience, and if you are really submitting your judgement so

that I can tell you what to think. Seeing that you are so sure of your own opinion and absolutely convinced that you are wasting your time, where does any submission of your judgement come in? Or can it be that you think my task is to tell you to waste your time? May God forbid that I should ever find myself doing harm to somebody when I cannot help the person!

[3] At another point you write, 'I am really very sorry to have thrown away all this time, during eight months, with that professor; if you are still convinced that we should waste time, then we will'. I distinctly remember that when you left here I told you that by the time you reached Paris, the course on the *Summulae*² would be two or three months under way: you should study Latin for four or five months to become more fluent, then dedicate three or four months to acquire an initial grasp of the *Summulae* course so that you would have some understanding when you began the full course the following year. It was your choice to follow your own opinion rather than mine and to insert yourself into a course that was already two or three months under way. Judge for yourself who has been responsible for your waste of time.

[4] Let me end this letter imploring God Our Lord in His infinite and supreme goodness to grant us the fullness of His grace that we may feel His most holy will and accomplish it fully.

12. Vocation doubts of a young man

1544

(No. 79 : I, 294–95 : Spanish)

The MHSI edition has the lurid title 'To a man tempted by a demon', and the distress of the person addressed can be easily imagined. The counselling technique adopted is very Ignatian.

Unknown addressee   28 November 1544
Unknown destination   from Rome

✛

Ihus

May the supreme grace and love of Christ Our Lord be always in our favour and assist us continuously!

[1] Given the great affection and goodwill I have for you there can be no question of my failing you in any way. So in reply to your letter and that of Master Laínez I shall simply put down briefly what my feelings in the Lord happen to be.

[2] 1. Re the suggestion that you go and live at home: I can think of nothing that in my opinion would be worse for you and that you should more detest. I have already written you at length on this topic, giving the reasons based on previous experience and other proofs.

[3] 2. Re the proposal that you keep a room and live in that house with ours: I don't think I can agree to this and don't feel happy that such a solution will be for the best. On the one hand, it is not as if you were finding the good you wanted there, which would be a reason for you to stay. On the other hand, both your relations and our men would be distressed because they would not be able to help you *in utroque homine* [= body and soul] as they would wish. So all things considered the surest solution, most likely to provide better and greater assistance to all in Our Lord, would be for you to spend the money that you would have spent at home in renting your own room in good company, quite separate from ours living there. You can then try living in it for a year, going to confession and having talks with some of ours a few times each week. In the rest of the time you can attend some lectures, more with a view to keeping your mind busy and strong than to mastering some

scholastic discipline for teaching others. You can take part in all sorts of good social contacts and such recreations that are not likely to lead to sin (it is preferable for us to avoid sin than to be lords over the whole world[1]). Once you have gained a certain peace and quiet of conscience with the help of internal consolations and spiritual joys,[2] then the time will come for you to study for the benefit of others, according to your mental and physical strength. Above all I would urge you, out of love and reverence for God Our Lord, when the past comes to mind, consider very carefully and not in any abstract way that this earthly home of ours is nothing but earth.

May God Our Lord, in His infinite and supreme goodness, grant us the fullness of His grace, that we may feel His most holy will and accomplish it fully.

Rome, 28 November 1544.

13. Borgia's early steps

1545
(No. 101 : I, 339–42 : Spanish)

The first extant letter of Ignatius to Borgia, but a sequel to others. Ignatius is aware that his addressee is already experiencing 'movements' of the spirit, but his direction remains at a very general level, with no hint of contact with a future candidate for the Society.

Francis Borgia,[1] Duke of Gandía   late in 1545
in Gandía   from Rome

My dear Lord in Our Lord,

May the supreme grace and eternal love of Christ Our Lord bring your Lordship salutation and visitation!

[1] [*Internal teaching*] On the last day of October I received a letter written by yourself on 24 July and was very pleased indeed in Our Lord to find in it references to matters that are more the fruit of experience and internal contact than of outside learning. These are usually communicated by God Our Lord in His infinite goodness to those persons who take for their base that goodness, which is the beginning, middle and end of all our prayers. May His supreme name be ever praised and honoured in all and by all creatures, all created and planned precisely for this eminently right and appropriate end.

[2] [*Ignatius's contacts with Borgia in God*] But to come down in particular to some points raised by you that seem to me to require comment. First, that I should not forget you in my prayers and maintain contact with you by my letters: the truth is that as I continued to comply with the first part of this request, as I still do every day (my hope in the Lord is that, if my prayers may win at least one favour, it will come simply and solely from above, descending from the divine goodness, my eyes fixed exclusively on God's eternal and supreme generosity and on the religious feeling and holy intentions of your Lordship), I was convinced that as I had you spiritually before my eyes every day, I was complying with the second part of your Lordship's request that you might find consolation in my letters. I like to think that when persons go

out of themselves and enter into their Creator and Lord, they enjoy continuous instruction, attention and consolation; they are aware how the fullness of our eternal Good dwells in all created things, giving them being, and keeping them in existence with His infinite being and presence. So I am easily convinced that one can find consolation in most things and with many other similar considerations. Those who love God completely find help in all things;[2] everything supports them in their deserving efforts and in their approach to, and union with, the Creator and Lord himself through their intense love.

[3] [*The obstacles we create*] This is true even if, as your Lordship points out, the creature often raises obstacles to the changes and great blessings the Lord wishes to bring about in the soul, and not only before the graces, gifts and delights of the Holy Spirit are given to assist us in our efforts, but even when they are present and felt – when a person has received visitations and consolations, when the darkness and troublesome worry have been dispelled, when many spiritual improvements have taken place, when a person has become happy and completely rapt in eternal things, those that are to last for ever in never-ending glory. We manage to distract ourselves with the most petty preoccupations and have no idea how to take care of the heavenly gifts we receive. We do indeed raise obstacles before the grace and influence of the Lord has made itself felt. And after it has been granted, we do the same, even though it is there so that we may take care of it.

[4] [*Plumbing the depths*] Your Lordship refers to these obstacles to show how little you value yourself before the Lord of all; and you also speak highly of us, who would prefer the lowest place. You affirm that the Society does not impede the work that the Lord wishes to accomplish in it. Perhaps you have in mind what Araoz[3] is doing in Portugal. For my part I am convinced that I am nothing but an obstacle, both earlier and later. But this gives me great contentment and spiritual joy in Our Lord; I cannot attribute to myself any good that may appear. The most certain thing in my opinion (though more intelligent persons may feel that there are other more important matters) is that very few persons in this life – and to press the point, I would say nobody – can calculate and form an appraisal of the degree to which they impede and undo the effectiveness of the Lord's influence on themselves. I am quite convinced that the deeper and the more advanced a person becomes in self-appraisal and love of God, the more conscious that person will become of the most delicate thoughts and of many other insubstantial things that impede and prevent, even if at first sight they may appear

slight and almost completely unimportant, being so faint themselves. It is not given us in this life to have full knowledge of our obstacles and failings: that is why the prophet asks to be freed from his unknown faults,[4] and Paul, while confessing that he does not know them, adds that not for that will he be found justified.[5]

[5] [*Pupils of the Lord*] In his infinite and characteristic mercy Our Lord has made your Lordship as well a pupil in the school of holiness (something you cannot deny when you reflect and deepen your self-knowledge, as I am quite sure from what I have gathered through your letters). My great desire in the Lord, who is to judge me for all eternity, is that you will study hard and do all you can to win over many fellow pupils. You should begin with those of your household, as we are more obliged to guide them by the most sure and direct way to the Divine Majesty. This 'way' is in fact Christ Our Lord, as He Himself said.[6] So I give great thanks to his divine goodness seeing that your Lordship (as I have been told here) is so assiduous in receiving the Lord [in communion]. In addition to the many other great graces one is granted on receiving one's Creator and Lord, there is one very important and special grace: the Lord does not permit one to remain in a prolonged and obstinate state of sin. As soon as one falls, even in the most minor failing (granted that no sin can really be called 'minor' when related to the one offended, the infinite, and indeed supreme, Good), the Lord swiftly lifts the person up with greater strength and with a greater resolve and determination better to serve the Creator and Lord. As you follow this 'way' thanks to the workings of divine assistance, and as you win over other people and your relatives, using the talent given to your Lordship by His Divine Majesty in His infinite and characteristic mercy, my own merit improves, without my deserving it, as my desire grows to follow your Lordship's example.

[6] [*Supervision of the College*] Seeing that you mention in your letter your wish to share in my undertakings, and as I am overburdened in Rome with the weight of responsibility – in accordance with our way of life, the supervision of our Society has been put upon me, either by divine command or by permission of the divine goodness because of my great and abominable sins – would your Lordship, out of love and reverence for God Our Lord, while helping me with your prayers, kindly assist me by undertaking the supervision and completion of a house or college in Gandía that has been planned for the scholastics of the Society (the house will be as much your Lordship's and that of Her Ladyship, the Duchess, and of her sister, Doña Joana,[7] as it will be ours)?

Already, thanks to your Lordship's request and command, some of ours[8] have been welcomed there, to my great spiritual joy. Please assist the house with your support and protection, in the way that your Lordship considers most appropriate in the Lord, and best suited to God's greater glory. At present we are all the more delighted in the goodness of God that a relative of the Duchess happens to be in the Jesuit house there,[9] to her Ladyship's pleasure as you mention in your letter. I commend myself warmly to her prayers and goodness, and those of Doña Joana, before the Lord. Let me close imploring the Divine Majesty to grant us the fullness of His grace so that we may feel His supreme will, and fulfil it completely.

From Rome, etc., 1545,

Ignatio

14. Conduct at Trent

1546

(No. 123 : I, 386–89 : Spanish)

Many of the Cardinals most supportive of the new Society were con-
vinced of the importance of a reforming Council, and Ignatius seems to
have shared their high hopes. However, the guidelines he drew up show
that the considerations preoccupying him were not confined to the
Council chamber, and probably reflect his own conduct and that of the
first companions.

Members of the Society of Jesus   early in 1546
in Trent[1]   from Rome

Instructions for the undertaking at Trent

✤

IHS

[PART I] ON SOCIAL RELATIONS

1   First: much can be gained, if God is willing, for the spiritual health
and progress of others by having social relations and contact with many
people. But unless we are vigilant and have Our Lord to help us, there
can be a counter-effect on us that will be a partial or a complete disaster. So, as it is not possible in our calling to avoid social relations, the
more forethought and planning we can adopt, the less we will have to
worry in Our Lord. The following points may be of some use in this
matter and are to be used freely as indications.

2   Anyone of ours should be slow to speak and show consideration and
sympathy, especially when dealing with doctrinal definitions that will or
may be discussed in the Council.

3   Along with his reticence, he should rely on a readiness to listen, keeping quiet so as to sense and appreciate the positions, emotions and desires
of those speaking. Then he will be better able to speak or to keep silent.

4   In these and similar discussions or in others, he should admit both

sides of the question and not appear to be self-opinionated, trying to avoid leaving either party discontented.

5 Unless the questions raised are of great moment, he should refrain from quoting authors, especially major ones; instead he should be friendly to all and avoid passionate support for one side.

6 When the questions raised invoke points of right that cannot or should not be passed over, he is to give his point of view as calmly and unpretentiously as possible, adding as a rider *salvo meliori iudicio* [= unless someone knows better].

7 Finally, when the subjects raised turn on experiential or infused knowledge, if one wants to take part, it will be a great help to forget completely one's own occupations and lack of time, i.e. my own convenience, and adapt myself completely to the convenience and requirements of the person I want to deal with, so that I can urge them on to God's greater glory.

[PART 2] ON HELPING OTHERS

1 Our main aim (to God's greater glory) during this undertaking at Trent is to put into practice (as a group that lives together in one appropriate place) preaching, confessions and readings, teaching children, giving good example, visiting the poor in the hospitals, exhorting those around us, each of us according to the different talents he may happen to have, urging on as many as possible to greater piety and prayer. All of this is undertaken so that they and we may implore God Our Lord that His Divine Majesty kindly infuse His divine spirit into all those due to discuss the questions proper to such a lofty gathering, in order that the Holy Spirit may descend with greater abundance of gifts and graces on this Council.

2 In their preaching they should not refer to points of conflict between Protestants and Catholics, but simply exhort all to upright conduct and to ecclesiastical practice, urging everyone to full self-knowledge and to greater knowledge and love of their Creator and Lord, with frequent allusions to the Council. At the end of each sermon, they should (as has been mentioned) lead prayers for the Council.

3 They should do the same with readings as with sermons, trying their best to influence people with greater love of their Creator and Lord as they explain the meaning of what is read; similarly, they should lead their hearers to pray for the Council, as has been mentioned.

4 In hearing confessions, they should remember to repeat to their penitents what they are saying in public, and in all the confessions they should give as penance some prayers for this intention.

5 When giving [the] Exercises or other conferences, they should bear in mind what they are saying in public. Incidentally the first week of the Exercises can be given indiscriminately to anyone, but no more of the Exercises except to certain exceptional individuals who are ready to dispose their future lives in the light of a retreat election. However even when such persons are in the election process, or in the Exercises, they should not be allowed to make religious promises, nor should they be allowed to enter enclosed orders, especially at the beginning. Later the situation may change with time, but one should always try to moderate them, above all if on occasion it seems right to give all the Spiritual Exercises in their complete form. And one should recommend throughout prayers for the Council.

6 They should spend some time, as convenient, in the elementary teaching of youngsters, depending on the means and disposition of all involved, and with more or less explanation according to the capacity of the pupils. At the end of such teaching and exhortation sessions they should lead prayers for the purpose mentioned.

7 Let them visit the almshouses once or twice a day, at times that are convenient for the patients' health, hearing confessions and consoling the poor, if possible taking them something, and urging them to the sort of prayers mentioned above for confessions. If there are three of ours in Trent, each should visit the poor at least once every four days.

8 When they are urging people in their dealings with them to go to confession and communion, to say mass frequently, to undertake the Spiritual Exercises and other good works, they should also be urging them to pray for the Council.

9 It was said that there are advantages in being slow to speak and measured in one's statements when doctrinal definitions are involved. The opposite is true when one is urging people to look to their spiritual progress. Then one should be eloquent and ready to talk, full of sympathy and affection.

[PART 3] ON LOOKING AFTER OURSELVES

[1] We should set an hour aside every evening for all of us to inform one another what has been done during the day and what should be done on the following day.

[2] We will take votes or use some other way to get agreement on what is past and what is still to come.

[3] One night one can ask the others to point out any faults they may have noticed, and the person criticized should not reply unless he is asked to explain why he did what was found wrong.

[4] Another night another will do the same, and so in turn, so that all can help one another to grow in charity and good influence all around.

[5] Each morning we should look at what we intend for that day, then make examen of conscience twice during the day.

[6] This time-table is to be put into effect five days after our arrival in Trent. Amen.

15. Refusing episcopal dignities
1546
(No. 149 : I, 450–53 : Spanish)

*Courtly letters of the sixteenth century are even more difficult to inter-
pret than others. However, in this case the polite wrapping can be easily
removed to disclose a decided negative to a royal request.*

Ferdinand I, King of the Romans[1]   (December?) 1546
in Vienna (?)   from Rome

✠

[1] [*The King's goodwill*] We are aware of the goodwill under God
which Your Highness has always had for this very minor Society, and
especially for some individual members of it. You now want to make a
further practical expression of this by choosing our companion Master
Claude Le Jay[2] for appointment to an ecclesiastical dignity, and re-
quiring him to accept it. You believe that this will further the service of
God Our Lord, and be a favour to us all. Your Highness's holy desire in
showing us, despite our great unworthiness, such great goodness and
kindness in Our Lord is evident to all, namely your wish to provide for
the Society in a way that will lead to the greater glory of God and to the
greater spiritual growth of its members. For all of this we are eternally
grateful to Your Highness before His Divine Majesty. May it please God,
in His infinite graciousness, to favour Your Highness in every way. May
He be pleased to fulfil my hope, implanting and engraving in your mind
and heart ways in which you can show favour to us more and more as
we go forward in our very minor way of life.

[2] [*The danger of bishoprics*] Truly this will be the case when Your
Highness, as we desire from the bottom of our hearts, decides to make
use of us without our being given any ecclesiastical dignities. It is our
conscientious opinion that to take any dignity would be for us to ruin
the Society, so much so that if I wanted to imagine or think up ways of
wrecking and destroying this Society, this way, the acceptance of a bishopric, would be one of the main ones, or even the most important of all.
There are three reasons for this, among many others.

[3] [*Need for mobility*] First: this Society and its members have been

brought together and united in one common spirit, namely to travel abroad from one part of the world to another, among believers and unbelievers, according to the orders of the Supreme Pontiff. Thus the spirit of the Society is to move on from one city to another in complete simplicity and modesty, and from one district to another, not to settle ourselves in one specific place. That this is characteristic of the very spirit of the Society is confirmed by the Holy See, as we have it in the Bulls, where we are said to be 'inspired, as may reverently be believed, by the Holy Spirit', etc.[3] Thus if we abandoned our simplicity, the abandonment would be of everything, destroying our spirit, and revoking completely the religious profession we have publicly made. After such undoing, the Society would be completely wrecked. Quite plainly, by doing something good in one particular place we would be doing a harm outweighing that good everywhere else.

[4] [*Tried policy*] Secondly, as the Society moves forward in this spirit, God Our Lord has shown Himself in a quite special way through it, bringing about greater spiritual benefit for people. If in German territories the land has been less fertile, in those parts of the Indies possessed by the King of Portugal there has been a year in which one[4] of ours has converted 80,000 people. Another[5] of our number who is in Portugal has done much useful work in that kingdom and has sent more than twenty persons[6] to the Indies, all of whom have renounced worldly concerns. He has another hundred scholastics who want to go there too, or elsewhere if they can be of greater service to God Our Lord. If it were not to take too long we could talk at length about Castile, Barcelona, Valencia and Gandía, as well as about many places in Italy, and recount how much God Our Lord has seen fit to work through this Society, as it follows the spirit which the Divine Majesty has imparted to it.

[5] [*Domino effect*] Thirdly, up till now we are only nine professed members.[7] Four or five of us in the Society have already been offered various bishoprics, and we have taken the line of refusing them.[8] If now some member accepted one, another would be caught in a policy of doing the same, and so on with all the others. Thus not only would we lose our spirit, but the Society would be completely destroyed, and then the greater good would be lost for the sake of the lesser.

[6] [*Material for scandal*] Fourthly, if one of us accepted a bishopric, everything would go sour, especially now, when the Society and its members are so well respected and esteemed wherever their travels have taken them, and when so much good has been done for people. Those who like

us, and who are getting something from us for their spiritual growth, would be shocked and scandalized; there would be bad feeling among those who have not taken up any position about us, and yet who also want to grow spiritually; and those who feel suspicious about us would be even more shocked and scandalized. We would provide much ammunition for widespread gossip and criticism, scandalizing many people, people for whom Christ Our Lord died on a cross. Already when any of us go into the palaces of the Pope, of princes, of cardinals or of nobles, so corrupt has the world become that people think we are being ambitious. If we now accepted a bishopric, it could very easily set off talk and gossip that would cause offence to God Our Lord.

16. Ideals for newcomers

Coimbra 1547

(No. 169 : I, 495–510 : Spanish)

Since 1545 reports had begun to reach Ignatius of weird penitential practices[1] adopted by the young Jesuit students in Coimbra, partly at the instigation of their superior (Fr Rodrigues). These seemed to threaten the very promising beginnings of the Society in a key country that was the gateway to India, Africa and America. The following letter (probably much indebted to the newly appointed secretary, Polanco), only hints at the historical context, which is nevertheless a necessary backdrop if one is to appreciate its nuances.

Students [of the Society of Jesus]   7 May 1547
in Coimbra[2]   from Rome

May the eternal grace and love of Christ Our Lord always favour and assist us! Amen.

[1] From letters of Master Simão [Rodrigues][3] and also of [Fr] Santa Cruz[4] I am always getting news about you all. God, from whom all that is good descends, knows how much consolation and joy I get from knowing how He helps you, both in your academic studies and in your efforts to grow in virtue. The good reputation to which this gives rise encourages and helps many people grow spiritually in other places far from your country. Although any Christian must rejoice at this, on the strength of the common obligation we all have to love God's honour and to work for the good of God's image, this image which is redeemed by the life-blood of Jesus Christ, yet I have many grounds to be particularly glad in Our Lord at what I hear about you, for I hold you close to my heart with a special affection.

[2] As every good thing, every grace, flows from the generosity of our Creator and Redeemer, may He be constantly blessed and praised for it all, and may it please Him each day to open more widely the fountain of His graciousness in order thus to increase and carry forward what He has begun in your minds and hearts. I have no doubt that God's generosity and love will indeed bring this about. The supreme generosity of

God is so supremely eager to spread its own riches; and the eternal love, with which God wants to give us our final fulfilment, is a desire to give far greater than ours to receive. If this were not so, Jesus Christ would not say, 'Be perfect as your heavenly Father is perfect',[5] encouraging us to strive for what we can receive from His hand alone. It is certainly the case that He for His part is ready, if only we for ours have a humility and desire capacious enough to receive His graces, and if only He can see us using well the gifts we have received, and asking eagerly and lovingly for His grace.

[Part I: Words of encouragement]

[I. THEIR CALLING]

[3] Along these lines I shall not stop giving you encouragement, even those of you making great strides. For I can certainly say to you that you must make great efforts, both with studies and virtue, if you are to live up to the expectations which so many people have of you, not just in Portugal but also in many other places. They look at all the forms of preparation and help that God is giving you, both for inner resources and practical skills, and quite reasonably expect for the future something very much out of the ordinary. It is certainly the case that what is merely average will not satisfy the great obligation you have to do good. If you consider what your vocation actually is, you will see that what in others would not be inconsiderable would indeed be so for you. God has not only 'called you out of darkness into His marvellous light',[6] and transferred you 'to the kingdom of His beloved Son',[7] as with all other believers; it has also pleased Him to take you out of the dangerous gulf of this world, so that you can better remain pure and upright, and centre your affections on the things of the Spirit, the things of His service. Thus your consciences will not be at risk from the tempests often stirred up in us by the wind of desire, a desire at one moment for wealth, at another for being honoured, at yet another for sensual pleasure, or else by the opposite of desire, the fear that all this might be lost.

[4] But God's intention goes further: so that your minds and hearts be not taken up with these paltry things, nor scattered in various directions, He would have you become converted, all united together, occupying yourselves in the purposes for which God created you, the honour and glory of God, your salvation, and the assistance of others.

[5] It is true that all the institutions of Christian religious life are de-

signed for these purposes. However God has called you to this one, and here you must make a sacrifice of yourselves continuously, for the glory of God and the salvation and well-being of others, not just a matter of general orientation, but throwing your whole life and everything you do into this enterprise. You must co-operate in this work for others, not just by good example and by prayers of desire, but also through the other, publicly visible means, arranged by His Providence for us to use in helping each other. Thus you will see how noble and royal a way of life you have adopted. There is no more noble activity for human beings, or even for angels, than that of glorifying one's Creator and, as far as they are able, of drawing creatures back to Him.

[6] Consider well, then, your calling, so that on the one hand you can give great thanks to God who has given you something so great, and on the other so that you can ask God for a special favour in order to be able to respond to it. Help one another too with enthusiasm and hard work, for this is very much a necessity if you are to achieve such goals. As for slackness, for half-heartedness, and for boredom, whether with studies or with the other good things you do for love of Our Lord Jesus Christ, recognize these as enemies set against your purpose.

[II. THEIR KEENNESS]

[7] Each one of you should take as his model to encourage himself, not those you think slack, but the most determined, those who make most effort. Do not allow the children of this world, as they seek for the things which pass, to be more hard-working and intent than you, who are seeking for the things of eternity.[8] You should be ashamed that they are running towards death more quickly than you towards life! If a courtier were to wait more attentively on an earthly prince to gain his favour than you to gain that of the heavenly prince, or if a soldier were to prepare himself and struggle for the honour of victory and for some spoil more keenly than you for victory and triumph over the world, the devil and your own selves, for the eternal kingdom and glory, then count yourselves good for nothing.

[8] For the love of God, do not be slack or half-hearted. As the saying goes, 'Tension may break the bow, but slackness the spirit',[9] and on the contrary, 'the soul of the diligent will be richly supplied',[10] so Solomon tells us. See that you maintain a holy, discriminating verve as you work to acquire both learning and virtue. With both of these one intently

performed act is worth more than a thousand done lackadaisically, and what a slacker will not get done in many years, a hard worker will achieve in a short space of time.

[9] In the field of studies the difference between one who works hard and one who is lazy is obvious, but that difference is there too when it comes to overcoming the wild passions and weaknesses that affect our nature and to acquiring virtues. For it is clear that slackers, owing to their failure to struggle against themselves, take longer to attain peace of mind and soul, if indeed they ever do. Nor do they ever completely acquire any of the virtues. By contrast, those who are keen and who work at these things make quick progress, both in studies and also in the personal sphere. Experience shows us that the contentment that can be had in this life is to be found not among the lazy, but rather among those who are bubbling over with keenness for God's service. This stands to reason. These people are making an effort of their own to overcome themselves and get rid of self-centredness. This means they also get rid of the roots of all the wild passions and trouble. Moreover they are acquiring virtues as habits, and so come as a matter of course to act spontaneously and cheerfully in accord with those virtues.

[III. THEIR MOTIVATION]

[10] Further, if we consider the matter in terms of God, the most generous of consolers, such people are making themselves ready, through this effort of theirs, to receive His holy consolations: 'To the one who conquers I will give the hidden manna.'[11] Half-heartedness, by contrast, causes one always to be living with burdens. It prevents one from getting rid of what causes them, namely self-love. It fails to win God's favour. So you must encourage one another to put great effort into your praiseworthy activities. Then even in this life you will sense how you gradually become afire with holiness. It is not just a matter of the perfection of your souls: it can be seen also in contentment with this present life. If you ponder the reward of eternal life, as you should do often, St Paul will readily convince you: 'These present sufferings are not of the same rank as the future glory which is to be revealed in us',[12] because 'this light and momentary affliction of ours brings about in us an eternal abundance of glory, far outweighing that affliction in sublimity'.[13]

[11] If this is the case for all Christians who honour and serve God, you can see how great your crown will be if you conform to our Institute,

namely, not only to serve God yourselves, but to attract many others to God's honour and service. Regarding such people, Scripture says, 'Those who instruct others in righteousness shall shine like the stars of the firmament for ever and ever'.[14] Those who take care conscientiously to fulfil their duty may take this as applying to themselves, both later, when they are actually using their weapons, and earlier, when they are making the weapons ready. It is certainly not enough merely to have theoretical knowledge about intrinsically good deeds. Jeremiah tells us, 'Cursed is the one who does the work of the Lord negligently',[15] and St Paul that 'In the stadium many run, but only one receives the prize'[16] (i.e. the one who has worked well). Again, 'Athletes are not crowned unless they compete according to the rules'[17] (and this too means those who have worked well).

[12] But above all I would like you to be uplifted by the pure love of Jesus Christ,[18] together with the desire for His honour and for the salvation of the souls that He has redeemed. In this 'company'[19] you are His soldiers with a special rank and a special pay. I call them 'special' but of course there are other more general obligations laid upon you to work for His honour and service. The pay He gives is everything in the order of nature which you are and possess. He gave you life and being, and He preserves them, together with all the various good things of soul, body, and the world around us. Again, the pay from Him consists of the spiritual gifts of His grace, with which He is always kindly and generously there before you, wherever you go, and which He continually provides even though you are awkward and rebellious with Him. His pay is the incalculable gifts of His glory that He has prepared for you and promised you, without His gaining anything. He imparts to you all the treasures of His bliss so that through 'eminent' participation in His divine perfection you can be what He is through His essence and nature. Finally, His pay is the whole universe and what it contains, both bodily and spiritually. For not only has He put everything under heaven in service to us, but also His whole noble and exalted court, sparing none of the heavenly hierarchies, for 'they are all spirits apt for service, for the sake of those who are to gain the inheritance'.[20] And as if all these payments were not enough, He has made Himself our pay, giving Himself to us as our brother in our flesh, on the cross as the price of our salvation, in the Eucharist as our sustainer and companion for our pilgrimage. What a miserable soldier a man would be if all these payments were not enough to make him work for the honour of such a prince!

[13] For we know that Christ our King willed to prepare our path in

advance with such incomparably precious gifts, so as to bind us to desire and seek His glory all the more eagerly. In a certain sense He stripped Himself of the endowments of His perfect bliss in order to make us sharers in them. He took on Himself our wretchedness so as to free us from it. He chose to be sold to redeem us, despised that we might be glorified, poor that we might be enriched. He took on a death of enormous shame and torment, in order to give us immortal and blessed life. What ungrateful, hard-hearted persons would fail to see themselves as bound by all this to serve Christ eagerly and to work for His honour!

[IV. THEIR TASK]

[14] Now then, if you are aware of your obligations, and if you desire to be of service in furthering this honour of His, you are certainly in a period when there is abundant need for your desire to be demonstrated through action. Just think if there is any place where the Divine Majesty is honoured, where His immense grandeur is held in awe, where His wisdom is known, along with His infinite goodness, or where His holy will is obeyed! Instead you will see with much sadness how much His holy name remains everywhere unknown, devalued, and blasphemed. The teaching of Jesus Christ is set aside, His example forgotten. In some way the ransom of Christ's blood is lost, as far as we are concerned, in that so few make the most of it.

[15] Look also at the people around you and realize that they are an image of the Holy Trinity. They have potential for the glory of Him to whom the universe is subject. They are members of Jesus Christ, redeemed through His many pains and insults, redeemed through His blood. Look, I repeat, at the wretched state they are in, the deep darkness of their ignorance, the storms of their vain fears, desires and other passions, the enemies who attack them, visible and invisible. Look at the risk they are running, not merely of losing their income or their earthly life, but rather the eternal kingdom and its bliss, and of falling into the unbearable pain of eternal fire!

[16] To recapitulate in a few words, my message is this. Consider well how great your obligation is to take up position in order to further the honour of Jesus Christ, and to help in the salvation of the people around you. See how imperative it is to make yourselves ready, with all possible effort and exertion, so that you become instruments of divine grace suitable for this purpose, especially since these days there are so

few workers of whom it can truly be said, 'They seek not their own interests, but those of Jesus Christ'.[21] Since God fashions for you in this calling and with these resolves so special a grace, you must make all the more effort to make up for the shortcomings of others.

[Part II: Words of warning]

[17] What I have said so far has been meant to wake up those of you who are asleep, and to spur on those dawdling and loitering on the way. It is not meant to be a licence for going to the opposite extreme, undisciplined enthusiasm. Disorders in the life of the spirit arise not only from coldness of heart (ailments like tepidity), but also from overheating, as when there is excessive fervour. St Paul talks of 'the worship due from rational creatures',[22] because he knew the truth of what the Psalmist said, 'The honour of the king loves sound judgement',[23] i.e. discretion. The point was prefigured in Leviticus, where it says, 'With all your offerings you shall offer salt'.[24] Thus it is as St Bernard says, that the enemy has no mechanism so effective for removing true charity from the heart than that of making the heart's growth in charity something reckless, out of keeping with spiritual common sense.[25] The philosophical dictum 'Nothing in excess' applies to everything, even justice itself, as you read in Ecclesiastes, 'Do not be excessively just'.[26] When such moderation is absent, good is transformed into bad and virtue into vice, and many problems arise for those taking this path, blocking their basic purpose.

[I. THE DANGERS OF EXCESS]

[18] 1st. Such persons cannot serve God over the long haul, rather as horses that get very tired in the first day's journeying often fail to arrive at their destination, and other people often have to spend their time looking after them.

[19] 2nd. The gains from excessive haste often do not last, because 'Riches soon won are soon spent'.[27] Not only do such gains waste away, but they also tend to trip one up ('The one who is fleet of foot stumbles'[28]), and should such people fall, the higher they are the more dangerous it is, as they will not stop until they hit the bottom of the ladder.

[20] 3rd. They do not take proper care to avoid the danger of overloading the boat. Admittedly it is dangerous to sail it empty, because

then it will be pulled hither and thither by temptations, but it is even more dangerous to overload it, as then it sinks.

[21] 4th. It sometimes happens that the 'crucifixion of our former nature'[29] ends up being the crucifixion of the new one as well, when weakness makes one incapable of actually living out the virtues. According to St Bernard[30] four things are lost by this kind of excess: the effectiveness of the body, the affections of the spirit, the testimony for others, and the honour due to God. From this he goes on to say that whoever thus mistreats the living temple of God is committing sacrilege, and is to blame for all these losses. He talks about loss of testimony for others because he says that one person's fall brings scandal to others. The same St Bernard rightly calls those who scandalize others 'spoilers of unity and enemies of peace'.[31] The sight of one person's fall does frighten many others and retards their spiritual growth, and the people concerned run the risk of pride and vainglory, following their own judgement rather than anyone else's, or at least taking over a role that is not rightly theirs, as they have become judges in their own cases when by rights it should be the Superior.

[II. THE NEED FOR SOUND JUDGEMENT]

[22] Apart from these, there are still further problems caused by over-enthusiasm. It is like loading oneself up with so many weapons that one cannot actually use them, like David with Saul's,[32] or like giving a naturally impetuous horse spurs and no rein. So it is that in this area there must be sound judgement. Virtuous practices must be kept on a course between two extremes. St Bernard[33] gives good advice on this: 'One must not always act out of a generous impulse, but rather curb it and keep it under control, especially as a beginner.' Otherwise those who want to be good for others will be destructive of themselves. 'Who can be good to others who is evil to oneself?'[34]

[III. OBEDIENCE]

[23] If sound judgement seems to you a rare bird not easily held, you should at least make use of a substitute, obedience, which will always be a secure guide.[35] If anyone wants to go further with their own way of seeing things, they should heed what St Bernard would say to them, 'If

anything happens without the will and consent of the spiritual director, it is to be counted as vainglory, not as merit'.[36] Also remember what Scripture says, 'The iniquity of idolatry consists in the refusal to obey, the sin of divination in disobedience'.[37] So if you want to hold on to the middle course between the two extremes of half-heartedness and ill-judged enthusiasm, confide in the Superior and rely on obedience. If you have great desires to die to yourselves, use these to break your wills and to submit your judgements under the yoke of obedience, rather than in weakening your bodies and hurting yourselves without due moderation, especially now during the time of studies.

[24] I would not want you to think, on the basis of all I have written, that I do not approve of what people tell me about certain of your ways of mortification. I am well aware that the saints made use of these and other holy aberrations and made progress through them. Such practices are useful for overcoming oneself, and for growing in grace, especially at the beginning. But for those who now have greater control over their self-centredness, I think that what I have written about their restricting themselves to staying on balance and keeping to moderation is more appropriate. Such people should not act against obedience. That is the ideal I hold up to you, and insist upon, along with the other virtue, summing up all the others, on which Jesus Christ insisted so much that He called the commandment enjoining it His own commandment, 'This is my commandment, that you love one another'.[38] However you should not be content to preserve lasting unity and love among yourselves, but should spread it to all people. Take care to sustain in your minds and hearts burning desires for the salvation of others, valuing each person at the price they cost, the blood, indeed the life, of Jesus Christ. By advancing with your academic work on the one hand, and growing in brotherly love on the other, may you come to be completely instruments of divine grace, and co-workers in that most sublime task, the bringing back of God's creatures into God's Kingdom, their ultimate end.

[Part III: The period of studies: ways of being useful]

[25] During this intermediate period of studies, do not think that you are of no use to others. Beyond the fact that you are making progress yourselves, for a proper understanding of charity requires, 'Be kind to your own self, fearing the Lord',[39] you are even now serving others in many ways and furthering the honour and glory of God.

[26] FIRSTLY, with your present work there is your intention in taking it on, directing it to the building up of others. When soldiers are occupied in equipping themselves with weapons and ammunition for a future campaign, it would be wrong to say that their work is not in the service of their prince. Death may cut someone short before they have begun to deal with others in public, but even so this does not undo the service given to others in the work of preparation. So, in addition to having an intention for the future, all should offer themselves every day to God for others. If God in His goodness deigns to accept them, they can be no less instruments for helping others than sermons or confessions.

[27] SECONDLY, there is your making yourselves into virtuous good people. Then you will become people fit to make others the way you yourselves are. God wills a certain system to obtain with reproduction in the material realm, and He wills something analogous in the spiritual realm as well. Both philosophy and experience will tell you that when a human being or some other animal comes into being, more is at work than general causes, such as the heavens; one needs also another cause or direct agent from the same species. This latter enables the product to have the form that the agent wishes to be carried over to a new subject. Thus it is that we say, '*Sol et homo generant hominem*' [= Humans are begotten by the sun and by humans].⁴⁰ Similarly, if God wants to shape people in the forms of humility, prudence, charity and so on, it follows that God also wants the direct cause used to shape others in this way, i.e. the preacher or the confessor to be humble, patient and charitable. So if you yourselves are growing personally in every virtue in the way I spoke of earlier, you are being of great service to others. By making moral progress you are no less (but rather more!) instruments for the grace to be conferred on them than you are by your learning, though obviously God's instruments should be fully developed in both.

[28] THIRDLY, you can help others by the testimony of your way of life: on this point, as I have already said, God's grace is making the good repute you have in Portugal spread and have a good effect on others abroad. I trust in the Author of all good that He will continue and increase His gifts in you so that each day, as you move forward towards every kind of perfection, the holy reputation you have, and the encouragement of others under God that follows from this, will grow all the more without your seeking it.

[29] FOURTHLY, a way of helping others which is very wide-ranging consists in prayers and holy desires. Study does not give you time for

very long prayers, but those who make all their activities into a continual prayer, entering into them only for God's service, can make up in desires for the time not spent formally praying. However with this as with everything else, you have people nearer to you with whom you can discuss the matter in detail. I could for this reason have left out some of what I have written, but since I write so seldom, I wanted this to be a long letter, from which I myself, along with you, could draw some consolation.

Conclusion

[30] No more for now, except that I pray to God, our Creator and Redeemer, that He may be pleased to continue His gifts in all of you and increase them, just as He was pleased to give you such great grace in calling you, and in giving you an effective desire by which you could resolve to spend yourselves completely in His service. May you always persevere, growing in His service, with much honour and glory to Him and great benefit to His holy Church.

From Rome,

Yours in Our Lord,

Ignacio

17. Need for structures of government

Gandía 1547

(No. 182 : I, 551–62 : Spanish)

This letter, written to justify the need for a Superior at Gandía, reveals a great deal about Ignatius's conception of his own role (all other superiors are essentially his 'substitutes'), and about his experimental approach to government in the early years of the Society. There is a startling contrast between the (theoretical) Part I and the (practical) Part II, each corresponding to different aspects of Ignatius's character.

My brothers in Our Lord who wish to join the
Society of Jesus   29 July 1547
in Gandía   from Rome

May the grace and love of Jesus Christ Our Lord be always alive and increasing in our minds and hearts, Amen!

[1] An obligation goes with the weighty responsibility to which I have been appointed. Moreover God our Creator and Lord has seen fit to give me a love and affection that accompany my sense of duty and greatly increase my resolve. I have to consider what might best foster the good of this Society of ours and its members, and thus bring about the honour and glory of God. It is my desire for this that leads and obliges me to provide affectionately, as far as I can, what I judge in Our Lord to be most conducive for the Society's greater good.

[2] One of these things which I feel to be very important is that wherever a number of members of the Society have to live together for a certain time, there should be a head or superior among them. And the others should accept to be ruled or governed by him, just as they would be by the General Superior[1] were he present. This provision has been made in Portugal and Padua, and it is on the point of being made at Louvain.[2] And I think the same thing should happen at Gandía.

[3] So in this letter I shall first tell you what makes me believe, in Our Lord, that it is right to have a substitute for myself among you, as being more for Our Lord's honour and praise, and better for the individuals and the religious group in Gandía, and in general for the whole body of

the Society. Then I shall tell you how you are to choose this person, and how you are to obey whoever is chosen, again as seems to me appropriate in the Lord.

Part I. On superiors and obedience in general

[A. HISTORICAL PRECEDENTS]

[4] In fact, in Part I, where I shall give some account of what makes me put in this substitute superior, I plan to expand on the matter rather more than might be necessary so as to convince you about this step which is so holy and so needful. However my intention is not simply to show you that this decision has been properly taken, but much more to encourage you to accept it, and then to persevere cheerfully and with dedication in this style of obedience.

[5] So, coming to the point, one of the many factors that influence me is the precedent given to us by all races, without exception, who live together in any kind of civil society, whether in kingdoms, cities or particular groupings and houses within cities, and whether past or present. Government always tends to be concentrated in the one figure, a superior, so as to get rid of confusion and disorder and to keep the crowd in order. If we follow the general consensus of thinking people, this arrangement must certainly be considered the most appropriate, most natural and most fitting one.

[6] But still more cogent is the vivid example of Christ Our Lord. When he was in the company of his parents, 'he was obedient to them',[3] just as Our Lady, the Mistress of us all, was to Joseph. Thus it is to Joseph, as the head, that the angel says, 'Take the child and his mother.'[4] Again, when Christ Our Lord lived in company with the disciples, he saw fit to be their superior, and when he had to go away from them, in his bodily existence, he left St Peter over the others and over the whole of his Church, entrusting their government to him, 'Feed my sheep'.[5] And so Peter remained, even after the apostles were filled with the Holy Spirit. Now if they needed a superior, other groups must need one all the more.

[7] We gather also that the earliest church in Jerusalem made James the Less superior. In the seven churches of Asia there were the seven superiors, whom St John in the Apocalypse calls 'angels'. In other religious groups too there were superiors, set in place by the apostles, and St Paul tells people to obey them, 'Obey your leaders and submit to them'.[6] The

successors of these groupings have kept to these commands right up to this day. This applies most particularly of all to religious, starting from the anchorites and the first founders of religious orders, right down to our time. You will always find this principle observed: where people live gathered together, there is one among them who is head, governing the other members, and ruling with authority.

[B. THE INDIVIDUAL'S ADVANTAGES]

[8] Moreover quite apart from precedent there are persuasive intrinsic arguments for taking this step. For we should regard a way of life as better to the extent to which more pleasing service is given within it to God. Now this principle must apply when all are obliged to obedience, which is more acceptable than all sacrifices ('Behold, obedience is better than sacrifice, and to hearken better than the fat of rams'[7]). And with good reason, for more is offered to God when persons give their own judgement and will and freedom, the heart of the human person, than when they offer to God anything else.

[9] Besides, such a way of living helps to bring about every virtue; as St Gregory says, 'Obedience is not so much a virtue as the mother of virtues'.[8] This is no surprise, for obedience brings it about that we obtain from God whatever we ask for. St Gregory again: 'If we are obedient to our superiors, God will obey our prayer.'[9] And before him the Bible, speaking of Joshua, who was a model of obedience towards Moses, his superior, not only says that the sun obeyed him, stopping in its course at his voice ('Sun, stop thou still at Gabaon'[10]), but even that God almighty, who made the sun and all creatures, obeyed him ('The Lord hearkened to a human voice'[11]). Thus great benefits for the increase in virtue accrue to those under a superior, as the One who is the source of virtues is obedient to their prayer, and also, to quote a sage, 'What you take away from your own will, you will add to your virtue'.[12]

[10] This way of life in which you follow the will and judgement of the superior also enables you to avoid many mistakes arising from your own judgement, as well as shortcomings and sins from your own will. This applies not only in individual matters, but in the overall choice of manner of living. Each of you, to the extent you abandon yourselves into God's hands through the obedience you give to God's delegate, is laying all the greater an obligation (to use a turn of phrase) on Divine

Providence to rule you and direct you. The delegate here is any superior to whom you subject yourself for love of God.

[11] In addition, having a superior nearby helps people overcome any temptation and weakness to which they are subject. They can conform to the superior's way of seeing things, and be governed by him ('The obedient man speaks of victories'[13]). Thus they triumph over themselves, the most noble of all triumphs. It is clear that this method, the practice of submitting one's own will and judgement through holy obedience, leads very directly to these triumphs, yet one could not use this method were the superior not nearby. Moreover for those who know how to make the best of it, this way of life has a special value in so far as it is like being martyred. One is constantly being beheaded, i.e., deprived of one's own will and judgement, and in their stead taking on those of Christ as represented through his delegate. It is not just a single will, that for survival, that is being cut off, as in the case of the martyr, but the whole array of one's longings.

[12] Merit also grows, as all good works are greatly increased in value if they are done under obedience.

[13] It should also be remembered that obedience will enable you to proceed with less restlessness, and to make quicker progress on the road towards heaven. You will be like a person who travels using someone else's footsteps, not having to rely always on your own understanding and desire. Obedience will enable you to travel on the road to heaven in and through everything, things like sleeping and eating, constantly acquiring merit. You will be like sailors, who move towards their journey's end even as they are at rest. After all, it is this journey's end which is the most important thing. Obedience will empower you to obtain the key with which to enter heaven, and to hold onto it more securely, just as disobedience caused and continues to cause the loss of heaven. In fact obedience is itself this key, yet even during the labours of our present condition, during our pilgrimage and our exile, this way of life gives a powerful foretaste of the unburdening we will experience in our heavenly home. Not only does it free us from perplexity and doubt, but it also helps us get rid of the enormous weight of our own desires and care for ourselves, and to place these on the shoulders of the superior. Thus it gives peace and serenity.

[14] If persons are under obedience and have superiors nearby and yet do not feel this serenity within themselves, they should consider the situation carefully and make sure that it is not their own fault, arising from their turning back and busying themselves with their own affairs

after they had entrusted themselves to the hands of the superior. Listen to what St Bernard says to such people: 'Once you have entrusted the care of yourselves to us, why turn back to interfere in your own affairs?'[14] So if people know of the benefit God is doing them, it is a great relief and source of calm when they have someone to obey near at hand. But not just a source of calm: it ennobles and raises the status of a person enormously. It makes a person become stripped of themselves and clothed in God, the supreme good. God makes our minds and hearts expand in so far as He finds us empty of our own will. Such people (if their obedience is from the heart) can say of themselves, 'I live, no longer I, but Christ lives in me'.[15]

[15] Now someone might say that all these benefits could accrue to any individual who obeyed, in the Lord, the general Superior of the Society, but I am certain that they would be less, and very much less, than the benefits gained by those who live together as a religious group having someone nearby to obey out of obedience to Our Lord himself.

[C. CORPORATE ADVANTAGES]

[16] As well as all the spiritual benefits already mentioned, which apply mainly to individuals, this way of life is important for the corporate survival of your religious group. It simply is the case that no crowd of people can stay together in one body unless it is united, nor can the body be united without order, nor can there be order without a head, a head to which all the other members are subordinated through obedience. If you want the nature of our group to be maintained, this necessarily means you must desire someone to be your head.

[17] Apart from the survival of the group there in Gandía it is very important for its good government that you have someone nearby who understands everything that is going on, and can make suitable provision in the way I would if I were there. Experience is now showing us that it is impossible to make provision from here [in Rome] for many important things. This is partly because one cannot write and let us know everything (not everything can be confided in writing), and partly because often the time for making a decision runs out while people are asking our opinion here and we are sending a reply.

[18] Moreover for anyone holding down my heavy responsibility this is a great and appropriate relief, or rather a necessity; when he cannot per-

sonally attend in detail to all the obligations he has, he can at least deal with them through others.

[19] Even apart from all this, there is no small benefit here for the survival of the Society as a whole. For this to be achieved it will be very useful if the present students and their successors are well practised in obedience, i.e. in not taking any account of who the delegates of Christ Our Lord might be personally, but rather recognizing Christ in each one of them, and obeying Christ himself through his delegate. The reason for such benefits is as follows: granted that in any religious group this virtue of obedience is very necessary, it is especially so in ours, for our group has learned people, people who are on mission from the Pope and from other Church dignitaries, people who are scattered in places far, far away from where the superior lives, people with influence among nobles. Given all these and many other factors it does not seem possible to keep control over such people unless their obedience is outstanding. Thus I regard no form of training as more suitable and necessary for the common good of the Society than this one, namely top-quality obedience.

[20] Moreover if a person is going to know how to be in charge over others and to rule them, that person needs first to become proficient in obedience, and given that it is of very great benefit to the Society to have people who know how to govern, it follows equally that it is of very great benefit for it to have some way of getting people to learn how to obey. In this connection we normally have two Ministers[16] here in this house, one subordinate to the other, and anyone who is in the house must obey either of these, even though they may not be ordained, just as they have to obey me and whoever might take my place.

[21] Finally, if we can take the successes and failures of others as lessons indicating how we should imitate and follow them, we see that in many religious groups there have been not a few mistakes arising from the fact that they do not have superiors with sufficient authority to rule the others, and not unimportant mistakes either! By contrast, one also sees the advantages of government in places where all obey one superior.

[22] Enough has been said for Part I of this letter concerning the reasons and considerations behind making this useful and necessary provision of a Superior, and the willingness and dedication with which you must accept this provision. It remains to move on to Part II, how to choose this Superior, and how to obey the one who is chosen.

Part II. How to elect the Superior[17]

[23] Regarding the choice: all of you who live in Gandía should get together for three days, without communicating with each other on matters connected with the choice. The priests should say mass with the rightness of the choice as a special intention, and the rest of you should entrust the matter deeply to God Our Lord in your prayers. During this time each of you should consider who would be most suitable for such a responsibility. You should bear in mind only what would be better for the government of your religious group in Gandía, and would be of benefit to it, so that there be honour and glory for God. It should be as if each of you were taking the election onto your own conscience, and as if you had to give account of it to God Our Lord on that momentous day when you are to be judged. In this spirit each one of you should personally write out your vote and sign it by the third day. These should all be put together in a box or in some other place, where no one should touch them until the following day. Then the votes should be taken out with everyone present. Whoever has most votes is to be your Superior or Rector, whom I approve until such time as you hear from me to the contrary. You may use this procedure for as long as there is no professed Father in Gandía, and until the Constitutions are finally published.

Part III. How the new Superior is to be obeyed

[24] Now for how you are to obey this person after you have elected him. It seems to me that you should obey him in the same way as you would me were I present, or anyone who held my post. For were I with you, I would want you to recognize me as an authority, so that I could help you better and that thus there would be greater honour and glory for God Our Lord. This purpose likewise leads me to wish that the Rector be respected in just the same way. The respect you pay him should not be in any way different from that you would pay to me personally. Better still, you should think in terms of paying respect neither to him nor to me, but rather to Jesus Christ Our Lord, whom you are obeying through both of us. It is for Him that you obey His delegates.

[25] Anyone not prepared to obey and allow himself to be governed in

the way stated above should prepare himself to take on a different way of life, leaving your group and the common life it has. This applies to those currently at Gandía and to those who will be your successors, and it applies both with respect to whoever becomes Rector now and with respect to any other who might, by decision of some future General Superior of the Society, take his place. It is quite unsuitable for your group that there be anyone living in it who is unable or unwilling to subject himself to obedience in the way I have specified.

[26] This letter should be an unambiguous indication for all who live in Gandía of my mind on this subject, under the Lord, and of my desires and wishes concerning what should be put into practice in order to further the spiritual growth of the Society's present students there. May this be for the greater service, praise and glory of God Our Lord and Creator.

[27] May this God be pleased in His infinite and supreme goodness to give us the fullness of His grace so that we may feel His most holy will and fulfil it completely, Amen.

From Rome, 29 July 1547,

Ignacio

18. Experience of poverty

Padua 1547

(No. 186 : I, 572–77 : Italian)

This letter, quite clearly not written by Ignatius,[1] is included to show the contrast between his style and that of his secretary: Polanco writes in clear, slightly rhetorical prose, carefully marshalling his Latin quotations and showing the orderly precision that made him an ideal secretary, cautious not to add anything of his own (except perhaps a sophisticated polish) to Ignatius's line of thought, and giving no indication of the tortuous complexity that produced it.

Members of the Society   6 August 1547
in Padua (from Fr Polanco, by commission)   from Rome

May the grace and true love of Jesus Christ Our Lord be always in our hearts and increase every day until our final consummation. Amen.

Dear Fathers and beloved brothers in Jesus Christ,

[1] A letter from our mutual friend, Pietro Santini, written to Fr Master Laínez at Florence, has reached us; we learn there, among other things, of your love for the poverty you have chosen out of love for Jesus Christ poor. Quite often there have not been wanting opportunities to undergo suffering because of the lack of necessities, as the financial resources of Mgr della Trinità[2] have failed to match his generous and charitable character. Now although it is not necessary to exhort to bear suffering those who bear in mind their state of life and have before their eyes Jesus Christ naked on the cross, especially as it is clear from that same letter what a welcome experience it is to all of you when poverty makes itself felt, yet, as I have been commissioned by our Fr Master in Jesus Christ, Ignatius, who loves you like a real father, I will take comfort along with you in that grace which His infinite Goodness bestows on us, both here and there, namely that of experiencing holy poverty. I do not know to what extent this happens where you are, but here we experience poverty to an extent very much in keeping with our profession. I call poverty a 'grace' because in a special way it is a gift of God. As Scripture says, 'Poverty and wealth are from the Lord'.[3] His only Son shows us

how much God loves it, who 'leapt from his royal throne',[4] and wished
to be born in poverty[5] and grow up in it. Nor did He love it only during
his lifetime, suffering hunger and thirst and 'having nowhere to lay his
head',[6] but even in death He wished to be stripped of his clothing and to
go without everything, even water when thirsty.

[PART I. THE EXCELLENCE OF POVERTY]

[2] Wisdom, which cannot be deceived, wished, according to St Bernard,[7] to show the world how precious was that jewel of poverty, whose
worth was unknown in the world, by choosing it Himself; thus His
teaching, 'Blessed are those who hunger and thirst, blessed are the poor,
etc',[8] would not seem to be at variance with His life.

[3] How greatly God appreciates poverty likewise appears when we see
that His chosen friends, especially in the New Testament, beginning
with His holy mother and the apostles, and on through the ages until
our own time, were usually poor – like subjects imitating their king, or
soldiers their captain, or the members their head, Christ.

[4] So great are the poor in the sight of God that Jesus Christ was sent
on earth especially for them: '"Because the poor are despoiled, because
the needy groan, I will now arise," says the Lord',[9] and in another place,
'He has sent me to preach good news to the poor'.[10] This recalls the
words of Jesus Christ when he sent an answer to St John, 'The poor
have good news preached to them'.[11] They are preferred to the rich to
the extent that Jesus Christ wished to choose the most holy college of
the apostles from among the poor, and to live and have dealings with
them, and to leave them as princes of His Church, and to appoint them
as judges 'over the twelve tribes of Israel',[12] that is, of all the unbelievers,
whose assessors will be the poor. So exalted is their standing!

[5] Friendship with the poor makes us friends of the eternal king. Love
of that poverty establishes kings, even on this earth, and kings not of
earth but of heaven. This is evident because while the future heavenly
kingdom may be promised to others, it is promised here and now to the
poor and those who suffer tribulation; it is the abiding Truth who says,
'Blessed are the poor in spirit, for theirs is the kingdom of heaven'[13] –
'even now they have a right to the kingdom'.[14]

[6] Not only are they kings, but they make others sharers in the kingdom, as Christ teaches us in St Luke when he says, 'Make friends for
yourselves by means of unrighteous mammon, so that when it fails they

may receive you into the eternal habitations'.[15] These 'friends' are the poor, thanks to whose merits those whom they help enter into dwellings of glory, especially if they are poor of their own free will. According to St Augustine[16] these are the little ones of whom Christ says, 'Anything you did for one of the least of these, you did for me'.[17]

[7] In this way the excellence of poverty becomes evident. Poverty does not think it worthwhile to heap up treasures out of dung or base earth, but, with the full power of its love, buys that precious treasure in the field of holy Church,[18] whether it be Christ himself or his spiritual gifts, from which he is never separated.

[PART II. THE USEFULNESS OF POVERTY]

[8] To appreciate the true utility of poverty, how far it really has a place among the means suitable to gain our final end, one should reflect on the many sins from which we are preserved by holy poverty, since it does away with the stuff of which they are made, *quia non habet unde suum paupertas pascat amorem.*[19] It slays pride, that worm of the rich, and cuts out those infernal leeches of excess and gluttony, and of so many other sins. And should we fall, through weakness, it helps us to get up quickly, because there is none of that amorous attachment which, like glue, binds the heart to the earth and to the things of the earth, and leaves no freedom to get up again, to come to one's senses and to turn to God. Poverty makes it easier in every case to hear better the voice, i.e. the inspiration, of the Holy Spirit, removing any obstacles in its way. It also makes prayers more effective in the sight of God, 'The Lord heard the prayer of the poor'.[20] It speeds us along the way of the virtues like a traveller relieved of every burden. It frees us from that slavery common to so many of the great of this world, in which *all things obey or serve money*'.[21] It fills with every virtue, if it is poverty in spirit, for the soul emptied of attachment to the things of earth will be that much fuller of God by reason of His gifts. Certainly, poverty cannot but be very rich, since it has been promised one hundred per cent gain,[22] even in this life. Although this promise is fulfilled in temporal matters only when expedient, it cannot but be true in spiritual matters. Thus they must needs be rich in divine gifts who voluntarily become poor in human things.

[9] This same poverty is that soil, fertile in strong men, *fecunda virorum paupertas,*[23] as the poet said, words far more applicable to Christian than to Roman poverty. This is that furnace that tests our progress in

strength and virtue, and in which is seen what is gold and what is not.[24] This is the moat that makes safe the camp of our conscience in religious life. It is the foundation on which Jesus Christ seems to have shown that the edifice of perfection is to be built when he said, 'If you would be perfect, go, sell what you possess and give to the poor, and follow me'.[25] This is the mother, the nurse and the guardian of religious life, for it bore, nourished and preserves it, just as affluence in temporal things on the contrary diminishes, spoils and ruins it.

[10] Hence it is easy to see how great is the utility, in addition to the excellence, of this holy poverty, since it is principally due to it that we are finally saved by the One who 'will save the humble (and the poor)',[26] and we obtain the everlasting kingdom of that same person who says that the kingdom of heaven is for the 'poor in spirit';[27] nothing else of value can be compared with this.

[PART III. THE HAPPINESS OF POVERTY]

[11] So although holy poverty is harsh, it should be embraced voluntarily. In fact, however, it is not harsh, but rather a source of great joy to those who take it on voluntarily. Even Seneca says that the poor laugh more heartily, having no other worry.[28] Experience too shows us that in the case of ordinary beggars, if one looks just at their degree of contentment, one finds that they live more cheerfully and happily than great merchants, magistrates, princes and other great persons. But if this is true of those not voluntarily poor, what shall we say of those voluntarily so? These people, not having or being attached to the things of this earth, enjoy imperturbable peace and utmost tranquillity in their regard, while the rich are tossed in constant storms. The former are in endless joy, at a kind of perpetual banquet, thanks to the security and purity of their conscience. This is especially true since they are ready, thanks to this same poverty, to receive divine consolations, which are usually that much more numerous in God's servants as they are lacking in the things and possessions of earth, provided they know how to fill themselves with Jesus Christ, so that He can supply their every need and be in place of everything.

[CONCLUSION]

[12] However, this is not the place to take the matter any further. Let what has been said be enough for our mutual consolation and exhortation, both yours and mine, to love holy poverty. The excellence, value and happiness mentioned above reside fully only in that poverty which is loved and voluntarily embraced, not imposed or involuntary. I will add only this: they who love poverty must love its effects, as far as depends on them, such as eating badly, dressing and sleeping poorly, and being looked down upon. Otherwise anyone who would love poverty, but is not willing to experience privation or any of its consequences, would be too fussy a poor man, and would surely show that he loved being called poor rather than possessing poverty, or else that he loved it more with his tongue than with his heart.

[13] All that remains in this letter is to pray Jesus Christ, the master and true example of spiritual poverty, to grant us all the possession of this precious inheritance which He bestows on His brethren and co-heirs, so that the spiritual riches of grace, and finally the unutterable riches of His glory, may abound in us. Amen

From Rome, 6 August 1547.

19. En route to the *Constitutions*

Louvain 1547

(No. 234 : I, 659–63 : Latin)

Flemish priests began to join the Society only after its foundation in 1540, but the departure of the non-French Jesuit students from Paris in 1543 (when Francis I and Charles V were at war) brought a group of nine students to live in Flanders, in the house of a priest, Fr Wischaven, who though a novice had not yet taken his first vows. In the following years the small community experimented, setting up the infrastructure of religious life, with no Constitutions to guide them, although Pierre Favre and others close to Ignatius (like Fr Doménech) were with the group at different times. In 1546 quite detailed instructions were sent out and Fr Paeybroeck was authorized to set up a formal community. This letter gives some idea of how fluid the situation remained, as these early Jesuits groped towards a new way of life, while Ignatius, many miles (and several wars) away tried to give a pattern that would be valid for the Society as a whole.

Fr Daniel Paeybroeck   24 December 1547
in Louvain   from Rome .

May the grace and peace of Our Lord Jesus Christ be always present and increase in our hearts. Amen.

[1] [*Introduction*] We received your two letters, written on the 4th and 18th of March. They gave us great joy in the Lord, and this fills us with love for you and for all the companions along with whom you are so closely joined in aims and intentions to the glory of the same Lord Jesus Christ. His love alone is the glue[1] which must hold together and sustain the whole Society.

[2] [*Advantages of communal living*] I approve highly of all you tell me both about your communal life together and about your method of selecting candidates for admission. I hope that both will redound to the honour and glory of our Creator, and to the benefit of all these candidates in good numbers, but provided that 'your light shines before men, so that they glorify your Father in heaven',[2] and that your example spurs

others to a holy emulation. It is really a great obligation that you have undertaken to live a holy and devout life, since you will be separated from others in your lodging and your manner of life, and thus exposed to the eyes and tongues of all. But I am confident that you will succeed, through Him 'from whom comes every good and perfect gift'.[3] You have consecrated yourselves totally to Him, and it is by His goodness that you have received this vocation and these holy desires – no ordinary pledge! Yet I also think it will be very valuable for you to live together, so that brother may help brother up again after a fall, support the unsteady and spur on the lazy by word and example. In this way you will share with each other the grace you have received[4] and prepare yourselves to receive still more from 'the Father of lights',[5] since the Truth Himself has promised that 'whenever two or three agree in asking for something',[6] He will hear and answer.

[3] [*Criteria for candidates*] Just as I approve the decisions you have made up to now regarding this Institute, so I urge you to keep the same method of selection. I would not like us to have to say, 'Thou hast multiplied the nation' but not 'increased its joy'[7] – or virtue! So take care that those you admit are commended by their upright life. If they are not all highly educated, they ought certainly to have the capacity and motivation for learning. Above all, they should enjoy sufficient health and strength for the activities which our way of life demands. Outside the Society, of course, we are entirely ready to help and look after the sick and infirm; but we have learned from experience that we should not admit them as members, because they are more likely to be a hindrance than a help to this Institute and way of life which we have chosen for the honour of God and the salvation of souls.

[4] [*Superiors*] As for your opinion that Jacob Lhoost of Jodoigne [Geldenaken] would be suitable to be your Superior, I share it. Admittedly he is in Sicily, labouring in the Lord's harvest, but I promise to do my best to have him come your way soon, unless he is kept back by occupations which it would cause too great loss to abandon. You can see that I am hoping for equally great profits from where you are, to the benefit of souls and the glory of Our Lord, Jesus Christ. I will add this one point with reference to your group: I think you should take special care to win the approval and love of your bishop, so that you may grow in numbers and virtue with your father's blessing, to the praise of Him who created and redeemed us, Our Lord Jesus Christ, who is blessed above all for ever.

[5] [*Provisional constitutions*] The constitutions or rules which you sent

me I readily approve, and I think they are suitable for this first phase of your group. As time passes you will learn by experience whether anything needs changing or adding, and if I judge that there is anything that I should draw to your attention I will be glad to do so. For the time being there are two points that I must mention.

[6] [*Women*] The first is where you say in the 4th Constitution, 'No one, male or female, is to be admitted to this group who has taken a vow . . .', etc. Here you seem to allow for the female sex, though lower down you rightly say that women are not to be received under obedience by vow. On this please note that our Society does not and cannot admit women so as to take responsibility for them,[8] except by way of advice and the other ministries that cannot be refused to anyone on grounds of social status or sex. We took a lot of trouble to obtain this from the Supreme Pontiff, so as to protect ourselves and our successors in office from having to neglect activities of greater value for God's honour and help to souls, in favour of others of smaller value and liable to involve much nuisance. This has in fact already been granted to us.

[7] [*Vow, not just promise, to enter*] The other point I noted is that you expressly pronounce vows of poverty and chastity, but as regards entering the Society only a firm resolution, not a vow. Now I would not wish to encourage anyone towards our Institute who was not called to it by God, but I advise you that it is our practice not to take on as subjects, under our responsibility, any who have not confirmed by a vow their resolution to enter the Society. You would be a very powerless Superior of people who could withdraw when they felt like it. Therefore if you have in mind for us to send you one of our members (for example, Jacob Lhoost, as you have suggested), I cannot see my way to grant this unless either we depart from our practice, which was not established lightly, or you all confirm your resolution to enter by a vow, as others do.

[8] [*The granting of faculties*] As regards the faculties and privileges that have been granted to this Society for the help of souls, please do not interpret the fact that I am not offering these immediately as implying any doubt of your honesty or prudence in making use of them. My conscience bears me witness that I have the highest opinion and hopes of you. But this treasury of graces was entrusted to me 'for building up, not for breaking down',[9] so that I might dispense them to our members as I may find each suited, and according to the needs of each. Therefore it is my duty to make use of them cautiously and with moderation, remembering that my job is to be a dispenser, not a disperser. Further, there are many today who, by abusing privileges granted to them, have

justly been deprived of them. (I am not referring to any of our own members; by God's grace none of them, to my knowledge, has either committed such abuse or suffered such deprivation.) This ought to make us all the more careful, so that, by using the faculties granted to us properly and with moderation, we may let them become established. They are so unusual that they could expose us to envy unless we temper liberty with moderation.

[9] [*Profession in the Society*] I have said all this so that you will not be surprised if I want to know what I grant and to whom. Therefore anyone who desires any favour of this kind for the spiritual benefit of others should write to me, individually, about his personal qualities and desires, how far he is advanced in his studies, and whatever may make him personally fitted to exercise such faculties. Next he should name the faculty he wants, whether singly or two together. Only then, if I grant something – and I do intend to do so – shall I be able to render an account to God or human judge, if it were demanded, for my dispensation. For the time being I must warn you about all these faculties that are destined for those who are professed in this religious order. No one may publicly claim them as his own till he is professed, because we received this grant from the Supreme Pontiff by word of mouth, not by documents. This, I say, concerns those not yet professed in the Society, for the professed will be able to show their privileges publicly by means of a brief or document.[10] Nevertheless in the forum of conscience it is just the same to have received the faculties by word of mouth, as far as the security of the one dispensing and the profit of the one being dispensed is concerned.

All best wishes in Our Lord Jesus Christ. May He be pleased to fill us with knowledge of His will and give us strength to fulfil it by His grace.

Rome, 24 December 1545,[11]

Yours in the Lord,

Ignatius

20. Defining obedience as an ideal

Coimbra 1548

(No. 243 : I, 687–93 : Spanish)

The precise occasion for this letter, written less than a year after the more general Letter 16, is not known, but clearly Ignatius was uneasy about the guidelines likely to help young Jesuits. The veiled references to ostentatious self-humiliations (§7) hint at a great anxiety, which would explain the exaltation of obedience almost to the exclusion of personal initiative in the particular context of Coimbra at this time. However, a new process of reflection is also under way, grappling with an obedience 'of the mind' that would be solidly based on tradition (notably the writings of St Bernard) and valid also for mature independent adults.

Rector and students of the College   14 January 1548
in Coimbra   from Rome

May the grace and peace of Jesus Christ Our Lord and God be constantly felt and grow in our minds and hearts, Amen!

[1] [*Initial satisfaction*] My necessary business has been covered in what I have written to Master Rodrigues,[1] and given my poor health[2] and overwork I might reasonably be excused from doing what is not strictly necessary. However Jesus Christ Our Lord has placed you all in my mind and heart with so great a love that I have no desire to avail myself of any possible excuse. I know that your devotion to the bond of obedience is such that you are consoled in Our Lord by the letters written to you from here. Likewise all of us here are greatly consoled in Our Lord by the good news we hear in Rome of your spiritual growth in learning and in virtue. I hope in God, our Creator and Lord, that He will make this rejoicing of ours grow daily rather than diminish, as the progress which gives rise to it also increases rather than slackens. Then you will be like those whom the sage describes in Proverbs, 'The path of the just grows ever brighter like the light of dawn, opening out into full day'.[3]

[2] [*God's blessings*] Therefore I ask the One who is source of this day, like a sun of wisdom and justice, to carry through in His great generosity what He has begun in you, until His work reaches fulfilment and

He allows you to find and know 'the pasture-grounds, the resting-place under the noon's heat',[4] displaying the richness of His omnipotent hand and His infinite splendour in the spiritual gifts within your minds and hearts, and through you, in those of many others. Through Him I ask you also, dear brothers in Jesus Christ Our Lord and God, to make yourselves open for His coming and His spiritual treasures. This openness comes through purity of heart, true humility, a common mind among you all, a common desire, and peace within and without, which is what makes a dwelling place in your soul for the One who is called 'Prince of Peace',[5] enabling Him to be Lord within you. In short, my prayer is that you be completely united, indeed simply one entity, in Our Lord Jesus Christ.

[3] [*Need for obedience*] However such unity among a number of people is not achieved without order, and order is not achieved without the necessary bond of obedience between subjects and superiors. This we can see from the whole natural order, the hierarchies of angels, and well-ordered human constitutions. These are united, preserved and governed through subordination. So holy obedience is the ideal I hold up to you, and insist upon: each of you should observe it, regarding your superiors in a way corresponding to whatever level of authority over you they have, minor officials of the house in what pertains to their office, confessors in matters of personal conscience, the Rector generally. Similarly, the Rector himself, just like all the others, must in general be subject to the Provincial Superior, especially since God Our Lord has made use of this particular person[6] to make a start to this work of His. And the Provincial must in the same way be subject to whoever God Our Lord might give him as General Superior, and the General Superior in his turn must be subject to whoever is supreme above all. In all superiors, it is Jesus Christ Our Lord whom one acknowledges, for it is to Him and through Him that all obedience should be given whoever it is that people obey.

[4] [*Grades of obedience*] If unity is to come about and be preserved through this obedience, it must not be simply a matter of practical directives observable in public. It must also extend, as it were, to a person's desires (as St Bernard put it, 'Those who do not make the wish of the Superior their own have not reached even the first stage of obedience'[7]), and similarly to the understanding, for union of wills will not last and cannot be preserved if divergent opinions are maintained. I mean situations where what is done and what is desired is, to be sure, what the Superior has directed, but people's basic intuitions are different

from his, and they live out of their own opinions rather than out of the Superior's. Apart from where some matter of sin is in question, or where the understanding simply cannot but recognize something as an error, it is well established that true obedience does not subject only actions to the Superior, but also wishes; and not only wishes, but also opinions. In this way unity is made firm and lasting, and under this holy and gentle yoke, peace and stability cannot be ruffled, at least to the extent that our present blighted state will allow.

[5] [*The good made bad*] Those people who do things against the intention of the Superior will see, from what has been said, how little they have entered into obedience, even though the things in themselves might be praiseworthy and good, such as mortification, contemplation and other practices. They are acting in conflict with what has been commanded them; they are following their own wishes rather than those of the Superior. How utterly unacceptable the sacrifice is that a person makes to God when one offers Him against the mind of the Superior some deed to which one is not obliged, even if the deed considered in itself is excellent! Such people will have to learn what St Bernard says: what is offered to the Holy Spirit is not acceptable if one fails to fulfil one's obligations. And for a subject, obligation means obeying one's Superior, of whom almighty God says, 'The one who hears you, hears me, and the one who rejects you, rejects me'.[8]

[6] [*Biblical examples*] It seems that the sacrifice made by Saul was like this, contrary to obedience towards God Our Lord as presented to him through Samuel the prophet. Saul says, 'The people have spared the best of the sheep and the oxen to sacrifice them to the Lord your God'. But what does the prophet reply? 'Why did you not listen to the voice of the Lord, but did what was evil in the sight of the Lord?' And when Saul appealed to his sacrifices, 'Has the Lord as great delight in burnt offerings and sacrifices as in obeying the voice of the Lord? For obedience is better than victims, and to hearken better than to offer the fat of rams. For, like a sin of divination is disobedience, and like the iniquity of idolatry the refusal to obey.'[9] Similarly too, Cain's sacrifice of the fruits of the earth was of little value, and did not deserve to be noticed by God. This is what pains and afflictions of body or soul, and any other sort of deed, are like if they are offered without appropriate obedience and charity. On the contrary, 'The Lord had regard for Abel and his gifts', because he offered 'from the firstlings of his flock and of their fat portions'.[10] And this sacrifice of Abel's is like the noble sacrifice 'sweetly fragrant',[11] of one's own will and understanding offered

through dedicated obedience to the Divine Majesty in the person of His delegates. When anyone offers his or her body through hurting it or in some other way, contrary to obedience, the sacrifice does not have the salt that it says in Leviticus every sacrifice must have.[12] This is not the 'living sacrifice', fitting for rational creatures and pleasing to God our Creator and Lord, that St Paul recommends.[13]

[7] [*Proud humiliations*] I would like you to be well aware of a truth spoken by St Bernard, and to have it fixed in your memories: 'If anything happens without the will and consent of the spiritual director, it is to be counted as vainglory, not as merit'.[14] But then, how much more is this the case when the action concerned is actually against the spiritual father's will? What greater pride could there be than that of preferring one's own wishes and opinions to those of the one whom you have formally acknowledged to be your superior in the place of Jesus Christ? This is why, as experience certainly bears out, such people are proud. As such they deserve that what are normally healthy antidotes (namely the mortifications in question, when accepted rightly at the wish of the Superior) become poison for them and lead to their death.

[8] [*Danger of ruin*] Great is the relish enjoyed by the Enemy of our nature on seeing persons going forward recklessly, unrestrained by anyone who knows how to rule and direct them! This is even more true if they are in very high and sublime reaches. Then the Enemy can expect their ruin all the more probably, and all the more serious will be their fall. The dedication that would be something holy if regulated under obedience comes to be a most effective weapon and instrument for the devil to rid the heart of the true love of God, and thus to put an end to a person's whole spiritual life. Remember how even the children of Israel, as they wanted to enter the promised land contrary to obedience, were defeated by their enemies, and thus be wary of acting against obedience, even in things that are very spiritual. Remember how when they were but few, and yet went forward under obedience, they would often defeat enemies large in number. When by contrast they went forward as a large, disobedient group, they were often defeated by a small force.

[9] [*Conclusion*] Since 'all this is written so that we can learn from example and be built up by it',[15] as you well know, be happy to let yourselves be governed as far as possible by this holy and safe counsel of perfection, obedience. Be convinced, under Our Lord, that thus you will proceed without going astray. Have faith that you will be shaped according to the divine will when you have trampled down under your feet the will that is our own, and have placed over your head and before your

eyes the will of your Superior. Have faith that Divine Providence is to rule and guide you by such means, so that you attain greater personal perfection, and give greater help to others.

[10] May it please His Divine Majesty to bring all this about, so that His holiest of names may be more greatly honoured and glorified in everything for ever.

From Rome, 14 January 1548,

Yours in Our Lord,

Ignacio

21. Developments in the spiritual life

Borgia 1548

(No. 466 : II, 233–37 : Spanish)

This letter was written to Borgia when he was coming to the end of his two-year 'novitiate', in answer partly to a letter from the Duke and partly to disquieting reports that he was under stress (not surprising given his passionate character and his Superior's notable lack of common sense). Put very crudely, Ignatius's message is: 'Hold your horses – less prayer time, less fasting, and less self-floggings!'

Francis Borgia,[1] Duke of Gandía   20 September 1548
in Gandía   from Rome

✛

IHS

My Lord in Our Lord,

May the supreme grace and eternal love of Christ Our Lord always favour and assist us continuously!

[1] [*Previous letter*] On hearing of your programme, of your way of approaching spiritual matters, of your physical regime, and of how all this is directed towards your spiritual growth, I have certainly been given new cause for great rejoicing in Our Lord. As I was thanking the Eternal Majesty for this, I could not attribute it to anything other than His divine goodness, the source of all that is good.

[2] [*Developments*] *At the same time I have the feeling in Our Lord that*,[2] just as at one time in our lives we need some particular exercises, both spiritual and physical, so at another, different time of our lives we need correspondingly different ones. For what has been good for us at one period is not *always* such at another. Your Grace has commanded me to explain my feelings on the matter, and I shall say *before the Divine Majesty* everything in this regard that suggests itself to me.

[3] [*Times for prayer*] First, regarding the hours to be directed to pious mental and bodily exercises: I would recommend your cutting out half of them. At the times and to the extent that the thoughts arising either from ourselves or from our enemy lead us to think of inappropriate, vain and unlawful things, and draw our understanding towards

them, then in such situations we should normally try to increase the internal and external exercises, in order to stop the will delighting in such things and consenting to them. This depends on individuals and on the range of such thoughts or temptations, and victory comes from correct adaptation *to the individuals concerned*. By contrast however, to the extent that such thoughts are becoming weak and dying off, good thoughts and holy inspirations come along spontaneously. *And we must make plenty of room for these, opening fully the gates of our minds and hearts.*

[4] [*Study, etc, in place of prayer*] As far as I can sense the matter in the Lord from what Your Grace tells me, you do not need as many weapons to conquer your enemies as you are currently using. I would therefore think it better that you make over half of the time you are currently spending on them to study (for there will always be a need and a use for the knowledge we acquire, as well as for what God infuses directly), to the administration of your property, and to spiritual conversations. You should always take care to maintain your soul in peace, in quiet, and in readiness for whatever Our Lord might wish to do within it. There is no doubt that it is a greater virtue in the soul, and a greater grace, for it to be able to relish its Lord in a variety of duties and in a variety of places, rather than simply in one. In order to attain this we are very much required to take steps ourselves, within the sphere of His divine goodness.

[5] [*Norms for fasting*] On the second point, *regarding fasting and abstinence*, I would recommend *for Our Lord's sake* that you take care of your digestion and strengthen it, along with your other natural faculties, rather than weakening them. *First*, when a person is prepared and set in such a way that he or she would prefer to lose life on earth completely rather than commit a deliberate offence, however slight, against the Divine Majesty, and *secondly*, when the person is not troubled by any particular temptations from the enemy, the world or the flesh – and I think that Your Grace, by God's grace, fulfils these conditions, *both the former positive and the latter negative one* – I would very much like Your Grace to convince yourself that the body along with the soul is the property of our creator and Lord, and that you will have to give a good account to God with regard to everything. Thus you should not allow your body to become weak. If that occurs, the inner self will not be able to function.

[6] [*Ignatius's experience with fasting*] I used to be all in favour of fasting, prolonged abstinences, and going without normal meals; for a

period of time all this seemed delightful to me. But in future, for the reasons given, I cannot recommend such a programme as I have seen that the stomach will not function properly owing to the fasting and abstinence involved; it cannot digest even normal meats or other foods that give proper sustenance to the human body. Now I would be in favour of doing everything possible to make people eat all legitimate kinds of food as often as these foods would benefit them without scandalizing others. We should cherish and love the body to the extent that it obeys and helps the soul, and to the extent that the soul, obeyed and helped in this way, is better fitted for the service and praise of our creator and Lord.

[7] [*Corporal penances*] On the third point, *re. inflicting pain on one's body for Our Lord*, I would recommend omitting anything that might draw blood, even a drop. I am convinced in the Divine *Goodness* that *His Divine Majesty* has given you the grace for this and for all that has been mentioned. But from now on it is much better for you to abandon such penances, without my giving explanations and arguments for this opinion.

[8] [*Tears*] Instead of drawing blood and somehow trying to force it out in some way, you should seek more directly from the Lord of everyone His most holy gifts, for example, a flow or even a sprinkling of tears. These may come, (1) over your own sins or those of others, (2) over the salvific events of the life of Christ Our Lord, here or in heaven, (3) from thinking of the Divine Persons, or from love of them. The more sublime the thoughts and reflections that give rise to these tears, the more valuable and precious they are. But though the third of these reflections is in one sense better than the second, and the second than the first, what is best for each individual is that in which God Our Lord imparts Himself more fully, displaying His holiest of gifts and his spiritual graces. It is God who sees and knows what is better for a person, and God, knowing everything, shows the person the way forward.

[9] [*Trial and error*] However for our part, to find that way through the medium of His grace we will be greatly helped if we search about and make many kinds of experiments, so that we can follow the route *that He most clearly shows to one*, the happiest and most blessed route in this life, completely governed and directed towards that other life, which is without end, embracing and united to these *most holy* gifts.

[10] [*The higher gifts*] By these I mean those gifts which are not in our *very own* power to summon *when we wish*, but which are purely gifts from the One who gives all that is good, and can do all that is good,

gifts such as the following (always understood as being directed and aimed at His Divine Majesty): intensity of faith, of hope, and of love; *spiritual rejoicing and repose*; tears; intense consolation; the raising up of the mind; impressions or illuminations from God; and all the other spiritual relishings and intuitions that lead to such gifts, together with humility and reverence towards our holy mother, the Church, and towards the rulers and teachers who have been appointed within her. Any of these *most holy* gifts must be preferred to any physical activities. These latter are good in so far as they lead to the attaining of the former gifts, *or some part of them*. I do not mean that we should seek these gifts *only* in order to take pleasure in them, or to enjoy them, but rather so that all our thoughts, words and deeds can be warm, clear, and just, and thus be of greater service to God. For we know within ourselves that without such gifts our thoughts, words and deeds get mixed up, becoming cold and confused. Thus we should desire such gifts, or parts of such gifts, or such spiritual graces, to the extent that they can help us, and thus be of greater glory to God. So when the body is at risk from too much hardship, it is the healthiest course to seek these gifts by using one's understanding and by other moderate exercises. Then it is not just the soul that will be healthy; we will have a sound mind in a sound body,[3] and thus everything will be healthier and better fitted for the divine service.

[11] [*Conclusion*] *As to how to proceed in more detail, I do not think in the Lord that I should talk about that. I am confident that the same divine Spirit that has guided and directed your Grace up till now will guide and direct you further, and that thus there will be greater glory for His Divine Majesty.*

22. Dealing with a radical crisis

Borgia 1549

(No. 790 : II, 494–95 : Spanish)

Both this[1] and the following letter shed light on one of the major crises faced by Ignatius as Superior General, a crisis that called in question – no doubt with the best of intentions – the whole orientation of the new Society.

Francis Borgia, SJ, Duke of Gandía[2]   27 July 1549
in Gandía   from Rome

If all that is being written to us is true, it appears that both those persons, B. and C.,[3] have found (to somewhat different degrees) the desert they were first after, and both seem to be heading for an even greater desert, unless they learn how to be humble and let themselves be guided in accordance with the religious profession they have made. Quite clearly a solution is urgently needed, and it may be provided either directly or by someone fully competent, who is willing for their sake to be God's instrument. In line with the first possibility we are invited to prayer and sacrifices in the presence of His divine goodness. As for the second, if there are any means at all that can be instruments of divine grace, your own authority and influence may be very effective.

In this situation I must bear in mind my obligations in conscience. I am absolutely convinced, without any doubt whatsoever, and declare openly before the tribunal of Christ Our Creator and Lord, who one day is to judge me for ever, that these people have gone astray. They have been deceived and disoriented. Sometimes they are on the right path; sometimes they stray, persuaded by the father of falsehood; it is part of his technique to assert or suggest one or even many truths in order to slip in a lie and leave us entangled in it.[4] So, your Grace, out of love and reverence for God Our Lord – it is to His divine goodness that I entrust everything – please reflect very carefully on this case, and be vigilant and far-seeing in dealing with it. Please do not give free rein in these matters that are so prone to cause great scandal and immense harm in all areas. My prayer is that the situation will be altered to the complete service of the Divine Majesty, and that the persons mentioned will be fully healed in order better to serve, praise and glorify Him, for ever and ever.

From Rome, 27 July 1549,

Ignatio

23. On prophecies and revelations

Gandía 1549

(Appendix 6, No. 3 : XII, 632–52 : Spanish)

This complex document, called an 'Instruction' but really a 'report' drawn up after a committee meeting, was added to the previous letter to Borgia. The crisis that both are dealing with sprang from the chance conjunction in Gandía of four persons: the Duke himself, clearly inclined initially (as Letter 21 testifies) to excessive prayer and penance; the Superior of the Jesuit community, Fr Andrés de Oviedo, a saintly but hardly normal personality[1]; a young French scholastic, François Onfroy, a tragic (almost operatic) figure, the prey to religious exaltation and tuberculosis; and the Franciscan friar Fray Juan de Tejeda, whom Ignatius most mistrusted, one of Borgia's earliest spiritual directors, a visionary prophet while still a student of theology. The last three were convinced that the new Society of Jesus needed 'reform', with men and time devoted much more to prayer (Oviedo wanted some eight hours a day), and its ideals directed to Church reform under the leadership of an angelic Pope. Ignatius acted in two ways: he assured himself of the support of Borgia (Letter 22) and he had a committee investigate teaching current in Gandía so that a full judgement could be sent to those concerned. This document was written by his secretary, Polanco, but can justifiably be attributed to Ignatius himself, both because he whole-heartedly supported the findings of his committee and because he went carefully through Polanco's text, toning down the harshness of some phrases and adding phrases of his own invention. More fundamentally, his 'Rules for the discernment of spirits'[2] underlie the discernment process illustrated here. He was helped by circumstances – both Onfroy and Tejeda dying in 1550 – but also by the exemplary cooperation of Borgia and Oviedo. The crisis was defused in twelve months, even if its traumatic effects, especially on Borgia, and through him on the Society, were more lasting.[3]

Francis Borgia, SJ, Duke of Gandía⁴   July(?) 1549
in Gandía   from Rome

[General principles]

Before we come on to details, *it seems to us good in the Lord of all* to say a few things which may be *of service towards the greater glory of His Divine Majesty* in dealing with this matter.

[1] [*Prophecy possible*] To start with, it is an accepted principle that not all prophecies subsequent to Christ Our Lord are to be rejected, for we see them attributed to St John,⁵ Agabus⁶ and the daughters of Philip.⁷ Also St Paul warns, 'do not despise prophecies'.⁸ Equally, credit is not to be given to all those who say they are prophets, nor are their prophecies to be accepted, since so many deceits of various kinds arise in this connection. The same first-mentioned apostle warns us, 'Let us not believe every spirit, but test the spirits to see if they are of God'.⁹

[2] [*But rash assertions also to be avoided*] Similarly it is an accepted principle that in the case of contingencies in the future, one cannot say with certainty that an eventuality that could conceivably occur is in fact impossible. Equally, to believe that all possible eventualities actually will occur would demonstrate *superficiality*. As the Wise man tells us, 'Rash is the heart that lightly trusts'.¹⁰ And those who have had experience of tricks of this kind – there are many significant examples these days! – are to be less easily excused.

[3] [*Need for discernment*] Thus *it is very appropriate and a matter of great necessity* to examine spirits of this kind, discriminating between them. According to St Paul, as this is a matter of great importance, God Our Lord bestows for this purpose on those in His service a special grace, *gratis data*,¹¹ 'for the discernment of spirits'.¹² This grace is helped by human effort and operates along with it, in particular with prudence and sound theology.

[4] [*Applying discernment*] Presupposing discernment of this kind, some of the prophecies or revelations that occur may be accepted in a spirit of reverence, if they do not contain anything that common sense or good theology would reject, if they foster people's growth rather than the contrary, and in particular if the person who utters them and the quality of the utterances are such as to make the messages trustworthy. Even so, sensible and holy people, without making condemnations, normally reserve judgement on such messages, and wait to see how things turn out before holding them to be certain. For even the prophets themselves do

not always see everything in their prophetic lights as clearly and without qualification as their expressions suggest. Thus it happened that Jonah said without qualification, 'Yet forty days and Nineveh shall be over-thrown!'[13] and it did not happen, or at least he did not express the condition which God Our Lord's eternal disposition had attached to that statement, namely, 'unless they did penance'.

[5] But it can also happen that a true prophet makes a mistake, stating what is not true because not really perceived through prophetic light, but rather with the light of natural common sense and reasoning. Thus Nathan was mistaken when he told David in God's name that he would build the Temple. But afterwards he saw the opposite, in the true and certain and supernatural light, and thus he told David that it would not be he who would build it because he had shed much blood, and so on.[14] With these warnings from Scripture itself it becomes clear how much more tentative people must be when it comes to trusting those who are not yet known to be prophets. In so many ways they can take falsehood to be truth.

[6] [*Some prophecies to be rejected*] When there is something con-trary to right thinking (even though there may be nothing immoral or heretical) in revelations or prophecies of this kind, it is legitimate and right not merely not to believe them, but even to speak out against them, unless the revelations or prophecies are confirmed by miracles or other proofs that are superior. But when they contain something that common sense, sound theology and a healthy attitude towards life would reject, and when they would do more harm than good if they were to be believed, then it is certain that to believe such prophecies is superficial and ignorant. It is right to contradict them and discredit them, and this furthers salvation as it promotes truth and justice and hence is pleasing to the Source of truth and justice.

[The particular case of François Onfroy]

[7] [*Initial feeling of distrust*] We come now to the case in question: these prophetic statements or revelations of B. [François Onfroy[15]]. Under obedience we have been ordered to commend the matter to God Our Lord, and then deliver our opinion. Looking at things in the light of His divine goodness, we judge that these statements should be placed in the last of the categories just described.[16] Some of the grounds for this judgement are extrinsic, others are to do with the person concerned,

others arise from the statements themselves. It is true, however, that as soon as we had read them, our minds were quite spontaneously inclined to think ill of them, before thinking about any grounds at all. *We felt great compassion* at seeing such an attitude on the part of those responsible, whom we love intimately in Jesus Christ. But both truth and falsehood often move the understanding of their own accord, without any reasoning for or against. A person who thinks that God Our Lord has imparted to us some grace for distinguishing between spirits might attribute this feeling of ours more to this gift than to other grounds. But the reasons that subsequently reinforced our conviction are as follows.

[I. GENERAL REASON I]

[8] [*Discredited teaching*] Firstly, this spirit of prophecy or these feelings, especially about the reformation of the Church and the angelic Pope,[17] etc, have existed for many years and must be regarded with good reason as highly suspect. It seems that the devil has taken to unsettling everyone he finds prone to believe such things by these means. Some of these have been people quite remarkably endowed with gifts of nature, of learning and, so they thought, of grace. Look at Amadeo,[18] not to begin any further back, or at Savonarola,[19] a man of such outstanding gifts. The sight of a person of such common sense and learning, and also of such great virtue and holiness (as far as one could see), being led astray, should be enough really to terrify anyone who gets mixed up in things of this kind. This man really wanted, in so many ways, to test his spirit to see whether it was of God, and yet, despite this, he was mistaken: for now we see that the time for his prophecies to come true has passed.

[9] [*Recent examples*] But to come to recent times. It is quite astounding how many people of our own day have got themselves caught up in this business, and cardinals among them, like Galatino:[20] it is public knowledge (and I shall keep quiet about what is not public knowledge for the sake of people's reputations) that they were and still are quite convinced that there must be angelic popes to reform the Church. That famous servant of Pope Paul's, called Ambrogio, also seemed to have this idea stuck in his mind; apparently he did not undervalue the papacy he sold.[21]

[10] [*Angelic anti-popes*] Then again, the other day in Urbino, a person with this spirit got so far as to dress up as a Pope and create cardinals. He began to acquire so many followers that the Duke of Urbino decided

it would be a great blessing if he could get rid of him and send him out of his territory. In the same way there has been another one recently in other areas of Italy, including Spoleto and Calabria, a Minim.[22] He likewise claimed that there had to be an angelic Pope, and went on about reform and so on. His election should have taken place last May, but nothing happened.

[11] [*A novitiate case*] Guillaume Postel[23] (and Your Grace will be aware of how talented he was) let himself be taken over by this same craze, and for that reason they got rid of him from the house here. In Venice where he is now he has waited, but the time within which he said his prophecies would be fulfilled is now elapsed. King Francis [I] of France, whom Postel wanted to be the monarch in the temporal sphere, is dead. Yet despite all this he still sallies forth and defends his prophecies as not being lies. He says that King Francis hindered what God had planned by not believing what he said. His son will fulfil the prophecy, just as Joshua fulfilled the prophecy that had been spoken by Moses – that he would lead the children of Israel into the promised land.[24] His ideas are now as fixed as they ever were, or more so. He has not moderated his views, but rather the poor man has fallen into other errors that are so outrageous as to give a good indication of the spirit he has. So much so that not only are they regarding him as a hopeless case, but have also forbidden him to preach. Even the Inquisition wants to get its hands on him.

[12] [*Two Portuguese cases*] In the last few days someone else has come from Portugal, talking about the need to reform the Church. Our Father tried to talk some sense into him here in the house. Another person from the same country says that he is absolutely certain to be elected Pope before the end of next August. He was agitating to get one of the churches here (a rather uncomfortable one) to live in, because it seemed to him that he would make a fine exit from there when he was elected Pope.

[13] [*Papal illusions*] Not to go on with so many individual cases, I will just mention one more, who came recently to talk to our Father and discuss his situation with him. This person showed quite an acquaintance with things of the spirit. According to what he was saying, he had already been elected Pope from more than 200 miles away. He was quite sure that Cardinal Farnese,[25] among others, had been present at his election. Apparently all that was left was for him to take possession of the papacy. I think, however, that our Father replied politely, saying that papal elections did not happen unless the see was vacant. He should find

out if Pope Paul was still alive or not, so as to see if his election had really happened, etc.

[14] [*Summary of Reason 1*] However, to come back to where I began, the first of the reasons influencing our decision comes from seeing these cases and others like them. Even if the prophecies were better grounded, things of this kind would render them suspect, deservedly so, and discourage one from getting mixed up with them.

[I. GENERAL REASON 2]

[15] [*Argument from authority*] The second of the reasons governing our decision comes from seeing that neither Fr Master Araoz[26] in Spain nor Fr Master Ignatius here approve of any of this. Rather, they hold it to be false, a deceit of *the enemy of human nature*. The mere agreement or disagreement of people like these is very significant for us. This is because, firstly, they are superiors who by virtue of their office are meant to govern. Thus they are normally more strongly influenced by the gifts of God necessary for the government of those under their charge. Secondly, because they are so dedicated to God Our Lord. In testing a particular spirit to see if it is of God or not, it is more reasonable in doubtful cases to rely on people like this, even without there being particular reasons, rather than on others who have lots of reasons. Our Lord says, 'If a person wishes to do the will of the one who sent me, that person will know whether the doctrine is of God'.[27] Certainly, virtue is very important in discernment. Thirdly, because both in the case of the one and in that of the other, *it seems that* by a gift of Jesus Christ, the source of all that is good, they have this grace of discerning spirits. *And it is much more appropriate and logical that they, rather than outsiders, have this gift in a particular way with regard to those under them.* Considering also their great prudence and experience, it seems very right to believe them regarding a matter about which they are so certain and have no doubt. It is their place to know about this, especially our Fr Master Ignatius.

[I. GENERAL REASON 3]

[16] [*Lack of good purpose*] The third reason is that when God Our Lord reveals things of this kind that are out of the ordinary, he normally

does so for some good purpose, seeking to bring about something that will help people. According to St Paul[28] and the doctors of the Church it is characteristic of these graces 'gratis datae'[29] that they be for the good of others. However if we look at what purpose the prophecies we have here might be serving, we find nothing helpful, but rather things that are harmful for those in the Society, should they believe the prophecies, and that cause scandal to outsiders. These people are saying that the Society has not been properly founded, and that it should be founded better. Now this would certainly lead anyone believing it not to be at peace in the Society. In their expectations for the future they would cease to be faithful here and now. Moreover if one is going to make something of being in the Society, it helps to have a good sense of it and a love of it. Thus whatever leads a person to lose this good sense or love would do harm.

[17] [*Positive harm*] As for those outside, it is clearly of little help to them to say that the Society's growth in numbers, even in the early years, has been matched by its falling off in spirit, and that there are such great deficiencies in it, etc. Just as the harm done within is obvious, so there seems no point at all in noising such things abroad, especially when those concerned do not want to tell the Superior of the Society how it is to be reformed. In sum, we say that in regard to doubtful claims a person should be inclined to believe what would, if accepted, help people and foster growth in preference to claims that would have the opposite effect, and consequently with these things that are not helpful, one must be inclined to hold them for the falsehoods that they in fact are.

[18] [*Summary*] Thus, recapitulating the reasons given so far: seeing that feelings of this kind lead so many people astray *so often* these days, seeing what Fr Araoz in Spain and Fr Master Ignatius here feel – who are superiors, people dedicated to God Our Lord, and wise people – and seeing that nothing is coming of such revelations, but only harm, we judge that they are not of a good spirit.

[II.] REASONS RELATED TO THE PERSON [OF FR ONFROY][30]

[19] [*A confused mind*] There are also reasons connected with B.'s [Fr Onfroy's] personality leading us to repudiate the claims discussed above. We take it as read that in the natural order the influence of a natural agent requires an individual well prepared to receive it fruitfully, and

that the same applies in the supernatural order. Admittedly in particular cases the opposite can happen, as infinite power does not need the material to be prepared. We are talking here about what obtains most often (even if with a supernatural agency there is no necessity for an individual to be prepared). Consequently, if one saw an individual who was well prepared for graces of this kind, one would be inclined with good reason to believe that that individual had them. And also, when one sees an individual who is not well prepared, but rather who has a tendency to let himself be deceived, one inclines to the opposite. We can see that B. has such a tendency to be deceived principally from the sort of mind he has. If, as he tells us when he is discussing C. [Fr Andrés Oviedo], we should take into consideration a person's natural openness for the gift of prophecy, then he himself is not a suitable person for this gift. For his mind is muddled, as C. tells us. This is why C. says[31] that B. is not a good person to teach others. A clear and discriminating mind would be better adapted for prophetic illumination: not only would such a mind be more apt to receive the illumination as such, but it would also be able to distinguish within the illumination what was absolute from what was conditional, and what was known through natural light from what was known through prophetic light. If these are experienced together indiscriminately, the one can easily be taken for the other.

[20] [*Inflexibility*] Another indication that he has been led astray is that he is a person who is quite content with his own judgement, and is too fixed in it. No. 24 shows this, and many of the other numbers.[32] His extended and disorderly prayers, his mental exercises, and his bodily mortifications will have helped him develop this stubbornness and inflexibility regarding his own ways of seeing things. Quite naturally the more one cuts oneself off from material things, the more the understanding becomes inflexible regarding what one apprehends as true or false. It often happens that such people take things that are doubtful, indeed false, for absolute truth, especially if they are blinded by the smoke of some passion (as seems to have occurred with this person).

[21] [*Physical and mental illness*] There are other factors also that contribute to his misguided state. Just as his inappropriate physical and mental activities leave him with a damaged body (as we gather from the reports reaching us of his spitting blood and other ailments), so I fear from other obvious signs that the seat of his imaginative faculty has been impaired. Moreover his thinking and evaluative powers have been damaged, those powers by which one judges particular issues, sorting out the true from the false and the good from the bad. If this sense is in

a bad state, it is quite normal for delirium to occur, *etc.* It may be (though God forbid it!) that by the time this arrives he will have given clearer indications of this *or of greater errors connected with it.*

[22] [*Impassioned will*] One can also see how easily his misguidance occurs if one looks at his will and his affectivity. For if the will is inclined to go one way or another, it will draw the understanding after it, and will not leave it free to judge what is right. Thus it follows that people are not good judges in their own cases. Now, with B. [Onfroy], it can be seen that he has a marked inclination towards long meditations and prayers, so much so that he would like to go off to the desert. It has distressed him, apparently, that they have gone against this self-love of his. And it is from this, it seems, that these prophecies and statements have arisen (Nos 8, 9, 10, 26, 27, 30 and 31), for in all of these this self-love is quite patent.

[23] [*Lack of integrity*] If a person has integrity before God in all that he or she does, seeking God's will in every way, it helps that person avoid being misguided. Indeed such integrity is a sign that a person is not misguided. In the same way, the lack of such integrity in B. indicates the opposite. I say 'lack of integrity' because it can be taken for certain that his will does not operate in conformity with the divine will, which is the supreme rule of integrity. For it does not conform in obedience with that of the Superior, as we see in Nos 10, 30 and the rest. Rather his will judges that of the Superior and condemns it.

[24] [*Unfaithfulness to the Society*] If a spirit leads a person to keep faith with all his or her obligations in serving God Our Lord, and to love them, it is a sign that the spirit is good. In the same way, a spirit that leads a person in the opposite way is bad. One can see this in No. 9 and others, where he shows the meagreness of his devotion to the way of life he has adopted and has promised by vow to observe. For in his view the Society has not been well founded and he would like it to be set up again, according to his taste. But those who do not feel good about something are not normally very assiduous or punctilious about keeping faith with it.

[25] [*Lack of humility*] If a spirit makes a person humbler and less presuming, if it gives greater self-knowledge in the light that God Our Lord imparts, it is a sign that this spirit comes from God. By the same token the spirit under discussion here *shows itself to be from God's enemy and ours. We can see this from how it incites and implants* great pride in B. [Onfroy]. Thus he judges and condemns *the one whom he has taken as his Superior in the place of Christ Our Lord,* and what that Superior orders and the Society's Institute, etc.

[26] [*Absence of modesty*] It is also a sign of a good spirit when one works to destroy spiritual vices, such as ostentation and vainglory. Thus to see these tendencies here with nothing being done against them indicates something wrong. This lack of control comes through in many of the statements of his that were written down, especially in Nos 20 and 21, when he talks of those who are in a supernatural state, or who will be very soon. If he had really had revelations of these things, *it does not seem he should have been* so quick to make them known. Those who receive supernatural or extraordinary communications from God Our Lord normally take to heart what Isaiah says: 'My secret to myself, my secret to myself'.[33] Yes, 'my secret to myself.' If they do make something public, they do so to the extent they judge God wishes it to be made known, a judgement they make by assessing how far it will help others grow, or else they are commanded to make it known.

[27] [*Inquisitiveness*] To this last reason one might add the following: inquisitiveness, rashness and a tendency to meddle. All this will appear in the third part of this letter shortly below. They are strong indications that the spirit in him is evil, just as their opposites indicate goodness.

[28] [*Summary*] We can thus sum up what has to be said regarding his personality. His understanding is confused *as the evidence shows*; his personal judgement is inflexible; the organs of his body (especially his thinking faculty) have been damaged; his will is impassioned, misguided with regard to obedience, and careless about keeping obligations; what he says shows pride, ostentation, inquisitiveness and rashness. All these indicate that the spirit that has dictated what he says is bad, and should rightly be opposed, *for it is our opponent, the father of lies, and the enemy of all that is good.* But let us come on to the third set of arguments, those arising from the statements themselves.

[III.] REASONS ARISING FROM SOME OF B.'S [FR ONFROY'S] STATEMENTS

[29] Nos 1, 2, 3 [*Acceptance of prophecies*] These and other statements relating to prophecies, although not impossible, cease to be acceptable in themselves given the other inappropriate and false things that have already been said, and will be said later. If the spirit were good, it would speak out well throughout. Secondly, if we consider the reasons why these things supposedly had to be revealed, we shall not find any useful purpose, but only the opposite, disturbances, etc. Thirdly, looking at

how things are currently going, there is no reason, *speaking in terms of reason*, to believe such new-fangled ideas. If we are meant to accept them as transcending or going against normal reason, any person tempted by them needs to be given some sort of warrant for believing that truths of this kind are revealed by God *Our Lord*, a warrant that will satisfy the understanding and its need for some kind of rationality. If such a warrant is not available, there is no reason for people to put themselves in danger of hare-brained error, particularly as even with those who are true prophets we are not obliged to believe everything they say, for they can be mistaken regarding matters that are not clearly shown them. Sometimes they will say things that have not been shown them in prophetic enlightenment, but rather what they have come to understand through their own natural reflection, just as we said above had occurred with certain people.[34] Now if things are like this with true prophets, we must be all the more hesitant about believing people of whom we do not know whether they have the gift of prophecy, and who seem to be narrating visions *that come from our enemy, or from their own moods*. And there are so many examples of this nowadays.

[30] Nos 4, 5. [*Dispute about the Pope*[35]] It does not seem appropriate to have strife or contention over the Vicar of Christ. Nor does martyrdom in such a situation seem very desirable. Secondly, it seems equally unlikely that *the Creator and Lord of all* would leave the Pope so bereft in matters regarding the overall governance of the Church. God has never done this regarding spiritual matters. Thirdly, it seems very improbable that the Pope will persecute the Society, which is so much his and so dedicated to his service, though of course the matter is in itself possible.

[31] No. 8. [*Decadence in the Society*] He says that over the last three years the Society has experienced a growth in numbers matched by its falling off in spirit. *As far as it is possible reasonably to judge*, we believe in Our Lord, *without any possibility of doubt*, that the opposite is true. The first ground for this is the test of reality. With regard to those of whom we have information here, professed and non-professed, it would seem on the contrary that they have grown in spirit, in virtue, and in the interior life over the last three years. A second ground is that God, *our Creator and Lord*, has brought about great growth in the Council at Trent as well as among various peoples here in Italy and Sicily, together with great fruit in many hearts and minds, through members of the Society in Venice, Padua, Belluno, Verona, Ferrara, Bologna, Florence, Perugia, Foligno, Rome, Naples, Messina, Palermo, and many

other places. This much can be inferred in part from reports being sent here to Rome, both currently and in the past. And among yourselves too, you know this, as much from what is happening on your doorstep in Spain as from the furthest reaches of the Indies and the Congo and Africa. Quite obviously we see that *God's Divine Majesty* is making great use of members of the Society. And since He Himself teaches us the signs by which we can get to know people when He says, 'You will know them by their fruits',[36] and since the externally visible fruit is of such quality, it seems that there is no lack of foundation for our supposition that the interior spirit and goodness have grown. A third ground is our Father's own sense of how things are. I think he is a reliable authority in this matter. As it is his job to know about this, he seeks out such knowledge and he is well capable of having it.

[32] No. 9. [*Defects in the foundation of the Society*] He says that the Society has not been well founded and that there will be a more spiritual foundation. *To strengthen our belief in this statement there is no reason for us to try and convince ourselves that the Holy Spirit dictated it*, the 'Spirit of truth',[37] who 'takes cognizance of every sound'[38] and cannot be ignorant of anything. Rather *it is obvious it must be the opposite spirit of his own*. For he is simply ignorant of how things stand with the Society. Matters of foundation, beyond the necessary and substantial, are still in process. The Constitutions are partly written, partly still being written. Moreover in the Papal Bulls some things have begun to be *reconsidered. The whole business has been entrusted to God Our Lord, with plenty of masses, prayers and tears; it is not that we want to relax what has been well established, but rather to develop it more fully, so that for the greater glory of God we can move on from what is good to what is better.* We do not have to wait for his prophecy to be fulfilled, a prophecy that seems to be based on his belief that the whole matter of the Society is now officially settled.

[33] [*More spirit?*] Secondly, the official establishment of the Society in so far as it is set out in the Briefs and Bulls available to B. [Fr Onfroy], contains nothing against spirit, even on his understanding of the matter (according to which 'spirit' is a matter of shorter or longer prayer), for up till now no limit has been placed on members of the Society, nor on its scholastics. Nothing is fixed in this regard. And if this is so, what in fact is the establishment that is apparently wrong, and that should be reconstituted in more spirit?

[34] [*Harmful regulations*] Thirdly, the Holy Spirit does not dictate nor order to be promulgated things of no use for the future, and of harm

here and now to anyone believing them, in that they lead people to lose devotion towards the Society's way of life, and thus to observe their obligations less conscientiously. For a low opinion of something would make anyone lose emotional commitment to the obligations it implied, together with any concern about its survival.

[35] No. 10. [*Revelations not to be disclosed to the Superior*] Regarding his not wanting to tell even the Superior[39] about matters concerned with the reformation, firstly one gets a whiff of the wrong ideas he has about the office of superior, minimalist to say the least. For he sees the Superior as not being capable of receiving his revelations, something that seems incredible given that God made him the very origin of the Society, not in any dream or fantasy, but really and truly. It serves only to give more evidence of his own self-importance, as if he were the only one capable, etc. Secondly, one senses also the spirit which 'hates the light'[40] and thus avoids holy people such as will not be ignorant of his tricks and who will make his deceits plain. Thirdly, one is given a sense of a spirit with little obedience or respect towards those who are obeyed in the place of Christ. Fourthly, this sort of revelation seems of no benefit, in that it has not been imparted to a person *under circumstances where it could lead to some spiritual growth.*

[36] No. 13. [*Predispositions to prophecy*] Here he seems to be exhibiting his old ideas and desires about the desert, as well as his own feelings towards the persons about whom he is prophesying. But quite apart from that, the substantive point must be ruled out of order. When God wants to give the gift of prophecy, He does not normally wait to give it until people give themselves totally to Him in prayer. We see this in Moses, David, and the other prophets: they were publicly occupied and so on. And one can see from the case of Balaam, an evil man, how little God needs in the way of predispositions. We are told that his mind was capable, although his will was evil, etc. Look at his ass, and see if it had the predispositions for speaking prophecy that B. [Fr Onfroy] demands. Secondly, either this predisposition is natural, something like a powerful intellect or a clear mind (in this case others are more likely to have it than C. [Fr Oviedo]) or it is supernatural, either some sort of special grace (*gratum faciens*[41]) or else a gift of the Holy Spirit like the gift of understanding or wisdom. Now it has never been the case that such things as these should be regarded as predispositions for prophecy, nor have they ever been called such. Many have had these gifts who were never prophets, just as others have been prophets without being in grace nor having such gifts from the Holy Spirit. So it is

not easy to see how C. is supposed to be well disposed for being a prophet. Finally, these things seem quite imaginary, *superficially* felt and expressed.

[37] No. 14. [*References to Fray Tejeda's predictions*[42]] These too seem imaginary, the result of his attachment [to Tejeda]. Although everything is possible for God, these things are not very likely. Since they do not touch on what is needful, we will not elaborate here. We will simply say that it would appear that T. [Fray Tejeda] ought not to have fallen short in this way regarding some points of *perfect* obedience, if he were to be the means for the reformation of his order. When he was here, he did not deny this shortcoming, etc.[43] This may have been the result of a secret dispensation from God, but it would be rash to believe so before it was demonstrated, a rashness shown by C. [Fr Oviedo] and B. [Fr Onfroy], to whom something of his [Fray Tejeda's] conversation may well have stuck.

[38] No. 15. [*Fray Tejeda greater than St Francis?*] Since he is in doubt here, it is clear that there is no revelation of these matters: they are opinions. Firstly, it seems irreverent to compare living mortals with the saints, especially with St Francis. Secondly, a judgement of this kind is over-hasty. Although B. is aware of great things regarding T. [Fray Tejeda], *he does not know everything about St Francis. Thirdly, from what we know of T. here*, and it can be envisaged that there is more to him still, a question like, 'Who has done greater things?' would cause us little difficulty. Such a doubt seems to come from a blind attachment.

[39] No. 18. [*Borgia the angelic Pope*[44]] Admittedly it is possible that R. [Francis Borgia[45]] will become the angelic Pope. It would be very easy for the Lord of all to do this, and here in Rome we would rejoice in that same Lord of ours at any great enterprise in which His Divine Majesty might wish to use R. Probably no one would rejoice more than ourselves! However it seems better for us to keep clear of thoughts about *such a dignity* until time tells, leaving God's divine goodness to conduct the whole business.

[40] Nos 20, 21. [*Tejeda and the continual presence of God*] Firstly, great rashness is shown by his saying what he says under these headings, in that only God is the one who weighs what people deserve. It is beyond belief that such intimate matters regarding the past and the future have been revealed to him and are still being revealed to him so continuously ('he [= Tejeda] will soon come to a supernatural state', he says), especially since so many things in him [= Tejeda] are obstacles. Secondly, on

the supposition that the revelation actually had occurred, he ought not to have published such deep and secret matters in such a trivial way. Thirdly, publication does not make such things bear fruit. In such cases they deserve to be condemned as demonstrating vainglory and presumption. If things of this kind were ever revealed to the saints, it was not their wont to speak them out in this way without any reason. *St Paul was in the desert for 14 years and so far as we know, the revelations made him by God when he was taken up to the third heaven were not made known.*[46] Fourthly, what B. says about a supernatural state and the continual presence of God seems fantastic and false. Some people dedicated to God can keep God more continually in their memories than others, and can think of God more frequently. But not even among great saints does one read about what is said here. Fifthly, what he says seems impossible in the normal course of events, even among very spiritual and holy people. This sort of continual presence of God requires the mind to be directly and intently, or rather immovably, engaged. This is not compatible with the situation of one merely on the way to God. Even the most dedicated in God's service complain about how their minds wander and never stay still. We read that St John sometimes came away from his contemplations, *bringing his mind down from the heights to a bird which he held in his hands.*[47] He told one of his disciples, who was not impressed by this, that just as his bow could not always be stretched tight, nor could the mind, and so on. Many people in God's service have from time to time, or even often, great and lively insights into God's eternal truths, insights that are certain and unshakable. But that they remain permanently in such a state *is not to be believed.*

[41] No. 22. [*Hostile reports to Rome*] This fear is based on a mistake. Here we have had no reports except what has come from Gandía, partly from C. [Oviedo] himself, partly from Fr Araoz.[48] If then the spirit is saying to him that there is someone else sowing discord,[49] then *it must be feared that the spirit that dictated this to him* is the spirit of which it was said, 'he is a liar, together with his father'.[50]

[42] No. 23. [*Polanco's hostility*] He talks about a liberty that was taken.[51] It was done in obedience to the Superior and with the sole intention of helping C. [Oviedo]. Perhaps it was an excess, but at least it was not the fruit of discord. Master Polanco knows this for certain. If B.'s spirit is saying that Polanco was used by the devil to sow such discord, Polanco can see quite certainly from his experience that B.'s spirit is not 'the spirit of truth'.[52] Polanco's conscience gives witness before God Our Lord that he loves C. sincerely in the Lord and has always loved him in

the Lord. He is very far from being accustomed to sow discord in this way, and by God's grace has always been so. Secondly, this point regarding Master Polanco is either a revelation or a suspicion. If it is, despite the point just made, a revelation, he should not be apprehensive, but know for certain, because it is, after all, a revelation. If it is a suspicion, he should be careful that it not be an offence against charity, or at least that it not be over-hasty.

[43] No. 24. Firstly, here we see a spirit of disobedience and pride. He does not defer in his understanding even to the highest of his superiors. Secondly, it is a spirit of vanity. He wants to give people the idea that he knows everything in a supernatural fashion. Thirdly, the general opinion here (as we said) is that it is pure fantasy and wrong where he says, etc.

[44] No. 25. [*Use of quotations*] Either he has this claim through a revelation or not. If he does, then surely people who know something through the light of prophecy do not need any other basis for their knowledge, at least not for themselves (although they might look round for arguments and precedents to satisfy others). If he does not, then he was clearly unjustified in being so insistent, for the three authors he cites may be in error. They are not all authoritative in the way he says, and even if what they say is good, it is possible that his understanding and interpretation of them is not. One of them, Henry Herp,[53] undoubtedly stands in need of careful glossing in some places if what he says is to be accepted. The point was made by a writer who wrote a massive preface to Herp's short work (the name escapes me), and certainly, although the preface was generally sympathetic to Herp, that is what it said.

[45] Nos 26, 27, 28. [*Reform of the Society*] Some of what is relevant here has already been said under No. 8. Granted all that, there is no doubt that we need God daily to increase us in spirit and virtue, and we hope that God will do so. But there is no excuse for B.'s rashness in saying things about which he has no knowledge. It is difficult not to pick up a note of arrogance, even contempt for the Society, when he regards himself as so spiritual.

[46] No. 29. [*Hours of prayer*] He says that no religious way of life has less prayer. If his belief is that the Society's regulations have set a shorter time-limit than others, he is wrong. Up till now, no limits have been set. If he is making a point about individuals in the Society, and saying that in no religious way of life do they pray less than we do in ours, he is wrong. One only has to look at what in fact goes on. Moreover he would always have to bear in mind that it is one thing to be in

colleges for study, and another to be in houses of the Society and out of studies.

[47] No. 30. [*Limitations on prayer*] Here we see where his real problem lies and where all these prophecies come from. And he is wrong. Firstly, he does not get beyond presumption in condemning his Superior in a matter about which he is ignorant. On the contrary, those who have some knowledge of these matters will know that the Superior is very much on the mark. For it is clear that the Superior is not forbidding prayer, which is indeed commanded by Christ and which is necessary for our well-being. Rather he is placing limits on some individuals who take too long over it. This is in keeping with the will of God, who is pleased by anything reasonable and moderate that conforms to his wisdom. Secondly, he shows that he has not renounced his private judgement and does not really know what obedience is.

[48] No. 31. [*Two-hour-long prayer? Example of Christ*] The idea that prayer for one or two hours is not real prayer, and that more hours are necessary, is bad theology and goes against the intuitions and practice of the saints. We see this firstly through the example of Christ: although he sometimes spent the whole night in prayer, at other times he was not so long, such as in the prayer at the Last Supper, or the three times he prayed in the Garden. B. [Onfroy] can never deny that these were real prayer, nor can he say that each of them went on for more than one or two hours; it seems they lasted no more than one, given that the other saving events of the Passion and so on must also have happened in what was left of that night.

[49] [*The Our Father*] We see this secondly through the prayer that Christ himself taught. Brief though it is (one does not have to take more than one or two hours to say it!), Christ called it a prayer and therefore *it cannot be denied* that it is a prayer.

[50] [*Desert Fathers*] We see this thirdly through the example of the holy Fathers who were anchorites. They generally had prayers that did not amount to one hour. In Cassian[54] we see that they used to say a fixed number of Psalms at one go, as is the custom with the Office or breviary. Does he not want this to be prayer either?

[51] [*Contemporaries*] We see it fourthly in the contemporary practice of believers, even devout ones, not all of whom (*rather, only a small minority*) spend two hours at a stretch in prayer.

[52] [*Definitions of prayer*] Fifthly, prayer is 'the request of what is appropriate from God', or to define it more generally, it is 'the raising up of the mind to God through a faithful and humble heart'.[55] If this can be

done in less than two hours, and even in less than half an hour, how can he want to deny the name and the reality of prayer to what does not go on for longer than one or two hours? Sixthly, those short exclamatory prayers, so much praised by Augustine[56] and the saints, would not count as prayer. [53] [*Conditions for life of study*] Seventhly, how much more time does he in fact want students to give to prayer, students who are studying for the service of God and the good of the Church as a whole, if they are meant to keep their mental faculties in shape for the work of learning, and to keep their bodies healthy? It would be good for him to reflect that God does not make use of people only when they are praying. If that were the case, prayers for anything less than physically possible in the 24 hours of the day would be too short, for everyone must give themselves as completely as possible to God. But in fact God makes more use at appropriate times of other things than of prayer. If it is God's pleasure that prayer should be left aside in favour of these things, then all the more so when it comes merely to shortening prayer. Thus one must understand properly the obligation to pray at all times without ceasing,[57] as the saints and the wise understand it.

[54] No. 32. [*Local practices*] The truth or otherwise of this assertion will be best seen on the spot, if Your Grace thinks it important.

With this much it seems that enough has been said about B. himself and the statements by him that have been written down. Now more briefly something will be said about the opinions of C. [Oviedo].

[The particular case of C. (Fr Oviedo)]

REGARDING THE OPINIONS OF C.

[55] Nos 1, 2. [*Fray Tejeda's miraculous conversations*] We do not really understand here [in Rome] this new kind of miracle because we cannot see how T.'s [Fray Tejeda's] communications go beyond nature, or how they are so rare as to be dignified with such a name. The title of miracle is given to certain rare deeds of God that go beyond the normal course laid down by the divine wisdom. We do not see how it can be applied to T.'s communications. Secondly, it was never said of St Peter, St Paul, or even of Our Lady that it was a miracle when they talked to people or communicated, nor even of Christ himself. Thirdly, then, one sees an excessive attachment on C.'s part, an attachment which has had the result of hampering his mind.

[56] No. 3. [*Presence of God*] For this, what was said above[58] about the continual presence of God is sufficient. The general opinion here is that such an affirmation is not worthy of belief if it is understood literally, i.e. as really a continual presence rather than as a frequent presence which he is calling 'continuous'.

[57] No. 4. [*Hearing God in Tejeda*] 'To hear T.'s own considered words is to hear God speaking': firstly, this statement seems to show so great an affection for a created being, and so high an opinion of him, that it ends up diminishing the glory of the Creator, the One known to exceed in all respects everything that has been created, and who must be understood and spoken of as such. Secondly, what makes things worse is that he is talking about T.'s 'own, considered words', i.e. he refers primarily to the speech that comes from deliberation and after thought. What C. says about hearing T. being like hearing God would be less irrational if C. meant that God was speaking in T., moving the parts of his body and so on, rather than T. talking of his own reflective accord. Thirdly, when C. says 'hear God speaking', it is not clear whether this is meant to be indirectly (rather as God spoke to Abraham and the other patriarchs supposedly through the person of an angel), or directly, as C.'s expressions suggest. In either case he should be asked whether he has ever heard God speaking. If not, how can he make such a comparison without actually knowing to what he is comparing T.'s words? On the surface it would seem that C. should be regarded as being so familiar with the conversations of God that he has come to regard them as of no great matter, or, to put it better, that he has not really experienced such conversations if he can compare the conversation of any created being with them. Fourthly, what he says is false. If the comparison is one of power, one is not going to say of T. that by his word 'the heavens were made'.[59] If it is one of truth, uprightness, or any form of perfection, such a comparison cannot ultimately be tolerated. Nor does it seem that it could come from a true person of the Spirit or from a person reflective about what he or she perceives and says.

[58] Nos 5, 6, 7, 8. [*The marvels of Fray Tejeda*] These things are easy for God, and if God wants to impart them to His creatures, He can do so without difficulty. But people loyal and sensible in their commitment to the Lord would want to see more adequate evidence before feeling compelled to believe them to be of God (as with the prophecies mentioned above). All the more so given that some of these things are so unusual, or rather have never been heard of, such as the trance lasting four months, and are therefore not worthy of belief. Secondly, we can

also say that here [in Rome], when something of what he was like came across, and when, we think, he revealed the best of what he had, he did not leave us in any state at all of admiration towards him. Still less was it a case of those who dealt with him on any matter being awestruck, as No. 8 says, but quite the contrary! He himself acknowledged that he had fallen into some important errors in behaviour, leaving aside any possible speculative ones.[60]

24. Spreading God's word in
a German university

1549
(App.1, No. 18 : XII, 239–47 : Latin)

This document, an instruction with its numbered parts rather than a letter, illustrates the careful thought given by Ignatius to new projects, in this case a proposed new university college in Ingolstadt. This text effectively demolishes the portrait of Ignatius as a military general marshalling his troops for battle against the Protestant heretics that his pugnacious disciple, Pedro de Ribadeneira, so successfully propagated in Spain's Golden Age.

Companions setting out to Germany   24 September 1549
from Rome

IHS

THINGS THAT MAY BE HELPFUL TO THOSE
SETTING OUT FOR GERMANY

The aim that they should have above all before their eyes is that intended by the Supreme Pontiff [Paul III] who has sent them: to help the University of Ingolstadt, and as far as is possible the whole of Germany, in all that concerns purity of faith, obedience to the Church, and firmness and soundness of doctrine and upright living.

Their secondary aim will be to advance the Society's purposes in Germany, especially by working for colleges of the Society to be set up in Ingolstadt and elsewhere, for the general good and God's glory.

These two aims are closely connected, and so are the means that will conduce to them, but some means can be seen to relate to both equally, others mainly to the first or to the second. It will be convenient, therefore, to treat them in this same order.

MEANS COMMON TO BOTH THE ABOVE AIMS

1st   What will help first and foremost will be to place all hope in God with a generous heart and no confidence in self, and to have a powerful desire, awakened and fed by charity and obedience, to fulfil the intended aim. In this way they will remember their aim and keep it before their eyes, commend it to God in their prayers and sacrifices, and undertake energetically all the other appropriate means.

2nd   This is to lead a life which is excellent in itself and consequently an example to others, such that they avoid not only all evil but even any appearance of it, and present models of modesty, charity and all virtues. Germany has great need of such examples, and will be correspondingly helped by them. Even with no word uttered, the Society's purposes will be advanced, and God will fight on their side.

3rd   They must both have and show sincere charity for all, especially those who have most power for the common good, such as the Duke [William IV][1] himself. They should present their apologies to him for not arriving sooner, and assure him of the love that both the Supreme Pontiff [Paul III] and Holy See, as also the Society, have for him. They must courteously promise their effort and energy to help his subjects, etc.

4th   They must prove by their works that their love is true, and win the gratitude of many, both by helping them spiritually and by external charitable activities (on which see below).

5th   Let it be clear that they are not out for 'their own interests but for those of Jesus Christ',[2] that is, his glory and the salvation of souls. This is why they do not accept any remuneration either for masses, for preaching or for the sacraments, nor can they have any income.

6th   They should make themselves liked, becoming 'all things to all'[3] by their humility and charity. As far as the Society's Institute permits, they should fit in with the customs of the country. If possible they should never let anyone go away saddened (unless it is for that person's good); but, while trying to please others, they must respect their conscience, and not let too much familiarity breed contempt.

7th   Where opposed factions or parties are active, they should show that they regard neither side as enemies, but hold a middle position and love them both.

8th   Much will depend on their moral authority and their reputation (if well founded) for sound doctrine, to their own credit and that of the whole Society, both with the general public and especially with the Duke and other leading figures. Such authority owes much not only to inner qualities, but also to outward behaviour: gravity in procedure and gesture, propriety in dress, and above all thoughtfulness in speaking and maturity in giving advice, both on practical affairs and on matters of doctrine. Such maturity implies not giving an opinion hastily when a case is not straightforward, but taking time to reflect, study or talk it over with others.

9th   Special attention should be given to maintaining the goodwill of those in positions of political power. It would be no bad thing if the Duke himself, and the more influential members of his court, could be helped by means of confession and the Spiritual Exercises. Likewise the friendship of university teachers and others of high standing should be won by services humbly and modestly rendered.

10th   It follows that, if they learn that the Society or they themselves are being criticized, especially to persons of influence, they should take prudent steps to counter this, and to make the Society's (and their own) true character better known, for the glory of God.

11th   It will be useful to understand people's character and customs, and to anticipate possible reactions in various circumstances, especially in more critical issues.

12th   It will help if all our members maintain unity both in thought and in word, dress the same way, and observe the same formalities and other practices.

13th   All the brethren should take trouble to reflect personally on what actions are appropriate to the aims stated above, and should discuss matters together; when the Superior has listened to the others, he will decide what is to be done or not.

14th   They must be careful to write to Rome, whether to ask for necessary advice or to report how things are going. This should be done frequently, as it can prove helpful in all kinds of ways.

15th   They should, every now and again, read through the above points, those that follow and any others they see fit to add, to refresh their memory of anything they might have begun to forget.

MEANS MORE RELATED TO THE FIRST PURPOSE: STRENGTHENING THAT NATION IN FAITH, DOCTRINE, CHRISTIAN LIFE, ETC

1st   The first concerns public lectures, which are the main purpose for which they have been asked for by the Duke and sent by the Supreme

Pontiff. They must be very competent in them, and teach solid doctrine without many technical terms (which are unpopular), especially if these are hard to understand. The lectures should be learned yet clear, sustained in argument yet not long-winded, and delivered with attention to style. As for disputations and other academic exercises, prudence will dictate how far to go in for them.

2nd   In order to get the biggest audiences and to help them draw the maximum profit, besides what feeds the mind, a bit of devotion to feed the heart should be mixed in, so that the hearers may go home not only wiser but also better people.

3rd   Besides these academic lectures, it seems opportune on feast days to hold sermons or Bible readings, more calculated to move hearts and form consciences than to produce learned minds. This should be possible either in Latin in the University or in German by Master Canisius[4] in the church where most people go.

4th   As far as the above indispensable occupations permit, they are to give time to hearing confessions. This is where the fruits are gathered from what has been cultivated by means of lectures and sermons. I mean confessions not of little old ladies or ordinary people (who should be directed towards other confessors), but rather of young and gifted persons who are capable of becoming apostolic workers, and of others who, with spiritual help, could make a greater contribution to the common good. Since it is impossible to meet the needs of all, priority ought to be given to those who give hope of greater profit in the Lord.

5th   They should make efforts to attract their students into a friendship of spiritual quality, and if possible towards confession and making the Spiritual Exercises, even in the full form, if they seem suitable to join the Society. More of them can be allowed (or even invited) to undertake the exercises of the First Week, and some method of prayer, etc, but still mainly those who give hope of greater good, and whose friendship seems more worth cultivating for God's sake.

6th   For the same reason, conversation and friendship with this same kind of people should be cultivated. Then, though it may sometimes be right for the sake of human interest to take up extraneous subjects, that appeal to the human intellect, one should draw the conversation back to things that are of real profit, so that such conversations may not be useless.

7th   On occasion they should give time to works of mercy of a more visible character, such as in hospitals and prisons and helping other kinds of poor; such works arouse a 'sweet fragrance' in the Lord.

Opportunity may also arise to act as peacemakers in quarrels and to teach basic Christian doctrine to the uneducated. Taking account of local conditions and the persons concerned, prudence will dictate whether they should act themselves or through others.

8th They should make efforts to make friends with the leaders of their opponents, as also with those who are most influential among the heretics or those who are suspected of it yet seem not absolutely immovable. They must try to bring them back from their error by sensitive skill and signs of love. Some rules have been written on this elsewhere.

9th They must be well trained in cases of conscience. If any arise which involve difficulties, it would be best, as was said above, to take time for study or consultation; just as it is inappropriate to be too scrupulous and anxious, so also one should not be too lax and easygoing, with danger of spiritual harm both to oneself and to others.

10th All must try to have at their finger-tips the main points concerning dogmas of faith that are subjects of controversy with heretics, especially at the time and place where they are present, and with those persons with whom they are dealing. Thus they will be able, whenever opportunity arises, to put forward and defend the Catholic truth, to refute errors and to strengthen the doubtful and wavering, whether by lectures and sermons or in the confessional and in conversations.

11th As regards their manner, they must remember to behave with prudence and adaptability, accommodating themselves to people's character and feelings, and not 'putting new wine into old skins',[5] etc.

12th They should defend the Apostolic See and its authority, and attract people towards true obedience to it, in such a way as not to lose credibility, as 'papists', through ill-judged partisanship. On the contrary, their zeal in countering heresy must be of such a quality as rather to reveal love for the heretics themselves and a compassionate desire for their salvation.

13th They will be helped by wise use of the faculties to absolve granted by the Supreme Pontiff both to the Society and to themselves in particular. These are to be used 'for building up, not for breaking down',[6] with liberality but also with prudence.

14th It will be helpful to lead people, as far as possible, to open themselves to God's grace, exhorting them to a desire for salvation, to prayer, to alms and to everything that conduces to receiving grace or increasing it.

15th To help their hearers the better to take in, retain and put in practice what has been set before them, they should consider whether it would be useful to hand out any written notes, and if so, to whom.

16th   It will be very useful to choose a convenient place where they can say mass, hear confessions and preach, and where they can be found when people want them; this can be arranged with the help either of the Duke or of Leonard Eck,[7] or of other friends.

17th   It will be helpful for the priests of the Society to discuss their studies and sermons together and to evaluate each other's lectures, so that, if these contain any defects, through being admonished at home they may become all the more acceptable and helpful to their hearers.

MEANS TO THE SECONDARY AIM: NAMELY, THE ADVANCEMENT OF THE SOCIETY'S PURPOSES IN GERMANY

Besides those mentioned above, which might have been enough without proposing any other means, a few more particular points will be added. They practically reduce to this, that the Duke, and anyone else who has effective power, should be willing and authorized to have seminaries for the Society in their territories.

1st   Firstly, then, the task of setting up a college should be undertaken in such a way that it does not seem to be our members who are doing it, or at least so as to make it clear that they are doing it for the good of Germany, with no hint of seeking power or self-interest. It must therefore be made known that from its colleges the Society wants nothing for itself but hard work and the exercise of charity; and that the income is disbursed again to support poor students, so that, when they have completed their studies, they may become all the better workers in Christ's vineyard.

2nd   Those who are able to influence the Duke of Bavaria and those close to him (such as Eck) in the direction of founding a college should try to put the idea in their minds without actually suggesting its realization; thus they themselves will gently draw the conclusion from the premisses provided.

3rd   It will contribute to this end if they form a good opinion of the Society's Institute. Let them learn interesting facts relevant to it, and how by God's grace it has developed in so few years and in so many parts of the world. Such accounts will be heard all the more effectively if the Duke himself has begun to experience some benefit in his territories.

4th   Let the Duke understand how valuable it will be, not only for his own subjects but also for the whole of Germany, to have seminaries for such men, acting without motives of power or gain, who help others by their sound doctrine and exemplary life. Let him know how much good it has done to the King of Portugal [John III], who from one single college[8] of the Society has been able to supply apostolic workers for so many regions of the Indies, Ethiopia and Africa, and even beyond his territories.

5th Let him understand, too, how greatly the University of Ingolstadt could be strengthened if there were a college there, as in Messina and Gandía, offering languages and philosophy, not merely theology, with academic exercises modelled on the Paris system.[9]

6th Let him understand also what glory it will mean for him if he is the first to introduce into Germany seminaries in the form of such colleges, to foster sound doctrine and religion.

7th To show how easy an operation it can be, it should be made clear to him how colleges of this kind can be set up and endowed by amalgamation of benefices, either from some abbey or from some other religious foundation that has lost its usefulness, especially since the Supreme Pontiff and the leading cardinals are strongly in favour of founding colleges in this way.

8th If so many were to join the Society that the religious body being maintained at the Duke's expense were to grow rather large, he might be more easily persuaded to free himself from concern with expenses and teachers' salaries by endowing the institution with a permanent income.

9th A large part of these matters could, I think, be handled more fittingly and suitably by persons in the Duke's confidence, such as Eck and other friends of the Duke, especially people of importance, such as Cardinals who will be able to confirm by letter what the Supreme Pontiff thinks. Such action will be all the more effective if it is encouraged by successful results.

10th If the Duke or others should seem inclined to favour a freer regime in colleges, with the possibility of others besides religious living in, it may be indicated to him that they can be set up so as to consist partly of religious, partly of others, provided that the administration is entrusted to those who by teaching and example can help others to advance both in their studies and in religious commitment.

11th They should see whether any private individuals who have so rich an income or other means as to be able to start a college, may feel moved by God to do so. Steps should be taken to attract such people and other national figures in that direction, for the good of Germany as a whole.

12th   Apart from colleges, the Society's purposes can be advanced among young people and those of mature age (especially if they are better educated) by attracting them to join the Society. This will be effected by good example, by friendly contact through the Exercises and spiritual conversation, or by other means which are dealt with elsewhere. If such people cannot be supported on the spot, or if it is best for them not to stay, they should be sent to Rome or to some other centre of the Society; conversely others, if need be, could be summoned from elsewhere (for example, from Cologne or Louvain) and transferred to Ingolstadt.

25. Placating a parent over a son's vocation

1549
(No. 958 : II, 603–06 : Italian)

How does one reason with a man who is furious at his son joining the Society, especially when the father is a person of rank, brother of the Bishop of Tivoli, and ready to use force and ecclesiastical pressure to force his son's return? At one level, Ignatius agreed to move the novice far from Rome and defended the case (with success) at the Papal court. But it is at the level of appeal to good sense that this letter is most revealing.

Gerolamo Croce   4 December 1549
in Tivoli   from Rome

✝
JHS

Your Excellency,

May the supreme grace and everlasting love of Christ Our Lord be always in our favour and assist us continually, Amen.

[1] A few days ago, I wrote to Your Excellency at some length, but as I understand my letter was not given to you, I am rewriting the same letter now. The reason is that I have heard that Your Excellency has a grievance against us and appears very upset over your son, Lucio. As I am sure this results from your not having correct information on all that has taken place, I want to provide it, so that you may understand that our intention has been to do service to God, as well as to Your Excellency, in a matter that concerns you so greatly. Although there is no need for me to apologize in a matter in which the counsels and teaching of Jesus Christ are well known, yet for Your Excellency's comfort, and to honour the friendship we have in common with that of Our Lord, I wanted to write both the previous letter and this one.

[2] Your Excellency should realize that Lucio came to confession in our church without being recognized or having ever spoken to the confessor or anyone else in the house. He manifested to him his desire to withdraw and serve God according to our way of proceeding, insisting that the said confessor should get me to receive him. The confessor had recourse

to Master Polanco, who usually examines those who wish to enter our Society, and the next day brought Lucio for an interview with Master Polanco. The latter, on questioning him about his age and intention, and what moved him to that purpose, and for how long he had had the desire, was courteously informed that he was nineteen years old, and that it was his devotion to follow our Institute in order to detach himself from the sins of the world and better save his soul in greater service of God Our Lord, and that all his life he had found himself inclined to do good, although the company of some people had misled him somewhat, and that for upwards of about a year or thereabouts he had had this desire. Likewise in the other matters on which he was questioned concerning the religious life and the difficulties to be encountered therein, he showed himself very willing, and ready even to serve in hospitals, and to go on pilgrimage like a penniless beggar, and to serve in the kitchen, and at menial tasks.

[3] When Master Polanco saw his good disposition and the testimony his confessor gave, believing it was an inspiration from God, he made me a report, saying that during the interview he learnt that he was Your Excellency's son. In view of all this and to test his constancy, we thought it good that he should return to the house of Monsignor, the Bishop, and remain a few days in the usual way, during which he could come to our house to be fully examined. This he did, staying for eleven or twelve days. When Master Polanco (as I myself did not speak with him) invited him, if he wished, to come to our house, he showed a desire to go somewhere further away from his own home, so that he should not be upset in his plans. When it was suggested to him that he might go to Bologna or even to Padua, he intimated that he wanted to go even further away than that.

[4] It so happened that we were to send two persons from our house to Sicily, where there are two colleges of our Society, at Messina and Palermo. So we sent him along with them, as he showed that he greatly desired this and insisted on it. That same day they all received the holy sacrament at San Sebastiano, and rode with the post as far as Naples, and embarked there. We know that they have reached Sicily safely, where he will have every opportunity to acquire not only virtue, but learning of every kind, namely the humanities, philosophy and theology, reading up all these subjects with great diligence in our colleges under the guidance of very competent persons. Since Your Excellency and your brother, the Bishop, planned to make an ecclesiastic of this son of yours, I think you should regard it as a favour that you are relieved of the

worry and expense that you were incurring over him, and that Lucio is placed where he will become virtuous and educated, as I believe he will, doing honour and giving great comfort to Your Excellencies, as well as giving spiritual assistance, as I hope, to your city by means of the spiritual help that God wishes to effect through this instrument. As far as we are concerned moreover, Your Excellencies can well perceive that our only interest is the service of God and the help given to his soul and that of others who may be aided by him. Moreover he has not yet been admitted to our Society, nor will he be professed in it, even if he so wished, for eight or ten years, until his education be complete. Your Excellency can be quite certain, as I have said, that he will not be admitted to profession for many years to come, and in the meanwhile you will be able to see him and take comfort with him in Our Lord; at least on our part there will be no objection. Once this is understood, I leave it to you to consider whether you have more reason to be grateful to us for the service we have done you than to be annoyed with us.

[5] Sgr Luis de Mendoza[1] knew nothing until Lucio had left, and then I told him and the Pope's vicar in confession. When however I saw what had happened to your son, Master Alexander[2] (for whom we grieved as any reasonable person would have done, even if we hope, seeing his good character, that the Lord God has transferred him from this temporal to the eternal life), when, as I say, I saw what had happened, in order to save Your Excellency from having one sorrow on top of another, I gave Sgr Mendoza permission to inform you that your son, Lucio, was alive and well. I also had a letter sent to Lucio, telling him to write to Your Excellency from Naples.

[6] There is nothing else for the moment, except to pray God to grant us all His grace in abundance always to feel His holy will and to fulfil it completely. May He grant Your Excellency so much light and burning charity in His service that you may give heartfelt thanks to the divine Goodness for having placed your young son where he now is.

From Rome, 4 December 1549

26. Letter of resignation

1551

(No. 1554 : III, 303–04 : Spanish)

An autograph resignation document, announcing to the assembled Fathers, called together after the first ten years of the Society's existence, Ignatius's firm decision to request a replacement. The request in the letter was rejected with only one father objecting that such a holy man must be right ...

Ours in the Lord who are brothers in
the Society of Jesus 30 January 1551
in Rome from Rome

✠

IHS

1 As during various months and years something has been thought over and considered by me, without my feeling that any internal or external perturbation was coming into play, I want to express in the presence of my Creator and Lord, who is due to judge me for ever, all that I feel and understand, for the greater praise and glory of His Divine Majesty.

2 When I look realistically and, as far as I can see, without passion at my many sins, my many imperfections and my many sicknesses, internal and external, I have come to the honest conclusion on many and different occasions that I fall short, by an almost infinite degree, of possessing the proper qualities needed to hold my present post in the Society, which I hold by appointment and imposition.

3 My desire in the Lord is that careful consideration be given and another person elected, who would better (or not so badly) carry out my present charge of governing the Society.

4 Similarly my desire is that such a person, once elected, be entrusted with this post.

5 In addition to my feeling this desire, it is my judgement supported by very good reasons, that this post be transferred not only if whoever holds it will do better or not as badly, but even if he will do no better than I.

6   In consideration of all this, in the name of the Father, the Son and the Holy Spirit, my sole God and Creator, I depose and renounce completely and utterly the post that I now hold. My request and the supplication I make with all my soul to the professed fathers and to any others who may wish to join the meeting on this subject, is that they accept this petition of mine, which is so justified in the Divine Majesty.

7   In the case of there being, for the greater divine glory, a disagreement among those who are to receive and judge my request, I implore them out of love and reverence for God Our Lord kindly to commend it with great fervour to His Divine Majesty that in all things His most holy will be done to His greater glory and to the greater universal good of souls and of all the Society, and that they bear in mind in all things the greater praise and glory of God for ever.

In Rome, today Friday, 30 January 1551,

Ignacio

27. Consoling a sister on her brother's death

1551

(No. 1587 : III, 326–27 : Spanish)

*This letter illustrates the kindliness with women shown in a notable
proportion of the Ignatian correspondence, and hints at their affection
for him.*

Isabel de Vega[1]   21 February 1551
in Sicily   from Rome

✛

IHS

My Lady in Our Lord,

May the supreme grace and eternal love of Christ Our Lord salute
and visit you, bringing His most holy gifts and spiritual blessings.

I received your letter (11 January) and the presents you kindly sent
with it for this season of Lent.[2] May He who inspires your thoughtfulness and charity welcome and repay such charity with an overflowing
increase in this life and with the full perfection of it in His eternal glory.

You mention the envy you feel for your brother, Don Hernando, now
in God's glory, because you see that he is out of danger of ever offending
God Our Lord in this evil world. And on the other hand you say that
you worry continuously because he was called at such an early age. My
comment would be that such envy is holy and good, and so is the worry
– but on condition that the envy does not lack a willingness to conform
to the divine will in the continuation of this pilgrimage, however weari-
some it may be and for as long as may be needed for God's greater
service, and that the worry does not lack a very firm hope that God our
Creator and Lord already holds in His holy glory, or on the path that
will soon lead him there, the late beloved Don Hernando.

Given submission to God, just as old age does not of itself increase
the merits of eternal life, so neither does youth diminish them. On
the contrary, no matter how old a person is, whoever shares most fully
in the merits of Christ – thanks to the merits which He gives – is the
richest. There are many who replace many years and great works in
His service by their great willingness to serve God. And I trust Don

Hernando will have done that, thanks to God's infinite kindness, because the indications he gave in life and in death lead one reasonably to believe this. When all is said and done, we have so good a God, and so wise and loving a Father, that we should not doubt that His benign Providence draws out His children from this life at the best instant there is for entering the next. So I shall not write further about that.

You are quite right to say that there is no need for you to remind me in your letters to keep His Excellency, Don Juan de Vega, in my poor prayers and masses. May the divine and supreme Goodness deign to hear the constant supplication that I raise for His Excellency and for all his house and affairs.

Master Laínez[3] had already left for Florence (at the same time as the Duke[4]) so I shall have a copy of what you write in your letter sent on to him.

All here are in good health (although these last few days I have not had much of it myself) by the grace of God Our Lord.

May He in His infinite and supreme goodness grant His full grace to all of us, so that we may always feel His most holy will and accomplish it fully.

From Rome.

28. Refusing a Cardinal's hat[1]

Borgia 1552

(No. 2652 : IV, 283–85 : Spanish)

A letter of key importance: it shows the process of spiritual introspection when making an election.

Fr Francis Borgia   5 June 1552
in Spain[2]   from Rome

+

IHS

May the supreme grace and eternal love of Christ Our Lord always favour and assist us continuously!

[1] [*Observing his feelings*] In this business of the hat I think it will be best if I give you some account of the process of my feelings, as if I were examining my soul for myself, for the greater glory of God. As soon as I was informed for certain that the Emperor [Charles V] had given your name, and that the Pope [Julius III] was happy to make you a cardinal, I felt a kind of agreement or inspiration that I should prevent it as far as I could. At the same time *tamen* [however], as I was not certain about the divine will – so many reasons occurred to me for and against – I gave an order in our house that all priests should celebrate mass, and the laymen say prayers, during three days, asking that I might be guided in all things for the greater glory of God. During this period of three days, there were times, as I turned over the matter in my mind and debated it, when I felt some sort of fear and I lost that freedom of spirit to speak out and prevent the business. 'How do I know what God Our Lord wants me to do?' I thought, and I could not feel sure about preventing it. But at other times, when I began the normal meditations, I could feel these fears vanishing. I continued with this petition on several occasions, occasionally feeling fear, and occasionally the opposite. *Tandem* [at last], on the third day, I felt during the normal meditation, and ever since constantly, that my mind was quite made up and that I was decided – in a way that was gentle and left me feeling quite free – to impede the nomination to the best of my ability before Pope and cardinals. If I did not act thus, I would be (and indeed am) quite certain in myself that I would not give a

good account of myself before God Our Lord, rather a wholly bad one.

[2] [*To differ not to condemn*] Despite all this I was also convinced, and still am, that while it was God's will that I should adopt a clear position, if others adopted a contrary view and you were given this dignity, there would not be any contradiction whatsoever. The same Spirit could inspire me to take up one point of view for some reasons and inspire others to the contrary for other reasons, and what takes place would be the appointment requested by the Emperor. May God Our Lord bring about – in all things, in whatever way, and at all times – His own greater praise and glory.

[3] I think it would be appropriate for you in reply to the letter that Master Polanco is writing to you on my behalf[3] to explain what you feel about this business, and to what decision God Our Lord has prompted you in the past and at present. The letter should be so written that it can be shown whenever needed, leaving everything to God Our Lord so that His most holy will may be accomplished in all our affairs.

[4] There will be separate letters in reply to the points raised in yours of 13 March. I hope God Our Lord has granted success to your undertaking and to all your actions, as we all here in Rome have prayed to His divine Majesty, and may this letter find you in full health, of mind and body, as I desire and constantly ask of God Our Lord in my poor and unworthy prayers, to the greater glory of His divine Majesty. In His infinite mercy, may He always favour and assist us.

From Rome, 5 June 1552,

All yours in Our Lord,

Ignacio

29. Students experiencing poverty

1552

(No. 3107 : IV, 564–65 : Italian)

In sharp contrast to Letter 18, written by his secretary, this brief note has all the personal characteristics of Ignatius.

Students of the Society of Jesus   24 December 1552
in various parts of Europe   from Rome

Pax Christi,

[1] From various letters we gather that God Our Lord visits you with the effect of holy poverty, in other words, discomfort and lack of certain temporal things, such as would be necessary for health and well-being of the body. It is no small grace that His divine goodness deigns to grant this real taste of something that should always be desired by us in order to be conformed to our guide, Jesus Christ, in accordance with the vow and the holy Institute of our order.

[2] In fact I know of nowhere in the Society where the communication of this grace is not felt, although in some places more than in others. Moreover, if we compare ourselves with those brethren of ours in India, who in the midst of such great bodily and spiritual hardship are so badly provided for as regards food – in many places not eating bread, still less drinking wine, getting by with a little rice and water, or suchlike things of little nutritive value – being poorly dressed too, and in short destitute of all outward things, I do not think our suffering is too hard. We too can reckon ourselves to be in our Indies, which are to be found in all places.

[3] Given this, if the person whose duty it usually is to provide what is necessary cannot do so, we can resort to holy begging, whereby it may be possible to satisfy our needs. When despite all this God Our Lord wills that there should be something to suffer, the sick must not go short. Those who are in better health will be better able to exercise patience, and may Jesus Christ Our Lord, who made patience so lovable by example and teaching, grant it to us all, bestowing love of Him and delight in His service in place of all else.

30. Agreeing to be royal confessors

1553

(No. 3220 : IV, 625–28 : Spanish)

Ignatius clearly felt under very great obligations to John III of Portugal, a generous and devoted patron from the first year of the Society (1540), an exemplary Christian, and the door to the far Eastern mission of Xavier and many others.

Fr Diego Mirón[1]   1 February 1553
in Lisbon   from Rome

May the supreme grace and eternal love of Christ Our Lord always assist and favour us!

[1] [*A request refused*] We have learned from a number of letters received from Portugal that when His Highness [John III] asked with real devotion that you and also Fr Luis Gonçalves[2] should be his confessors, you both declined. This was not for fear that you may not be able in good conscience to have dealings with His Highness, whom you consider a good person (as you say in your letters), but because you considered such a dignity should be avoided no less than a bishopric or a cardinal's hat in that kingdom. For this same reason I believe that Fr Luis Gonçalves has stopped being confessor even to the prince.

[2] [*Criticism of the refusal*] For my part I can only whole-heartedly approve your intentions, and be edified as I weigh up your motives and see that they are grounded in humility and a sense of security: these are usually found more in a low position than in a high one. However when I take an overall view I am convinced that you have missed the mark by such decisions, bearing in mind the greater service and glory of God Our Lord. Firstly, because your religious profession and institute require you to administer the sacraments of confession and communion to people of all classes and ages. The same need for you to give spiritual consolation and help to a neighbour obliges both in the case of the very low and in that of the very high.

[3] [*Obligations to the King of Portugal*] Moreover, the whole Society from its very beginning owes a particular obligation to Their Highnesses,

one that exceeds that to any other Christian ruler, whether one considers their material help in good works or the exceptional affection and love shown, which of themselves should win our hearts. I cannot imagine any reason sufficiently strong to excuse us from giving our services to Their Highnesses in a matter that is so proper to our profession, when they have indicated that this would give them spiritual consolation and contentment. If one bears in mind the universal good and the greater service of God, then as far as I can see in the Lord, the greater benefit will result from this. For all members of the body share in the advantage of the head, and all subjects in that of their rulers. So the spiritual help given to Their Highnesses should be esteemed more valuable than that given to other people. As proof of this, simply consider one example: the influence that a reminder from a confessor would have had in bringing to a happy conclusion the business of the Patriarch of Ethiopia,[3] which is of such great importance to the salvation, I won't say only of many persons, but of many cities and provinces. While on that point, whether or not one of you does act as confessor to His Highness, please do not omit to remind him of this business, nor to write to me about what you have done, each time that you write to Rome.

[4] [*Personal danger*] But to return to the reasons why you should not decline this invitation, my own opinion is that even the argument based on your personal safety is not relevant. Obviously if our religious profession had no other purpose but to ensure our security, and if we were supposed to subordinate the good we do to keeping clear of danger, then we would not have to live among people and have contact with them. But according to our vocation, we have contact with everyone. As St Paul said, 'We ought to become all things to all people, so that we may gain all in Christ'.[4] If we go about with our intention upright and pure, 'seeking not our own gain but that of Christ',[5] then Christ Himself will look after us in His infinite goodness. Unless our profession clings to His powerful hand, it will not be enough to draw back from such dangers to avoid falling into them or even greater dangers.

[5] [*What people will say* . . .] As for the judgements that people may pass about your wanting honours and dignities, they will fall of their own accord under the force of truth and with the proof of your way of life, when they see that you maintain the lowliness that you chose in God Our Lord. So you ought not to avoid what may result in great service of God Our Lord, of Their Highnesses and of the common good, just because of what the multitude may say and think.

[6] [*Conclusion*] To conclude, in order to satisfy my conscience in this matter once and for all, I order you and Fr Luis Gonçalves in virtue of holy obedience to do what Their Highnesses may order you in this matter, either one or other of you, or some other member of the Society if you think best and His Highness agrees to his taking this position. Be confident in the divine goodness that all will turn out for the best by your following this path of obedience. You are to inform His Highness of this order imposed on you, showing him this very letter, if he wants to see it, or at least giving him the gist of it.

[7] Master Polanco will write at length about other matters, so I will not say more, except to commend myself greatly to your prayers and sacrifices. I beg God Our Lord to give us all the fullness of His grace, so that we may always feel His most holy will and accomplish it completely.

From Rome, 1 February 1553,

Yours in Our Lord,

Ignacio

31. The final word on obedience

1553

(No. 3304 : IV, 669–81 : Spanish)

This famous letter brings together strands of reflection and often phrases from letters over several years: the grades or degrees of obedience, the disputed doctrine of 'blind obedience', the vicar-of-Christ motif, and the chain-of-command model.[1] Obedience had not figured in the first promises of the companions, and Ignatius himself had little experience of its practice, as many of the theoretical considerations and idealistic examples of the letter make very clear. But since 1545 he had been alarmed by reports from Portugal, and in 1552 had learned that many members of the Society were refusing to accept orders, as indeed did Simão Rodrigues the Provincial. Ignatius sent a plenipotentiary, who moved Rodrigues to Spain and expelled a large proportion of the Province. In 1553, at the suggestion of Gonçalves da Câmara,[2] he prepared this letter. The precise context – the Portuguese crisis – must be borne in mind when assessing its doctrine.

Fathers and Brothers   26 March 1553
in Portugal   from Rome

Jhus

May the supreme grace and eternal love of Christ Our Lord greet you and visit you with his holy gifts and spiritual graces.

[§1] [*Desire for perfection*] It is a great consolation for me, dear brothers in Our Lord Jesus Christ, to hear how keenly and effectively you long to strive for your own perfection and for God's service and glory. These are longings that have been granted to you by the One who in His mercy has called you to this way of life. He it is who keeps you in this way and directs you to the blessed end which His chosen ones reach.

[§2] [*Obedience for members of the Society*] The truth is that, although I would like you to attain full perfection in all the virtues and spiritual graces, it is especially in obedience, more than in any other virtue (as you will have heard from me on other occasions[3]), that God fills me with longing to see you outstanding. I want this partly because of the extraordinary advantages that obedience of itself brings (that is why it is so highly recommended in word and example by Holy Scripture, both the Old and the New Testaments), but also because as St Gregory says, 'Obedience is the sole virtue that grafts the other virtues upon the mind and protects them when they are grafted'.[4] As long as obedience is flourishing, all the other virtues will be seen to flourish and to bear the fruit that I would like to see in your souls. Obedience is what He demands who through His obedience redeemed the world that had been lost through disobedience, 'becoming obedient unto death, even a death upon the cross'.[5]

In the case of other religious orders we can accept the fact that their members may excel us in fasting and vigils and the other mortifications that they observe, in all sanctity, following their way of life. However when it comes to the authenticity and perfection of obedience, with a real deposing of our own wills and a denial of personal judgements, my great desire, dear brothers, is that those who have chosen the Society as their way of serving God Our Lord should be outstanding, and I would like this obedience to be the distinctive sign of the Society's legitimate sons. They are not to regard the persons of the particular superiors they happen to obey, but always in them Christ Our Lord because of whom they obey.

[§3] [*The key principle*]   It is not because superiors happen to be very prudent, or very good people, nor because they are endowed with any other gifts of God Our Lord, that they are to be obeyed, but because they stand for Him and have His authority. As the eternal Truth says, 'He who listens to you, listens to me; he who despises you, despises me'.[6] On the contrary, just because some people are less prudent, they are not to be disobeyed in the areas where they are superiors. They are representatives of the One who is infallible Wisdom and who makes up for whatever may be lacking in His ministers. The same holds in cases where kindness and other good qualities may be missing: Christ Our Lord, after mentioning that 'The scribes and pharisees have sat upon the chair of Moses', stated explicitly, 'Do whatever they have told you to do, but do not follow their way of acting'.[7]

So no matter who your superiors are, I would like you all to practise recognizing in them Christ Our Lord, and to reverence and obey in them His divine Majesty with complete devotion. You will find this less of a novelty if you consider that St Paul orders obedience to be given even to secular and pagan superiors as if it was being given to Christ, from whom all properly ordered power descends. As he writes to the Ephesians: 'Obey your earthly masters with fear and trembling, single-mindedly, as serving Christ. Do not offer merely the outward show of service, to curry favour with others, but, as slaves of Christ, do whole-heartedly the will of God. Give the cheerful service of those who serve God not humans'.[8]

[§4] From this quotation you can deduce the status to be given in their hearts by members of religious congregations to those they have accepted not only as their superiors, but quite explicitly as substitutes for Christ Our Lord, so that He can direct and govern them in His divine service. You can also work out if these religious should regard them as just human beings or rather as vicars of Christ Our Lord.

[§5] [*From simply doing to wanting*]   Another principle that I would like to see firmly embedded in your minds is that the first degree of obedience, which consists in the performance of what is ordered, is a very low one and does not deserve the title of obedience because it fails to have the value of that virtue; it does not rise to the second degree, where the superior's wishes are made one's own. There should be not merely effective execution, but affective agreement, with an identifica-tion in wishing and not wishing. For that reason Scripture says, 'Obedi-ence is better than sacrificial victims'.[9] As St Gregory explains, 'In the case of sacrificial victims, the flesh of other beings is sacrificed; in the case of obedience, one's own will'.[10] Given the exceptional value of our wills, the sacrifice of them, offered in obedience to their Creator and Lord, is correspondingly great.

Perverting the order]   How great then is the misapprehension and danger that threatens those who think that they can legitimately set aside the wishes of their superiors! And here I am talking not only of matters associated with weaknesses of human nature, but even more about those areas normally considered as spiritual and holy, like fasts and prayers and any other sort of devotional practices. Cassian's wise words, in the 'Conference' attributed to Abbot Daniel, are worth noting: 'To disobey a superior's express order is exactly the same sort of disobedi-ence no matter if committed through attachment to work or out of a penchant for idleness. The damage is the same if a monastery's rules are broken for the sake of a vigil or for the sake of a nap. Finally, it is just as serious to neglect the abbot's order because you want to study as it is because you want to sleep.'[11] The busy occupation of Martha was excel-lent and so was the contemplation of Magdalen,[12] and her compunction and tears as she washed the feet of Christ Our Lord.[13] But all this had to take place in Bethany, which is said to mean 'the house of obedience'. As St Bernard remarks, it is as if Christ Our Lord wanted us to draw the conclusion, 'Neither the energy put into good work, nor the leisure of holy contemplation, nor the tears of repentance, could have been welcome to Him outside Bethany'.[14]

[§6] [*Offering one's freedom*]   Try then, dear brothers, to set aside completely your own wishes. With great liberality, offer the liberty that He gave you to your Creator and Lord present in His ministers. Consider that it is no small privilege of your freedom of will to be able to return it completely in obedience to the One who gave it to you. You do not destroy it in this way; rather you bring it to perfection as you put your own wishes in line with the most sure rule of all rightness, the will of God. For you the interpreter of that will is the superior who rules you in the place of God. Obviously you ought never to try and drag the wishes of your superior (wishes that for you ought to be considered those of God) behind your own. Otherwise instead of using God's will to guide your will, you would be using yours to guide God's, a perversion of Wisdom's order. The error of thinking that one observes obedience when a subject attempts to drag a superior to want what the subject wants is all too obvious; it is characteristic of minds that have been blinded by self esteem. St Bernard's words, those of a man of experience, are worth quoting: 'Those who openly or secretly intrigue so that their spiritual fathers will order them to do what they themselves already want, are deceiving and flattering themselves under the guise of obedience; instead of obeying their superiors in such matters, the superiors are obeying them!'[15]

Let me end this part: anyone who wants to rise up to the virtue of obedience must be prepared to rise to this second degree of obedience, which goes beyond the mere performance of an order to the adoption of the superior's wishes. Rather, it is a question of stripping oneself of one's own wishes and putting on the divine wishes interpreted by the superior.

[§7] [*From wanting to agreeing*]   However, those who set their sights on the complete and perfect offering of themselves to God must not stop at their wishes, but include their thoughts. Here appears another grade, the loftiest, of obedience. Not only should there be a single wish, but also a single sense with the superior. We have to subordinate our own judgements to the superior's, in so far as it is possible for a judgement to be moved by a pious desire.

[§8] Normally the understanding does not have the liberty proper to the will; it must assent to what is presented before it as true. Yet there are many instances where the probative force of the known evidence is not absolute, and where an option of the will may be made for one rather than another judgement. It is in cases such as these that truly obedient persons should bend themselves to see things as the superior does.

[§9] [*Offering one's mind*] Obedience is nothing less than a holocaust. It is there we can offer ourselves completely, without excluding any part of ourselves, in the fire of love to our Creator and Lord at the hands of His ministers. By obedience one puts aside all that one is, one dispossesses oneself of all that one has, in order to be possessed and governed by divine Providence by means of a superior. It seems self-evident that obedience cannot be restricted to the effective performance of an action coupled with a wish to go along with it. Included in obedience must be one's understanding, so that one feels that the superior is right in the order given, to the extent (as has been mentioned) that an option is possible.

[§10] [*Universal order*] Would to God that this sort of obedience of the understanding could be understood and practised by all those who belong to religious congregations as much as it is essential to them and pleasing to God Our Lord! When I say it is 'essential' I make a parallel with the heavenly bodies: for the lower to feel the pull and influence of the higher, it is essential for it to be in a proper inferior position, with due subordination and order from one body to another. Similarly, for one rational creature to be moved by another (as happens in obedience) it is necessary for the one moved to be below and subordinated so that one person can receive the pull and force from the person who moves. Such an inferior position and subordination cannot exist unless there is a conformity of both will and understanding between the subject and the superior.

[§11] [*Guidance*] Again, let us look at the matter with an eye on the purpose of obedience. Just as one may have desires that are wrong, so one may have ideas that are not right. To find a radical solution, we may opt for the expedient of agreeing to the wishes of a superior in order to ensure that our desires are not misdirected, and similarly one should be ready to adapt one's opinions to those of a superior in order to ensure that one's ideas are not misguided. 'Do not support yourself only on your own prudence', the Scriptures tell us.[16] (§12) That is why even in ordinary human affairs it is common wisdom that truly sensible people do not rely exclusively on their own judgements, especially where one is personally involved (as normally one is least competent to judge when passionately involved in a case oneself). (§13) But if in our personal affairs we ought to follow other people's judgements, even though they do not happen to be our superiors', rather than our own, surely *a fortiori* we ought to accept the opinion of a superior specially chosen by us as a guide in God's place for the interpretation of God's will. (§14) And the need in question becomes even more obvious in the sphere of spiritual things and persons. Great danger exists for anyone racing along the spiritual road if the brake of discretion is missing. So Cassian writes in the 'Conference' of the Abbot Moses: 'No other stratagem better serves the devil for dragging a monk headlong to death than to persuade him to neglect the advice of the elders and trust solely on his own judgement and decision.'[17]

[§15] [*Smooth functioning*] But there is another argument. When obedience does not include opinions, it is impossible for it to include successfully desires and actual performance. By nature the soul's power to desire follows the grasp of the understanding, so that in the long run it will be a great strain to maintain an obedience of will against one's own judgement to the contrary. Even if one can obey for a certain time – on the basis of the general principle that one must obey even when wrongly ordered – the best one can say is that it will not be for long and perseverance is impossible, or at least the perfection of obedience will be lost, viz. the love and joy of obeying. Whenever one is going against what one feels, it is impossible while that repugnance lasts to obey with love and joy. All the alacrity and promptness go. The person who is only half convinced will be half in doubt if it is worth doing what has been ordered. That simplicity of blind obedience, which has been so highly praised, is also lost. People start debating with themselves if the order given is right or wrong, and perhaps the superior will be criticized for ordering something to be done which does not please. Humility is lost as one prefers oneself in one way to the superior, though subordinating oneself in another. Fortitude in adversity is lost, and to sum up, so is all the real perfection of this virtue.

[§16] [*Strains and tensions*] And, conversely, when we fail to subordinate our opinions, our obedience is mixed with discontent, unhappiness, slowness, negligence, criticisms, excuses and other considerable imperfections and drawbacks. These impair the value and merit of obedience. Thus St Bernard rightly describes people who are unhappy, because ordered by the superior to do things with which they disagree, as follows: 'If you begin to be irritated, to criticize superiors and inwardly condemn them, then even if outwardly you comply with the order given, there is no real virtue of patience here, but a cloak of malice.'[18] [§17] Clearly the peace and tranquillity of the obedient will never reach those who keep in their hearts a source of constant unrest and disturbance, the personal conviction of the error of an order that obedience imposes. [§18] To prevent that, and to encourage the unity needed by every religious congregation to stay alive, St Paul is so insistent 'that all should have one mind and one voice'.[19] It is union in thought and will that preserves them. On the other hand, if unity is required between the head and the members, it is easy to decide if the head should consent to the members or the members to the head. And therefore one can conclude from all that has been said how essential is an obedience that includes the understanding.

[§19] [*The high point*] To form an idea of the exceptional intrinsic value of this obedience in the eyes of God Our Lord, one should weigh both the worth of the noble sacrifice offered, involving the highest human power, and the completeness of the self-offering undertaken, as one strips oneself of self, becoming 'a living victim'[20] pleasing to the Divine Majesty. Another indication is the intensity of the difficulty experienced as one conquers self for love of God, opposing the natural human inclination felt by us all to follow our own opinions. Strictly speaking obedience is a function of our wishing powers, as it makes us ready to fulfil the wishes of the superior, but as we have shown, it has to involve our judgement as well, bringing pressure upon our opinions so that they become those of the superior. In this way we can proceed, with all the forces of our minds, both wishes and opinions, to the prompt and perfect execution of an order.

[§20] [*Ways to attain obedience*] By now, dear brothers, I feel that you will be saying that you are well aware of the importance of this virtue, but you would like to know how to become perfect in it. My reply will be that of Pope Leo: 'Nothing is too lofty for the lowly, and nothing too rough for the gentle'.[21] Let us be unpretentious and let us be gentle! God Our Lord will grant the grace to enable you, gently and lovingly, to maintain constantly the offering you have made to Him. But now, leaving those recommendations to one side, there are three ways that I want to describe for you, which will be a great help to attain that summit of obedience where the understanding itself submits.

[§21] [*Christ in the superior*] FIRSTLY, as I said to you at the beginning, you ought not to pay any attention to whoever happens to be your superior, a person subject to human errors and failings. Instead, try to see who it is you are obeying in that person, Christ, the supreme wisdom, immense goodness, infinite love, incapable (as you well know) either of being tricked or of wanting to trick you. You have the certainty that it is out of love for Him that you have placed yourselves under obedience, submitting to the opinion of a superior in order to be most in agreement with the will of God. You can be equally certain that He will not fail, in His fidelity and love, to steer you by the means He has chosen for you. When the voice of your superior is heard giving an order, recognize it not as the voice of the person you know, but as the voice of Christ. This is what St Paul means when he exhorts the Colossians that subordinates should obey their superiors: 'Whatever you are doing, put your whole heart into it, as if you were doing it for the Lord and not for men ... Accept Christ as your master'.[22] Similarly St Bernard says: 'Whether God or a human person, as standing in for God, gives a particular order, it is to be accepted with equal care and deferred to with equal reverence, provided of course that the human person gives no order contrary to God'.[23] If you proceed in this way, using not the eyes of the flesh to look at the external person but the eyes of the soul to see God, then you will have no difficulty in bringing your desires and opinions into conformity with the rule you have adopted for your actions.

[§22] [*Pro rather than con*] The SECOND way is to be quick always to look for arguments on behalf of superiors' orders or wishes rather than against them. It will be easier to do this if one has affection for what obedience orders us to do, and the side-effects will be joy and facility in obeying. As St Leo says, 'One can hardly be forced by harsh constraint to serve when one is fond of serving'.[24]

[§23] [*Asking no questions*] The THIRD way to subordinate one's opinions is even easier and surer, and was practised by the holy fathers. It consists of adopting as a presupposition and belief, rather as we do when questions of faith are involved, that whatever orders are issued by the superior are really regulations of God Our Lord and expressions of His holy will. One then proceeds to do what is ordered quite blindly, without any further inquiry and with all the verve and promptness of a person wanting to obey. Presumably this is how Abraham set about complying with the order he was given to sacrifice his son Isaac.[25] Similarly in New Testament times, some of those holy fathers described by Cassian acted like this, e.g. Abbot John, who did not spend time wondering if what he had been ordered was something useful or not (on one occasion, the laborious watering of a dry stick for a year[26]), or if it was possible or impossible (like trying with all his force when ordered to move a stone that a great gang of men could not budge[27]).

[§24] [*Confirmed by examples*]   In order to encourage belief in this form of obedience we find cases of God Our Lord occasionally collaborating with miracles, e.g. a disciple of St Benedict, Maurus, was able to walk into a river without sinking when ordered by his superior;[28] and another disciple, ordered to bring his superior a lioness, captured her and brought her along.[29] There are other examples that you know about. My point is that the saints were in the habit of practising this way of subordinating their own opinions, simply presupposing that anything they were ordered to do was holy and in conformity with the will of God, without asking any more questions. So it ought to be imitated by those who want to be completely obedient in all things, where no obvious sin is involved.

[§25] [*Just representation*]   All that has been said does not exclude your bringing before your superiors a contrary opinion that may have occurred to you, once you have prayed about the matter and you feel that it would be proper and in accord with your respect for God to do so. However, to avoid feeling a suspicion that you may be acting out of self-interest and personal judgement it is important to remain quite indifferent as to the outcome, both before and after you have put your case. By 'indifferent' I mean ready not merely to do or not to do what is in dispute, but ready even to be happier with, and to consider better, whatever the superior may order.

[§26] [*The chain of command*]   All that I have said about obedience applies just as much to individuals in relation to their immediate superiors as it does to Rectors and local Superiors in relation with Provincials, to these in relation with the General, and to the latter in relation with the one appointed by God Our Lord as his superior, viz. Christ's vicar on earth. In this way a complete range of subordination[30] can be safeguarded – and as a result the union and love without which the wellbeing and government of the Society cannot be maintained (nor indeed those of any other religious congregation).

[§27] [*Celestial models*]   Such is the model on which divine Providence 'gently disposes all things',[31] so that the lower via the middle, and the middle via the higher, are led to their final ends. For example, among the angels there is a subordination of one hierarchy to another, and similarly in the heavens and in the movements of all bodies there is a pull from the higher to the lower, and among the higher, each in its due order, up to the supreme mover.   [§28]   The same can be seen upon the earth with respect to all secular constitutions that are duly established, and with respect to the ecclesiastical hierarchy, which is subordinated to a single overall vicar of Christ Our Lord. So much the better is the government where such subordination is safeguarded, and if this subordination is faulty in any society, the failings become all too obvious. [§29] That is the reason why I am so anxious that in this Society, where God Our Lord has given me a certain responsibility, there should be such a perfect practice of obedience – as if the Society's whole future depended on it.

[§30] [*Conclusion*] Let me finish as I began with the topic of obedience, without touching any other matters. My request to you, for the love of Christ Our Lord, who not only gave the precept but led the way with his example of obedience, is that you should all make a great effort to attain obedience by winning a glorious triumph over yourselves, conquering self in the loftiest and most difficult part of yourselves, the area where desires and opinions are formed. Then the true knowledge and love of God Our Lord will be able to take possession and control of your inner souls during all this pilgrimage, until the day when He leads you, along with many others won through your means, to the final and most blessed goal of eternal happiness.

I commend myself warmly to your prayers.

From Rome, 26 March 1553,

Belonging to all of you in the Lord,

Ignatio

32. The last call to Francis Xavier

Japan 1553

(No. 3505 : V, 148–51 : Spanish)

Written in fact after Xavier's death (3 December 1552), this letter – apparently so business-like – perhaps rationalizes a deep desire that they might meet one last time.

Fr Francis Xavier   28 June 1553
in Japan   from Rome

Ihs

May the supreme grace and eternal love of Christ Our Lord always assist and favour us!

Dearest brother in Our Lord,

[1] We received your letters (dated 28 January 1552[1]) later than was reasonable, because of the difficulty of the crossing from Portugal to Rome. That is why you will not have received a reply as soon as I would have wished. We have heard of the door that God Our Lord has opened to the preaching of His Gospel and to the conversion of the people in Japan and China by your ministry, and we find great consolation in the Divine Majesty, hoping that His knowledge and glory will spread wider every day, especially among people capable of consolidating and carrying further what has been gained, with the favour of God.

[2] [*The place for a superior*] I also think that it was a wise move to send Master Gaspar[2] and others to Japan and to China. But although I shall approve if you yourself have gone to China (you mentioned your intention of going there if you were not held back by affairs in India), as I can convince myself that it is the eternal Wisdom that is guiding you, still as far as one can judge from here in Rome, my opinion is that God Our Lord will make more use of you if you have stayed in India, and sent others with directions to do what you would have done. The reason is that in this way you will be carrying out in many places what you personally could do in only one place. But I shall go further: having considered the greater service of God Our Lord and the best way of spiritually helping most persons in those countries, and bearing in mind how much their good depends on Portugal, I have decided to order

you in virtue of holy obedience to select among the many routes open to you that which will bring you back to Portugal as soon and as safely as possible. So I order you in the name of Christ Our Lord to do this, even if it will be so as to return soon to India.

[3] [*Reasons for a return to Europe*] In order to help you convince those there who may want to detain you for the good of the Indies, I shall explain the reasons that here in Rome have persuaded me, while bearing in mind the needs of those countries.

[4] [*The King of Portugal*] Firstly, you are well aware how important for the upkeep and advancement of Christianity in those lands, as also in Guinea and Brazil, is the good order that the King of Portugal can grant from his kingdom. When a prince of such Christian desires and holy intentions as is the King of Portugal receives information from someone of your experience about the state of affairs in those parts, you can imagine what influence this will have on him to do much more in the service of God Our Lord and for the good of those countries that you will describe to him.

[5] [*The Roman Apostolic See*] Next, it is clearly important that correct and full information about the Indies should reach the Apostolic See, coming from someone who has the confidence of the See, so that proper provision may be made for the spiritual requirements that may appear necessary or very advisable for the good of that new Christianity, as also for the good of former Christians who live there. Now you are the most suitable to fulfil this office of all those living there, both because of the information you have, and because of the information about you that the Holy See has.

[6] [*Future missionaries*] You are also aware how important it is for the good of the Indies that the persons sent there should be suitable for the aim that one is pursuing in those and in other lands. Your coming to Portugal and Rome will be a great help in this respect, as not only will many be moved with the desire to go out there, but also you would be able to weigh up among those moved in this way who are suitable and who are not, who should go to one place and who to another. You can see for yourself how crucial it is to judge rightly in this matter. Moreover, all that you write from there to help people here understand the situation is not enough, unless you yourself (or someone with equivalent knowledge) deal with and come to know those who should be sent.

[7] [*Side-effects in other missions*] Quite apart from all these reasons, which apply to furthering the good of India, it seems to me that you would fire the King's enthusiasm for the Ethiopian project, which has

been planned for so many years without anything effective having been seen. Similarly, with regard to the Congo and Brazil, you could give no small help from Portugal, which you cannot do from India as there are not the same commercial relations. If people in India consider that your presence is important given your post, you can continue to act as superior no less from Portugal than from Japan or from China, and probably much better. Just as you have gone away on other occasions for longer periods, do the same now, and appoint the Rectors that you think fit, along with someone with overall responsibility for that area, along with the consultors that you consider appropriate, and God Our Lord will be with them.

[8] On other matters I rely on Master Polanco to inform you,[3] and commend myself whole-heartedly to your prayers. I implore the divine and supreme Goodness to give everyone the fullness of His grace so that we may always feel His most holy will, and fulfil it perfectly.

From Rome, 28 June 1553.

When you reach Portugal, you will be under obedience to the King to do whatever he will dispose for yourself to the glory of God Our Lord.

Completely yours in Our Lord,

Ignatio

33. Criteria in the choice of parish work

1554

(No. 4184 : VI, 347–48 : Latin)

An example of Ignatius dealing with pressure from an outsider, and trying to combine firmness with courtesy in defending a key principle for the Society's future work.

Sig. Giovanni Andrea Schenaldo[1]   24 February 1554
in Morbegno[2]   from Rome

✛

IHS

Grace, peace, etc.

[1] Despite all too little acquaintance with the one to whom I am writing, I must not seem to neglect my duty, and so I thought I should briefly reply to your kind letter, in which you try hard to persuade me that we should undertake the care of parishes, and on those grounds that you should keep our Father Andrea Galvanello[3] by you.

[2] It is true that our Society puts all its efforts into work to help and advance the salvation of souls. The principles both of charity and of our Institute impel us in that direction; the great spiritual need all over the world urges us ever more and more, and spurs on our own willing feet. What our Constitutions forbid is not that: it is the obligation that arises from pastoral responsibility and the contract of a parish priest. The professed members of this Society of ours have to be free and unencumbered, so that they may fly rapidly to any place on earth where greater hope of God's glory and the salvation of souls summon us like beacons; we must not stick to this or that place (unless we have a college or house there), but devote our efforts now to these, now to those, for a short term, freely and without charge.

[3] It should, however, go with modesty and indeed with prudence that, when others do something reasonably and in order, and are aiming purely to do God's will, we either approve, or at least do not disapprove without adequate reflection. Everyone who is a soldier for Christ under the banner of holy Church and with His approval should be allowed 'to be fully assured in his own mind'.[4] Nevertheless I take in good part what

you have written, and put it down to your piety and your charitable concern for your own people.

I will not mention anything else, since I have written to the authorities of your commune.

Best wishes in the Lord Jesus Christ.

Rome, 24 February 1554.

34. Financial worries

1555

(No. 5256 : VIII, 552 : Spanish)

Although in the hand of Polanco, these lines capture the voice of Ignatius and disclose an important aspect of his personality.

Fr Alfonso Román (by commission)   14 March 1555
in Zaragoza[1]   from Rome

Postscript

The copy ends here, and I have nothing to add except for a more detailed memorandum on the financial budget (I am sending a copy to Fr Tablares).

Apart from what is in the memo Fr Francis [Borgia] will have learned the other news, such as that about the Princess[2] and other unforeseen events and happenings in other regions.\

Please bear with my talking of financial matters as if they had top priority. As I have more than 160 hungry mouths to feed, not to mention the upkeep of the buildings, it is quite true that the letters likely to bring me most comfort will be letters of credit. They help me run the colleges, so I run after them for the colleges' sake – primarily out of holy obedience that has placed me in this and similar affairs. May Christ Our Lord accept all this activity! It is certainly true that even if obedience were not there to make me see how important all this is, it would be enough to consider how great and how outstanding in God's service this work is, for which such activity is very necessary.

I commend myself to your prayers.

35. Norms for dealing with Superiors

1555

(No. 5400ᵃ : IX, 90–92 : Spanish)

An Instruction rather than a 'letter', the first seven norms have in mind the strong-willed characters who, paradoxically, are often attracted to the obedience of a religious life; somehow their contribution has to be encouraged, while protecting their Superiors' independence of decision.

Fathers and Brothers   29 May 1555
anywhere in the world   from Rome

✢

IHS

THE WAY TO TREAT AND HAVE DEALINGS WITH ANY SUPERIOR

1st   Anyone having to deal with a Superior should previously have digested and weighed up the issues, either on his own or with others according to the greater or lesser importance of the matter. However, should this be of slight importance or very urgent and there is no time to ponder and consult, each should use his discretion and decide without further ado if he should bring it to the Superior's notice or not.

2nd   Once the issues have been digested and weighed up, let him propose them saying, 'Such a point has been considered by me or by others' (as the case may be); 'my/our opinion was that it might be best to act in this/that way', but he should never say to a Superior in his dealing with him that so and so 'will' be the best, but always use the hypothetical form, that it 'might' or 'may' be the best.

3rd   Once the matter has been presented in this way it will be up to the Superior to reach a decision or to wait a while in order to weigh up the issues, or to consult afresh with the person or persons already consulted, or to appoint others to examine and decide the issue, according to its greater or lesser importance and difficulty.

4th   If an answer seems called for to a decision or reaction of the Superior and it has been presented, once the Superior has repeated his decision there should not be any further answer or discussion for the time being.

5th   After the Superior has come to a certain decision, should the person bringing up the issue feel that a different course of action would be better, or if he has the impression that it has a certain weight, even though he suspends his judgement, then three or four hours later or on another day he can consult the Superior again if this or the other would not be better, but always having recourse to such a form of language and choice of words that no disagreement or quarrel may result or appear to result, keeping quiet once a decision has been reached on that occasion.

6th   Nevertheless, although a matter has been decided once and then again, one may bring up in the same way what one feels or the thoughts one has on that decision, perhaps a month later or after an even longer period. For one discovers many aspects by trying things out over a period, and things also change in time.

7th   Again, the person dealing with a Superior should adapt himself to the latter's disposition and natural capacities, speaking clearly and distinctly and at times that are suitable as far as possible.

[NORMS FOR OFFICIAL LETTERS]

8th   If one plans to write to catch the post on a Saturday (or on some other regular or special post-day to places outside Italy), as far as possible one should not wait for the day itself or the day before to write in a hurry. Instead an effort should be made to consider and take note of what is to go with the Saturday post from the previous Sunday to the end of Wednesday, so that as little as possible remains to be answered to previous letters. Then one has Thursday, Friday and Saturday in hand to consider and reply if something of importance crops up later.

9th   Letters to Italian houses should be on a monthly basis, and Rectors of houses are to be informed of this regulation, except when matters occur that cannot wait that long.

10th   Letters further afield are to be on a three-monthly basis, unless there is something important, or the postal system requires otherwise.

[THE ADMISSION OF CANDIDATES]

11th   With regard to accepting new members to the Society in Italy, copies are sent to all the colleges of the points to be considered, dealing with the qualifications required in those to be admitted to the Society. Nobody should be admitted in other houses nor sent to Rome until information has been supplied on each of the points mentioned.

12th   Nevertheless if the candidates very clearly possess all the qualifications mentioned in the points, so that no doubt is possible, then if they are able to join, they can be admitted or even sent to Rome, if such action appears to be strongly advisable given their exceptional quality or the danger involved in waiting (the decision being left to the good judgement of the Superiors). However it is far better to inform the General in Rome and wait for a reply, as it may not be convenient for the house in Rome even if it would be for the candidates.

13th   The same documents and regulations drawn up for those in Italy and Sicily (the latter should always be understood when Italy is mentioned) are to be sent to all other regions. As a general rule it will be useful if the other regions are informed about what is customary here, so that they can make the best possible use of it. But it is quite true that in areas very far away from Rome, in other kingdoms, there is no need to consult the General about admitting candidates and sending them to Rome. Instead it will be up to the Commissioner or Provincial to use his charity and discretion in place of such a consultation, and lower Superiors or Rectors should consult with them, as there could well be cases that would not benefit from the delay involved with the General.

[DISTRIBUTION OF THIS INSTRUCTION]

14th   The arrangements mentioned here are to apply wherever those of our Society happen to be present. So a copy of what is written should be sent to them and entered in the Register[1] kept here in Rome, with a footnote saying that it has been sent to all areas and noting where it has been received; then reference to the dispatch and the request for notification of receipt should be made every time that letters are written until the notification is received.

15th   This same letter should be sent to India, and the Provincial there should send on the Instruction to the furthest areas of his jurisdiction, and from Portugal the same dispatch can be sent to Brazil and the Congo. However, in the case of such far-off lands, especially among people without the faith or only recently Christianized, although they can make use of the present letter as far as they can, it is up to the discretion of those in charge, bearing in mind the nature and special circumstances of those lands, to proceed in the way that they consider most appropriate for the greater glory of God and the greater spiritual good of all.

36. The Society and the Inquisition
1555
(No. 5471 : IX, 226–27 : Spanish)

Ignatius's own brushes with the Inquisition had marked him deeply, and he was well aware of the limitations restricting the work of its officers. Yet a request from the King of Portugal, the Society's most enthusiastic and efficacious supporter, carried great weight. In this letter he tries to limit the damage caused by too facile an acceptance of the offer of responsibility for the Portuguese Inquisition, and although the lines say 'yes', the message to be read between them is 'only if explicitly ordered by the Pope', which seems a polite way of saying 'No, thank you'.

Fr Diego Mirón[1]   20 June 1555
in Portugal   from Rome

Pax Christi,

May the supreme grace and love of Christ Our Lord always assist and favour us!

[1] I have learned from your letter (4 May) that His Majesty [John III] is inclined to urge our Society to take charge of the Holy Office of the Inquisition in Lisbon (now that the person responsible for it under the Cardinal Infante has died), provided this does not clash with our Institute; and also of your reply to His Majesty.

[2] It is certainly true that this business requires much reflection, and that there are strong arguments either way. So in addition to considering the question myself and commending it to God Our Lord in my prayers, I appointed a committee of six (Master Laínez, Master Salmerón, Master Bobadilla, Dr Olave, Dr Madrid and Master Polanco) to offer mass during three days and to consider and discuss the matter, acquiring additional information from Luis Gonçalves, apart from that you have sent from Portugal, and talking about it with him. They were then to give me their opinions in writing.

[3] The summary of what we finally decided in Our Lord is that everything should be left to His Highness, and that we would obey in whatever way he thought we should for the glory of God Our Lord. To

undertake such a task does not clash with our Institute, so there is no reason why our Society, which considers itself to belong to His Highness in Our Lord, should refuse to undertake work that is of such importance in his service and for the purity of religion in that kingdom.

[4] However we also feel it advisable, if many disadvantages are to be avoided, that His Majesty should kindly write to the Pope [Paul IV] asking him to order us to accept this task. As His Holiness, when still Dean of the Cardinal Inquisitors, wanted the Society to undertake similar duties in this regard, such a move would not be contrary to his wishes. It would also help if a letter were written to our Protector, Cardinal de Carpi, who is at present Dean of the Inquisitors; and another letter to the King's ambassador, so that he can undertake the business.

[5] Still, if His Majesty considers it unsuitable to write these letters, we shall still do whatever His Majesty orders us to God's glory. Should he order us to accept the charge, then representation will be made to His Highness pointing out that in view of the goal at which we are aiming, several arrangements² should be made that will help the Society to perform this holy task with greater efficacy and edification.

[6] If His Highness decides that we should not wait for a reply from the Pope before beginning to take part in the proceedings, then one or two could start to lend their services in this department until they assume full responsibility on orders from His Holiness. However, I have already written that, once representation has been made, one should do whatever is more to the pleasure of His Highness.

For other matters I leave the answers to Master Polanco, commissioned by me to write further. I only add that I commend myself very much to your prayers.

From Rome, 20 June 1555.

37. Catechizing the sign of the cross

(Appendix, No. 10 : XII, 666–67 : Italian)

An extract chosen to give some idea of how Ignatius would have preached, sometimes to children, using very simple words and gestures to illustrate theological points.

PRÉCIS OF MASTER IGNATIUS'S PREACHING ON CHRISTIAN DOCTRINE

... To make the sign of the cross we put a hand to the head to indicate God the Father, who proceeds from no one.

When we put our hand to the middle it indicates His Son, Our Lord, who proceeds from the Father and who came right down to the womb of the most holy Virgin Mary.

When we put our hand to one side and then to the other it indicates the Holy Spirit, who proceeds from the Father and the Son.

When we join our hands, this indicates that the Three Persons are one true essence.

When we place the sign of the cross on the mouth,[1] it signifies that in Jesus, our Saviour and Redeemer, the Father and the Son and the Holy Spirit are only one God, our Creator and Lord, and that the divinity was never separated from the body of Christ at his death ...

38. Consoling the mother of a student

1556

(No. 6087 : X, 483–84 : Spanish)

The widow addressed here, a relative of the Duke of Nájera, Ignatius's former employer, had encouraged her son in his vocation to the Society (1554). Ignatius clearly felt sympathy for her, and wrote two letters[1] to thank and console her.

Juana de Valencia   8 January 1556
in Malaga   from Rome

✢
Jesus

The highest grace, etc.

[1] After I had replied to a letter of yours received a few months ago I received another dated 10 April. Truly, the more one sees in your letters how great is your motherly love for Don Fadrique, the more you hearten us by the conformity of your will with that of God!

[2] The same Spirit that drew Don Fadrique from the world into the religious life seems to have instructed you to be calm and content with his decision, making up by the strength of grace for the weakness of nature. May the same Spirit be pleased to increase always His light and charity in your soul, so that every day you may find greater consolation when you see that the person you so love is employed in the service of the Person who should be loved above all things, and in whom and for whose glory all those other things should be loved.

[3] For the rest, Don Fadrique is now yours in the Lord, as much as (indeed even more than!) ever before. The latter's love will bring to perfection the natural love which he should have as a son. Once he has made progress in his preliminary literary studies (and this should not take long, given the flair he has) he will be able to visit you one day in person. In the meanwhile, thanks to the merit he gains by his virtue, his religious observance and exemplary conduct, he cannot fail to win our highest esteem and to be greatly loved in Christ by all who have contact with him. As you recommend it so strongly, special care will be taken of his health.[2]

May the supreme goodness of God guard your own health for His divine service, and may His perfect grace be granted to all of us always to feel and fully accomplish His most holy will.

From Rome, 8 January 1556.

39. Norms for food in Louvain

1556

(No. 6454 : XI, 374–75 : Latin)

One appreciates the problems facing the founder of a religious order in which Spanish and Flemish Jesuits were to eat together. Here the author of the 'Rules for Eating'¹ was perhaps urged on by his favourite disciple, Pedro de Ribadeneira, who found himself in Flanders and unhappy with beer.

Fr Adrian Adriaenssens (Rector)   12 May 1556
in Louvain   from Rome

✢

IHS

Pax Christi,

[1] We have received your letter of the end of March. To reply briefly to what occupies almost the whole of it: we praise, as far as is possible, your frugality, economy and good example to others in what concerns food. However, we judge that it is not a good idea to cut down on what is necessary for maintaining or restoring health, as is prescribed by a doctor (who will be aware of our poverty and religious profession). So much in general.

[2] More in particular, for those who are well and in good condition, it is good to get used to ordinary and easily procured kinds of food and drink; this is in accord with reason and with our Institute, which says that our members should keep to an ordinary standard of fare. So if someone's health allows him to get used to beer or even water, or cider where that is the common drink, he should do so, and not drink imported wines, which cost more and make a less good impression.

[3] Nevertheless some may have really poor health, such as (in your community) Masters Adrian Witte, Bernard [Olivier] and Pedro de Ribadeneira. If they treat their poor bodies kindly, they can keep well enough to do religious and charitable work, helping souls and building up the faith of others. But if they do not, they get ill and prove less useful to others, indeed a burden, as happened to Masters Adrian and Bernard in Italy. I would judge that they ought not to have to get used to

food and drink of poorer quality, except in so far as they could do so without harm to health. I would rather that the good things God offers were given to servants of God, and to those who are ready to bear heavy burdens for Christ, than to others who are of less service to the common good. All the same, care should be taken that superfluities do not creep in in place of necessities, or what gratifies the senses in place of what is best for health; a good custom must not grow into an abuse. If someone should have occasion to consume in public a diet that doctors have prescribed as necessary for him, but which could make an unfavourable impression, he should take it in private.

[4] To conclude: short of causing offence, catering should be based on what is good for health. So much in general: it will be for prudence to go into particulars and decide on them in the light of circumstances.

May the Lord give us the light of holy discernment, so that we may use created things by the light of the Creator. Amen

Rome, 12 May 1556.

P.S. To have different kinds of food or drink served at the same table, as is required respectively for the well or unwell, is neither unusual nor disapproved of by spiritual masters. If there are present any people of less mature understanding who might take offence, prescribed diets can be consumed somewhat apart, keeping in mind what Paul says about not giving offence to the 'weaker brethren'.[2]

40. Reacting to obstacles in Zaragoza

1556

(No. 6677 : XII, 119 : Spanish)

In 1555 the Archbishop of Zaragoza had launched a threat of excommunication against the Jesuits when they celebrated mass in his cathedral city without due permission; an intervention by the Princess Regent of Spain (a secret member of the Society) helped to pacify the situation, but animosities remained. Shortly before his death Ignatius dictated this characteristic little note to encourage the Rector.

Fr Alfonso Román   14 July 1556
in Zaragoza   from Rome

It is a matter of common experience that greater good follows wherever there has been greater opposition, and the Society's foundations tend to improve in such circumstances. So it looks as if there will be a very large and imposing spiritual construction in Zaragoza given that such deep foundations of opposition have been laid. Such is the hope we should have in what God Our Lord will do.

THE SPIRITUAL EXERCISES

Introduction

As mentioned in the Preface the *Spiritual Exercises* was the only work of Ignatius published during his lifetime (in a very limited edition) and strictly speaking no author's copy has survived.[1] However it has become customary to refer to a Spanish manuscript preserved in the Roman archives of the Society of Jesus as the 'Autograph' because, although not written by Ignatius, it bears numerous notes and corrections in his hand, probably dating from about 1550. In addition there is a very literal Latin translation,[2] which is of particular importance as it seems to antedate the Autograph by over ten years and Ignatius may well have had a hand in the translation. Finally, there is another Latin translation, the *Vulgata*, the work of André des Freux, a French Jesuit well trained in classical Latin, which was commissioned in order to be submitted for Papal approval in 1548 and therefore couched in a more elegant style. Although some have claimed that this should be regarded as the authoritative text, most scholars are agreed that its preoccupation with elegance exacts a certain lack of fidelity.

The reluctance shown by Ignatius to any wide dissemination of his text is easily understandable when one accepts that it was always through the *spoken* word that he introduced people to the *Exercises*. Somebody is required to 'give' the exercises, and only persons who have experienced the process that these exercises set in motion can do this.

The process itself is no great mystery, as the very first Annotation (Exx. 1) makes clear: a person wants to dispose him/herself before God, so that the inner heart can face God with honesty. In some ways this is no more mysterious than walking or running, but just as most people would agree that reading a book is not the most helpful way to learn to walk or run, so anybody who has actually experienced praying to God for light about the honesty of one's life will acknowledge that books are no great help.

Ignatius prepared these notes so that somebody could instruct somebody else in the steps of the process, and would have some warning of the sorts of reactions that may occur – from outright rejection to wild enthusiasm (both equally dangerous). The idea is to bring the retreatant gently into a state where prayer before God can be undertaken while at the same time one looks honestly at the failings or drawbacks which hinder that prayer. Eventually the attention focuses more and more on the figure of Jesus Christ, and on his liberating message. It is in the light of the One who claimed to be the Way, the Truth and the Life that the exercitant examines whether the life he or she is leading is as it should be. And frequently it is the shock of this self-questioning that arouses great personal emotions, doubts, joy and pain. Usually somebody is then needed to help one cope with the test. And the resolutions taken have to be able to stand the questions raised by the death of Christ, and by His glory.

However, this general process gives rise to a wealth of remarks about a series of techniques (concerning self-knowledge, ways of praying, making choices, etc) to which Ignatius returns constantly in his other writings, and which of themselves justify the inclusion of the *Exercises* here. In any case Ignatius's text is now an acknowledged heirloom in the spiritual heritage of the world.

In the translation the Autograph has served as the basic text, though there are references to the Latin translations in the notes. The paragraph numbers follow standard convention for reference purposes. The English translation has passed through almost as many hands as did the original text: it stems from a version made by William Yeomans, and was then radically revised by Michael Ivens and Joseph Munitiz, with the help of further suggestions by Philip Endean.

NOTES

1 The fundamental work on the manuscripts of the *Exercises* was completed by two Spanish Jesuits, José Calveras and Cándido de Dalmases. A useful survey is included in the latter's edition (see Bibliography).

2 Slightly shortened; there are two slightly different versions, dubbed *Versio prima* 1 and *Versio prima* 2, with minimal differences.

Annotations

JHS

[1] ANNOTATIONS[1] (OR NOTES) TO PROVIDE SOME EXPLANATION OF THE SPIRITUAL EXERCISES THAT FOLLOW. THEY ARE INTENDED TO BE OF ASSISTANCE BOTH TO THE PERSON GIVING THEM AND TO THE PERSON WHO IS TO RECEIVE THEM.

ANNOTATION 1. The term 'spiritual exercises' denotes every way of examining one's conscience, of meditating, contemplating, praying vocally and mentally, and other spiritual activities, as will be said later. For just as strolling, walking and running are exercises for the body, so 'spiritual exercises' is the name given to every way of preparing and disposing one's soul to rid herself of all disordered attachments,[2] so that once rid of them one might seek and find the divine will in regard to the disposition of one's life for the good of the soul.

[2] ANNOTATION 2. The person who gives to another a way and a plan for meditating or contemplating must provide a faithful account of the events to be meditated or contemplated, simply running over the salient points with brief or summary explanations. For if a person begins contemplating with a true historical foundation, and then goes over the historical narrative and reflects on it personally, one may by oneself come upon things that throw more light on the history or better bring home its meaning. Whether this results from one's own reasoning or from the enlightenment of divine grace, this is more gratifying and spiritually profitable than if the director[3] had explained and developed at length the meaning of the history. For it is not so much knowledge that fills and satisfies the soul, but rather the intimate feeling and relishing of things.

[3] ANNOTATION 3. In all the spiritual exercises that follow we bring the intellect into action in order to think and the will in order to stir the deeper affections. We should therefore note that the activity of the will, when we are speaking vocally or mentally with God Our Lord or with His saints, requires greater reverence on our part than when we are using the intellect to understand.

[4] ANNOTATION 4. The exercises that follow are made up of four

Weeks, corresponding to the four parts into which these Exercises are divided: namely, the First is the consideration and contemplation of sins; the Second is the life of Christ Our Lord up to, and including, Palm Sunday; the Third, the Passion of Christ Our Lord; the Fourth, the Resurrection and Ascension, with the three ways of praying. However this does not mean that each Week necessarily lasts for six or eight days, for in the First Week some may happen to be slower in finding what they are looking for, namely contrition, sorrow, and tears over their sins. Then again, some may be more rapid than others, and some more stirred or tried by various spirits. Therefore it may be necessary sometimes to shorten the Week and at other times to lengthen it, and similarly in the subsequent Weeks one must always be seeking whatever is appropriate to the matter under consideration. But the Exercises should be completed in about thirty days.

[5] ANNOTATION 5. It is very profitable for the exercitant to begin the Exercises in a magnanimous spirit and with great liberality towards one's Creator and Lord, offering Him all one's power of desiring and one's liberty, so that the Divine Majesty may make use of one's person and of all that one has according to His most holy will.

[6] ANNOTATION 6. When the director giving the Exercises becomes aware that the exercitant is not affected by any spiritual movements, such as consolations or desolations, and is not being stirred by various spirits, the director should question the exercitant closely about the Exercises, whether they are being made at their appointed times, and in what way, and similarly whether the additions are being carefully followed. The director should inquire in detail about each of these points. There are remarks below on consolation and desolation [Exx. 316–24] and on the additions [Exx. 73–90].

[7] ANNOTATION 7. If the one giving the Exercises sees that the one receiving them is desolate and tempted, it is important not to be hard or curt with that person, but gentle and kind. Let the director give the exercitant courage and strength for the future, and lay open before that person the cunning tricks of the enemy of human nature, and encourage the person to prepare and make ready for the consolation that is to come.

[8] ANNOTATION 8. As the director giving the Exercises becomes aware of the particular needs of the receiver in the matter of desolations and cunning tricks of the enemy, as well as in the matter of consolations, the director will be able to instruct the exercitant about the rules of the First and Second Weeks for recognizing various spirits [Exx. 313–27, 328–36].

[9] ANNOTATION 9. The following should be noted when the exercitant is making the Exercises of the First Week. If it is a person with no previous experience of spiritual things, and who is tempted crudely and obviously, as for example by having obstacles suggested preventing advancement in the service of God Our Lord, such as fatigues, shame and fear inspired by worldly honour, etc, the director should not talk to that person about the Second Week rules for various spirits, because just as the First Week rules will be very profitable to such a person, so will those of the Second Week do harm, as they deal with questions too delicate and too elevated to be understood.

[10] ANNOTATION 10. When the giver of the Exercises sees that the receiver is being assailed and tempted under the appearance of good, that is the time to speak to such a person about the Second Week rules mentioned above. For normally the enemy of human nature tempts more under the appearance of good when a person exercises him- or herself in the illuminative life,[4] which corresponds to the Exercises of the Second Week. Such temptations are less common in the purgative [way of] life, which corresponds to the Exercises of the First Week.

[11] ANNOTATION 11. Whilst the exercitant is in the First Week it is better for such a person to know nothing of what will have to be done in the Second Week. Rather, the exercitant should strive to obtain what is being looked for in the First Week as if there were nothing good to be hoped for in the Second.

[12] ANNOTATION 12. The giver of the Exercises should remind the receiver frequently that since an hour has to be spent in each of the five exercises or contemplations to be made each day, one should always try to find contentment in the thought that a full hour has indeed been spent in that exercise – and more, if anything, rather than less! For the enemy usually leaves nothing undone in his efforts to procure a shortening of the hour of contemplation, meditation or prayer.

[13] ANNOTATION 13. It should also be noted that whereas in time of consolation it is easy and undemanding to remain in contemplation for the full hour, in time of desolation it is very difficult to last out. Consequently, in order to go against desolation and overcome temptations the exercitant must always stay on a little more than the full hour, so that one gets used not only to standing up to the adversary, but even to overthrowing him.

[14] ANNOTATION 14. If the giver sees that the receiver is going along in consolation and full of fervour, the giver should forewarn the exercitant against making any unthinking or precipitate promise or vow, and the

more unstable in temperament the person is known to be, the more should that person be warned and admonished. It is true that one person can legitimately move another to enter a religious order, with the intention of making vows of obedience, poverty and chastity, and it is also true that a good work done under vow is more meritorious than one done without a vow. Nevertheless careful consideration must be given to the individual temperament and capabilities of the exercitant, as well as to the helps or hindrances that may be met in fulfilling promises that such a person might want to make.

[15] ANNOTATION 15. The one giving the Exercises ought not to move the one receiving them more to poverty or to any particular promise than to their contraries, nor to one state or way of life more than to another. Outside the Exercises it can indeed be lawful and meritorious for us to move all who seem suitable to choose continence, virginity, religious life and every form of evangelical perfection, but during these Spiritual Exercises it is more opportune and much better that the Creator and Lord communicate Himself to the faithful soul in search for the will of God, as He inflames[5] her in His love and praise, disposing her towards the way in which she will be better able to serve Him in the future. Hence the giver of the Exercises should not be swayed or show a preference for one side rather than the other, but remaining in the middle like the pointer of a balance, should leave the Creator to work directly with the creature, and the creature with the Creator and Lord.

[16] ANNOTATION 16. For this, namely, that the Creator and Lord may work more surely in His creature, if the soul in question happens to be attached or inclined to something in an ill-ordered way, it is very useful for her to do all in her power to bring herself round to the contrary of that wrong attachment. This would be the case, for example, if a person were bent on seeking to obtain an appointment or benefice, not for the honour and glory of God Our Lord, nor for the spiritual good of souls, but for one's own advancement and temporal interests. One must then set one's heart on what is contrary to this, insisting upon it in prayers and other spiritual exercises, asking God Our Lord for the contrary, namely, not to want that appointment or benefice or anything else, unless the Divine Majesty gives a right direction to one's desires and changes the first attachment, so that the motive for desiring or keeping this or that thing be solely the service, honour and glory of the Divine Majesty.

[17] ANNOTATION 17. There is much to be gained if the giver of the Exercises, while not wanting to ask about or know the exercitant's self-

chosen thoughts or sins, is given a faithful account of the different agitations and thoughts brought by the different spirits; because depending on the greater or lesser degree of progress, the director can give the exercitant some spiritual exercises that will be appropriate and suited to the needs of a soul agitated in a particular way.

[18] ANNOTATION 18. The Exercises are to be adapted to the capabilities of those who want to engage in them, i.e. age, education or intelligence are to be taken into consideration. Hence someone uneducated or of poor health should not be given things that cannot be undertaken without fatigue and from which no profit is to be derived. Similarly, in order that each may feel more at ease and derive the best benefit, what is given to each exercitant should be in accordance with his or her dispositions. Hence, one who is hoping to gain some instruction and to reach a certain level of peace of soul can be given the particular examen [Exx. 24–31], then the general examen [Exx. 32–43]; also together with this, for half an hour in the morning, the way of praying about the commandments, capital sins, etc [Exx. 238–48]. Such persons can also be recommended to confess their sins each week, and if possible to receive communion every fortnight, and better still every week, if they are so inclined. This arrangement is more suited to unformed and uneducated people, to whom explanations can be given of each commandment, each of the capital sins, the precepts of the church, the five senses, and the works of mercy. Likewise, should the giver of the Exercises see that the receiver has poor health or little natural capacity, or that not much fruit is to be expected of such a person, it is more suitable to give some less demanding exercises until the person has been to confession. Afterwards some [topics for] examen of conscience can be given and the instruction to confess more frequently, so that such a person may maintain the progress made. One should not go on to the election material or to the other exercises that are outside the First Week, especially when the exercitant can gain greater profit from other exercises and there is no time for everything.

[19] ANNOTATION 19. When a person is taken up with public affairs or necessary business, and is someone who is educated or intelligent, such a person can set aside an hour and a half a day for the Exercises. Then one can talk with such a person about the end for which human beings are created, as well as giving a half-hour for the particular examen, then the general examen and method of confessing and receiving communion. On three days this exercitant can make for one hour each morning the meditation on the first, second and third sins [Exx. 45–53]; later for

another three days at the same hour the meditation on the sequence of sins [Exx. 55–61]; later for another three days at the same hour the meditation on the punishments that correspond to sins [Exx. 65–71] should be made, and during these three sets of meditations the ten additions [Exx. 73–90] should be given. For the mysteries of Christ Our Lord the same procedure will be followed, as is explained in detail further on in these same Exercises.

[20] ANNOTATION 20. To one who is more at liberty and desires to benefit as much as possible, all the Spiritual Exercises should be given in the exact order in which they are set down.[6] As a general rule in making the Exercises, the more one disengages oneself from all friends and acquaintances, and from all worldly preoccupations, the more profit will there be. For example, one can change residence and go to a house or room so as to live there in the most complete privacy possible, with the opportunity to attend mass and vespers each day without fear of acquaintances getting in the way.

This withdrawal will have three principal advantages, among many others. The first is that when one separates oneself from many friends and acquaintances as well as from distracting business in order to serve and praise God Our Lord, one gains no small merit before the Divine Majesty. The second is that in this state of withdrawal, with one's mind not divided amongst many things but entirely taken up with one thing alone, namely, serving one's Creator and doing good to one's soul, one is able to use one's natural powers all the more freely in the diligent search for what one's heart desires. The third, the more we are alone and by ourselves, the more capable we become of drawing near to and reaching our Creator and Lord, and the more we reach Him, the more we make ourselves ready to receive graces and gifts from His divine and supreme Goodness.

First Week

[21] SPIRITUAL EXERCISES HAVING AS THEIR PURPOSE THE OVERCOMING OF SELF AND THE ORDERING OF ONE'S LIFE ON THE BASIS OF A DECISION MADE IN FREEDOM FROM ANY ILL-ORDERED ATTACHMENT.

[22]   PRESUPPOSITION

So that the director and the exercitant may collaborate better and with greater profit, it must be presupposed that any good Christian has to be more ready to justify than to condemn a neighbour's statement. If no justification can be found, one should ask the neighbour in what sense it is to be taken, and if that sense is wrong he or she should be corrected lovingly. Should this not be sufficient, one should seek all suitable means to justify it by understanding it in a good sense.

[23]   PRINCIPLE AND FOUNDATION

The human person is created to praise, reverence and serve God Our Lord, and by so doing to save his or her soul. The other things on the face of the earth are created for human beings in order to help them pursue the end for which they are created. It follows from this that one must use other created things in so far as they help towards one's end, and free oneself from them in so far as they are obstacles to one's end. To do this we need to make ourselves indifferent to all created things, provided the matter is subject to our free choice and there is no prohibition. Thus as far as we are concerned, we should not want health more than illness, wealth more than poverty, fame more than disgrace, a long life more than a short one, and similarly for all the rest, but we should desire and choose only what helps us more towards the end for which we are created.

[24]   PARTICULAR DAILY EXAMEN
                    containing three times and two examens

The FIRST TIME is in the morning immediately on rising: the exercitant
makes a firm resolve to take great care to avoid the particular sin or
defect that he or she wants to correct and reform.

[25] The SECOND TIME comes after the mid-day meal, when one asks
God Our Lord for what one wants, i.e. grace to remember how often
one has fallen into that particular sin or defect, and to reform in the
future. Then the exercitant makes the FIRST EXAMEN: it consists of demanding of oneself an account of the particular point proposed for
correction and reform, running over each hour or each period of time,
beginning from the hour of rising, up to the hour and moment of the
present examen. On the first line of the diagram as many marks should
be made as times one has fallen into the particular sin or defect. Then
one should resolve again to do better up to the next examen to be made.

[26] The THIRD TIME is after supper, when the SECOND EXAMEN will
be made in the same way, going from hour to hour from the first examen
to this second one. On the second line of the same diagram as many
marks should be made as the times one has fallen into the particular sin
or defect.

[27]   FOUR ADDITIONS
          for getting rid of the particular sin or defect more quickly

ADDITION 1 Each time one falls into the particular sin or defect, one
should put a hand to the breast in sorrow for having fallen. This can be
done even in the presence of many people without their noticing.

[28] ADDITION 2 Since the first line of the diagram represents the first
examen, and the second line the second examen, the exercitant can see
at night if there is an improvement from the first line to the second, i.e.
from the first examen to the second.

[29] ADDITION 3 The second day should be compared with the first, i.e.
today's two examens with yesterday's two examens, to see if there is an
improvement from one day to another.

[30] ADDITION 4 One week should be compared with another to see if
there is an improvement between the present week and the preceding.

[31] NOTE The first two long lines in the following diagram[7] stand for

Sunday, the second shorter ones for Monday, the third for Tuesday, and so on.

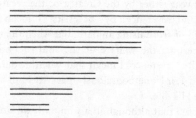

[32]   GENERAL EXAMEN OF CONSCIENCE
in order to purify the soul and to make a better confession

I presuppose that there are three sorts of thought processes in me, one sort which are properly mine and arise simply from my free will and choice, and two other sorts which come from outside, one from the good spirit and the other from the bad.

[33]   *Thoughts*

There are two ways of gaining merit when an evil thought comes from outside: the first – for example, if the thought of committing a mortal sin comes, I resist it promptly and it is overcome; [34] the second way of meriting is when the same bad thought comes to me and I resist it, it recurs again and again and I keep on resisting until the thought goes away defeated. This second way is more meritorious than the first.

[35] One sins venially when the same thought of committing a mortal sin comes and one gives ear to it, dwelling on it a little or taking some sensual enjoyment from it, or when there is some negligence in rejecting this thought.

[36] There are two ways of sinning mortally. The first is when one consents to a sinful thought in order to put one's consent into immediate action, or to act on it if one could [37]. The second way of sinning mortally is when that sin is actually committed, and this is more serious for three reasons – (i) because more time is spent, (ii) because there is more intensity, (iii) because greater harm is done both to others and to oneself.

[38]   *Words*

One should not swear either by the Creator or the creature except with truth, necessity and reverence. By 'necessity' I mean not when one swears to any kind of truth using an oath, but when the matter is one of importance, concerning the welfare of the soul or body, or involving temporal goods. By 'reverence' I mean that when invoking the name of one's Creator and Lord one consciously pays to Him the honour and reverence that are His due.

[39] It is to be noted that although in a vain oath we sin more seriously when we swear by the Creator than when we swear by the creature, it is more difficult to swear as we ought – with truth, necessity and reverence – by the creature than by the Creator for the following reasons: FIRST. When we want to swear by some creature, the choice of invoking the creature does not make us as careful and alert about telling the truth, or affirming it with necessity, as would the choice of invoking the name of the Lord and Creator of all things. SECOND. In swearing by the creature it is not as easy to pay reverence and submission to the Creator as when swearing by and invoking the name of the Creator and Lord Himself, because the intention of invoking God Our Lord brings with it more submission and reverence than is aroused by the intention of invoking created things. Therefore it is more permissible for the perfect to swear by the creature than it is for the imperfect, because the perfect, thanks to constant contemplation and to an enlightened understanding, are more in the habit of considering, meditating and contemplating how God Our Lord is in every creature according to His own essence, presence and power, and so when swearing by the creature are better prepared and predisposed to pay homage and reverence to their Creator and Lord than are the imperfect. THIRD. With persistent swearing by the creature, the imperfect are in more danger than the perfect of falling into idolatry.

[40] One should not speak 'idle words',[8] by which I understand those of no profit to either myself or to others, and those not directed to that end. Consequently to speak about anything that benefits or seeks to benefit my own soul or my neighbour's, or that is for the good of the body or for temporal welfare, is never idle. Nor is it idle even to speak of things that do not belong to one's state of life, e.g. if a religious speaks about wars or trade. Rather in all these cases there is merit in speaking to a well-ordered purpose, and sin in ill-directed or aimless talk.

[41] One should say nothing to defame another or to spread gossip,

because if I make known a mortal sin which is not public knowledge, I sin mortally, and if the sin is venial, I sin venially, while if it is a defect, I show my own defect. But when there is a right intention there are two possible ways of speaking of the sin or fault of another: WAY 1. When the sin is public, as in the case of a public prostitute, and where a sentence has been passed in court, or a public error poisons the minds of those with whom one deals. WAY 2. When a hidden sin is revealed to someone so that such a person can help the sinner to rise from sin; however there should be some expectation or probable likelihood that help can be given.

[42]   *Deeds*

One should take as subject-matter the Ten Commandments, the precepts of the Church and the recommendations of superiors; any action done against any of these three is a greater or smaller sin depending on the greater or lesser importance of the matter. By 'recommendations of superiors' I mean e.g. fasting dispensations and other indulgences, such as those granted for peace treaties, which can be obtained by confession and reception of the Blessed Sacrament, as there can be no little sin in inciting others to act or acting oneself against the religious exhortations and recommendations of those in authority.

[43]   WAY OF MAKING THE GENERAL EXAMEN
                  containing five points

POINT 1: to give thanks to God for the benefits received.
POINT 2: to ask for grace to know one's sins and reject them.
POINT 3: to ask an account of one's soul from the hour of rising to the present examen, hour by hour, or from one period to another, first about thoughts, then about words and finally about deeds, following the order given in the particular examen [Exx. 25].
POINT 4: to ask God Our Lord for pardon for sins.
POINT 5: to determine to do better with His grace, ending with an Our Father.

[44] GENERAL CONFESSION AND COMMUNION

Anybody wanting of one's own accord to make a General Confession will find in it three particular benefits amongst many others: (i) while granting that a person who goes to confession every year is not obliged to make a general confession, yet if such a person does make one, there is greater profit and merit because of the greater present sorrow being felt for all the sins and wrongs of one's whole life; (ii) during the Spiritual Exercises one gains a greater interior knowledge of sins and of their malice than when one is not engaged in the same way with matters of the inner life; with the greater knowledge and grief for sins, one will have greater profit and merit than would previously have been had; (iii) as a consequence of making a better confession and being better disposed, the person is better prepared and readier to receive the Blessed Sacrament (the reception of which helps us not only to avoid falling into sin, but also to keep on increasing in grace). It is better to make this General Confession immediately after the exercises of the First Week.

[45] The First Exercise

A MEDITATION WITH THE THREE POWERS ON THE FIRST,
SECOND AND THIRD SINS
*containing – after a preparatory prayer and two preambles⁹ – three
principal points and a colloquy*

[46] PRAYER The preparatory prayer is to ask God Our Lord for grace that all my intentions, actions and operations may be directed purely to the service and praise of His Divine Majesty.

[47] PREAMBLE 1 This is the composition,¹⁰ seeing the place.

It should be noted here that for contemplation or meditation about visible things, e.g. a contemplation about Christ Our Lord who is visible, the 'composition' consists in seeing through the gaze of the imagination the material place where the object I want to contemplate is situated. By 'material place' I mean e.g. a temple or a mountain where Jesus Christ or Our Lady is to be found, according to what I want to contemplate. Where the object is invisible, as is the case in the present instance dealing with sins, the composition will be to see with the gaze of the imagination and to consider that my soul is imprisoned in this body which will one day disintegrate, and my whole composite self as if exiled in this valley among brute beasts. When I say 'my whole composite self', I mean body and soul together.

[48] PREAMBLE 2 This is to ask God for what I want and desire.

The request must be adapted to the matter under consideration, so e.g. in contemplating the Resurrection one asks for joy with Christ joyful, but in contemplating the Passion one asks for grief, tears and suffering with the suffering Christ. Here I will ask for personal shame and confusion as I see how many have been damned on account of a single mortal sin, and how many times I deserved to be damned for ever on account of my numerous sins.

[49] NOTE Before any of the contemplations or meditations the preparatory prayer should always be made without any change, and also the two preambles mentioned, the latter being adapted at times to suit the matter under consideration.

[50] POINT 1 Bring the memory to bear on the first sin, which was that of the angels, then apply the intellect to the same event, in order to reason over it, and then the will, so that by seeking to recall and to comprehend all this, I may feel all the more shame and confusion, comparing the one sin of the angels with my many sins, for while they went to hell for one sin, how many times have I deserved hell for my many sins! When I say 'bring to memory the sin of the angels', I mean how they were created in grace, but as they did not want to avail themselves of their liberty in order to give reverence and obedience to their Creator and Lord, and fell into pride, they became changed over from grace to malice and were cast out of heaven into hell. Similarly afterwards one should go over the subject more in detail with the understanding, and then stir up the heart's affections[11] with the will.

[51] POINT 2 In the same way bring the three powers to bear on the case of the sin of Adam and Eve, calling to mind the long penance they did on account of that sin, and the corruption that came upon the human race, with so many people going their way toward hell. When I talk about recalling the second sin, that of our [first] parents, I mean how after Adam had been created in the plain of Damascus and placed in the earthly Paradise, and Eve had been created from his rib, they were forbidden to eat of the tree of knowledge. But they ate and by doing so sinned. Afterwards, dressed in tunics of skins and cast out of Paradise, they lived all their life without their original justice, which they had lost, in great labours and much penance. Then go over the

subject in greater detail with the understanding, and use the will as has been explained above.

[52] POINT 3 Do the same for the third sin, the particular one of any individual who has gone to hell for a single mortal sin, and also the numberless other people who have gone to hell for fewer sins than I have committed. Do the same, I say, with regard to such a third sin, a particular one, calling to memory the gravity and malice of sin against one's Creator and Lord, reflecting with the understanding how someone who has sinned and acted against the infinite goodness has justly been damned for ever, then end with the will as has been said.

[53] COLLOQUY Imagining Christ Our Lord before me on the cross, make a colloquy[12] asking how it came about that the Creator made Himself man, and from eternal life came to temporal death, and thus to die for my sins. Then, turning to myself I shall ask, what have I done for Christ? what am I doing for Christ? what ought I to do for Christ? Finally, seeing Him in that state hanging on the cross, talk over whatever comes to mind.

[54] A colloquy, properly so-called, means speaking as one friend speaks with another, or a servant with a master, at times asking for some favour, at other times accusing oneself of something badly done, or telling the other about one's concerns and asking for advice about them. And then say an Our Father.

[55]   The Second Exercise

A MEDITATION ON SINS
*containing – after the preparatory prayer and two preambles –
five points and a colloquy*

PRAYER The preparatory prayer will be the same.

PREAMBLE I The first preamble will be the same composition.

PREAMBLE 2 This is to ask for what I want, and here it will be to ask for mounting and intense sorrow and tears for my sins.

[56] POINT 1 This is the record of my sins, i.e. I recall to my memory all the sins of my life, looking from year to year or from one period of time to another, and for this three things are helpful: (i) to see the place and house where I lived, (ii) the relations I have had with others, (iii) the occupation in which I have spent my life.

[57] POINT 2 I weigh up my sins, considering the intrinsic foulness and

malice of each capital sin committed, quite apart from its being forbidden.

[58] POINT 3 I look at who I am, diminishing myself by means of comparisons: (i) What am I compared to all human beings? (ii) What are all human beings compared to all the angels and saints in Paradise? (iii) What can I alone be, as I look at what the whole of creation amounts to in comparison with God? (iv) I look upon all the corruption and foulness of my body. (v) I look at myself as though I were an ulcer or an abscess, the source of many sins and evils, and of great infection.

[59] POINT 4 I consider who God is, against whom I have sinned, going through His attributes and contrasting them with their opposites in myself: His wisdom with my ignorance, His almighty power with my weakness, His justice with my injustice, His goodness with my malice.

[60] POINT 5 Exclamations of wonder, with intense feeling, as I reflect on the whole range of created beings, how ever have they let me live and kept me alive! The angels, who are the sword of divine justice, how have they endured me, and looked after me, and prayed for me! How have the saints been able to intercede and pray for me! And then the heavens, the sun, the moon, the stars and the elements, the fruits, the birds, the fishes and the animals, how have they kept me alive till now![13] As for the earth, how has it not opened to engulf me, creating new hells where I might suffer for ever!

[61] COLLOQUY I will conclude with a colloquy about mercy. All my thoughts will be about mercy and I will thank God for giving me life up till now, proposing to do better in the future with His grace. Our Father.

[62]   The Third Exercise

REPETITION OF THE FIRST AND SECOND EXERCISES
making three colloquies

After the preparatory prayer and the two preambles, repeat the First and Second Exercises, noting and dwelling upon the points where I have felt greater consolation or desolation or greater spiritual relish. I shall then go on to make three colloquies as follows.

[63] COLLOQUY I This is to be made to Our Lady, so that she will obtain grace for me from her Son and Lord for three things, (i) that I may feel an interior knowledge of my sins and an abhorrence for them, (ii) that I

may feel a sense of the disorder in my actions, so that abhorring it I may amend my life and put order into it, (iii) I ask for knowledge of the world so that out of abhorrence for it I may put away from myself worldly and aimless things. Then a Hail Mary.[14]

COLLOQUY 2 The second colloquy is the same but to the Son, that He may obtain this for me from the Father. And then an Anima Christi.

COLLOQUY 3 The third, the same but to the Father, so that the eternal Lord Himself may grant me this. And after it an Our Father.

[64]   The Fourth Exercise

RECAPITULATION OF THE THIRD EXERCISE

When I use the word 'recapitulation' I mean that the intellect, carefully and without digressing onto any other subject, should range over the memory of matters contemplated in the previous exercises, and make the same three colloquies.

[65]   The Fifth Exercise

MEDITATION ON HELL
*containing – after the preparatory prayer and the two preambles –
five points and a colloquy*

PRAYER This should be as usual.

PREAMBLE 1 The composition here is to see with the eyes of the imagination the length, breadth and depth of hell.

PREAMBLE 2 The second preamble is to ask for what I want. Here it will be to ask for an interior sense of the suffering which the damned endure, so that if through my faults I should ever forget the love of the eternal Lord, at least the fear of punishments may help me not to fall into sin.

[66] POINT 1 This will be to look with the eyes of the imagination at the great fires and at the souls appearing to be in burning bodies.

[67] POINT 2 To hear with one's ears the wailings, howls, cries, blasphemies against Christ Our Lord and against all the saints.

[68] POINT 3 To smell with the sense of smell the smoke, the burning sulphur, the cesspit and the rotting matter.

[69] POINT 4 To taste with the sense of taste bitter things, such as tears, sadness and the pangs of conscience.

[70] POINT 5 To feel with the sense of touch, i.e. how those in hell are licked around and burned by the fires.

[71] COLLOQUY As I make a colloquy with Christ Our Lord, I should recall to my memory the persons who are in hell, some because they did not believe in His coming, others who believed but did not act according to His commandments, so dividing them up into three categories, the first, those before His coming, the second, those during His lifetime, and the third, those after His lifetime. And with that I should give thanks to Him for not allowing me to fall into any of these categories by putting an end to my life. Likewise I should thank Him for His constant loving kindness and mercy towards me right up to the present moment. One concludes with an Our Father.[55]

[72]   NOTE

The First Exercise will be made at midnight, the Second on rising in the morning, the Third before or after mass, as long as it is made before lunch, the Fourth at the time of vespers, the Fifth an hour before supper. I intend this timetable (more or less) to be applied always during the Four Weeks in so far as the age, constitution and temperament of the exercitant allow the person to do five exercises or fewer.

[73]   Additions

THE PURPOSE OF THESE ADDITIONAL PRACTICES IS
TO HELP THE EXERCITANT TO MAKE THE EXERCISES BETTER,
AND TO FIND MORE COMPLETELY WHAT HE OR SHE DESIRES.

ADDITION 1 After going to bed and when wanting to go to sleep, I should think for the space of a Hail Mary at what time I have to get up, and for what purpose, going over the exercise I have to make.

[74] ADDITION 2 When I wake up I turn my attention at once (so as not to leave room for stray thoughts) to the subject I am about to contemplate in the First Exercise at midnight, arousing myself to confusion for my many sins by using comparisons, such as that of a knight coming

before his king and all the court, full of shame and confusion on account of offences committed against the lord from whom in the past he has had many gifts and favours. Similarly for the Second Exercise, I see myself as a great sinner in chains, that is to say, as about to appear, bound, before the supreme and eternal Judge, recalling how chained prisoners appear for the death penalty before a judge here on earth. It is with thoughts like these, or others adapted to the subject matter under consideration, that I should dress myself.

[75] ADDITION 3 One or two paces before the place where I have to contemplate or meditate, I shall stand for the space of an Our Father with my mind raised up to consider how God Our Lord looks at me, etc, and then make a genuflexion or some other act of humility.

[76] ADDITION 4 I start on the contemplation, sometimes kneeling, sometimes prostrate on the ground, sometimes stretched out face upwards, sometimes seated, sometimes standing, but always intent on the search for what I want. We should pay attention to two points: (i) if I find what I want whilst kneeling, I shall go no further, and similarly if prostrate, etc; (ii) at the point at which I find what I want, I shall settle down, without any anxiety about going further until I have had my fill.

[77] ADDITION 5 At the end of the exercise I shall either sit down or walk around for a quarter of an hour while I consider how the contemplation or meditation has gone. If badly, I shall look to see what was the cause, and having found it, repent in order to do better in the future; and if well, I shall thank God Our Lord and proceed in the same way next time.

[78] ADDITION 6 We should not want to think about agreeable or glad things, e.g. final glory or resurrection etc, because feelings of grief, pain and tears for our sins are only impeded by thoughts about joy and gladness. Instead I should keep before me my wish to grieve and feel sorrow, and remind myself more of death and judgement.

[79] ADDITION 7 In order to obtain these same feelings I should deprive myself of light, closing shutters and doors whilst I am in my room, except when reciting the Office, reading and taking meals.

[80] ADDITION 8 I should avoid laughing or saying anything likely to provoke laughter.

[81] ADDITION 9 I should put a guard over my eyes, except when I receive or take leave of someone with whom I speak.

[82] ADDITION 10 This consists of penance, which can be divided into interior and exterior, the interior being grief for one's sins with the firm

determination not to commit those or any others, and the exterior, which is the fruit of the former, being the punishment we impose on ourselves for sins committed. There are three ways of inflicting it.

[83] (i) The first is in regard to food. In the matter of food, to go without the superfluous is not penance but temperance; penance begins when we go without what is in itself appropriate, and the more one does this, the greater and better is the penance, as long as the penitent's health is not undermined and no serious illness results.

[84] (ii) The second regards the way we sleep. Here once again it is not penance to go without what is of finer quality and more comfortable, but penance begins when we go without what is suitable in the way we sleep; again the more this is done the better, as long as the penitent is not harmed and no serious illness results, and provided an exercitant does not go without the sleep needed, unless the person happens to have the bad habit of sleeping too much, and then only in order to arrive at a just mean.

[85] (iii) The third consists in chastising the body, i.e. inflicting physical pain, which can be done by wearing haircloth or cords or iron chains next to the skin, or by whipping and bruising oneself, and other sorts of austerities.

[86] NOTE The most practical and safest in regard to penance seems to be that the pain should be felt in the flesh and not penetrate to the bone, so that the result is pain and not illness. Therefore the most appropriate seems to be to strike oneself with thin cords, which cause external pain, rather than in some other way that may cause some possibly serious internal illness.

[87] NOTES ON THE ADDITIONAL PRACTICES

NOTE 1 Exterior penances are done chiefly to produce three results: (i) to make reparation for past sins, (ii) to master oneself, i.e. to make one's sensual nature obedient to reason, and to make all the lower parts of the self more submissive to the higher, (iii) to seek and find some grace or gift that a person wants and desires, for instance, one may desire to have interior contrition for one's sins, or to weep much either over one's sins, or over the pains and sorrows endured by Christ Our Lord; or one may want to resolve some perplexity in which one finds oneself.

[88] NOTE 2 One should notice that Additions 1 and 2 are to be put into practice for the midnight and dawn exercises, but not for the exercises

made at other times. Addition 4 is never to be put into practice in church in the presence of other people, but only in private, e.g. at home, etc.

[89] NOTE 3 When the exercitant does not find what is desired, e.g. tears, consolations, etc, it is often very advantageous to make some alteration in eating, and sleeping, and in other penitential practices, so that the exercitant practises some penances for two or three days and then leaves them off for another two or three. This is because it suits some people to do more penance, and others to do less, and also because quite often we give up penance through sensuality or wrongly judging that the human physique cannot withstand the stress without serious illness, and at other times on the contrary we overdo penance thinking that the body can endure it. As God Our Lord knows our nature infinitely better than we do, He often allows us to perceive through such alterations what is suitable for each.

[90] NOTE 4 The particular examen is to be directed towards getting rid of faults and negligences in the practice of the Exercises and Additions. This holds for the Second, Third and Fourth Weeks as well.

Second Week

[91]   THE CALL OF THE EARTHLY KING[16]
WILL HELP US TO CONTEMPLATE THE LIFE OF
THE ETERNAL KING.

PRAYER The preparatory prayer will be the same.
PREAMBLE 1 This is the composition, seeing the place, and here it
will be to see with the eyes of the imagination synagogues, towns and
villages where Christ Our Lord went preaching.
PREAMBLE 2 I ask for the grace I want; here I ask Our Lord for grace
not to be deaf to His call, but alert to fulfil His most holy will to the
best of my ability.

[92]   [PART I]

POINT 1 I put before me a human king chosen by the hand of God Our
Lord, to whom all Christian leaders and their followers give their
homage and obedience.
[93] POINT 2 I watch how this king speaks to all his own saying:
'My will is to conquer all the land of the infidels! Therefore all those
who want to come with me will have to be content with the same food
as I, the same drink, the same clothing, etc. Such persons will also have
to work with me by day, and keep watch by night, etc, so that in this way
they will afterwards share with me in the victory, as they have shared
with me in the labours.'
[94] POINT 3 I consider what reply good subjects should make to such
an open and kindly king, and on the other hand, if anyone refused to
accept the request of such a king, how greatly such a person would
deserve to be blamed by everyone and to be judged an unworthy knight.

[95]   PART II

consists in applying the above example of the earthly king to Christ Our Lord, following the three points mentioned:

POINT 1 If such a call made by an earthly king to his subjects is worthy of our consideration, how much more is it worthy of consideration to see Christ Our Lord, the eternal King, and before Him the entire human race, as to all and to each one in particular His call goes out, 'My will is to conquer the whole world and every enemy, and so enter into the glory of my Father! Therefore all those who want to come with me will have to labour with me, so that by following me in my suffering, they may also follow me into glory.'

[96] POINT 2 We should consider that all who have judgement and reason will offer themselves completely for the task.

[97] POINT 3 Those who will want to respond in a spirit of love, and to distinguish themselves by the thoroughness of their commitment to their eternal King and universal Lord, will not only offer themselves bodily for the task, but rather by going against their sensuality and their carnal and worldly love will offer greater and more important sacrifices, saying, [98] 'Eternal Lord of all things, I make my offering, with your favour and help, before your infinite Goodness, and before your glorious Mother and all the saintly men and women of the court of heaven! My resolute wish and desire, and my considered determination – on the sole condition that this be for your greater service and praise – is to imitate you in enduring every outrage and all contempt, and utter poverty, both actual and spiritual, if your most holy Majesty wants to choose me and receive me into that life and state.'

[99] NOTE 1 This exercise will be made twice in the day, viz. on rising in the morning and one hour before dinner or supper.

[100] NOTE 2 For the Second Week, as well as for the future, it is very helpful to read from time to time from the *Imitation of Christ*, or from the Gospels, or lives of saints.

[101]   First Day: First Contemplation

ON THE INCARNATION
*containing the preparatory prayer, three preambles, three points
and a colloquy*

PRAYER The usual preparatory prayer.

[102] PREAMBLE 1 The first preamble is to recall the narrative of the
subject to be contemplated, in this case how the three Divine Persons
were looking at all the flatness or roundness of the whole world filled
with people, and how the decision was taken in Their eternity,[17] as They
saw them all going down into hell, that the second Person would
become human to save the human race. Thus when 'the fullness of
time'[18] came They sent the angel Gabriel to Our Lady [Exx. 262].

[103] PREAMBLE 2 The composition, seeing the place, which here will
be to see the great extent of the round earth with its many different
races; then, in the same way, see the particular house of Our Lady and
its rooms in the town of Nazareth in the province of Galilee.

[104] PREAMBLE 3 I ask for what I want: here I ask for interior knowledge of the Lord who became human for me so that I may better love
and follow Him.

[105] NOTE It may be well to note here that this same preparatory
prayer (without any change, as was mentioned at the beginning [Exx.
49]), along with the same three preambles, should be made in this Week
and in those following, but adapting the form according to the matter
under consideration.

[106] POINT 1 This is to see the various kinds of persons: first, those on
the face of the earth, in all their diversity of dress and appearance, some
white and some black, some in peace and others at war, some weeping
and others laughing, some healthy, others sick, some being born and
others dying, etc; second, I see and consider the three divine Persons, as
though They are on the royal throne of their Divine Majesty, how They
look down on the whole round world and on all its peoples living in
such great blindness, and dying and going down into hell; third, I see
Our Lady and the Angel who greets her. And I should reflect in order to
draw profit from such a sight.

[107] POINT 2 This is to hear what the people on the face of the earth
talk about, i.e. how they talk with each other, how they swear and

blaspheme, etc. In the same way what the Divine Persons are saying, viz., 'Let us bring about the redemption of the human race, etc'. Then what the Angel and Our Lady are talking about. And I should reflect to draw profit from their words.

[108] POINT 3 Next I look at what the people on the face of the earth are doing, e.g. wounding, killing, and going to hell, etc, and in the same way, what the Divine Persons are doing, that is, accomplishing the sacred Incarnation, etc, and similarly, what the Angel and Our Lady are doing, the Angel fulfilling his role of legate and Our Lady humbling herself and giving thanks to the Divine Majesty. Then I reflect in order to profit from each of these things.

[109] COLLOQUY At the end a colloquy is to be made. I think about what I ought to be saying to the three Divine Persons, or to the eternal Word incarnate, or to His mother, Our Lady, and I make a request, according to my inner feelings, so that I may better follow and imitate Our Lord, thus newly incarnate, saying an Our Father.

[110]   SECOND CONTEMPLATION
                            on the Nativity

PRAYER The usual preparatory prayer.

[111] PREAMBLE 1 The narrative here will be how Our Lady, almost nine months pregnant (as we may devoutly think of her[19]) and seated on a donkey, with Joseph and a servant girl, taking with them an ox, set out from Nazareth for Bethlehem to pay the tribute which Caesar had imposed on all those lands [Exx. 264].

[112] PREAMBLE 2 Composition, seeing the place. Here it will be to see with the eyes of the imagination the road from Nazareth to Bethlehem, considering the length and breadth of it, whether it is a flat road or goes through valleys or over hills; and similarly to look at the place or grotto of the Nativity, to see how big or small it was, how low or high, and what was in it.

[113] PREAMBLE 3 The same, and in the same form, as in the preceding contemplation [Exx. 104].

[114] POINT 1 This is to see the people, i.e. Our Lady, and Joseph, and the servant girl, and the child Jesus after his birth. Making myself into a poor and unworthy little servant, I watch them, and contemplate them, and serve them in their needs as if I were present, with all possible submission and reverence; and afterwards I reflect within myself to derive some profit.

[115] POINT 2 I watch, and notice and contemplate what they are saying, and then reflect within myself to derive some profit.

[116] POINT 3 I watch and consider what they are doing, e.g. their travel and efforts, so that Christ comes to be born in extreme poverty and, after so many labours, after hunger, thirst, heat and cold, outrages and affronts, he dies on the cross, and all of this for me; then I reflect within myself to derive some spiritual profit.

[117] COLLOQUY I end with a colloquy as in the preceding contemplation [Exx. 109], and then an Our Father.

[118]   THIRD CONTEMPLATION
          the repetition of the First and Second Exercises

After the preparatory prayer and the three preambles the repetition of Exercises 1 and 2 will be made, attention always being given to any more important places where one has experienced new insight, consolation or desolation, and making a colloquy in the same way at the end, with an Our Father.

[119] [NOTE] In this and all subsequent repetitions the same order of procedure will be followed as in the repetitions of the First Week, changing the matter and keeping the form.

[120]   FOURTH CONTEMPLATION
        *the repetition of the First and Second Contemplations
         made in the same way as the preceding repetition*

[121]   FIFTH CONTEMPLATION
          *this is to bring the five senses to bear[20]
           on the First and Second Contemplations*

After the preparatory prayer and the three preambles, it is helpful to pass the five senses of the imagination over the First and Second Contemplations in the following manner.

[122] POINT 1 To see the persons with the imaginative sense of sight, meditating and contemplating their circumstances in detail, and to draw some profit from what I see.

[123] POINT 2 To hear with the sense of hearing what they say or could say, and to reflect within oneself to draw some profit from this.

[124] POINT 3 To smell and to taste, with the senses of smell and taste, the infinite gentleness and sweetness of the divinity, and[21] of the soul, and of its virtues, and of everything else (according to whoever the person contemplated may be), and to reflect within oneself and draw profit from this.

[125] POINT 4 To touch with the sense of touch, for example, embracing and kissing the places where these persons tread and sit, always seeking to derive profit from this.

[126] COLLOQUY One should finish with a colloquy as in the First and Second Contemplations [Exx. 109, 117], and with an Our Father.

[127]   [NOTES]

NOTE 1 It should be noted that in the course of this and the following weeks I should read only the mystery of the contemplation that I have to make immediately; thus for the time being I should not read any mystery that is not to be made on that day or at that time, so that the consideration of one mystery may not interfere with the consideration of another.

[128] NOTE 2 The first exercise on the Incarnation is to be made at midnight, the second at dawn, the third at mass time, the fourth at the time of vespers, and the fifth before supper; an hour is to be spent on each of the five exercises, and the same order will be kept in all that follows.

[129] NOTE 3 It should be noted that if the exercitant is old or weak, or if this person, although robust, has been left weakened in some way by the First Week, it is better for such an exercitant at least occasionally in this Second Week not to rise at midnight, but to make one contemplation in the morning, another at mass time, another before dinner, and a repetition of these at the time of vespers, and finally to make the prayer of the senses before supper.

[130] NOTE 4 In this Second Week, changes should be made to some of the Additional practices mentioned in the First Week, viz. the second, the sixth, the seventh and (partly) the tenth [Exx. 74, 78, 79, 82].

RE ADDITION 2 Immediately on waking I shall put before myself the contemplation which I have to make, with the desire to know all the more the eternal Word Incarnate, so as the better to serve and follow Him.

RE ADDITION 6 I shall frequently call to mind the life and mysteries of Christ Our Lord, beginning from His Incarnation as far as the place or mystery that I am engaged in contemplating.

RE ADDITION 7 In the use to be made of darkness or light, and of agreeable or unsettled weather, the criterion is the profit and help the exercitant can derive in the search for what that person desires.

RE ADDITION 10 The exercitant must act in harmony with the mysteries being contemplated, as some demand penance and others do not.

In this way all the ten Additional practices are to be very carefully observed.

[131] NOTE 5 In all the Exercises, except those at midnight and in the morning, the equivalent of the second Additional practice [Exx. 74] is to be observed as follows: as soon as I remember that it is time for the exercise I have to do, before beginning I put before myself where I am going and into whose presence, and I run briefly over the exercise to be done; then I make the third Addition [Exx. 75] and start on the exercise.

[132]   SECOND DAY

One should take for the First and Second Contemplations the Presentation in the Temple [Exx. 268] and the Flight into Egypt as into exile [Exx. 269]; two repetitions and the bringing to bear of the senses should be made on these two contemplations, in the same way as on the preceding day.

[133]   NOTE

Sometimes it is helpful for the exercitant, even if robust and in the right dispositions, to change the timetable from this second day until the fourth (inclusive), in order better to find what one desires, and to make only one contemplation at dawn and another at the time of mass, then to make the repetition on these at the time of vespers and to make the prayer of the senses before supper.

[134]   THIRD DAY

Contemplate how the Child Jesus was obedient to His parents at Nazareth [Exx. 271], and how afterwards they found Him in the Temple
[Exx. 272], then later make the two repetitions and the prayer of the senses.

[135]   PREAMBLE FOR THE CONSIDERATION OF
                           STATES OF LIFE

The example given us by Christ Our Lord of the first state of life, the
observance of the Commandments, has been considered in the contemplation of His obedience to His parents; we have considered too his
example of the second state, evangelical perfection, when He stayed in
the Temple, leaving His adopted father and natural mother, to devote
Himself to the exclusive service of His heavenly Father; now we shall
begin, at the same time as we contemplate His life, to inquire and ask in
which life or state the Divine Majesty wishes to use us. By way of
introduction to that we shall see (in the first exercise that follows) the
intention of Christ Our Lord and on the contrary that of the enemy of
human nature, as well as the attitudes we must acquire to reach perfection in whatever state of life God Our Lord may offer us for our choice.

[136]   Fourth Day

                   A MEDITATION ON TWO STANDARDS,
           one that of Christ our Commander-in-Chief and Our Lord,
         the other that of Lucifer, the deadly enemy of our human nature

PRAYER The usual preparatory prayer.
[137] PREAMBLE 1 This is the narrative: here it will be how Christ calls
and desires all to place themselves under His standard, and how Lucifer
on the contrary wants everyone under his.
[138] PREAMBLE 2 The composition, seeing the place: here it will be to
behold a great plain extending over the entire region around Jerusalem,
where the Commander-in-Chief of all the good is Christ Our Lord, and
another plain in the region of Babylon, where the enemy leader is
Lucifer.

[139] PREAMBLE 3 I ask for what I want: here it will be to ask for knowledge of the deceptions practised by the evil leader and for help to guard against them, and also for knowledge of the true life revealed by the supreme and true Commander, and for grace to imitate Him.

[140] POINT 1 This point is to imagine the leader of all the enemy powers as if he were enthroned in that great plain of Babylon, upon something like a throne of fire and smoke, a horrible and fearsome figure.

[141] POINT 2 To consider how he calls up innumerable demons, and how he then disperses them, some to one city and others to another, thus covering the entire world, omitting no region, no place, no state of life, nor any individual.

[142] POINT 3 To consider the address he makes to them, ordering them to lay traps for people and to bind them with chains. They are to tempt them first to crave after riches (the enemy's usual tactic), so that they might come more readily to the empty honours of the world, and in the end to unbounded pride. Therefore the first step is riches, the second, honour, and the third, pride; from these three steps the enemy leads people on to every other vice.

[143]   *On the other hand, we are to apply the imagination to*
          the supreme and true commander, Christ our Lord

[144] POINT 1 This is to consider Christ Our Lord taking his stand in a great plain in that region of Jerusalem, in a lowly place, His appearance comely and gracious.

[145] POINT 2 To consider how the Lord of all the world selects so many persons, as apostles, disciples, etc, and sends them out over the whole world spreading His sacred doctrine among all people of every state and condition.

[146] POINT 3 To consider the address which Christ Our Lord delivers to His servants and friends as He sends them out on this enterprise. He recommends them to be ready to help everyone; first, by drawing everyone to the highest spiritual poverty; and if His Divine Majesty be thereby served and should be pleased to choose them for it, not less to actual poverty; and secondly, by drawing everyone to the desire for insults and contempt. For from these two things follows humility. Therefore there are three steps, first, poverty as opposed to riches, second, insults and contempt as opposed to worldly fame, and thirdly, humility as opposed to pride; from these three steps they can lead everyone to all the other virtues.

[147] COLLOQUY 1 A colloquy with Our Lady, asking her to obtain for

me grace from her Son and Lord that I be received under His standard, first in the highest spiritual poverty, but also, if His Divine Majesty requires this and should be pleased to choose and receive me for it, in actual poverty, second, in suffering insults and reproaches, so as to imitate Him more closely, provided only that I can suffer these without sin on the part of any other person and without displeasure to His Divine Majesty; and then a Hail Mary.

COLLOQUY 2 To ask the same of the Son that He may obtain it for me from the Father, and then say an Anima Christi.

COLLOQUY 3 To ask the same of the Father that He would grant it to me Himself, and say an Our Father.

[148] NOTE This exercise will be made at midnight and again in the morning, with two repetitions (at the time of mass and at the time of vespers); it should always conclude with the three colloquies, with Our Lady, with the Son, and with the Father. The following exercise, on the Three Classes, is to be made at the hour before supper.

[149]   ALSO ON THE FOURTH DAY
                    the meditation on three classes of persons,[22]
                    so that we may embrace whatever is the better

PRAYER The usual preparatory prayer.

[150] PREAMBLE 1 The first preamble is the narrative. Three persons have each acquired 10,000 ducats; but not purely, and as would have been right for the love of God. Since they all want to be saved and to meet God Our Lord in peace, they wish to become free from the burden and obstacle arising from the attachment they feel to the thing they have acquired.

[151] PREAMBLE 2 Composition, seeing the place: here it will be to see myself standing in the presence of God Our Lord and of all His saints in order to desire and to know whatever is more pleasing to His Divine Goodness.

[152] PREAMBLE 3 To ask for what I want: here it will be to ask for the grace to choose what is more for the glory of His Divine Majesty and for the salvation of my soul.

[153] CLASS 1 The first class of person would like to be rid of their attachment to what he or she has acquired, in order to meet God in peace and ensure their salvation, but they take no means to bring this about until the hour of their death.

[154] CLASS 2 Those of the second class want to be free of their attachment, but they want this to be in such a way that they will still retain possession of what they have; so God is to approve what they themselves want, and there is no decision to relinquish it (in order to go to God), even if it might be better for them if they did.

[155] CLASS 3 Those of the third class want to be rid of their attachment; moreover they want to be rid of it in such a way that they also have no inclination to retain their acquisition or not to retain it, but all they want is simply that their wanting or not wanting it should be in accordance with whatever God Our Lord inclines them to want, and as might appear to be more for the service and praise of His Divine Majesty. In the meantime they want to act as if they had already given up the whole sum, as far as their affections are concerned, and they draw upon all their powers to want neither this particular thing nor anything else, unless it be solely the service of God Our Lord that moves them. Thus it is the desire to be better able to serve God Our Lord that will move them to accept the thing or leave it.

[156] THREE COLLOQUIES Make the same three colloquies that were made in the preceding contemplation on the Two Standards.

[157] NOTE It is to be noted that when we feel attachment [to riches] or repugnance with regard to actual poverty, when we are not indifferent towards poverty or riches, it is a great help towards extinguishing such a disordered attachment to ask in the colloquies (even though it goes against our natural inclination) that Our Lord should choose us for actual poverty, and to desire, request, indeed beg for this, provided it be for the service and praise of His Divine Majesty.

[158]   FIFTH DAY
contemplation on the departure of Christ Our Lord from
Nazareth and His journey to the River Jordan, and his baptism
                          [Exx. 273]

[159] NOTE 1 This contemplation is to be made at midnight, and again in the morning, with two repetitions, at mass time and at the time for vespers, and before supper one should bring the senses to bear upon it. At the beginning of each of these five exercises come the usual preparatory prayer and the three preambles, in accordance with all that has been explained in the contemplation on the Incarnation [Exx. 101] and the Nativity [Exx. 110]; and one should end with the triple colloquy of

the three classes of persons [Exx. 156, 147] or according to the Note which follows the three classes [Exx. 157].

[160] NOTE 2 The particular examen after dinner and supper will be made on the faults and negligences in the Exercises and Additional practices of this day, and similarly for the following days.

[161] SIXTH DAY
a contemplation on how Christ Our Lord went from the River Jordan into the desert (inclusive[23]) [Exx. 274]

keeping to the same arrangement in everything as on the Fifth Day.

SEVENTH DAY
on how St Andrew and others followed Christ Our Lord [Exx. 275]

EIGHTH DAY
on the Sermon on the Mount, i.e. on the eight beatitudes [Exx. 278]

NINTH DAY
on how Christ Our Lord appeared to His disciples on the waves of the sea [Exx. 280]

TENTH DAY
on how the Lord preached in the Temple [Exx. 288]

ELEVENTH DAY
on the raising of Lazarus [Exx. 285]

TWELFTH DAY
on Palm Sunday [Exx. 287]

[162] NOTES
NOTE 1 In the contemplations of this Second Week, the exercitant can prolong or shorten the week according to the time that one may want to give, or according to the progress being made. To lengthen it one can take the mysteries of the Visitation of Our Lady to St Elizabeth, of the shepherds, of the Circumcision of the child Jesus, the three Kings, and

others as well; and to shorten it, one can even drop some of the mysteries proposed, because what is given here is an introduction and method so that afterwards contemplation may be better and more fully made.

[163] NOTE 2 The material dealing with Elections will be taken up from the contemplation on Nazareth to that on the Jordan (including the latter), i.e. the Fifth Day, in the way that is explained in what follows.

[164] NOTE 3 Before beginning on Elections, it will greatly help the exercitant to embrace whole-heartedly the true teaching of Christ Our Lord if he or she considers attentively the following three kinds of humility, spending time occasionally during the whole day turning them over, and in the same way making the three colloquies, as will be explained later [Exx. 168].

[165]   [Three kinds of humility]

FIRST KIND OF HUMILITY This is the kind that is necessary for my eternal salvation, and consists in subjecting and humbling myself, as far as I can, so that I obey the law of God Our Lord in everything; so much so that even if I were made the lord of all created things in this world, or even if my own life on this earth were at stake, I would not deliberately set about breaking any law, whether divine or human, that obliges me under pain of mortal sin.

[166] SECOND KIND OF HUMILITY The second is more perfect than the first. I have it if I find myself at a point where I do not desire, nor even prefer, to be rich rather than poor, to seek fame rather than disgrace, to desire a long rather than a short life, provided it is the same for the service of God and the good of my soul; and along with this I would not deliberately set about committing a venial sin, even for the whole of creation or under threat to my own life.

[167] THIRD KIND OF HUMILITY This is the most perfect humility. It is present when – given that the first and second kinds are included, and supposing equal praise and glory of the Divine Majesty – in order to imitate Christ Our Lord and to be actually more like him, I want and choose poverty with Christ poor rather than wealth, and ignominy with Christ in great ignominy rather than fame, and I desire more to be thought a fool and an idiot for Christ, who first was taken to be such, rather than to be thought wise and prudent in this world.

[168] NOTE For anyone who desires to obtain this third kind of humility it will, therefore, be a great help to make the three colloquies mentioned for the three classes of persons [Exx. 156, 147], asking that Our Lord may be pleased to choose one for this third higher and best level of humility so as the better to imitate and serve Him, provided that it may be for the equal or greater service and praise of the Divine Majesty.

[Elections]

[169]   PREAMBLE FOR MAKING AN ELECTION

In[24] every good election, in so far as it depends on us, the eye of our intention must be simple, looking only at what I have been created for, viz. the praise of God Our Lord and the salvation of my soul, and therefore whatever I choose must help me towards the end for which I have been created, and I must not make the end fit the means, but subordinate the means to the end. But what happens in fact is that many first of all choose marriage, which is a means, and secondly the service of God in married life, although this service of God is the end; and similarly there are others who first of all want church benefices, and afterwards to serve God in them. The result is that such people do not go straight to God, but they want God to come straight to their disordered attachments. They make a means of the end, and an end of the means, and so they put last what they ought to put first. Our objective should be in the first place the desire to serve God, which is the end, and in the second place, to accept a benefice or to marry, should one of those be better for me, since those are means to the end. To sum up, nothing ought to induce me to take up or reject such means except the service and praise of God Our Lord and the eternal salvation of my soul.

[170]   DIRECTIVES
     for finding out the matters on which an election should be made
                    containing four points and a note

POINT I It is necessary that all the things about which we want to make an election be morally indifferent or good in themselves, and that they are on the side of our holy mother, the hierarchical Church, and are not bad or opposed to the Church.

[171] POINT 2 Some things involve an unchangeable choice, e.g. the priesthood, marriage etc., others a changeable one, e.g. accepting or giving up benefices, acquiring or renouncing material possessions.

[172] POINT 3 In the case of an unchangeable election, if such has already been made, there are no further grounds for election since it cannot be undone. So in the case of priesthood, marriage etc., the only point to be considered is that if the election has not been made properly and with due order (i.e. without disordered attachments), one should repent and try to lead a good life within the state one has chosen. It does not look as if such an election is a divine vocation, since it is disordered and biased, even though many deceive themselves in this, considering that a vocation can be divine which comes from a biased or bad election, whereas a divine vocation is always pure and clear, without any mingling of lustful inclination or of any other disordered attachment.

[173] POINT 4 In matters that fall under changeable choice, if the election was made in a proper and rightly ordered way, without admixture of natural inclination or worldly criteria, about things that are subject to a changeable choice, there is no reason for making the election once more, but rather one should try to become perfect to the best of one's ability in the way of that choice.

[174] NOTE It should be noted that when such a changeable election has not been made sincerely and in due order, then if the exercitant really wants to bear outstanding fruits, very pleasing to God Our Lord, it will be to the exercitant's advantage to make it properly.

[175]   THREE TIMES
              in any of which a sound and good election can be made

FIRST TIME This is when God Our Lord so moves and attracts the will that without doubting or being able to doubt, such a dedicated soul follows what is shown, just as St Paul and St Matthew did when they followed Christ Our Lord.

[176] SECOND TIME A time when sufficient light and knowledge is received through experience of consolations and desolations, and through experience of the discernment of different spirits.[25]

[177] THIRD TIME This is a tranquil time. One considers first of all the purpose for which human beings exist, viz. to praise God Our Lord and to save their souls. Desiring this end, one chooses as means some life or state within the limits set by the Church, in order to find thereby a help

to the service of one's Lord and the salvation of one's soul. I called this a 'tranquil' time as then the soul is not disturbed by different spirits and can use her natural powers freely and calmly.

[178] If the election is not made in the first and second times, there follow here two ways of making it in the third.

THE FIRST WAY
to make a sound and good election in the third time
containing six points

POINT 1 To put before myself the subject about which I want to make the election, e.g. a position in life or a benefice to be accepted or refused, or anything else that is subject to a changeable election.

[179] POINT 2 It is necessary to keep as my objective the end for which I was created, viz. to praise God Our Lord and save my soul, and at the same time to be in an attitude of indifference, free from any disordered attachment, so that I am not more inclined or attracted to accepting what is put before me than to refusing it, nor to refusing it rather than to accepting it. Rather I should be as though at the centre of a pair of scales, ready to follow in any direction that I sense to be more to the glory and praise of God Our Lord and the salvation of my soul.

[180] POINT 3 To ask God Our Lord to be pleased to move my will and bring to my mind what I ought to do that is most for His praise and glory about the matter before me, while I use the powers of my understanding well and faithfully, and choose in conformity with His most holy will and good pleasure.

[181] POINT 4 To consider and think over rationally the advantages or benefits I would gain by holding (solely for the praise of God Our Lord and the good of my soul) the proposed position or benefice, and on the other hand to consider in the same way the disadvantages and dangers in holding it. Do the same with the alternative; look at the advantages and benefits of not holding it, and conversely the disadvantages and dangers in not holding it.

[182] POINT 5 After having thought over and reflected in this way from every point of view on the matter before me, I shall look to which side reason most inclines, and thus it is according to the stronger movement of the reason, and not through any sensual inclination, that one should make up one's mind on the matter before one.

[183] POINT 6 Once such an election or deliberation has been made, the

person who has made it should turn with great diligence to prayer, placing him- or herself before God Our Lord, and offering Him this election, so that His Divine Majesty may be pleased to accept and confirm it, if it is to His greater service and praise.

[184]   THE SECOND WAY
to make a sound and good election in the third time
containing four rules and a note

RULE 1 This rule is that the love which moves me and makes me choose something has to descend from above, from the love of God; so the person who makes the choice must first of all feel interiorly that the love, greater or lesser, felt for the object chosen is solely for the sake of one's Creator and Lord.

[185] RULE 2 I should look at the case of a person whom I have never seen or known, and for whom I desire full perfection; I consider what I would tell such a person to do and what election to make for the greater glory of God Our Lord and the greater perfection of that person's soul. Then as my case is the same, I should do the same myself, and keep the rule that I lay down for another.

[186] RULE 3 If I were at the point of death, consider what procedure and what criteria I would then wish to have followed in making the present election. Make my own decision entirely according to this rule.

[187] RULE 4 I should look at and consider my situation on the Day of Judgement, and think how at that moment I would want to have chosen in the present matter; and adopt now the rule that I would then want to have observed, so that then I may be filled with happiness and joy.

[188] NOTE Following the rules just mentioned for my salvation and eternal rest, I shall make my election and offering to God, in accordance with Point 6 of the First Way of making an election [Exx. 183].

[189]   FOR THE AMENDMENT AND REFORM OF
ONE'S PERSONAL LIFE AND STATE

In the case of those already established in ecclesiastical positions or in marriage (whether or not they are well off in material possessions), this is to be noted. If such people lack either the occasion or the readiness to make a choice about matters that are subject to a changeable election, it can be very helpful for them, instead of making an election, to be given a framework and method by which to amend and reform themselves in their personal lives and states. This requires them to commit their existence, life and state to the glory and praise of God Our Lord and the salvation of their souls. In order to reach and attain this end, each one, by means of the Exercises and the ways of election explained above, should consider and ponder: what size of house and staff one should have, how one ought to manage and direct it, what should one's words and example inculcate there, and with regard to one's income, how much should be allocated to the dependants and house, how much should be given to the poor and to other good works. In such matters one should seek nothing other than the greater praise and glory of God Our Lord in and through everything. Thus everyone must bear in mind that one will make progress in spiritual things in the measure in which one shall have put off self-love, self-will and self-interest.

Third Week

First Day

FIRST CONTEMPLATION, AT MIDNIGHT,
*how Christ Our Lord went from Bethany to Jerusalem,
including the Last Supper* [Exx. 289],
*containing the preparatory prayer, three preambles,
six points and a colloquy*

PRAYER The usual preparatory prayer.

[191] PREAMBLE 1 This is to recall the narrative; here it is how Christ Our Lord from Bethany sent two disciples to Jerusalem to prepare the supper, and afterwards went there Himself with the other disciples; after having eaten the paschal lamb and finished supper, He washed their feet and gave His most holy body and precious blood to His disciples. After Judas had gone off to sell his Lord, he spoke to them at length.

[192] PREAMBLE 2 Composition, seeing the place; here it will be to consider the road from Bethany to Jerusalem, whether it is broad or narrow, level etc; similarly, the place of the supper, whether it is large or small, and what it looks like.

[193] PREAMBLE 3 To ask for what I want; here it will be for grief, deep feeling and confusion because it is for my sins that the Lord is going to the Passion.

[194] POINT 1 To see the people at the supper, and by reflecting within myself to try and draw some profit from them.

POINT 2 To hear what they are saying, and in the same way draw some profit from it.

POINT 3 To watch what they are doing, and draw some profit.

[195] POINT 4 To consider what Christ Our Lord suffers in His human nature, or is willing to suffer, depending on the episode that one is contemplating; and here I should start to draw upon all my powers to grieve, to feel sorrow and to weep; in the same way I should labour through each of the other points that follow.

[196] POINT 5 To consider how the divine nature goes into hiding, i.e. how Christ as divine does not destroy His enemies, although He could

do so, but allows Himself in His sacred human nature to suffer most cruelly.[26]

[197] POINT 6 To consider how He suffers all this for my sins, etc, and what I myself ought to do and suffer for Him.

[198] COLLOQUY To end with a colloquy to Christ Our Lord, and finally with an Our Father.

[199] NOTE It should be noted, as has already been partly explained, that in the colloquies we should talk things over and make petitions according to our present situation, i.e. depending on whether I am in a state of temptation or consolation, on whether I desire to have this or that virtue, on whether I want to choose one direction or another, on whether I want to grieve or rejoice over what I am contemplating; to sum up, I ask for what I most earnestly desire concerning certain particular things. In this way I can make a single colloquy to Christ Our Lord, or if the topic or a special devotion moves me, I can make three colloquies, one to the Mother, one to the Son, one to the Father, in the form indicated in the Second Week in the meditation on the three classes of persons [Exx. 156, 147], with the Note there [Exx. 157].

[200]   SECOND CONTEMPLATION, IN THE MORNING,
          from the Last Supper to the garden (inclusive) [Exx. 290]

PRAYER The usual preparatory prayer.

[201] PREAMBLE 1 The narrative here will be how Christ Our Lord with His eleven disciples came down from Mount Sion, where He had had the supper, to the valley of Josaphat; here He left eight of them in a place in the valley and the other three in a part of the garden, and putting Himself in prayer, His sweat became like drops of blood; next he prayed three times to the Father and awakened His disciples; next, at His voice, the enemies fell to the ground, and Judas gave Him the kiss of peace; St Peter cut off the ear of Malchus, and Christ put it back in place; He was arrested as a criminal, and they take Him down into the valley and up the slope to the house of Annas.

[202] PREAMBLE 2 One sees the place: here it will be to consider the road from Mount Sion to the valley of Josaphat, and also the garden, whether wide, whether long, whether of one form or of another.

[203] PREAMBLE 3 It is proper to prayer on the Passion to ask for grief with Christ in grief, to be broken with Christ who is broken, and for

tears and interior suffering on account of the great suffering that Christ has endured for me.

[204]   [NOTES]

NOTE 1 In this Second Contemplation, after the preparatory prayer with the three preambles mentioned above, the same method of procedure for the points and colloquy will be followed as in the First Contemplation (of the Last Supper). Two repetitions will be made on the First and Second Contemplations at the times of mass and vespers, and before supper the prayer of the senses should be made on the same two contemplations, always beginning with the preparatory prayer and the three preludes, adapted to the matter under consideration, in the way mentioned and explained in the Second Week [Exx. 119, 159].

[205] NOTE 2 In accordance with the age, constitution and temperament of the exercitant, all five exercises or fewer will be made each day.

[206] NOTE 3 In this Third Week there are modifications to be made to the Additional practices, viz. the second and the sixth [Exx. 74, 78].

RE ADDITION 2 As soon as I wake up, I put before myself where I am going and for what purpose, and I run briefly over the contemplation I want to make, whatever the mystery may be, making a great effort, while getting up and dressing, to sorrow and grieve over all the great grief and suffering of Christ Our Lord.

RE ADDITION 6 The modification here is that I shall make no attempt to evoke joyful thoughts, not even good and holy ones about subjects like resurrection and final glory, but rather bring myself to grieve, to suffer and to feel broken, calling frequently to mind the labours, weariness and grief suffered by Christ Our Lord from the moment of His birth up to the mystery of the Passion, in which I am at present engaged.

[207] NOTE 4 The particular examen will be made on the Exercises and these Additional practices, as in the previous Week [Exx. 160].

[208]   SECOND DAY

At midnight, on what happened from the Garden to the house of Annas (inclusive) [Exx. 291]; in the morning, from the house of Annas to the house of Caiaphas [Exx. 292]; later the two repetitions and the prayer of the senses, in the way that has already been said [Exx. 204].

THIRD DAY

At midnight, from the house of Caiaphas to Pilate (inclusive) [Exx. 293]; in the morning, from Pilate to Herod (inclusive) [Exx. 294]; and then the repetitions and the senses in the way that has already been said [Exx. 204].

FOURTH DAY

At midnight, from Herod to Pilate [Exx. 295], taking in and contemplating the first half of the mysteries which happened in Pilate's house; then in the morning exercise, the other mysteries which happened in the same house; the repetitions and senses as has been said [Exx. 204].

FIFTH DAY

At midnight, from the house of Pilate up to the nailing to the cross [Exx. 296]; in the morning, from the raising up on the cross to His death [Exx. 297]; later, the two repetitions and the senses [Exx. 204].

SIXTH DAY

At midnight, from the taking down from the cross to the tomb (not including the last mystery) [Exx. 298]; in the morning, from the tomb mystery (to be included) up to the house where Our Lady went after her Son was buried.

SEVENTH DAY

A contemplation of the Passion as a whole in the exercises at midnight and in the morning, and instead of the two repetitions and the senses, one should consider throughout the whole day, as frequently as possible, how the most holy body of Christ Our Lord remained detached and separated from the soul, and where and how it was buried: similarly, one should consider the loneliness of Our Lady with her grief and exhaustion, and then, on the other hand, the loneliness of the disciples.

[209] NOTE It should be noted that anyone who wants to spend more time on the Passion should take fewer mysteries in each contemplation, e.g. in the first, only the Last Supper, in the second, the washing of the feet, in the third, the giving of the Eucharist to the disciples, in the fourth, Christ's discourse, and so on for the other contemplations and mysteries. Again, after finishing the Passion, one can take half of the entire Passion for one full day, the other half on a second day, and the whole Passion on a third day. On the other hand, someone wanting to spend less time on the Passion can take at midnight the Last Supper, in the morning, the garden, at the time of mass, the house of Annas, at the time of vespers, the house of Caiaphas, and for the hour before supper, the house of Pilate. In this way, without repetitions or the prayer of the senses one can make five different exercises each day with a different mystery of Christ Our Lord in each exercise. After finishing the whole Passion in this way, such a person can on another day make one exercise on the whole Passion, or several exercises, or whichever seems likely to be more profitable.

[210]   Rules for the future ordering of one's life
                     as regards eating

RULE 1 There is less to be gained in restraint from eating bread, since bread is not a food about which the appetite is usually as uncontrolled, or the temptation as urgent, as is the case with other foods.

[211] RULE 2 With regard to drink, restraint seems more appropriate than in the eating of bread; so one ought to observe carefully what is beneficial and to be admitted, and what is harmful and to be cut out.

[212] RULE 3 Where delicacies[27] are concerned, one ought to observe the strictest and most complete restraint, for since in this matter the appetite is more inclined to excess, so temptation is more urgent. Restraint in order to avoid disorder with regard to delicacies can be practised in two ways: (i) by getting into the habit of eating plain fare, (ii) by taking delicacies only in small amounts.

[213] RULE 4 Provided one takes care not to fall ill, the more one can cut back on one's normal intake, the sooner will one arrive at the just mean in eating and drinking. There are two reasons for this: (i) by predisposing and adapting oneself in this way, very frequently one will

experience increased inner promptings, consolations and divine inspirations, enabling one to discover what is the just mean; (ii) if one finds that in cutting back in this way one lacks either the bodily strength or the inclination for spiritual exercises, one will easily come to a decision about what is more suitable for the sustenance of the body.

[214] RULE 5 While eating one should imagine that one is seeing Christ Our Lord eating with His apostles, considering the way He drinks, the way He looks, and the way He talks, and then try to imitate Him; thus the higher part of the mind is taken up with considering Our Lord, and the lower with feeding the body, and so one attains a more perfect harmony and order in the way one should behave and conduct oneself.

[215] RULE 6 At other times, when eating, one can think over the lives of the saints, or some religious contemplation, or some spiritual matter that has to be undertaken; for when attention is given to something like this, less pleasure and sensual enjoyment is taken in the body's food.

[216] RULE 7 Above all, one should take care not to become wholeheartedly engrossed in what one is eating, and not to be carried away by one's appetite at meals; instead one should be in control of oneself, both in the manner of eating and in the quantity eaten.

[217] RULE 8 To become free from disordered habits it is very helpful to decide after dinner or supper, or at some other time when one has no appetite for food, what amount of food will be enough for the next dinner or supper, and similarly each day to decide the amount that it is fitting to eat; then no matter how hungry and tempted one may be, one should not exceed this quantity, but rather, if tempted to eat more, one should eat less, the better to overcome one's disordered appetite and the temptation of the enemy.

Fourth Week

FIRST CONTEMPLATION
How Christ appeared to Our Lady [Exx. 299]

PRAYER The usual preparatory prayer.

[219] PREAMBLE 1 The narrative. After Christ died on the cross His body remained separated from the soul, but still united with the divinity, and His blessed soul, also united with the divinity, descended into Hell; from here He released the souls of the just; then returning to the tomb and having risen, He appeared in body and soul to His blessed Mother.

[220] PREAMBLE 2 Composition, seeing the place. Here it will be to see the arrangement of the Holy Sepulchre, and the lodging or house of Our Lady, looking in detail at all its parts, with her room, oratory, etc.

[221] PREAMBLE 3 To ask for what I want, and here it will be to ask for grace to feel gladness and to rejoice intensely over the great glory and joy of Christ Our Lord.

[222] POINTS 1, 2, 3 These three points will be the usual ones that we had for the Last Supper of Christ Our Lord [Exx. 194].

[223] POINT 4 To consider how the divine nature, which seemed to go into hiding in the Passion, now appears and reveals itself so miraculously in the most holy Resurrection, producing really true and holy effects.

[224] POINT 5 To observe how Christ Our Lord fulfils the office of consoler, and to draw comparisons with the way friends are accustomed to console one another.

[225] COLLOQUY To finish with a colloquy, in accordance with the matter under consideration, and an Our Father.

[226]   [NOTES]

NOTE 1 In the following contemplations all the mysteries of the Resurrection are to be gone through in the way indicated below [Exx. 299–312], up to and including the Ascension. For the rest, the same arrangement and procedure are to be adopted and kept throughout the whole week of the Resurrection as were maintained in the week of the Passion

[Exx. 204]. Hence this First Contemplation on the Resurrection may be taken as a guide with regard both to the preambles, which are adapted according to the matter under consideration, and also the five points, which remain the same. The Additions given below [Exx. 229] also remain the same. In everything else, for example the repetitions, five senses, and the shortening or lengthening of the mysteries, etc [Exx. 204, 209], one can take as guide the arrangement of the Third Week of the Passion.

[227] NOTE 2 In this Fourth Week, it is usually more appropriate than in the three preceding weeks to make four exercises and not five: the first will be immediately on rising in the morning; the second, at the time of mass or before lunch in place of the first repetition; the third, at the time of vespers in place of the second repetition; the fourth, before supper, will be the prayer of the senses on the three exercises of the day; in this one should note and pause at the most important points and the places where greater movements of spiritual relish may have been experienced.

[228] NOTE 3 Though a fixed number of points, e.g. three or five, have been given in all the contemplations, the person who is contemplating can take more or fewer points as best suits that person. For this purpose it is very helpful before beginning the contemplation to estimate and number the particular number of points to be taken.

[229] NOTE 4 In this Fourth Week there are modifications to be made to the following out of the Additional practices: Additions 2, 6, 7 and 10 [Exx. 73–82].

RE ADDITION 2 As soon as I wake up, I put before myself the contemplation I have to make, deliberately wanting to be moved and to rejoice in the great joy and gladness of Christ Our Lord.

RE ADDITION 6 I call to mind and think about things that cause happiness, gladness and spiritual joy, such as final glory.

RE ADDITION 7 One can take advantage of the light and of the pleasures of the seasons, e.g. refreshing coolness in the summer, in the winter of the sunshine or the warmth of a fire,[28] in so far as one seems likely to be helped by these things to rejoice in the Creator and Redeemer.

RE ADDITION 10 Instead of practising penance one should look to temperance and the just mean in everything, except where the Church's precepts about fasting and abstinence apply, for these must always be observed, unless there is some legitimate impediment.

[Additional material]

[230] Contemplation for attaining love

NOTE It will be good to notice two things at the start: (i) love ought to find its expression in deeds more than in words; [231] (ii) love consists in mutual communication, i.e. the lover gives and communicates to the beloved whatever the lover has, or something of what the lover has or is able to give, and the beloved in turn does the same for the lover. Thus one who possesses knowledge will give it to the one without it, and similarly the possessor of honour or wealth shares with the one who lacks these, each giving to the other.

PRAYER The usual preparatory prayer.

[232] PREAMBLE 1 The composition, which here is to see how I am before God Our Lord, and before the angels and the saints who intercede for me.

[233] PREAMBLE 2 To ask for what I want. Here it will be to ask for interior knowledge of all the good I have received so that acknowledging this with gratitude, I may be able to love and serve His Divine Majesty in everything.

[234] POINT 1 This is to bring to memory the benefits received – creation, redemption, and particular gifts – pondering with great affection how much God Our Lord has done for me, and how much He has given me of what He has; and further, how according to His divine plan, it is the Lord's wish, as far as He is able, to give me Himself; then to reflect and consider within myself what, in all reason and justice, I ought for my part to offer and give to His Divine Majesty, that is to say, everything I have, and myself as well, saying, as one making a gift with great love:

'Take, Lord, and receive all my liberty, my memory, my understanding, and my entire will, all that I have and possess. You gave it all to me; to you Lord I give it all back. All is yours, dispose of it entirely according to your will. Give me the grace to love you,[29] for that is enough for me.'

[235] POINT 2 To see how God dwells in creatures – in the elements, giving being, in the plants, causing growth, in the animals, producing

sensation, and in humankind, granting the gift of understanding – and so how He dwells also in me, giving me being, life and sensation, and causing me to understand. To see too how He makes a temple of me, as I have been created in the likeness and image of His Divine Majesty. Again, to reflect within myself in the way indicated in Point 1, or in some other way I feel to be better. The same procedure is to be followed in each of the following points.

[236] POINT 3 To consider how God works and labours on my behalf in all created things on the face of the earth, i.e. 'He behaves in the same way as a person at work',[30] as in the heavens, elements, plants, fruits, cattle, etc, He gives being, conserves life, grants growth and feeling, etc. Then to reflect within myself.

[237] POINT 4 To see how all that is good and every gift descends from on high; so, my limited power descends from the supreme and infinite power above, and similarly justice, goodness, pity, mercy, etc, as rays descend from the sun, and waters from a fountain. Then to finish reflecting within myself, as has been said [Exx. 235].

[COLLOQUY] End with a colloquy and an Our Father.

---

[238]   Three Ways of praying

WAY 1   1. ON THE COMMANDMENTS

The first way of praying is concerned with the Ten Commandments, the Seven Capital Sins, the Three Powers of the Soul, and the Five Senses of the Body. This way of praying aims more at providing a framework, a method, and certain exercises by which to prepare oneself and make progress in order that prayer may be acceptable to God, rather than at giving any framework or method of prayer properly so-called.

[239] [PREPARATION] First of all, the equivalent of the second Additional practice, as explained in the Second Week [Exx. 131], should be made: i.e. before entering into prayer I shall allow the spirit to rest a little, by sitting down or strolling about, as seems best to me, while considering where I am going and for what purpose. This same Addition is to be observed at the start of each of the Ways of praying [Exx. 250, 258].

[240] PRAYER A preparatory prayer should be made, such as asking God Our Lord for grace to be able to know my failings in relation to the Ten Commandments. I should ask as well for grace and help to do

better in the future, and for a perfect understanding of the Commandments so that I may keep them better for the greater glory and praise of His Divine Majesty.

[241] [POINTS] This first way of praying should be made as follows: I consider and think over the First Commandment: how have I kept it? how have I failed to keep it? I stay with this as a rule for the time it takes to say three Our Fathers and three Hail Marys. If in this time I discover failings, I ask forgiveness and pardon for them, and say an Our Father. The same procedure is to be repeated for each of the Ten Commandments.

[242] [NOTE 1] It should be noted that if one finds one is not in the habit of sinning against the particular Commandment under consideration, there is no need to spend so long over it; but according as one offends more against a Commandment or less, so one should spend more time or less in the consideration and examination of it. This norm holds good for the capital sins as well.

[243] NOTE 2 After talking over all of the Commandments in this way, having acknowledged my sin with regard to them, and asked for grace and help to do better in the future, I should end with a colloquy to God Our Lord adapted to the matter under consideration.

[244]   WAY I (CONT.)   2. ON THE CAPITAL SINS

Concerning the Seven Capital Sins, after the Additional practice [Exx. 239] one should make the preparatory prayer, in the way already mentioned [Exx. 240]; the only change is that here the subject-matter is sins to be avoided, whereas beforehand it was Commandments to be observed; the same order and rule is to be followed as already explained, and the colloquy [Exx. 241–43].

[245] For a better knowledge of one's faults in relation to the Seven Capital Sins, one should look at their contraries; and similarly, the more surely to avoid these sins, one should resolve and endeavour by means of devout exercises to acquire and keep the Seven Virtues opposed to them.

[246] WAY I (CONT.)   3. ON THE POWERS OF THE SOUL

With regard to the Three Powers of the Soul, the same order and rule are to be followed as for the Commandments, making the Additional practice, the preparatory prayer and the colloquy [Exx. 239–43].

[247] WAY I (CONT.) 4. ON THE FIVE BODILY SENSES

With regard to the Five Bodily Senses, the same procedure is to be kept, changing only the subject-matter.

[248] NOTE Should one wish to imitate Christ Our Lord in the use of the senses, one should commend oneself to His Divine Majesty in the preparatory prayer, then after considering with each sense say a Hail Mary or an Our Father. And if one wishes to imitate Our Lady in the use of the senses, one should commend oneself to her in the preparatory prayer, so that she may obtain that grace from her Son and Lord, then after considering each sense, say a Hail Mary.

[249] WAY 2 OF PRAYING
consists in contemplating the meaning
of each word of a prayer

[250] ADDITION In this second Way of praying the addition will be the same as for the first [Exx. 239].

[251] PRAYER The preparatory prayer will be appropriate to the person to whom the prayer is directed.

[252] [POINTS] The second way of praying is as follows. One either kneels or sits, according to one's disposition and to the devotion one experiences. Keeping one's eyes closed or fixed on one spot, without allowing the gaze to wander, one says the word 'Father', staying with this word for as long as one finds meanings, comparisons, relish and consolation in considerations related to it. One should do this for each word of the Our Father, or for any other prayer that one may wish to take for praying in this way.

[253] RULE I One should spend an hour on the whole of the Our Father, keeping to the procedure just given; then after finishing this, one says the Hail Mary, the Creed, the Anima Christi and the Hail Holy Queen, vocally or mentally in the usual way.

[254] RULE 2 If the person contemplating the Our Father finds in one or two words rich matter for reflection, and much relish and consolation, that person should not be anxious to go further, even though the whole hour is spent on what has been found; when the hour is up, the remainder of the Our Father should be said in the usual way.

[255] RULE 3 If a person has spent a complete hour on one or two

words of the Our Father, when wanting to go back to the same prayer on another day, that person should say those one or two words in the usual way and then begin the contemplation on the word immediately following them, in the manner explained in Rule 2.

[256] NOTE 1 It should be noted that when the Our Father has been completed – either in one day or several – the same procedure should be followed with the Hail Mary, and then with the other prayers, so that over a period of time one will always be exercising oneself in one of them.

[257] NOTE 2 When a prayer is ended, one should turn to the person to whom the prayer has been addressed, and in a few words ask for the virtues or graces for which one feels greater need.

[258] WAY 3 OF PRAYING
by rhythm

ADDITION This will be the same as for Ways 1 and 2 of praying [Exx. 239, 250].

PRAYER The preparatory prayer will be the same as for Way 2 [Exx. 251].

[POINTS] The third Way of praying consists in praying mentally with each breath or respiration, by saying one word of the Our Father or of any other prayer being said, so that only a single word is pronounced between one breath and the next. In the interval between each breath, attention is especially paid to the meaning of that word, or to the person to whom one is praying, or to one's own lowliness, or to the distance between the other's greatness and one's own lowliness; one goes through the other words of the Our Father keeping to the same arrangement and rules; then one says the other prayers, i.e. Hail Mary, Anima Christi, Creed and Hail Holy Queen in the usual way.

[259] RULE 1 One should say the Hail Mary rhythmically on another day or at another time when one wants to pray, and then the other prayers in the usual way; and subsequently take the other prayers in turn and follow the same procedure.

[260] RULE 2 Whoever wants to remain longer on the prayer by rhythm can recite all the prayers mentioned above, or fewer of them, but keeping the same system of rhythmic breathing already explained.

[261] The Mysteries of the life of Christ Our Lord

NOTE In the following mysteries all the words in quotation marks are from the Gospel itself,[31] and the other words are not. For most of the mysteries three points are given to make it easier to meditate or contemplate the mysteries.

[262]   *The Annunciation of Our Lady*
                        Luke 1:25–38

1 The angel St Gabriel, greeting Our Lady, indicated to her the conception of Christ Our Lord: 'The angel, entering where Mary was, greeted her saying to her, "Hail Mary, full of grace; you will conceive in your womb and bear a son"'.

2 The angel confirms what he said to Our Lady by indicating the conception of St John the Baptist, saying to her: '"And behold, Elizabeth, your relative, has conceived a son in her old age"'.

3 Our Lady replied to the angel: '"Behold the handmaid of the Lord; may it be done unto me according to your word"'.

[263]   *The Visitation of Our Lady to Elizabeth*
                        Luke 1:39–56

1 When Our Lady visited Elizabeth, St John the Baptist, while in his mother's womb, became aware of the visit Our Lady had made: 'And when Elizabeth heard the greeting of Our Lady, the child felt joy in her womb; and Elizabeth, full of the Holy Spirit, cried out in a loud voice and said, "Blessed may you be among women, and blessed the fruit of your womb"'.

2 Our Lady sings the canticle, saying: '"My soul magnifies the Lord"'.

3 'Mary was with Elizabeth about three months, and then she returned to her house.'

[264]   *The Nativity of Christ Our Lord*
                        Luke 2:1–14

1 Our Lady and her husband Joseph go from Nazareth to Bethlehem: 'Joseph went up from Galilee to Bethlehem, to acknowledge his subjection to Caesar, with Mary, his wife, a woman already pregnant'.

2 'She bore her first-born son, and wrapped him in clothes, and placed him in the manger.'

3 'There came a multitude of the heavenly army, which said, "Glory to God in the heavens".'

[265]   *On the shepherds*
                   Luke 2:8–20

1 The nativity of Christ Our Lord is made known to the shepherds by the angel: '"I declare to you a great joy, because today the Saviour of the world has been born"'.

2 The shepherds go to Bethlehem: 'They came with haste and found Mary, and Joseph, and the child placed in the manger'.

3 'The shepherds went back, glorifying and praising the Lord.'

[266]   *The Circumcision*
                   Luke 2:21

1 They circumcised the child Jesus.

2 'The name by which he is called is Jesus, the name given to him by the angel before he was conceived in the womb.'

3 They gave the child back to his mother, who felt compassion at the blood that flowed from her son.

[267]   *The Three Kings, the Magi*
                  Matthew 2:1–12

1 The three kings, the Magi, came guided by a star to adore Jesus, saying: '"We saw his star in the East, and we came to adore him"'.

2 They adored him and they offered him gifts: 'Prostrating themselves on the ground they adored him and they presented him gifts: gold, incense and myrrh.'

3 'They received a reply, while they were asleep, that they should not return to Herod, and they returned to their region by another way.'

[268]   *The Purification of Our Lady*
          and the Presentation of the child Jesus
                  Luke 2:22–29

1 They bring the child Jesus into the Temple, so that he can be presented

to the Lord as a firstborn, and they offer for him 'a pair of turtle doves or two young pigeons'.

2 Simeon, coming into the Temple, 'took him in his arms', saying, ' "Now, Lord, leave your servant in peace" '.

3 Anna, 'coming afterwards, acknowledged the Lord and talked about him to all who were waiting for the redemption of Israel'.

[269]   *The Flight into Egypt*
                          Matthew 2:13–15

1 Herod wanted to kill the child Jesus, and so he killed the innocents; and before their death, the angel warned Joseph to fly into Egypt: ' "Rise up and take the child and his mother and fly into Egypt" '.

2 He left for Egypt: 'Who, rising up at night, left for Egypt'.

3 He stayed there until the death of Herod.

[270]   *The Return of Our Lord from Egypt*
                          Matthew 2:19–23

1 The angel warned Joseph to return to Israel: ' "Rise up, take the child and his mother, and go to the land of Israel" '.

2 Rising he came to the land of Israel.

3 As Archelaus, the son of Herod, was ruling in Judaea, he withdrew to Nazareth.

[271]   *The Life of Christ Our Lord*
              from the age of twelve to the age of thirty
                          Luke 2:51–52

1 He was obedient to his parents. 'He grew in wisdom, age and grace.'

2 It seems that he practised the craft of a carpenter, as St Mark [Mark 6:3] indicates with the remark, ' "Is this man by any chance that carpenter?" '

[272] *Christ's coming into the Temple when he was aged twelve*
                          Luke 2:41–50

1 Christ Our Lord, at the age of twelve, went up from Nazareth to Jerusalem.

2 Christ Our Lord stayed in Jerusalem, and his parents did not know it.

3 After three days had gone by, they found him disputing in the Temple, and sitting in the midst of the doctors; and when his parents asked him where he had been, he replied: ' "Do you not know that it is appropriate for me to be in the things that are my Father's?" '

[273]   *The Baptism of Christ*
                         Matthew 3:13–17

1 Christ Our Lord, after having said farewell to his blessed mother, came from Nazareth to the River Jordan, where John the Baptist was.

2 Saint John baptized Christ Our Lord, and when he wanted to offer excuses, judging that he was unworthy to baptize Christ, the latter said to him: ' "Do this on the present occasion, because it is necessary for us to fulfil in this way all that is just" '.

3 'The Holy Spirit came and the voice of the Father from heaven asserting: "This is my beloved son, with whom I am very satisfied" '.

[274]   *The Temptations of Christ*
                        Luke 4:1–13, Matthew 4:1–11

1 After he had been baptized, he went to the desert, where he fasted forty days and forty nights.

2 He was tempted by the enemy on three occasions: 'The tempter, going up to him, says, "If you are the Son of God, tell these stones to turn into bread"; "Throw yourself down from here"; "All that you see, I shall give you if you prostrate yourself on the ground and adore me" '.

3 'The angels came and served him.'

[275]   *The Call of the Apostles*

1 It seems that St Peter and St Andrew were called on three occasions: (i) with a hint (cf. John 1:[35–42]); (ii) to follow Christ to some extent, but with the intention of returning to own what they had left behind (Luke 5:[1–11]); (iii) to follow Christ Our Lord for ever (Matthew 4:[18–22]).

2 He called Philip (John 1:[43–51]) and Matthew (Matthew 9:[9]).

3 He called the other apostles, even if the Gospels make no mention of their special vocations.

There are three other things that ought to be considered: (i) how the apostles were from the uneducated and lower classes; (ii) the dignity to which they were so gently called; (iii) the gifts and graces by which they were raised above all the fathers of the New and Old Testaments.

[276] *The First Miracle performed at the Marriage Feast at Cana*
John 2:1–11

1 Christ Our Lord was invited along with his disciples to the marriage.
2 The mother informs the son about the lack of wine, saying: ' "They have no wine" ', and orders the waiters, ' "Do whatever he tells you" '.
3 'He changed the water into wine, and showed his glory, and his disciples believed in him.'

[277] *Christ Our Lord drove the sellers out of the Temple*
John 2:13–25

1 He threw all the sellers out of the Temple with a whip made of cords.
2 He overturned the tables and coins of the rich bankers who were in the Temple.
3 To the poor who were selling pigeons he gently said: ' "Take those things away from here and avoid making my house into a market-place" '.

[278] *The Sermon on the Mount*
Matthew 5:1–48

1 He speaks separately to his beloved disciples about the eight beatitudes: ' "Blessed the poor in spirit, the gentle, the merciful, those who weep, those who undergo hunger and thirst for the sake of justice, the pure of heart, the peacemakers, and those who suffer persecutions." '
2 He exhorts them to make good use of their talents: ' "So may your light shine before all people that they may see your good deeds and glorify your Father, who is in the heavens" '.
3 He shows himself to be not a transgressor of the Law, but one who brings it to completion, explaining the precepts not to kill, not to commit fornication, not to perjure, and to love enemies: ' "I tell you that you should love your enemies and do good to those who abhor you" '.

[279] *Christ Our Lord stilled the tempest at sea*
Matthew 8:23–27

1 While Christ Our Lord was asleep at sea, there came a great storm.

2 His terrified disciples woke him, and he rebukes them for their little faith, saying to them: ' "What do you fear, men of little faith?" '

3 He ordered the winds and the sea to stop, and with their stopping the sea became calm, so much so that the men were amazed, saying: ' "Who is this, that wind and sea obey him?" '

[280]   *Christ Our Lord walking on the sea*
                        Matthew 14:22–33

1 While Christ Our Lord was on the mountain he made his disciples go to the little boat, and when he had sent away the crowd, he began to pray on his own.

2 The skiff was being threatened by the waves; then Christ came to it walking over the water, and the disciples thought that it was a ghost.

3 As Christ said to them, ' "It is I, do not be afraid" ', St Peter at Christ's command came to him, walking over the water; then having doubts, he began to splash about, but Christ Our Lord saved him, and he rebuked him for his little faith; later when Christ entered the skiff, the wind dropped.

[281]   *The Sending of the Apostles to Preach*
                        Matthew 10:1–42

1 Christ calls his beloved disciples and gives them power to expel demons from people's bodies and to cure all sicknesses.

2 He taught them about prudence and patience: ' "Look! I am sending you like sheep among wolves; therefore be prudent like serpents and simple like doves" '.

3 He instructs them how they should go: ' "Do not desire to possess gold or silver; whatever you receive free of charge, give out free of charge" ', and he instructs them on what they should preach: ' "Go and preach saying, 'The kingdom of heaven has drawn near' " '.

[282]   *The Conversion of the Magdalen*
                          Luke 7:36–50

1 While he was sitting at table in the house of the Pharisee the Magdalen entered there, carrying an alabaster vase full of ointment.

2 Taking a position behind the Lord, near to his feet, she began to sprinkle them with her tears and to wipe them with the hair of her head, and she kissed his feet and anointed them with the ointment.

3 As the Pharisee was accusing the Magdalen, Christ speaks in her defence saying: '"Many sins are forgiven her because she loved much", and he said to the woman, "Your faith has saved you, go in peace"'.

[283]   *The Feeding by Christ of the Five Thousand*
                        Matthew 14:13–21

1 As it was becoming late, the disciples ask Christ to send away the multitude of men who were with him.

2 Christ Our Lord ordered that the loaves should be brought to him, and ordered that all should sit down at table, and he blessed and broke and gave the loaves to his disciples, and the disciples gave them to the multitude.

3 'They ate and had their fill, and twelve baskets were left over.'

[284]   *The Transfiguration of Christ*
                        Matthew 17:1–9

1 Taking in his company the beloved disciples, Peter, James and John, Christ Our Lord transfigured himself, and his face shone like the sun, and his clothing like snow.

2 He talked with Moses and Elijah.

3 When St Peter said that they should make three tabernacles, a voice sounded from heaven saying, '"This is my beloved son; listen to him"', and his disciples on hearing this voice fell on their faces out of fear, and Christ Our Lord touched them saying, '"Rise up and have no fear: tell no one about this vision until the Son of man rises from the dead"'.

[285]   *The Raising of Lazarus*
                        John 11:1–45

1 Martha and Mary inform Christ Our Lord about the illness of Lazarus, and when he knew of it, he held back for two days so that the miracle might be more obvious.

2 Before he raises him, he asks both of them to believe, saying: '"I am the resurrection and the life; anyone who believes in me, though dead, will live"'.

3 After having wept and prayed, he raises him; and the way he raised him was by ordering him, '"Lazarus, come out"'.

[286]   *The Supper at Bethany*
                          Matthew 26:6–10

1 The Lord sups in the house of Simon the leper, together with Lazarus.
2 Mary pours the ointment over the head of Christ.
3 Judas speaks disparagingly: ' "Why all this waste of ointment?" ' But
Christ defends Magdalen once more, saying: ' "Why are you troubling
this woman, since she has performed a kindness to me?" '.

[287]   *Palm Sunday*
                          Matthew 21:1–17

1 The Lord sends for the ass and the colt, saying, ' "Untie them and
bring them to me; and if anyone says anything to you, say that the Lord
needs them, and at once he will allow you" '.
2 He mounted the ass that was covered with the apostles' garments.
3 People come out to receive him, spreading their clothes and the
branches of the trees on the road, and saying: ' "Save us, Son of
David! Blessed be he who comes in the name of the Lord! Save us on
high!" '

[288]   *The Preaching in the Temple*
                          Luke 19:47–48

1 He was teaching every day in the Temple.
2 When the preaching was finished, as there was nobody to welcome
him in Jerusalem, he would go back to Bethany.

[289]   *The Last Supper*
                          Matthew 26:17–30, John 13:1–30

1 He ate the Paschal Lamb with his twelve apostles, to whom he foretold
his death: ' "In truth I tell you that one of you is going to sell me" '.
2 He washed the feet of the disciples, even those of Judas, beginning
with St Peter, who did not want to consent to this, as he had in mind the
majesty of the Lord and his own lowliness, saying: ' "Lord, are you
washing my feet?" ' but he did not know that Christ was giving an
example of humility in this way, which is why he said, ' "I have given you
an example, so that you should do as I have done" '.
3 He instituted the most holy sacrifice of the Eucharist, as the greatest

sign of his love, saying: ' "Take and eat" '; when the supper is finished, Judas goes out to sell Christ Our Lord.

[290]   *The Mysteries performed between*
          the Last Supper and the Garden (inclusive)
              Matthew 26:30–46, Mark 14:26–42

1 When the supper was finished and the hymn had been sung, the Lord went to the Mount of Olives with his disciples, who were full of fear; and he left eight of them in Gethsemane with the words, ' "Sit down here while I go over there to pray" '.

2 Accompanied by St Peter, St James and St John, he prayed three times to the Lord, saying: ' "Father, if it is possible, may this chalice pass from me; nevertheless, not my will but yours be done" '; and being in an agony, he prayed all the more profusely.

3 He began to feel such fear that he said, ' "My soul is sad even unto death" ', and he sweated blood so abundantly that St Luke says, 'His sweat was like drops of blood that ran to the ground', which implies that his garments were full of blood.

[291]   *The Mysteries performed between*
          the Garden and the House of Annas (inclusive)
                Matthew 26, Luke 22, Mark 14

1 The Lord allows himself to be kissed by Judas and arrested like a thief, while saying to them: ' "You have come out to arrest me with sticks and arms as if I were a thief, whereas I was with you teaching every day in the Temple and you did not arrest me" '; and when he said, ' "Which person are you looking for?" ', the enemies fell to the ground.

2 St Peter wounded the servant of the High Priest; then the gentle Lord said to him, ' "Put your sword back in its place" ', and he cured the servant's wound.

3 Deserted by his disciples, Christ is brought to Annas, where St Peter, who had followed him from a distance, denied him once; and Christ was struck a blow in the face, with the words, ' "Is that how you reply to the High Priest?" '

[292]   *The Mysteries performed between*
        the House of Annas and the House of Caiaphas (inclusive)

1 They take him bound from the house of Annas to the house of

Caiaphas, where St Peter denied him twice, and under the gaze of the Lord, he went outside and wept bitterly.

2 Jesus spent the whole of that night in bonds.

3 In addition, those who were holding him prisoner mocked him, and wounded him, and blindfolded him, and struck him blows in the face; and they asked him, ' "Prophesy to us who has struck you" ', and they did other similar acts of blasphemy against him.

[293]   *The Mysteries performed between*
the House of Caiaphas and the House of Pilate (inclusive)
Matthew 27, Luke 23, Mark 15

1 The whole multitude of the Jews take him to Pilate, and they accuse him before Pilate saying, ' "We have found that this fellow was perverting our people, and was forbidding the payment of tribute to Caesar" '.

2 After Pilate had examined him once and then again, Pilate said: ' "I find no fault whatsoever" '.

3 Barabbas, a thief, was chosen in preference to him: 'They all shouted out saying, "Do not release this man, but Barabbas" '.

[294]   *The Mysteries performed between*
the House of Pilate and the House of Herod

1 Pilate sent Jesus, the Galilean, to Herod, tetrarch of Galilee.

2 Herod, who was curious, questioned him at length, and he did not reply to anything at all, even though the scribes and priests were constantly accusing him.

3 Herod and all his army treated him with contempt by dressing him in a white garment.

[295]   *The Mysteries performed between*
the House of Herod and the House of Pilate
Matthew 27, Luke 23, Mark 15, John 19

1 Herod sends him back once more to Pilate, thanks to which they become friends after having been enemies.

2 Pilate took Jesus and had him flogged; and the soldiers made a crown of thorns, and they put it on his head, and they clothed him in purple, and came up to him saying, ' "Hail, King of the Jews" ', and they struck him blows in the face.

3 He brought him out before them all: 'Jesus then came out, crowned with thorns and clothed in red; and Pilate said to them, "Here is the man", and as soon as the High Priests saw him, they shouted out saying, "Crucify him, crucify him!"'.

[296]   *The Mysteries performed between*
        the House of Pilate and the Cross (inclusive)
                John 19:13–22

1 Pilate, seated as a judge, handed Jesus over to them so that they might crucify him, after the Jews had denied him as king, saying, '"We have no king but Caesar"'.
2 He was carrying the cross on his back, and when he was not able to carry it, they forced Simon of Cyrene to carry it behind Jesus.
3 They crucified him between two thieves, putting up the notice, '"Jesus of Nazareth, king of the Jews"'.

[297]   *The Mysteries performed on the Cross*
                John 19:23–37

1 He spoke seven words on the Cross: he prayed for those who were crucifying him; he pardoned the thief; he commended St John to his mother, and his mother to St John; he cried aloud, '"I am thirsty"' and they gave him gall and vinegar; he said that he was forsaken; he said, '"It is finished"'; he said, '"Father, into your hands I commend my spirit"'.
2 The sun was darkened, the rocks split, the tombs opened, the veil of the Temple was torn into two parts from the top to the bottom.
3 They blasphemed, saying: '"You are the one about to destroy the Temple of God; come down from the cross!"'; his garments were divided; when his side was wounded by the lance, it poured out water and blood.

[298]   *The Mysteries performed from the Cross*
                to the Tomb (inclusive)
                John 19:38–42

1 He was taken from the cross by Joseph and Nicodemus, in the presence of his sorrowful mother.
2 The body was carried to the tomb, and anointed, and buried.
3 Guards were posted.

[299]   *The Resurrection of Christ Our Lord*
                      The First Appearance

1 He appeared to the Virgin Mary. Although this is not stated in Scripture, it is assumed to have been included in the statement that he appeared to so many others, for Scripture supposes that we are capable of understanding, as it is written: ' "Are you also without understanding?" '

[300]   *The Second Appearance*
                         Mark 16:1–11

1 Mary Magdalene [Mary] the mother of James, and Salome make their way very early in the morning to the tomb, saying: ' "Who will lift the stone from the door of the monument for us?" '
2 They see the stone lifted and the angel who says, ' "Jesus of Nazareth, whom you seek, is already risen from the dead; he is not here" '.
3 He appeared to Mary, who had stayed near the tomb after the other women had gone.

[301]   *The Third Appearance*
                        Matthew 28:8–10

1 These Marys come out of the monument full of fear and great joy, intending to announce to the disciples the resurrection of the Lord.
2 Christ Our Lord appeared to them on the way, saying: ' "May God bless you" ', and they came close and fell at his feet and adored him.
3 Jesus says to them, ' "Do not be afraid; go and tell my brothers to make their way to Galilee, because there they will see me" '.

[302]   *The Fourth Appearance*
                          Luke 24:9–12

1 As soon as St Peter heard from the women that Christ was risen from the dead, he went with haste to the monument.
2 Entering the monument, he saw only the cloths that had covered the body of Christ Our Lord, and nothing else.
3 While St Peter was thinking about these things, Christ appeared to him, and that is why the apostles were saying, ' "Truly the Lord has risen from the dead and has appeared to Simon" '.

[303]   *The Fifth Appearance*
                         Luke 24:13–35

1 He appeared to the disciples who were on their way to Emmaus talking about Christ.

2 He rebuked them, showing from the Scriptures that Christ had to die and rise from the dead: ' "You foolish people and slow of heart to believe all that has been talked about by the prophets! Was it not necessary that Christ should suffer, and so enter into his glory?" '

3 At their entreaty he stays there, and was with them until, on giving them communion, he disappeared; and then they returned and told the disciples how they had recognized him in the communion.

[304]   *The Sixth Appearance*
                         John 20:19–23

1 The disciples were gathered together 'for fear of the Jews', except for St Thomas.

2 Jesus appeared to them, the doors being closed, and while in their midst said, ' "Peace be with you" '.

3 He gives them the Holy Spirit, saying: ' "Receive the Holy Spirit: whose sins you forgive, they will be forgiven them" '.

[305]   *The Seventh Appearance*
                         John 20:24–29

1 St Thomas says in his unbelief, because he had not been present at the preceding appearance, ' "Unless I see it, I will not believe it" '.

2 A week later Jesus appears to them, the doors being closed, and says to St Thomas, ' "Insert your finger here and see the truth, and do not be unbelieving, but faithful" '.

3 St Thomas believed, saying, ' "My Lord and my God" ', and Christ says to him, ' "Blessed are those who did not see and believed" '.

[306]   *The Eighth Appearance*
                         John 21:1–17

1 Jesus appears to seven of his disciples, who were fishing; they had not caught anything during the whole night, but when they stretched out the net at his command, 'they could not pull it in because of the huge catch of fish'.

2 St John recognized him by this miracle and said to St Peter, '"It is the Lord"', and the latter threw himself into the sea and came to Christ.

3 He gave them some roast fish and a honeycomb to eat, and he entrusted the sheep to St Peter (after first examining him three times on charity) saying, '"Feed my sheep"'.

[307]   *The Ninth Appearance*
                             Matthew 28:16–20

1 At the Lord's command the disciples go to Mount Tabor.

2 Christ appears to them and says, '"All power in heaven and on earth has been given to me"'.

3 He sent them all over the world to preach, saying, '"Go and teach all peoples, baptizing them in the name of the Father and of the Son and of the Holy Spirit"'.

[308]   *The Tenth Appearance*
                             1 Corinthians 15:6

'Later he was seen by more than five hundred brethren together.'

[309]   *The Eleventh Appearance*
                             1 Corinthians 15:7

'He appeared later to St James.'

[310]   *The Twelfth Appearance*

He appeared to Joseph of Arimathaea, as is devoutly meditated upon and written about in the *Lives of the Saints*.

[311]   *The Thirteenth Appearance*
                             1 Corinthians 15:8

He appeared to St Paul after the Ascension ('Finally he appeared to me, as to one born out of due time'); he appeared also, in soul, to the holy fathers in Limbo; and after they had been brought out, and he 'took up once more' his body, he appeared many times to the disciples, and spoke with them.

The Ascension of Christ Our Lord
Acts of the Apostles 1:1–12

1 After he had been appearing during forty days to the apostles, giving many demonstrations and signs, and talking of the kingdom of God, he ordered them to wait in Jerusalem for the Holy Spirit that had been promised.
2 He brought them to the Mount of Olives, and in their presence he was raised up, and a cloud made him disappear from their sight.
3 As they were looking up to heaven, the angels say to them, ' "Men of Galilee, what are you looking at up in heaven? This Jesus, who is taken up from your eyes to heaven, will come in the way that you have seen him go to heaven" '.

[313] Rules by which to perceive and understand to some extent the various movements produced in the soul: The good that they may be accepted and the bad that they may be rejected

RULES MORE SUITABLE FOR THE FIRST WEEK

[314] RULE 1 With people who go from one mortal sin to another it is the usual practice of the enemy to hold out to them apparent pleasures; so he makes them imagine sensual satisfactions and gratifications, in order to retain and reinforce them in their vices and sins. With people of this kind, the good spirit uses the opposite procedure, causing pricks of conscience and feelings of remorse by means of the power of rational moral judgement.[32]

[315] RULE 2 In the case of people who are making serious progress in the purification of their sins, and advancing from good to better in the service of God Our Lord, the opposite to Rule 1 takes place, because then it is typical of the bad spirit to harass, sadden and obstruct, and to disturb the soul with false reasoning, so as to impede progress, while the distinctive trait of the good spirit is to give courage and strength, consolations, tears, inspirations and quiet, making things easy and removing all obstacles, so that the person may move forward in doing good.

[316] RULE 3 On spiritual consolation. I use the word 'consolation' when any interior movement is produced in the soul that leads her to become inflamed with the love of her Creator and Lord, and when, as a

consequence, there is no created thing on the face of the earth that we can love in itself, but we love it only in the Creator of all things.

Similarly, I use the word 'consolation' when one sheds tears that lead to love of one's Lord, whether these arise from grief over one's sins, or over the Passion of Christ Our Lord, or over other things expressly directed towards His service and praise.

Lastly, I give the name 'consolation' to every increase of hope, faith and charity, to all interior happiness that calls and attracts a person towards heavenly things and to the soul's salvation, leaving the soul quiet and at peace in her Creator and Lord.

[317] RULE 4 On spiritual desolation. 'Desolation' is the name I give to everything contrary to what is in Rule 3, e.g. darkness and disturbance in the soul, attraction towards what is low and of the earth, anxiety arising from various agitations and temptations. All this tends to a lack of confidence in which the soul is without hope and without love; one finds oneself thoroughly lazy, lukewarm, sād, and as though cut off from one's Creator and Lord. For just as consolation is contrary to desolation, so the thoughts born of consolation are contrary to the thoughts born of desolation.

[318] RULE 5 In time of desolation one should never make any change, but stand firm and constant in the resolutions and decision by which one was guided on the day before the desolation, or in the decision one had reached during the preceding time of consolation. For, just as in consolation it is more the good spirit who guides and counsels us, so in desolation it is the bad spirit, and by following his counsels we can never find the right way.

[319] RULE 6 Although in desolation we must make no changes in our former decisions, it is however very helpful to make an intense effort to change oneself in a sense opposed to this desolation, e.g. by more insistence on our prayer and meditation, by much use of examens, and by increasing our practice of penance in some suitable way.

[320] RULE 7 Anyone in desolation must consider how Our Lord has placed them in a trial period, so that they are to resist the various disturbances and temptations of the enemy by their own natural powers; and they are able to do this with the divine help which remains with them at all times, even though they may not clearly feel it. Although the Lord has withdrawn their great fervour, deeply-felt love and intense grace, He has still left them a grace which is sufficient for their eternal salvation.

[321] RULE 8 A person in desolation must endeavour to remain in an

attitude of patience, for patience is opposed to the annoyances that come upon one; one should keep in mind that consolation will soon come, if one uses all one's powers against this desolation, as has been said in Rule 6.

[322] RULE 9 There are three principal reasons for our being in desolation: (i) because we are lukewarm, lazy or careless in our commitment to the spiritual life, and so spiritual consolation goes away because of our faults; (ii) to test our quality and to show how far we will go in God's service and praise, even without generous recompense in the form of consolations and overflowing graces; (iii) to give us true information and understanding, so that we may perceive through experience that we cannot ourselves arouse or sustain overflowing devotion, intense love, tears or any other spiritual consolation, but that everything is a gracious gift from God Our Lord. So we do not build our nest where we do not belong, becoming elated in mind to the point of pride or vainglory, putting down to our own account things like devotion or the other features of spiritual consolation.

[323] RULE 10 When in consolation one must consider how one will bear oneself in the desolation that will follow later, and gather renewed strength for that moment.

[324] RULE 11 In consolation one should try to humble and lower oneself as much as possible by thinking how little one is worth in time of desolation without this grace or consolation. On the contrary, in desolation one should keep in mind that by drawing strength from one's Creator and Lord, one has great power (if grace is enough) to resist every enemy.

[325] RULE 12 The behaviour of the enemy resembles that of a woman in a quarrel with a man, for she is weak before strength, but strong when allowed her will. It is the way of a woman, when she is quarrelling with a man, to lose courage and take flight when the man shows a bold front; on the other hand, the moment the man gives way and loses courage, then the rage, vengeance and ferocity of the woman overflow and know no bounds. In the same way it is the nature of the enemy to weaken and lose courage, and to turn to flight with his temptations, when the person actively engaged in the spiritual life shows a bold front against those temptations and acts in a way diametrically opposed to them. If on the contrary the exercitant begins to be afraid and to lose courage in sustaining temptations, no beast on the face of the earth is as ferocious as the enemy of human nature in the intense malice with which he carries out his wicked purpose.

[326] RULE 13 The enemy also behaves as a false lover behaves towards a woman. Such a man wants to remain hidden and not be discovered; in using dishonest talk to try to seduce the daughter of a good father, or the wife of a good husband, he wants his words and inducements kept secret; on the other hand he is greatly put out when the daughter reveals his deceitful words and corrupt intentions to her father (or the wife to her husband), for then he clearly recognizes that his plans cannot succeed. In the same way, when the enemy of human nature brings his deceits and inducements to bear upon the just soul, he wants them to be received and kept in secret; but when they are disclosed to a good confessor or other spiritual person who knows his trickery and perversity, he is very displeased, realizing that once his tricks are revealed, his malicious purpose cannot succeed.

[327] RULE 14 Likewise, he behaves like a military leader setting about the conquest and seizure of the object of his desire. For the commander of an army, after setting up his camp and inspecting the fortifications and defences of a castle, attacks it at its weakest point; and in the same way the enemy of our human nature makes his rounds to inspect all our virtues, theological, cardinal and moral, and where he finds us weakest and in greatest need as regards eternal salvation, there it is that he attacks and tries to take us.

[328] Rules for the same purpose containing more advanced ways of discerning the spirits
RULES MORE APPLICABLE TO THE SECOND WEEK

[329] RULE 1 It is characteristic of God and His angels in the movements prompted by them to give true gladness and spiritual joy, while banishing all the sadness and distress inspired by the enemy, whose characteristic it is to fight against this joy and spiritual consolation by bringing forward specious arguments, subtleties and one fallacy after another.

[330] RULE 2 Only God Our Lord gives consolation to the soul without preceding cause; for it is the Creator's prerogative to enter the soul, and to leave her, and to arouse movements which draw her entirely into love of His Divine Majesty. When I say 'without cause' I mean without any previous perception or understanding of some object due to which consolation could come about through the mediation of the person's own acts of understanding and will.

[331] RULE 3 When there is a cause, consolation can be given by the good or the bad angel, but these give consolation for opposite purposes: the good angel for the soul's profit, so that the person grows and rises from good to better, the bad angel for the contrary purpose, so as eventually to draw the person into his own evil intention and wickedness.

[332] RULE 4 It is the characteristic of the bad angel to assume the form of 'an angel of light'[33] in order to enter the devoted soul in her own way and to leave with his own profit; i.e. he proposes good and holy thoughts well adapted to such a just soul, and then little by little succeeds in getting what he wants, drawing the soul into his hidden snares and his perverted purposes.[34]

[333] RULE 5 We must pay close attention to the whole course of our thoughts: if the beginning, middle and end are entirely good, and tend towards what is wholly right, this is a sign of the good angel; but if the course of the thoughts suggested to us leads us finally to something bad, or distracting, or less good than what one had previously intended to do, or if in the end the person is weakened, upset or distressed, losing the peace, tranquillity and quiet previously experienced, all this is a clear sign of the bad spirit, the enemy of our progress and eternal well-being.

[334] RULE 6 When the enemy of human nature has been detected and recognized by the evil end to which he leads, his serpent's tail, it is profitable for the person who has been tempted by him to retrace immediately the whole sequence of good thoughts he has suggested, looking for their starting-point, and noting how the enemy contrived little by little to make the soul fall away from the state of gentleness and spiritual joy she was in, until he drew her into his depraved intention; by recognizing and taking note of this experience one is put on one's guard in the future against his habitual deceits.

[335] RULE 7 With those who go from good to better, the good angel touches the soul sweetly, lightly and gently, like a drop of water going into a sponge, while the bad spirit touches her sharply with noise and disturbance, as when a drop of water falls on a stone; with those who go from bad to worse, these same spirits touch the soul *contrario modo* [in the opposite way]. The reason for this difference is the person's disposition of soul, either contrary or similar to those spirits: when the disposition is contrary, the spirits enter with noise and disturbance, making themselves felt; when the disposition is similar, they come in quietly, as someone comes into one's own home opening the door.

[336] RULE 8 When the consolation is without cause, even though there is no deception in it, as it comes from God Our Lord alone, as has been said [Exx. 330], nevertheless the spiritual person to whom God gives this consolation must scrutinize the experience carefully and attentively, so as to distinguish the exact time of the actual consolation from the period following it, during which the soul is still aglow and favoured with the after-effects of the consolation now passed. For during this second period it often happens, owing either to thinking based on conclusions drawn from the relations between our own concepts and judgements, or to the agency of the good or bad spirit, that we form various plans and opinions that are not directly given to us by God Our Lord. These therefore require to be examined with very great care before being given complete credence and put into practice.

---

[337] Rules to be observed in the ministry of alms-giving

[338] RULE 1 If I distribute alms to relations or friends, or to persons to whom I am attached, I should consider four things, of which some mention has already been made in connection with the election [Exx. 184–87].

Firstly, the love that moves me and makes me give the alms has to descend from above, from the love of God Our Lord; so I must first of all feel within myself that the love, greater or lesser, which I have for these people is for God's sake, and that in my motive for my loving them more God must shine forth [Exx. 184].

[339] RULE 2 Secondly, I should look at the case of someone whom I have never seen or known, and for whom I desire full perfection in their ministry and state of life. The norm which I would like such a person to observe in the way of distributing alms – for the greater glory of God Our Lord and the greater perfection of that person's soul – I myself shall keep to, acting in the same way, neither more nor less. So I will observe the rule and norm that I would want for someone else, and that I judge to be appropriate [Exx. 185].

[340] RULE 3 Thirdly, I should consider, supposing I were at the point of death, what procedure and what criteria I would then wish to have maintained in the duties of my administration; keeping to that rule, I shall put it into practice in my particular acts of distribution [Exx. 186].

[341] RULE 4 Fourthly, I should look at my situation on the Day of Judgement, and think how at that moment I would want to have fulfilled my duties and responsibilities in this ministry. I shall adopt now the rule that I would then want to have observed [Exx. 187].

[342] RULE 5 When one feels a preference and attachment for the people to whom one wants to give alms, one should stop and carefully ponder the four rules just given, using them to examine and test one's attachment; one should not give the alms until one has got rid of and rejected one's disordered attachment, in keeping with these rules.

[343] RULE 6 There is no fault in taking the goods of God Our Lord for distribution when one is called by our God and Lord to such a ministry. Nevertheless fault and excess are possible in regard to the amount and proportion that one should appropriate and allot to oneself out of the goods held for donation to others, so it is always possible to reform one's life and state by means of the above rules.

[344] RULE 7 For the foregoing reasons and for many others, it will always be better and more secure in what touches our person and standard of living the more we cut down and reduce expenses, and the closer we come to our High Priest, our model and rule, Christ Our Lord; it was in this spirit that the Third Council of Carthage (at which St Augustine was present) decided and decreed that the furniture of a bishop should be ordinary and cheap.

The same consideration applies to all walks of life, taking into account and making allowances for the circumstances and social position of individuals. Thus for marriage we have the example of St Joachim and St Anna, who divided their means into three parts: the first they gave to the poor, the second to the ministry and service of the Temple, the third they took for the support of themselves and of their household.

[345]   Helpful Notes
            for the perception and understanding of scruples
                   and of the insinuations of our enemy

[346] NOTE 1 People commonly give the name 'scruple' to something coming from our judgement and freedom, i.e. the situation when I freely take something to be sin which is not a sin, as would be the case if a person, having accidentally trodden on a cross formed by two straws, were to make the personal judgement that a sin had been committed. Properly speaking this is an error of judgement, not a scruple in the true sense.

[347] NOTE 2 After I have trodden on that cross, or indeed after anything I may have thought, said or done, the idea may come to me from outside myself [Exx. 32] that I have sinned, while on the other hand it seems to me that I have not sinned; *tamen* [however] I feel troubled about the matter, doubting and at the same time not doubting. It is this that is a 'scruple' properly so-called, and a temptation suggested by the enemy.

[348] NOTE 3 The first scruple (Note 1) is to be utterly abhorred, being as it is a total error. But for the person seriously committed to the spiritual life, the second (Note 2) is of no small benefit for a time. Indeed to a great extent it cleanses and purifies such a person, separating his or her spirit far from anything that even looks like a sin (as St Gregory says, 'It is the mark of a good soul to see a fault where there is none'[35]).

[349] NOTE 4 The enemy observes closely whether a person is of coarse or sensitive conscience: a sensitive conscience he tries to sensitize still further, to the point of excess, in order the more easily to cause trouble and confusion. For instance, he may see that a person consents neither to mortal nor to venial sin, nor anything that looks like deliberate sin at all, and in such a case, unable to make such a person fall into anything that seems to be sin, he endeavours to make that person see sin where there is no sin, as in some word or passing thought. But if the conscience is coarse the enemy tries to make it even more coarse. For example, if up to now a person took no notice at all of venial sins, he will try to make that person take little notice of mortal sins, and in the case of a person who up to now took some notice of them, he will try to diminish the sense of venial sin or eliminate it completely.

[350] NOTE 5 The person who wishes to progress in the spiritual life must always go *contrario modo* [in the opposite direction] to that of the

enemy; i.e. if the enemy is out to make the conscience coarser, one should seek to become more sensitive, and likewise if the enemy tries to refine the conscience to an extreme degree, one should seek to establish a position in the just mean, so as to become completely tranquil.

[351] NOTE 6 A person may wish to say or do something consistent with the Church and with the mind of the authorities, something that promotes the glory of God. In those circumstances, if a thought, or rather a temptation, comes from without not to say or do that thing, proposing specious arguments about vainglory or something else, then such a person ought to raise the understanding to our Creator and Lord, and if one sees that the proposed action is for God's due service, or at least not against it, one must act in a way opposed *per diametrum* [diametrically] to the temptation (like St Bernard in his answer to a similar temptation, 'I did not begin because of you, and I am not going to give up because of you'[36]).

---

[352] <center>Rules to follow
in view of the true attitude of mind that
we ought to maintain
[as members] within the Church militant</center>

[353] RULE 1 Laying aside all our own judgements, we ought to keep our minds open and ready to obey in everything the true bride of Christ Our Lord, our holy mother, the hierarchical Church.

[354] RULE 2 We should praise confession made to a priest, and the reception of the Blessed Sacrament once a year, much more its reception once a month, and very much more its reception once a week, given the duly required dispositions.

[355] RULE 3 We should praise frequent attendance at mass; also hymns, psalms and long prayers, whether in or out of church; and likewise, appointed hours at the appropriate times for all the divine services, prayers and the canonical Hours.

[356] RULE 4 We should praise greatly religious life, virginity and continence, and we should not praise matrimony to the same extent as any of these.

[357] RULE 5 We should praise the vows of religion – obedience, poverty and chastity – and other vows of perfection made voluntarily; it should be noted however that vows should not be made about matters that

withdraw from evangelical perfection, e.g. to be a merchant, to marry, etc., as a vow has to do with things that lead to that perfection.

[358] RULE 6 We should praise the cult of the saints, venerating their relics and praying to the saints themselves, praising also the stations, pilgrimages, indulgences, jubilees, dispensations and the lighting of candles in churches.

[359] RULE 7 We should praise the decrees about fasting and abstinence, e.g. in Lent, on the ember days, vigils, Fridays and Saturdays; similarly penances, not only interior but also exterior.

[360] RULE 8 We should praise the decoration and architecture of churches, also statues, which should be venerated according to what they represent.

[361] RULE 9 Finally we should praise all the precepts of the Church, being ready to seek arguments in their defence and never in any way to attack them.

[362] RULE 10 We should be more inclined to approve and praise the decrees and regulations of those in authority, and their conduct as well; for although some of these things do not or did not in the past deserve approval, more grumbling and scandal than profit would be aroused by speaking against them, either in public sermons or in conversations in front of simple people. In that way people would become hostile towards authority, either temporal or spiritual. But just as harm can be done by speaking ill to simple people about those in authority in their absence, so it can do good to speak of their unworthy behaviour to the actual people who can bring about a remedy.

[363] RULE 11 We should praise both positive theology and scholastic theology, for as it is more characteristic of the positive doctors, such as St Jerome, St Augustine and St Gregory, to move the heart to love and serve God Our Lord in all things, so it is more characteristic of the scholastics like St Thomas, St Bonaventure, the Master of the Sentences, etc, to define or explain for our times what is necessary for eternal salvation and for more effectively combating and exposing all errors and fallacies. This is because the scholastic doctors, being more recent, not only have the benefit both of the true understanding of Sacred Scripture and of the holy positive Doctors, but while being themselves enlightened and illuminated by divine grace, they can avail themselves of the councils, canons and decrees of our holy mother Church.

[364] RULE 12 We must avoid making comparisons between those of our own day and the blessed of former times, for there is no small error in doing this, i.e. in saying of someone, 'He knows more than St Augustine,'

or 'He is another St Francis or greater', or 'He is another St Paul for virtue, sanctity, etc'.

[365] RULE 13 To maintain a right mind in all things we must always maintain that the white I see, I shall believe to be black, if the hierarchical Church so stipulates; for we believe that between Christ Our Lord, the bridegroom, and the Church, His bride, there is the same Spirit who governs and directs us for the good of our souls because it is by that same Spirit and Lord of us all who gave the Ten Commandments that our holy mother Church is directed and governed.

[366] RULE 14 Even granting as perfectly true that no one can be saved without being predestined, and without having faith and grace, nevertheless much caution is needed in the way in which we discuss and propagate these matters.

[367] RULE 15 We must not make a habit of talking much about predestination, but if sometimes mention is made of it one way or another, our language should be such that simple people are not led into error, as sometimes happens with them saying, 'It is already decided whether I am to be saved or damned, so whether I do good or evil can change nothing'; paralysed by this notion, they neglect the works that lead to the salvation and spiritual progress of their souls.

[368] RULE 16 In the same way we must be careful lest by speaking about faith at great length and with much emphasis, without distinctions and explanations, we give people occasion to be dilatory and lazy in works, either before they have a faith informed by charity, or even afterwards.

[369] RULE 17 Similarly we must not talk of grace at such length and with such insistence as to poison people's attitude to free will. Thus our way of talking about faith and grace should result, as far as we can with God's help, in the greater praise of His Divine Majesty, but not in such a way and with such expressions (especially in times as dangerous as ours) that there is any prejudice against, or contempt for, good works and free will.

[370] RULE 18 Given that the motive of pure love in the constant service of God Our Lord is to be valued above all, yet we ought also greatly to praise fear of the Divine Majesty. The reason is that not only filial fear is a good and holy thing, but where someone is not capable of attaining anything better or more useful, even servile fear can be a great help to escape from mortal sin, and once free a person can easily reach the filial fear, which is wholly acceptable and pleasing to God Our Lord, as it is all one with divine love.

Appendix

Anima Christi (translated by John Henry Newman)

Soul of Christ, be my sanctification;
Body of Christ, be my salvation;
Blood of Christ, fill all my veins;
Water from the side of Christ, wash out my stains;
May Christ's Passion strengthen me;
O good Jesu, hear me;
In your wounds I fain would hide,
Never to be parted from your side;
Guard me when my foes assail me,
Call me when my life shall fail me.
Command me then to come to thee,
That I for all eternity
With your saints may praise thee. Amen.

Creed

I believe in God, the Father almighty, Creator of heaven and earth;

and in Jesus Christ His only Son, Our Lord, who was conceived by
the Holy Spirit, born of the Virgin Mary, suffered under Pontius Pilate,
was crucified, dead and buried; He descended into hell; the third day He
rose again from the dead; He ascended into heaven, and is seated at the
right hand of God the Father almighty; from thence He shall come to
judge the living and the dead.

I believe in the Holy Spirit; the holy catholic Church; the communion
of saints; the forgiveness of sins; the resurrection of the body, and life
everlasting. Amen.

Hail Holy Queen

Hail, holy Queen, mother of mercy; hail, our life, our sweetness, and our hope! To you do we cry, poor banished children of Eve; to you do we send up our sighs, mourning and weeping in this vale of tears. Turn, then, most gracious advocate, your eyes of mercy towards us, and after this our exile, show to us the blessed fruit of your womb, Jesus. O clement, O loving, O sweet Virgin Mary!

Hail Mary

Hail Mary, full of grace, the Lord is with thee; blessed art thou among women, and blessed is the fruit of thy womb, Jesus.

Holy Mary, Mother of God, pray for us sinners, now, and at the hour of our death. Amen.

Our Father

Our Father, who art in heaven, hallowed be thy name, Thy kingdom come, Thy will be done on earth as it is in heaven. Give us this day our daily bread, and forgive us our trespasses, as we forgive those who trespass against us. And lead us not into temptation, but deliver us from evil. Amen.

Notes

1 The stronghold in question was Pamplona, capital of Navarre, and the date is 20 May 1521. The incident takes its place in long-standing tensions between France and Spain. Legend has it that Ignatius was wounded by a cannonball, but his choice of words suggests something lighter. Recent research has established that Ignatius was probably wounded not during the major part of the battle, when heavy cannon was used, but in preliminary lighter skirmishes. See Luis Fernández Martín, 'Rendición de la fortaleza de Pamplona', in *Ignacio de Loyola en Castilla*, ed. Luis Fernández Martín and Rogelio García Mateo, Valladolid 1989, pp. 93–101.

2 It was standard medieval practice for lay Christians in danger, and in the absence of a priest, tó confess to each other. See, for example, Thomas Aquinas's *Summa Theologiae*, supplement, q.8. Technically, such confession was non-sacramental.

3 Coudray's Latin translation of c. 1560 adds that Ignatius remained in the same room he had occupied previously, and that he was looked after by the best doctors in the French army.

4 The two feast-days mentioned here are 24 June and 29 June.

5 Polanco's 1547–48 account of Ignatius's life mentions that, as a courtier, he had written poems in honour of Peter (FN II, p. 517).

6 According to Nadal (e.g. FN II, pp. 186–87) the life of Christ was that of Ludolf of Saxony (d. 1377), and the collection of saints' lives was that known as the *Golden Legend* (or *Flos Sanctorum*) compiled by the thirteenth-century Dominican Archbishop of Genoa, Jacopo of Varazze. Spanish translations of both texts were in circulation by the early sixteenth century. Nadal's witness is confirmed in part by the striking parallels between Ludolf's *Vita Christi* and the *Spiritual Exercises*. See E. Raitz von Frentz, 'Ludolphe le Chartreux et les Exercices de S. Ignace de Loyola', *Revue d'ascétique et mystique*, 25 (1949), pp. 375–88; Gilles Cusson, *Biblical Theology and the Spiritual Exercises*, St Louis, MO 1988, pp. 10–19.

7 *Motes*. The translation is conjectural, and the identity of the lady in question (assuming she was not a creation of Ignatius's fantasy) quite uncertain.

8 This word is being used in Ignatius's technical sense. See Glossary, Exx. 316 and Letter 4.

9 Ignatius's hyperbole here alludes to Aristotelian and Thomist theories of knowledge and sense-perception. We come to know a particular object through

its interaction with a 'likeness' (*species*) stored in the mind. See, for example, Thomas Aquinas, *Summa Theologiae*, I, q.84 a.7. obj.1 and ad.1.

10 Note Ignatius's characteristic link here between consolation and the desire for service.

11 There is a notable Charterhouse in Burgos, site of the grave of Queen Isabella.

12 Antonio Manrique de Lara, viceroy of Navarre 1516–21, in whose service Ignatius had fought at Pamplona. Later in the summer of 1521, the French victory in the May battle had been reversed and Manrique restored. However, he had been replaced in November 1521, and had thus moved from Pamplona to Navarrete. The probable date of the incidents recorded here is February 1522.

13 This name is Basque for 'you are among thorns'. In 1468, Our Lady had appeared to a shepherd boy in a thornbush, and the place soon became a Basque national shrine.

14 In 1554 Francis Borgia was concerned with the restoration of a monastery next to this shrine. At this point Ignatius wrote to him as follows: '. . . when God our Lord did me the mercy of my making some change in my life, I remember having received some profit in my soul from keeping vigil by night in the main body of that church' (*Epist.* VII, p. 422). Other early accounts of Ignatius's life speak of a vow of perpetual chastity which he made on the journey from Loyola to Montserrat. It seems attractive to conjecture that this took place here.

15 The language here, especially in the marginal note, echoes the characteristically Reformation concern with justification, and the bitter disputes that concern stimulated. But the narrative's theme here is probably not a technical one. Ignatius is charting his growth in the awareness of God by contrasting the rash and unreflective naïveté of this stage in his journey with the wisdom that comes later at Manresa.

16 This is the first point at which the text gives Ignatius this title.

17 The flesh of the gourd, a kind of pumpkin, would have been scraped out, and the rind used as a water container.

18 *Amadis of Gaul* was probably the most famous of the so-called 'tales of chivalry' in Spain at the time, and had been published in 1508. At one point, Amadis's son, Esplandián, keeps watch by night at the Virgin Mary's altar. See Pedro de Leturia, *Iñigo de Loyola*, trans. Aloysius J. Owen, Chicago 1965, p. 143.

19 The confessor was a Frenchman, Jean Chanon; the three days probably includes time taken for prayerful preparation. Montserrat, a Benedictine monastery on a Catalan mountain with striking rock-formations, was at this time in the vanguard of the Catholic Reformation. This was chiefly thanks to the initiatives of Abbot García de Cisneros (abbot from 1493 to 1510), whose spiritual treatise *Ejercitatorio de la vida espiritual*, published in 1500, was widely influential. The abbey was a major centre of the so-called *devotio moderna*, with its renewed stress on the interior life and a methodical approach to prayer. In the abbey church there is a famous statue of Our Lady with the face in black.

20 Here Nadal added 'having received the holy Eucharist' to the early Latin translation.

21 This passage suggests that Ignatius's original intention was to stay only a few days in Manresa. Why his stay was extended can only be conjectured. It may be that Ignatius wanted to avoid the retinue of the newly elected Adrian VI (Adrian Dedal, a Dutchman, formerly tutor to Charles V and regent of Spain), who had passed through the territory of Navarre (hence perhaps the shortage of money referred to in §13), and who left Barcelona for Rome in the spring of 1522.

22 The first of many sentences ending with 'etc.'. It is not clear whether this usage goes back to Ignatius himself or whether it indicates that Gonçalves da Câmara is conscious of having left something out.

23 Passages such as this and the vision of Our Lady recounted in §10 obviously suggest the possibility of a psychoanalytic interpretation. For an initial discussion of the issues involved, see W. W. Meissner, *Ignatius of Loyola: The Psychology of a Saint*, 1992.

24 Compare Letter 4.5.

25 The identity of this woman is unknown. Lay women – *beatas* – played a significant role in the Spanish spiritual renewal of this period. See Mark Rotsaert, *Ignace de Loyola et les renouveaux spirituels en Castille au début du XVIe siècle*, Rome 1982, pp. 66–72.

26 Weekly communion was in fact a rarity in the sixteenth-century Church. Later the Society of Jesus would become noted for encouraging the practice.

27 This reference to an *agujero* (literally 'hole') is curious. Perhaps Ignatius's memory is at this point so painful that he loses his grip on circumstantial detail and conflates his room with a cave outside.

28 See Exx. 87. The *Golden Legend* tells of how St Andrew once fasted for five days in order to obtain God's pardon for a hardened, long-standing sinner.

29 See Exx. 319.

30 The most attractive interpretation of the passage, though by no means the only possible one, is as an illustration of the general principles outlined in Exx. 333–34, 346–48. Ignatius's scruples are revealed as a strategy of the enemy's. Initially they seemed to proceed from a sensitive piety, and it is only at a later stage, when Ignatius realizes that they culminate in making him feel like reneging on his conversion, that their destructive effect becomes apparent. Painful though an experience of this kind always is, it yields its own wisdom. Through it one gains insight into how the destructive forces within the self characteristically work.

31 '*ayudar algunas almas*' or, elsewhere, '*ánimas*'. Though (or because?) no human being is able to help Ignatius as he is seized by God, the experience leads him to offer spiritual help to others. This is the first explicit use (but cf. §11, note 10) of a formula dear to Ignatius. It is quite wrong to interpret this phrase in terms of a Platonic or Cartesian dichotomy between soul and body; a case indeed can be made for translating *alma* or *ánima* as 'person'. The principal reason for maintaining the term 'soul' in translation is to preserve, however inadequately, the sense that the help in question is motivated by the Gospel. See *Constitutions*, pp. 77–78, n. 10.

32 It is in this kind of detachment from particular experiences that Karl Rahner, the noted twentieth-century theologian, locates Ignatius's original contribution to the spiritual life.

33 See Exx. 175, 330. Ignatius writes in these passages of an unquestionable divine irruption into consciousness, without reflecting on how such an event is to be understood theoretically. Commentators are seriously divided on the speculative issues raised by such claims.

34 According to Gonçalves da Câmara the major hiatus in the dictation process came after Ignatius had been 'in Manresa for some days'. On stylistic grounds it seems likely that the break came here or hereabouts. But see note 40 below.

35 'en figura de tres teclas'. This is a puzzling and obscure expression, and it may not be appropriate to seek out a precise meaning. The analogy may be with how three individual notes can contribute to a chord.

36 See Exx. 237.

37 In the manuscripts the '3' comes earlier (before the parenthesis immediately preceding). It has been transferred here first because it makes much better sense in this new position, secondly because it is clear that the copyists rearranged the material from which they were working at this point. Two of the most authoritative manuscripts have the following note: 'The three things following (referring to the incidents recounted in paragraphs 32–33) are interspersed between these five points. In the copying they will be placed after all five are finished, below' (FN I, p. 402).

38 These incidents are noted subsequently: §§ 41, 48.

39 Compare the testimony of Diego Laínez: 'I remember . . . having heard Fr Ignatius say, when speaking of the gifts our Lord gave him there in Manresa, that it seemed to him that, if, per impossibile, the Scriptures and the other documents of the faith were to be lost, the idea and the impression of things which our Lord had imparted to him in Manresa would be enough for him as regards the things pertaining to salvation' (FN I, p. 84).

40 Assuming that the date of dictation is 1555, this indicates that Ignatius was born in 1492 or 1493, and is therefore mistaken. If this passage was dictated in 1553 the reference would indicate what is probably the correct date: 1491. However, the context of the passage from Gonçalves da Câmara's Notebook cited in the following note and the evidence of his preface tell in favour of dictation in 1555. As noted above, there is some evidence that the arrangement of material here is the responsibility of the scribes; they may be drawing on information given during both periods of dictation.

41 This vision by the River Cardoner is clearly a high point in Ignatius's life, and one which he saw as decisively formative. On 17 February 1555 Gonçalves da Câmara asked Ignatius a number of questions about why he had laid down particular directives for life in the Society: no fixed dress, no office in choir, sending new recruits on pilgrimage, etc. 'And to all these things the reply is going to be, "through something that happened to me at Manresa"' (Notebook, n. 137; FN I, p. 610).

Some Jesuit commentators have held that Ignatius at this point received a kind of detailed revelation of the Society's future constitution. Ignatius's own account underplays any sense that God revealed particular information, and stresses the total transformation of the understanding, the change of identity wrought by conversion. Interpreters do well to respect his reticence.

42 Ignatius returns to the mysterious vision he recounted at the beginning of his time at Manresa, as if to show us that the purpose of his deepening in prayer was a growth in ability to discern the forces operating in his psyche. Ignatius's concern is not that we banish the evil spirit from our hearts, because this does not lie within our power. Rather, we are to learn to deal appropriately with it.

43 Behind Ignatius's horror of vainglory lies one of the convoluted issues of the Reformation, that of the senses in which we may and may not say with assurance that we are justified by God's grace. It is anachronistic to distinguish positions along official confessional lines prior to the first session of the Council of Trent in 1546. Trent's decree on justification presents a nuanced position: '. . . just as no devout person ought to doubt the mercy of God, the merit of Christ and the power and efficacy of the sacraments, so it is possible for anyone, while regarding themselves and their own weakness and lack of dispositions, to be anxious and fearful about their own state of grace, since no one can know, by that assurance of faith which excludes all falsehood, that he or she has obtained the grace of God' (Tanner, *Decrees of the Ecumenical Councils*, Washington and London 1990, p. 674 – translation slightly adapted).

For a telling account of how Ignatius is caught up in this religious upheaval, see Terence O'Reilly, 'The Spiritual Exercises and the Crisis of Medieval Piety', *The Way Supplement*, 70 (Spring 1991), pp. 101–13.

44 Baltasar de Faria was Portuguese ambassador to the Holy See from 1543 till 1551, and as such a significant figure in the early development of Jesuit ministries. Francisco Ferrer, born in Manresa in 1528, was a servant in his household.

45 Pilgrim ships normally left Venice in the early summer. Ignatius had also to fit in a visit to Rome in order to get the necessary permit. Allowing for unexpected delays, he needed to leave Manresa at roughly the turn of the year.

46 One of the principal nobles of Catalonia. His sister was married to the Duke of Nájera, in whose service Ignatius had been at Pamplona.

47 A small coin.

48 See §21.

49 Townspeople were nervous of visitors because of the plague.

50 Ignatius's application for permission to visit the holy places, together with a Curial indication of approval, has been preserved in the Vatican Archives and recently edited (FD, pp. 289–90). Here Ignatius is described as a 'cleric of the diocese of Pamplona', a point which is corroborated by documents from a 1515 legal process in which he claimed clerical status in order to escape the jurisdiction of the civil court (FD, pp. 229–46). Ignatius was therefore not, as many have claimed, a lay person during his most formative years, and he may in fact have had a significant religious history before the Battle of Pamplona.

51 §29.

52 Rhodes had been captured by the Turks on 12 December 1522.

53 Now Larnaka.

54 Two of Ignatius's fellow pilgrims have also left accounts of this journey, though neither expressly mentions Ignatius: Peter Füessli, a bell-maker from Zurich; and Philipp Hagen, a canon from Strasbourg. Peter Knauer, in his German translation of the *Reminiscences* (see Bibliography), gives a modern German version of part of Füessli's account, with details of the original texts (pp. 129–39 and p. 64 n. 131). According to Füessli they arrived at Jaffa on 25 August 1523 but were not allowed to leave the ship until 31 August. The master of the ship had to inform those in charge of the shrines that the pilgrims had arrived, and also to negotiate an escort through what was territory controlled by Turks.

55 Contrast this account of his purpose with what he envisaged on his Loyola sickbed (§9); and see note 31 above.

56 At this time the care of the holy places was entrusted to the Franciscans. 'Guardian' is a technical term for the superior of a Franciscan house.

57 '*a estas partes*' – to Europe, where the story is being narrated.

58 The Franciscan Provincial in question lived in Cyprus, but was visiting the houses in the Holy Land at the time of Ignatius's pilgrimage. See BAC, pp. 112–113, nn. 18–19.

59 22 September. There are references in the early sources to a fuller account of this pilgrimage written by Ignatius, but unfortunately the text is lost. See FN I, pp. 1–4.

60 A village near the Mount of Olives from which the Palm Sunday procession began. See Mt. 21:1 and parallels.

61 A name given to Syrian Christians, a group which did not accept the understanding of Jesus Christ defined at the Council of Chalcedon (451). The name evokes the belt with which they tied in their loose Arabic cloak. The circumlocution allows the narrative to suggest Ignatius's continuing attachment to the suffering Christ even as he has to leave the holy places.

62 According to Füessli they left Jerusalem on 23 September 1523, but were prevented by the Turks from reaching Jaffa before 3 October. They arrived in Cyprus on 14 October.

63 According to legend, the body of St James was miraculously transported from Jerusalem to Compostela. See Larrañaga, p. 233, n. 5.

64 '*tomar una tierra de la Pulla*'. From Coudray onwards (c. 1560), translators have taken this as a reference to Apulia. Knauer, however, conjectures that Ignatius landed at Pula, south of Trieste. Füessli also landed in this area, and the journey from Apulia to Venice could not have been covered on foot in the short time suggested by §50.

65 Ignatius has made explicit mention only of one person (§42), though it may be that he was taken into a house in St Mark's Square.

66 The relative values of the coins mentioned here and below have to be deduced from the text. *Quattrino* is a word still existing in modern Italian. Etymologically, it corresponds to the English 'farthing'; in terms of usage, it is sometimes simply the equivalent of 'cash' or 'coppers'. The *marchetto* was a copper coin

minted in Venice during the fifteenth and sixteenth centuries. The *giulio* was a more valuable, silver coin struck in 1504 by Pope Julius II (1503–13).

67 The war in question was once again the struggle between Francis I of France and Charles V, Holy Roman Emperor. At this point the dispute centred on possession of the Duchy of Milan. In 1525, after the Battle of Pavia, Francis was captured and taken to Madrid as a prisoner.

68 Contrast the visions of Christ as a white body (§29), a gold object (§44) or a sun (§99). It is not clear whether the 'representation' here is something distinct from a vision or merely a different kind of vision.

69 The point being made here depends on the different, more or less formal, modes of address still preserved in modern European languages other than English.

70 An interestingly down-to-earth and tiny example of discernment of spirits issuing in a decision. One presumes the cap is metaphorical.

71 In reality Portuondo. In 1524 Rodrigo de Portuondo had overseen the return of the Imperial fleet from Marseilles to Genoa after its admiral had been defeated and taken prisoner (FN II, p. 435). A letter of Charles V, written from Genoa in 1529, discusses the maintenance of ships under the supervision of 'Rodrigo de Portuondo, captain general of our galleys' (García-Villoslada, p. 257, n. 45). Note how Ignatius's ideals of strict poverty coexist quite unselfconsciously with his ability to draw on his courtly past in order to find powerful patrons.

72 Andrea Doria (1466–1560), a legendary Genoese seaman and mercenary, who fought for France from 1522, but by 1528 had switched allegiance to Charles V. Even as Ignatius was dictating his narrative, Doria, now more than eighty years old, was commanding a naval expedition in Corsica.

73 Ignatius would have arrived in Barcelona in late February or early March 1524. On Isabel Roser, see Letter 3, note 2; Letter 19, note 8. Jeroni Ardèvol held the chair of grammar at the Barcelona Estudi General in the academic year 1525–26, and may have been teaching there in a subordinate role in the years before. It is uncertain whether his teaching Ignatius without charge simply reflects the fact that students at the college customarily did not pay, or whether alternatively Ignatius is here remembering some kind of extra private tuition for which Ardèvol would normally have been remunerated. For an account of the documentary evidence, see two articles in Spanish by Cándido de Dalmases, the second of which he co-authored with José M. Madurell Marimón: AHSI 10 (1941), pp. 283–93; 37 (1968), pp. 370–407.

74 The identity of the monk remains uncertain. Contrast §37, where Ignatius speaks of how unsatisfied he was with the spiritual help available in Manresa and Barcelona.

75 But see §82, and compare §26, Exx. 326.

76 See §34.

77 The university of Alcalá had been established by Cardinal Jiménez de Cisneros in 1508, and quickly became a major centre of humanist learning. In the usage of medieval and Renaissance universities 'arts' was the name given to a general course of studies, including material we would now include under the

heading of 'science'. From this course a student could proceed to one of the higher faculties: law, medicine or theology.

78 These are named later in the narrative (§58). It may be significant that one of the manuscripts omits the whole section from here to §70, replacing it with a brief summary.

79 Named after its founder, and also known as the almshouse of Our Lady of Mercy.

80 Domingo Soto (1494/5–1560) had taught at Paris and Alcalá before entering the Dominican order in 1524. The Albert mentioned may be Albert the Great (1193–?1280), another Dominican, who wrote a commentary on book 8 of Aristotle's *Physics*. However, one source (FN II, p. 154) suggests that he could have been Albert of Saxony (1316?–90), rector of the universities of Paris and Vienna and later bishop of Halberstadt, who wrote a commentary on Aristotle's *Physics*. Peter Lombard, a twelfth-century theologian, was enormously influential, especially for his *Sentences*, a synthesis of scholastic theology. Ignatius was probably a private student in the city, since his name appears on no surviving university register. The range of material may have been over-ambitious (see below, §73).

81 Ignatius's ministry at Alcalá, as we shall see, was controversial and led to a trial. From the records of that trial it seems that he was giving only parts of what we now know as the *Spiritual Exercises* to the women who came to him. See note 105 below.

82 Gonçalves da Câmara has a marginal note here: 'I must remember the fear which he himself went through one night'. This may be elucidated by another marginal insertion, this time added by Polanco himself to the manuscript of his 1574 Latin life of Ignatius: 'However, he had a room in the part of that house which was infested with ghosts. He was thus agitated by some kind of terror during the night, which he decided was vacuous and not to be given in to, entrusting himself to God. He began to provoke the demons both mentally and vocally: "if you've got any power from God against me, use it. I'll willingly put up with whatever God pleases. You can't do anything more than God allows you". And that steadfastness of mind and heart, that steady faith and confidence in God, did not merely free him from every terror of the enemy then, but rendered him immune, with God's help, from nocturnal terrors of this kind subsequently.' (FN II, p. 545.)

83 Diego de Eguía later joined Ignatius in Venice, and as a Jesuit was to become Ignatius's confessor. His brother Miguel was responsible for printing Erasmus's *Enchiridion militis christiani* in Spanish translation, a book that was clearly both influential and controversial, and had also recently brought out a version of the *Imitation of Christ* (Exx. 100). The family was related to Francis Xavier. Scholars have sometimes picked up on this kind of reference to show how Ignatius at this stage was allied to expansive rather than repressive religious currents in Spain, and have contrasted this with his reserved attitude towards Erasmus in later years. Perhaps, however, the really significant point is how closely Ignatius is related to agencies carrying through a cultural and religious revolution through the new medium of the printed book.

On the complicated history of how Erasmus's writings were received in Spain, the standard work is Marcel Bataillon, *Érasme et l'Espagne* (Paris 1937), available also in Spanish. On how Ignatius may have interacted with this process, see two essays in English: John C. Olin, 'Erasmus and St Ignatius Loyola', in *Six Essays on Erasmus* (New York 1979); and Terence O'Reilly, 'Saint Ignatius Loyola and Spanish Erasmianism', AHSI 43 (1974), pp. 301–21.

84 At this point some currents of spiritual renewal in Spain were beginning to fall foul of authority, represented by the Inquisition. The term *alumbrado* or 'illuminist' was used legally to denote those adjudged heretics. Its theological content was shifting and imprecise, rather like 'modernist' in the early part of the twentieth century. The underlying problem is that of how to relate charismatic inspiration and ecclesial authority: a problem which is still unresolved in the Christian Churches. How far Ignatius and his companions were associated with *alumbrados* is a complex theoretical and historical question which awaits further research.

85 From this first process, we have records of testimony given in closed session by four witnesses, and of the interview described below. Further documentary evidence suggests that this first investigation, despite what Ignatius says, was not in fact provoked by his activity, but rather was part of a general systematic investigation of people suspected of illuminism. The inquisitors were simply gathering information, and leaving action to be taken by officials in the various towns. See FD, pp. 322–31, and Luis Fernández Martín, 'Iñigo de Loyola y los alumbrados', in *Ignacio de Loyola en Castilla* (as cited in note 1 above), pp. 155–264, here pp. 241–42.

86 From the official record: 'that for just causes leading him to this, he was commanding them and did command them, each one, by virtue of holy obedience and under pain of major excommunication which they would *ipso facto* incur if they did the opposite, to relinquish within the next eight days their said habit and mode of dress, and conform to the normal dress which clerics and lay people wear in these kingdoms of Castile' (FD, p. 331 – 21 November 1526). This may be reconcilable with Ignatius's account if one takes it that he and Arteaga were clerics; alternatively, Figueroa may have moderated the sentence on account of the companions' lack of means to buy new clothes (see §64). On Figueroa, cf. Letter 10 (with note 10).

We learn from the testimony of the almshouse warden that Juanico – Jean de Reynald – was a page of the then Viceroy of Navarre. He was injured in an Alcalá brawl and taken to the almshouse to recover (FD, pp. 329–30). Ignatius had presumably acquired the other companions in Barcelona.

87 At this point Gonçalves da Câmara wrote in the margin 'about what Bustamente told me'. Bartolomé de Bustamente, a controversial Provincial in Andalucía in the mid-1550s, joined the Society of Jesus in 1552. Prior to that he had been secretary to the Archbishop of Toledo, and hence was in a position to provide Gonçalves da Câmara with information relevant here.

88 Three women were interrogated on 6 March 1527 and asked about what Ignatius did when conversing with women. 'And he has spoken with them,

teaching them the commandments, and the mortal sins, and the five senses and powers of the soul, and he explains this very well. He explains it through the gospels and St Paul and other saints, and he says they should examine their consciences in front of a holy picture every day, bringing to mind things in which they have committed sin; and he advises them to go to confession every week and receive the Sacrament at the same time' (FD, p. 332).

89 The third process finished on 1 June 1527, and must therefore, if Ignatius is right about a confinement of six weeks, have begun in mid-April, a mere six weeks after the second.

90 Here Gonçalves da Câmara has a marginal note, 'M^a uno, y era confesor'. The MHSI editors conjecture, reasonably, that this should be translated 'Miona one of them, and he was his confessor'. Manuel Miona, a learned Portuguese priest, was Ignatius's confessor both here and in Paris, and joined the Society in 1545. See Letter 6.

91 This lady was noted as one concerned for prisoners and for the poor, and also for her devotion to the Eucharist, so much so that she was called 'the madwoman of the Sacrament'. For further information, see FN I, pp. 447-48.

92 A cryptic way of asking if Ignatius was a secret Jew. According to Polanco's 1547-48 account, Ignatius answered 'that on Saturday he had a devotion to Our Lady; he didn't know any other feasts, nor were there Jews in his part of the world' (FN I, p. 174). In 1492 Spanish Jews were faced with a choice between conversion or deportation, and in later years the religious authorities were permanently concerned with Jews who might outwardly have converted but who continued to practise their Judaism in secret. See James W. Reites, 'St Ignatius of Loyola and the Jews', Studies in the Spirituality of Jesuits, 13.4 (September 1981).

93 According to ancient Christian legend, a woman (known as Veronica – 'true image') wiped the face of Christ as he was carrying his cross, and the image of his face remained on the cloth. Jaén, in southern Spain (hence a long way from Alcalá), was one of a number of shrines purporting to possess this cloth.

94 A senior professor at the University, who had been nominated by Cardinal Jiménez himself as the first occupant of the chair named after Thomas Aquinas.

95 It was a pious custom for people to accompany the priest on his visits to the sick with the consecrated host.

96 According to Polanco's account of 1547-48, Ignatius had been visiting Calisto in Segovia when the two women had departed.

97 From the trial documents we learn that the two ladies indeed corroborated what Ignatius had said, and the accounts of the verdict correspond. However, it is clear that the authorities investigated Ignatius's dealings with a wider circle of women than the mother and daughter mentioned here (FD, pp. 333-44).

98 Alfonso de Fonseca, Archbishop of Toledo and Primate of Spain 1523-34, a patron of humanism and Erasmianism. He was in Valladolid for the baptism of the new prince, later to become Philip II. It is noteworthy that Ignatius is in a position to make this kind of contact over the heads of officials such as Figueroa.

Fonseca had founded a house in Salamanca for poor students, known either as the College of St James or as the Archbishop's College.

99 See §52. In the next sentence, 'on realizing . . . said' is supplied by the MHSI editors from the early Latin version.

100 Ignatius uses the same word, 'society' – *compañia* – to refer both to his group in Alcalá and Salamanca here and to what was to become the Society of Jesus.

101 In this same summer of 1527, there was a major meeting of theologians at Valladolid under the chairmanship of the Grand Inquisitor to consider Erasmian ideas. Dominicans from the Salamanca faculty were among the sharpest critics of Erasmus.

The name of the subprior was Nicolás de Santo Tomás. From his point of view Ignatius and his companions cannot but have resembled a number of heretical, indeed bizarre religious figures in the 1520s, and his suspicion is at least understandable. See V. Beltrán de Heredia, 'Estancia de San Ignacio de Loyola en San Esteban de Salamanca', *Ciencia Tomista*, 83 (1956), pp. 507–28.

One reason Ignatius expands so much on this incident may be that at the time of dictation the *Spiritual Exercises* were under suspicion in Spain, and Dominicans were in the forefront of those raising sharp questions. Moreover, Dominicans were raising campaigns against the Jesuits at the Spanish court as early as 1542, when there were only two members of the Society in Spain. Whatever happened at Salamanca, and at Alcalá beforehand, was remembered in influential places.

102 Ignatius stresses that this Frías is a bachelor in order to distinguish him from another Frías with a doctorate, mentioned below at §68. On the identity of the judges see B. Hernández Montes, 'Identidad de los personajes que juzgaron a San Ignacio en Salamanca', AHSI 52 (1983), pp. 3–51 (with summary in English, p. 51).

103 Other sources indicate he became a Franciscan.

104 See §62.

105 Exx. 35–37. We are in no position to assess how similar the Salamanca papers were to the text we now know as the *Spiritual Exercises*. In general the supple use of the word 'exercise' in the text (e.g. §67) should alert us to how Ignatius's method in the strict sense shades into everyday pastoral care. An editor or translator has to make a decision about capitalizing the word which a narrator can avoid. It is clear from the Alcalá trial records that Ignatius was at this stage making this distinction in his dealings with people (FD, p. 334), and the point may also be linked to his experience of scrupulosity at Manresa.

106 Francisco de Mendoza (1508–66), at that time a teacher of Greek in the University, later Archdeacon of Toledo, Bishop of Coria, and Cardinal. He was appointed to the see of Burgos in 1550.

107 By founding the Society of Jesus, Ignatius realized elements of both these visions. In this linguistically difficult passage Ignatius shows how he connected the ideals of following the suffering Christ (see, for example, Exx. 147) and apostolic service.

108 In the late summer and autumn of 1527 tensions between France and Spain were escalating, and war was declared on 22 January 1528.

109 From a letter we know that Ignatius arrived on 2 February 1528. Gonçalves da Câmara is obviously uncertain here. A marginal note refers to the birth of Philip II in 1527: 'When he was a prisoner in Alcalá the prince of Spain was born; from this one can calculate everything, also for the period before.'

110 One of approximately sixty colleges at the University of Paris, known for its strict discipline. Other students included Erasmus, Calvin and Rabelais.

'Humanities' here refers to the study of Latin, more linguistic than literary. Ignatius was repeating some of the material he had studied back in Barcelona. Later, at the College of Ste Barbe, he proceeded to the Arts course (see note 77 above).

111 According to the most recent French commentary on this text, that of Jean-Claude Dhôtel, one écu would have maintained a student for a month.

112 A regent would have been a teacher in charge of a number of students and sharing living-quarters with them.

113 Juan de Castro, who obtained a doctorate in 1532. See below, §§77–78, and Letter 4, note 9.

114 Ignatius needed to make only three such trips, in 1529 and the two following years, going to London during the last of these. According to the elderly Polanco, there were circles of merchants in Bruges, Antwerp and London who were accustomed to supporting students. In subsequent years the merchants simply sent Ignatius money, which enabled him also to help others. Ignatius is also said to have met the noted humanist, Luis Vives, on the first of these trips, and there was a slight altercation between them regarding Lenten fasts (FN I, p. 179; FN II, pp. 556–58). Unfortunately, none of the primary sources enables us to expand on Ignatius's visit to London.

115 Nothing further is known of Amador, except that he came from Pamplona and his fuller name was Amador de Elduayen; Pedro de Peralta was later a canon of Toledo cathedral.

116 Diego de Gouveia (?1470–1557), a Portuguese, and principal of the College of Ste Barbe, to which Ignatius indeed later moved. The threat recorded here came to nothing, but on a later occasion, when Ignatius began to acquire the companions who definitively stayed with him, Gouveia did get as far as summoning all the students to witness Ignatius being beaten. However, at the last minute he relented, and later became a significant patron of the Society. On him, see Letter 10 and Schurhammer, pp. 101–02, 136–43.

Magister Noster ('our master') was a conventional way in which students at Paris referred to their teachers. It recurs at §81.

117 From this point onwards the original is in Italian, and the narrative becomes noticeably more sketchy.

118 There was a Benedictine abbey at Argenteuil, eventually suppressed in 1791. It possessed what was thought to be a seamless garment woven for Christ by his mother. The garment is now in the parish church.

119 Leonor de Mascarenhas (1503–84), a Portuguese noblewoman and long-standing friend of the Society. She had been governess to the infant prince Philip, and Ignatius probably first met her when he went to Valladolid in 1527 to meet the Archbishop. See Hugo Rahner, *Saint Ignatius Loyola: Letters to Women*, pp. 417–33.

120 Original – '*India dello imperatore*'. The lady has been identified as one Catalina Hernández, a *beata*, one of six who sailed to Mexico in 1531 in the hope that they would direct a kind of school for native girls. The relationship between Calisto and Catalina gave rise to scandal, and he was banished from Mexico City to the interior of the country. He refused to comply and instead returned to Spain. See Marcel Bataillon, 'L'iñiguiste et la beata', *Revista de historia de América*, 31 (June 1951), pp. 59–75.

121 *Comendador* was the title given to a cleric granted the honours and salary of a knight. He in fact became tutor to one of Prince Philip's pages. In 1540 Paul III appointed him, at Charles V's behest, to the new diocese of Chiapas. Arriving ill at Veracruz, he journeyed towards Mexico City in order to recuperate, and on the journey the curious incident occurred that is recounted below. He died on 8 September 1541, and his replacement was the famous Dominican defender of the rights of the native population, Bartolomé de las Casas.

122 A colourless solution of mercuric chloride in water. Medically, such a toxic compound would probably have been used in an attempt to kill infections.

123 Matthieu Ory (d. 1557) from Brittany. In 1536 he was appointed by Francis I inquisitor for the whole of France, and in 1538 a canon penitentiary at St Peter's. He gave witness in favour of the companions during the Roman process in 1538 (see Letter 10; FD, pp. 553–56). From the report of his testimony: 'and, though the said witness told them [Ignatius and his companions] that they could not institute a new form of living without permission from pontifical authority, nevertheless, having learnt of and seen their habits, way of life and teaching, he declared them free from all suspicion of heresy, and drew up letters patent for the said Ignatius in his justification . . .'

124 1 October 1529. At this point Ignatius changed college from Montaigu to Ste Barbe.

125 Contrast §71.

126 It is noteworthy that Ignatius presents this momentous fact quite so baldly, though we can only speculate as to why. Favre and Xavier are referred to in several of the Letters (cf. 8, 32).

127 Jerónimo Frago was then a teacher of Scripture in the university. He died as a canon at Pamplona in 1537. The reference as it stands would have meant nothing to almost any Jesuit apart from the first companions: perhaps an indication of how the narrative at this stage loses focus.

128 '*quelli che studian le arti . . . pigliano una pietra*' – a piece of university jargon, the significance of which has not come down to us. Presumably it refers either to an examination or to some kind of graduation ceremony. For a discussion of various suggested interpretations, see FN I, pp. 478–79, n. 20.

129 On the basis of an autopsy performed after Ignatius's death we know that the pain was caused by gallstones.

130 Ignatius became a Bachelor of Arts in 1532, and was thirtieth out of about a hundred candidates in the licentiate examination of 1533. He passed the examination for the master of arts degree in 1534, but delayed actually taking the degree until the following year. In October 1536, the university issued a certificate to the effect that he had studied theology for a year and a half. See FD, pp. 384–92, 395–97, 523.

131 On 15 August 1534 Ignatius and six others (Favre, Xavier, Laínez, Salmerón, Rodrigues and Bobadilla) had made some kind of joint commitment to a life of poverty and service. The commitment made reference to a journey to Jerusalem, and also to the service of the Pope. The text of the commitment has not been preserved, and the early sources vary as to the precise details. See FN I, p. 37 for a list of further references. Again it is noteworthy that Ignatius does no more than allude to an event of capital importance for the founding of the Society. Cf. Letter 8.4.

132 'Vicar of Christ' is a set phrase referring to the Pope, but the root meaning of the word 'vicar' – substitute – may be operative here.

133 Other sources indicate that Ignatius also wanted to correct the bad example he had given in his home area (FN II, p. 568).

134 25 January.

135 The inquisitor on this occasion was a Dominican called Valentin Liévin. The judgment has not survived.

136 The province of Guipúzcoa, in which Loyola is situated.

137 *predetti*. An authoritative manuscript reads *preti* – priests. It is uncertain which of these two should be preferred.

138 From a contemporary official document: 'Since, as experience shows us, there result many troubles and excesses from there not being an orderly way in which the poor, in each jurisdiction and parish, are sustained and fed ... we therefore order, legislate and command that the mayors, faithful and governors of this town henceforth should elect and nominate every single year two good, conscientious persons, one clerical, one lay, from the jurisdiction of this town, who are to have charge of asking for and receiving alms on Sundays and feasts for all the poor in the jurisdiction' (FD, p. 457).

139 Ignatius's sojourn at home lasted around two months, and ended in July 1535. There is abundant independent documentation on the visit, in the forms of legal ordinances and of beatification processes, now edited in the *Fontes Documentales* and the *Scripta de S. Ignatio*. Indeed, Ignatius here omits at least one important achievement: that of bringing about a settlement in a long-standing dispute between the local clergy and a convent of Franciscan nuns. (See Dalmases, *Ignatius of Loyola*, pp. 133–34.)

The narrative as we have it sets a programme of catechetical and social ministry within a frame of marked expressions of detachment from his family, though another source does tell us that his sister-in-law persuaded him to visit the family house once in order to expel a concubine (FN III, p. 333). Currently we are learning to understand Christianity, and religion in general, not simply as matters of theoretical belief but also as social institutions. In this light, the

Azpeitia documentation appears as, at least potentially, a richly significant resource for the understanding of Ignatius, and one that has been largely neglected. Two interesting pioneer attempts to draw on this material are: Dominique Bertrand, *La politique de S. Ignace de Loyola*, pp. 367–71; Norbert Brieskorn, 'Ignatius in Azpeitia 1535: Eine rechtshistorische Untersuchung', AHSI 49 (1980), pp. 95–112. On Ignatius's relations with his brother, see Letter 2.

140 See §78. Other sources indicate that Ignatius's visit to the Charterhouse at Segorbe lasted a week.

141 Kahyr-Al-Dîn (1476–1546), one of a family of Turkish sea-warriors known in Europe as Barbarossa (Red Beard).

142 See §33.

143 Polanco's 1547–48 account adds that eventually Ignatius found his way to a Spanish college in Bologna, where he was fed and cared for. Ignatius continued his theological studies in Bologna, moving to Venice on account of the climate in December 1535 (FN I, p. 188).

144 On Pietro Contarini see Letter 9. Gasparo de Dotti was Vicar General to the Papal Nuncio in Venice. It was he who issued the document clearing Ignatius of the charges mentioned below at §93 (FD, pp. 535–37). In 1556, as governor of Loreto, he took some private version of Jesuit vows enabling him to have a personal link with the Society while not abandoning his official position. Rozas ('Roças' in the manuscript) cannot be identified.

145 Diego Hoces was a noble cleric from Andalucía. On his death at Padua in 1538 see §98. We know from other sources that Ignatius was joined at this point also by Diego de Eguía (see §57) and his brother Esteban.

146 Original 'Cette'. Though some commentators have suggested that this may refer to Ceuta in North Africa, it seems preferable to take it as Chieti. The bishop of Chieti was none other than Gian Pietro Carafa, of whom there is in any case mention below (§93), and who was at this stage resident in Venice. He was founder of the Theatines (a name based on the Latin form of Chieti); he was made Cardinal in December 1536, and was later to become Pope Paul IV in 1555. See Letter 7, and Peter A. Quinn, 'Ignatius Loyola and Gian Pietro Carafa: Catholic Reformers at Odds', *Catholic Historical Review*, 67 (1981), pp. 386–400.

147 The six companions remaining in Paris had been joined by three others: Claude le Jay, Paschase Broët and Jean Codure. Unlike the Eguía brothers, these three French recruits seemed to count as full members of the companions in the various deliberations that took place leading up to the formal establishment of the Society of Jesus in 1540, perhaps because they had taken part in renewals of the Montmartre vows in the years 1535 and 1536.

The narrative in this part of the *Reminiscences* is often elliptical, and some passages make sense only in the light of information given in Letter 8.

148 The year 1537 saw a heightening of tension in the Mediterranean involving the Turks and France on one side, the Emperor, Venice and the papacy on the other. 1537–38 was the only year in several decades when pilgrimages to the Holy Land were impossible.

149 The house was an abandoned monastery about a mile north-west of the city, San Pietro in Vivarolo.

150 The companion in question was Simão Rodrigues.

151 According to Polanco's life of 1547–48, it was during this time when the companions were all together at Vicenza that they decided that their group was to be called the *Compañía de Jesús* (FN II, p. 204).

152 See §93.

153 In fact the other companions did not go directly to Rome at the beginning of winter in 1537, but rather occupied themselves with ministry in Siena, Bologna, Ferrara and Padua, meeting up in Rome in the spring of 1538 (FN I, pp. 120–24). The precise interpretation of this passage is uncertain, given that we do not know the details of the commitment made by the companions at Montmartre.

The vision that follows took place at La Storta, ten miles north of Rome on the Via Cassia, and Jesuit tradition has seen it as centrally important. Motifs from it recur both in the *Exercises* (§147) and in the *Spiritual Diary* (e.g. 8, 23 February). Laínez's account of the matter, referred to in the interpolation below, is probably best represented in a talk he gave in 1559: 'As we were coming to Rome along the road from Siena, our Father ... told me that it appeared to him that God the Father was imprinting in his heart these words: "*Ego ero vobis Romae propitius*" (I shall be favourable to you in Rome). And our Father, not knowing what this was meant to mean, said, "I don't know what will become of us. Perhaps we'll be crucified in Rome". Then another time he said that he seemed to see Christ with the cross on his shoulder. And the eternal Father was close by, saying, "I want you to take this person as your servant". And thus Jesus took him, and said, "I want you to serve us".' (FN II, p. 133.) See *Spiritual Diary*, 23 February, and note 30.

For a classic discussion of the vision, see Hugo Rahner, *The Vision of St Ignatius in the Chapel of La Storta*, Rome 1979.

154 i.e. Francis Xavier.

155 Francisco de Estrada (?1519–84), a connection of Ortiz's. He had been dismissed from the service of Cardinal Gian Pietro Carafa, and was on his way to Naples to become a soldier when Ignatius persuaded him to return to Rome and make the Exercises. As a result he joined the Society.

156 The reference is to a house on Monte Pincio, placed at the companions' disposal when they first arrived in Rome by a nobleman named Quirino Garzonio. The companions moved from there in June 1538.

157 This suggests that Ignatius was walking for roughly four hours daily.

158 For a fuller and clearer account of the events recounted here, see Letter 10. 'Miguel' refers to Miguel Landívar, on whom see in particular note 8 to the Letter.

159 Ignatius here refers to the establishment of houses for Jewish and Muslim prospective converts to Christianity unable to remain in their homes, for reforming prostitutes, and for the relief of orphans.

160 At this point the style of the text changes. Gonçalves da Câmara's own presence becomes more explicit, and the writing resembles that in his *Notebook*. Though there is a case for not counting these exchanges as part of the

Reminiscences, they are retained here partly for convention's sake, partly because of the important information they give.

161 i.e. three days before his departure (1555).

162 Exx. 28–31.

163 There is in fact no explicit mention earlier of such a vision, but it may be that the reference is to §29. The difficulty led two early translators and copyists to read '*sole*' not as a noun meaning 'sun', but as an adverb meaning 'as was his norm'.

164 Ignatius must here be referring to what we now have as the *Spiritual Diary* (as the description makes clear), but it is uncertain how many, if any, papers were lost.

PROS AND CONS

1 This is the decision (taken in 1541) mentioned in the Introduction.

2 A new section began here, but was then crossed out: it seems to read: 'THE DISADVANTAGES ARISING FROM THE POSSESSION OF A PARTIAL INCOME (QUITE APART FROM BEING THE ADVANTAGES OF NOT HAVING ANYTHING) ARE THE FOLLOWING: 1st One Superior would have charge over those who are allowed this income, for he would superintend the distribution of it, and he would also have charge over those who are not allowed it; also he would have to take from the same house what is necessary for himself or for those of the Society; this does not seem right.'

3 Ignatius added one more argument, but then crossed it out: '16th There are three ways of maintaining the Society: 1st all members, or nearly all, should be men of letters; 2nd some means could probably be found to house and clothe the scholastics, and to pay their travelling expenses; 3rd for the equipment and other things the Society needs, even some of those who will probably enter could help.'

THE SPIRITUAL DIARY

PART I

1 Ignatius began by writing a whole paragraph at the start of this entry, but then crossed it all out: it reads: 'Last night I was greatly weakened by bad sleep; at prayer this morning, a quiet mind and considerable devotion; I felt moved in spirit, experiencing warmth and the impulse to weep. Later, on rising, I twice lost the feeling of weakness; later, on going to mass, devotion in prayer and the same on vesting, with an impulse to feel like weeping. During mass, continuous devotion, weakness, various impulses of spirit, a tendency to weep. The same after mass ['my will ever set on poverty', added then crossed out], peaceful throughout the whole day. Contrary to the tendency that formerly seemed predominant, all desire to continue with this election left me completely: the solution seemed plain, viz. complete poverty.'

2 Ignatius first added here 'and the Father and the Son' (as if he had perceived them also, and not just the Holy Spirit), but then crossed out these words. Fr Iparraguirre calls this correction 'the most mysterious and important' in the text: how could Ignatius have thought at one moment that he had seen the Father and Son, only to change his mind on further reflection? However the same editor points out that the passage has been altered in other ways: the reference to 'seeing in some way' was added, and originally Ignatius wrote only of 'perceiving' (feeling). Clearly he realized on reflection that a quite special contact had been momentarily established with the Holy Spirit, which was not the case with the other Persons.

3 This heading, along with the entries for Tuesday, Wednesday and Thursday, seem to have all been written on the evening of Thursday, and describe a phase that was caused by an event on Tuesday (see notes 6, 9), rather than something that had occurred the previous day.

4 'Wednesday' before correction (see note 9).

5 Probably Francisco Vanucci, Chief Almoner of Paul III.

6 A complete paragraph, which may be crucial for understanding the text, was added and then crossed out: 'Afterwards I disposed of a question or temptation that had occurred at dawn that morning, viz. if income might not be allowed for the church alone: I saw my path with great clarity and insights, and with considerable devotion. I wished most earnestly to refuse entry to such a suggestion: in great peace, understanding and thankfulness of heart towards the Divine Persons and also considerable devotion. The occasion of the temptation had been my rising from prayer to see if I could stop the noise or if it was inevitable, owing to the position of my room. Later, when I went to mass and during it, I felt that the warmth within was beset by the cold wind from outside; I could see that the clarity within was good and that the evil was without: so in the middle of mass I felt warmth and some devotion, not coldness, yet disturbances from those in the room and from whoever was hearing mass. When mass was over and I considered the matter, I remained undisturbed and with the same interior devotion.'

7 'Thursday' before correction (see note 9).

8 'Wednesday and Thursday' are an error (not noticed by Ignatius) for 'Tuesday and Wednesday' (as is clear from the corrections he made to the headings of the entries: see note 9).

9 Ignatius wrote the first letters of the word for 'Friday', realized his mistake and, having crossed them out, wrote the word for 'Thursday'. At this moment he made the corrections to the headings of the two previous entries.

10 Literally, 'Our Lady of the Temple', but the meaning is 'Mass of Our Lady, votive mass of the Presentation in the Temple, with the gospel account of Simeon'.

11 The brackets are Ignatius's, probably underlining the importance of this intuition.

12 Ignatius added here and then crossed out: 'at times my mind wandered, but

not to evil things; towards the end there was very great calm and a certain sweetness: I rose and dressed, and nothing worth mentioning occurred either one way or the other'.

13 Probably a reference to the annuities belonging to the Church of Our Lady of the Way, by a bull of Paul III these were transferred to the sacristy of the church when the Jesuits took it over.

14 On the Wednesday Ignatius had decided to delay before saying more masses of the Trinity; yet he feels his election must end with a mass in their honour.

15 Clearly a reference to the end of the election process, and not simply to the end of the prayer period: cf. Monday 18 Feb.

16 'You gladly bear with fools' (2 Cor. 11.19), from the readings of the mass of this Sunday.

17 Ignatius is premature in writing these words; the following morning he will change his mind, and the election process will continue until 12 March.

18 The word 'abraçándome' written by Ignatius here is ambiguous since it can derive from abrasar ('to burn') or from 'abrazar' ('to embrace'). All the interpreters seem to have opted for the latter sense, but Ignatius's frequent references to 'warmth' make the former sense more likely. The only other passage sometimes mentioned in support of 'embracing' is a non-starter: cf. 19 Feb. (with note 23).

19 'less than during the previous twenty days' (added then crossed out; only seventeen days have been recorded so far in this fragment of Ignatius's notes).

20 Probably the patriarchs of the Old Law.

21 Ignatius separated this paragraph from the preceding section with two lines: the notes now concentrate more on Trinitarian revelations, to which he appears to have attached particular importance. Cf. note 24 below.

22 Exceptionally this entry begins with the day of the week and the mass is written on the same line immediately after it, instead of above it in first place.

23 The words 'asta apretarme en los pechos' have been interpreted through a misreading of an earlier passage (18 Feb. §4, where see note 18) as a reference to Ignatius hugging himself for joy, but the more obvious parallels are with the frequent references to breathing difficulties he experienced.

24 This passage, and others in italics, were encircled by Ignatius with a line and then copied out by him on a separate sheet of paper now in Madrid (bound with other Jesuit documents, Biblioteca Nacional no. 692 Cartas de Jesuitas: cf. MHSI 63, pp. CCXLI–CCXLII).

25 A difficult passage: 'el apropiar las oraciones' has been interpreted 'with the appropriation for my own purposes of the mass prayers', but it probably refers to the attribution of operations in the Trinity.

26 2 Cor. 12:2.

27 The Gospel text for this votive mass is Mt. 28:18–20.

28 Ignatius added, then crossed out, the words: 'of salvation, and others at times wiping them out and at others preserving them', but this last phrase has been interpreted by the German translator as, 'at times thinking that the soul would be wiped out, at others that it would be preserved', and the Spanish is far from clear.

29 These words were added by Ignatius in the margin; cf. note 32 below.

30 The end of the italicized sentence is a reference to the vision at La Storta; cf. *Rem.* 96.

31 In the preliminary outline of the *Constitutions* it had been decided that the sacristies of churches should possess income.

32 Once again Ignatius added these words in the margin; cf. note 29 above.

33 He seems to mean the brazier placed in his room during the winter months.

34 Cardinal Rodolfo Pio da Carpi (1500–64): he was the Cardinal Protector of the Society of Jesus.

35 Filippo Archinto (1495–1558).

36 Cardinal Gian Domenico de Cupis, Archbishop of Trani (d. 1553): he was the Protector of the house of catechumens founded by Ignatius.

37 Cf. Mt. 11:25.

38 Literally, 'contradiction' (*'contradición'*), viz. between his desire for a conclusive Trinitarian consolation and the apparent reluctance on the Trinity's part to work in exactly that way.

39 The text is ambiguous as it is not clear if Jesus is to do the service (the interpretation adopted here), or if Ignatius is somehow to enter into service (*sic* Giuliani); however, the reflexive (*'se hiciese'*) is probably one more example of Ignatius confusing his grammar.

40 One of the three prayers said by the priest before the communion in the former Latin liturgy.

41 A difficult passage because Ignatius seems at first sight to be saying that he has already referred to a vision of Jesus in which the colour white was involved: but there has been no such reference, as Knauer (in a note to the German translation, p. 280, n. 107) points out. Later, in 1555, when dictating his *Reminiscences*, Ignatius once more speaks of the humanity of Christ 'like a white body' (§29), and says that such was a frequent vision at Manresa (in 1522).

42 The liturgy of this mass was formerly used on the first Friday after Ash Wednesday.

43 Probably the church of Our Lady of the Way (S. Maria della Strada), the church entrusted to the early Jesuits.

44 Ignatius uses the Latin tag *'ad utramque partem'* (literally, 'to both parts'), which here seems to mean that neither consolation nor desolation was predominant.

45 The Gospel for the day's mass dealt with Christ's temptations in the desert (Mt. 4:1–11).

46 In the Latin liturgy this prayer (*'Placeat tibi Sancta Trinitas'*) was said by the priest before the final blessing: cf. 4 March.

47 Ignatius writes 'at the 10th hour', but one calculated then from sunset of the previous day, which in March would have been about 6.30 p.m.

48 This curious distinction between the clarity with which he understood and the light that flooded his mind is noted by the editors of the *editio princeps* (p. 113, n. 61).

49 'Blessed be the Holy Trinity and the undivided Unity'.

50 Cf. 2 March, with note 46 above.

51 Cardinal Juan Alvarez de Toledo, then Archbishop of Burgos, a Dominican friend of Ignatius: as Inquisitor General he examined the *Spiritual Exercises*.

52 The autograph is full of corrections at this point, and Iparraguirre justly remarks: 'Nearly always when Ignatius adds many corrections to a phrase it is because a special mystical grace is being mentioned' (p. 350 [392], n. 208).

53 The first words of the former Canon of the mass, now the first eucharistic prayer.

54 The holder of the title 'de Sancta Cruce' in 1544 was Cardinal Cervini, later Pope Marcellus II (cf. MHSI 63, pp. XCII-XCIV).

55 This number is a mistake for 35, the first of several errors made by Ignatius in the numbering of the entries.

56 Jer. 1:6.

57 He is quoting (incorrectly) from memory the opening words of the Introit: 'Benedicta sit sancta Trinitas' (Mass of the Blessed Trinity).

58 Ignatius has found a middle region in which to keep his attention floating, avoiding both the presumption of forcing a revelation of the Trinity and the despondency of clinging to dead letters: it is the state of true indifference, poised to respond to God's will.

59 The prayer before the consecration in what is now the first eucharistic prayer.

60 Many have interpreted the reference to the 'fire' here as metaphorical, but Ignatius always uses the word *'fuego'* to mean the brazier except on one occasion (22 Feb.) where he makes it quite clear that a simile is being used.

61 Ignatius is here putting into practice the third degree of humility, as outlined in his *Spiritual Exercises* §167.

PART II

1 Second Week in Lent (1544).

2 The interpretation is difficult because the verbs *'tener'* and *'no tener'* may refer to the having of tears (*sic* Knauer and Giuliani) rather than of income and other possessions. The present entry replaces an earlier one: '. . . to the Divine, and reflected that for me it would be something of a rest to say mass without searching for tears and not having them. During . . .', where there is clearly no reference to anything but tears. On the other hand, the verbs mentioned are a sort of shorthand for the list of pros and cons used in the previous election period, and if Ignatius did decide to stop weighing up the phenomenon of tears, the entries for the following three days make very odd reading. Incidentally there are signs that he wrote up the entries for these three days all together on the Saturday.

3 The editors of the *editio princeps* have shown that these letters were used to signify: 'a' – tears before mass; 'l' – tears during mass; 'd' – tears after mass.

4 Third Sunday in Lent.

5 Giuliani draws attention to the use of the word 'sacrifice' instead of 'mass' at this point.

6 A reference to the parts of the *Constitutions* dealing with the Papal 'missions', i.e. the readiness to be sent wheresoever the Pope desires: cf. *Constitutions*, Exam. Gen., 1, 5; V 3, 3C; VII, 1 (tr. G. E. Ganss, pp. 79–80, 239, 267–71).

7 This sign indicates that the tears were less copious.

8 Ignatius added in the margin the sign for a vision.

9 Fourth Sunday in Lent.

10 Once more the marginal sign for a vision.

11 The Latin term *Secreta* was used until the Second Vatican Council for the 'prayer over the oblation' said by the priest immediately before the beginning of the Preface.

12 In the margin the sign for a vision.

13 Fifth Sunday in Lent.

14 The word for 'vision' in the margin.

15 'I should be a liar like you', John 8:55 (where the context well repays examination).

16 In the margin the word for 'vision'.

17 Palm Sunday, 1544.

18 Two numbered but blank spaces appear here; in 1544 Good Friday and Holy Saturday, when no private masses are celebrated, fell on these days. Ignatius separated the spaces from the other entries with two single lines.

19 First Sunday after Easter; the lines separating §§34 and 35 are in the autograph.

20 In the autograph appears, with lines drawn around it in an oblong, the solitary word *'Preparar'*: it seems to refer back to the heading above 17 March.

21 It is impossible to say precisely what Ignatius had in mind. He seems to be referring to some point of the *Constitutions*.

22 Ignatius repeats the numbers 30–39; similarly below he writes 40 instead of 60 after 59, and then continues 41 etc. All of these seem to be simply errors.

23 Second Sunday after Easter.

24 The first mention in the *Diary* of this mysterious *loquela* (a Latin/Italian word that means 'speech', 'discourse', 'talking'): the commentators discuss its possible classification among the mystic gifts mentioned by St John of the Cross, and the MHSI editors refer to the *Imitation of Christ* (III 1–3). References to it stop after 28 May.

25 Rogation day before the Ascension.

26 Whit Sunday, 1544.

SELECT LETTERS

1 Advice to a good woman (Inés Pascual 1524)

1 One of the first women to recognize the sanctity of Ignatius, and one of the most generous of his benefactresses; she helped him first in Manresa, and then in Barcelona, where he lodged in her house.

2 See note 5 below.

3 The sole copy of this letter notes that a few words in the original were illegible at this point.

4 Calisto de Sá (see *Rem.* 58, 80) was the first of several young men who were attracted by Ignatius and followed him during several years in Spain; but none went with him to Paris, and subsequently they followed different careers.

5 A later hand added here the year 1525, but the editors argue convincingly that the previous year is more likely to be correct.

6 The exact spelling (Ynigo, Iñigo, Inigo, Ignacio, Ignatius?) is rarely given here, as copyists and editors felt free to 'correct' as they thought best. G. Schurhammer (*Francis Xavier*, I, p. 562, n. 29) assures us that the Ynigo spelling was regularly used by Ignatius until he moved to Rome, but subsequent scholars have questioned this. He matriculated in Paris with the Latin name Ignatius, perhaps because it approximated to his Basque name, perhaps out of devotion to the first-century martyr whose works had been published shortly before (1498/9), and used this form for official occasions and in some of his private letters. But his friends continued to call him Iñigo in Rome.

2 Dealings with brother and nephew (1532)

1 Despite the confusing name the addressee is the second eldest brother of Ignatius; in 1507 on the death of his father, Martín inherited the title of Lord of the castle-tower of Loyola as his elder brother had already died.

2 A reference to some unknown good fortune that had befallen one of Martín's five daughters.

3 It is ten years since Ignatius left Loyola; he mentions below that for some five or six years he has thought of writing more frequently to his brother.

4 2 Cor. 12:7; in this and other quotations Ignatius seems to be writing from memory and the translation reflects his lapses.

5 Rom. 7:23.

6 Gal. 5:17.

7 Rom. 7:15.

8 Rom. 8:38–39.

9 Psalm 150:1.

10 1 Cor. 7:29–31.

11 These enigmatic words added to the Pauline quotation are far from clear.

12 Parish priest of Loyola, a nephew of Ignatius.

13 Magdalena de Araoz, wife of Martín and sister-in-law of Ignatius.

14 The first appearance of what will be a favourite closing formula for Ignatius.

3 Comfort among calamities (Isabel Roser 1532)

1 See H. Rahner, *St Ignatius Loyola: Letters to Women* for this letter, pp. 262–68, and his Introduction (pp. 10–11) on the circle of benefactresses in Barcelona.

2 This form of the surname is now commonly accepted, but the forms Rosés and Rosel(l) are also found (Ignatius himself is a most unreliable informant on the spelling of names). The lady addressed here (married into a well-known Barcelona family) helped Ignatius before his Jerusalem pilgrimage (1523) and became a close friend and admirer. As a widow she attempted (1543–47) to found a female branch of the Society in Rome (see Letter 19, note 8). Her friendship survived its failure and she entered a convent in Barcelona, dying in 1554.

3 In the following year Ignatius would finish his licentiate studies; he had the option of going on for an MA or not.

4 The honorific Catalan title meaning 'Mr', Isabel's husband.

5 Juan de Arteaga was one of the young men who joined Ignatius in his very early student days in Barcelona (where Isabel would have known him) and then moved with Ignatius to Alcalá and Salamanca, but did not follow him subsequently to Paris. For an account of his tragic death, see *Rem.* 80.

6 To judge from the sole surviving copy, Ignatius misspelt most of the names in the postscript.

4 Steps in discernment (Teresa Rejadell 1536)

1 Available in English translation, H. Rahner, *St Ignatius Loyola: Letters to Women*, pp. 329–68, with both the letters of Ignatius and those of Sister Rejadell (he always referred to her by her family name).

2 Exx. 313–36, 345–51; these Rules and Notes were not part of the first drafts of the Exercises, and their final formulation seems to date from as late as 1539 (when Ignatius reached Rome).

3 A nun at the Benedictine convent of Santa Clara mentioned in another letter (MHSI I, pp. 93–99), though it is not clear if she is the person mentioned there, nor if Ignatius had ever met her. Until her death (1553) Sister Rejadell was one of the leaders of a reform group within the convent, and thus in conflict with others there. Her group repeatedly sought some kind of incorporation into the Society, but Ignatius always refused.

4 Lope de Cáceres (to be distinguished from Diego de Cáceres who knew Ignatius in Paris, see MHSI I, pp. 132–34) is one of the three companions from Barcelona, Alcalá and Salamanca mentioned in *Rem.* 58. He returned with

Ignatius to Barcelona, but did not accompany him to Paris. Eventually he returned to his home city, Segovia (*Rem.* 80).

5 See *Rem.* 20 for a similar experience.

6 This Latin tag (= 'Do the opposite') encapsulates the teaching of Annotation 16 (Exx. 16).

7 Ecclus. 13:10 (Vulgate).

8 One scrupulous copyist baulked at the mention of an 'involuntary sin' and crossed out the words in brackets.

9 Juan de Castro had been one of Ignatius's professors in Paris (see *Rem.* 75), experienced a conversion while dealing with Ignatius, and subsequently (in 1542) became Prior of the Carthusian monastery near Valencia, where Ignatius visited him in 1535.

5 Prayer made easy (Teresa Rejadell 1536)

1 See Letter 4.

2 Mentioned in the previous letter to Sister Rejadell (Letter 4, note 4).

6 In praise of *The Spiritual Exercises* (Fr Miona 1536)

1 A devout Portuguese priest, professor at Alcalá (1526–27) where he became Ignatius's spiritual father and close friend. In 1532 he came to Paris for further studies, still acting as Ignatius's confessor. In 1544 he entered the Society in Rome, becoming professed in 1549. He worked for several years in Sicily before returning ill to Rome, where he died in 1567 (G. Schurhammer, *Francis Xavier*, I, pp. 239–40).

2 The word here (*centella*) would mean in Spanish something like a 'spark' or 'glitter', but Ignatius seems to have been influenced by the Italian *cento*.

3 Pierre Favre, the first priest-companion among the Paris friends of Ignatius.

4 Cf. Mt. 18:24f.; 25:15f.

5 Luke 19:22–23.

7 Blueprint for a religious order (Mgr Carafa 1536)

1 The text of this letter has survived in Ignatius's own hand. However, the copy lacks the name of the addressee and the date, both conjectured by the editors (MHSI). In a detailed study Georges Bottereau has argued against the probability of the letter ever having been sent, but also indicates the importance Ignatius himself attached to the letter, as a sort of blueprint for his own order: Georges Bottereau, 'La "lettre" d'Ignace de Loyola à Gian Pietro Carafa', AHSI 44, 1975, pp. 139–52.

2 At this point still known as Bishop of Chieti, a member of a powerful

Neapolitan family, who had renounced his ecclesiastical privileges (as archbishop and bishop) to spearhead the reform movement with the Theatines (see note 4 below). He was nominated a Cardinal in December, and there is a hint at Ignatius's problems with him in *Rem.* 93.

3 Cf. Mt. 19:30 and parallels.

4 The Theatines were a group of clerks regular founded partly by St Cajetan and partly by Carafa in 1524; they practised strict poverty and worked for the internal reform of the Church.

5 The text here, as indeed in the previous two lines, is very obscure.

6 Again an ambiguous phrase.

7 In 1536 Carafa was about sixty years of age; he became Pope Paul IV in 1555 when nearly eighty, dying in 1559.

8 1 Cor. 6:12.

9 The term is used in a technical, canon law, sense.

8 Early years in Italy (1536–37)

1 First edited in vol. I, pp. 118–23; the second edition used the autograph copy that had been discovered in Spain, and is now in Salamanca, cf. B. Hernández Montes, 'Original de la carta de San Ignacio a Mosén Verdolay', *Manresa* 56 (1984), pp. 321–43.

2 The recipient of this letter, a young Aragonese priest and 'Master' in theology active in Barcelona, who had befriended Ignatius and knew his other friends there, eventually joined the Society, but only in 1556 when 52 years of age, shortly after the death of Ignatius. Some seven years later he left the Jesuits to become a Carthusian monk (cf. B. Hernández Montes, loc. cit., pp. 334–35).

3 In 1535 Ignatius had visited Spain (moving down from Loyola to Toledo and then across to Valencia), but not Barcelona (as far as one can judge from the records): see *Rem.* 90.

4 One of the different forms of this name (Roser, Rosell) found in the letters.

5 Francis Xavier, Diego Laínez, Alfonso Salmerón, Nicolás Bobadilla (the four Spaniards); Paschase Broët and Jean Codure (Frenchmen); Pierre Favre and Claude Le Jay (from Savoy); Simão Rodrigues (Portuguese). A tenth companion was already in Venice, Diego Hoces (a Spaniard). See *Rem.* 93.

6 Dr Pedro Ortiz, Ignatius's former professor and harsh critic in Paris, was in Rome as an agent for the Emperor Charles V over the question of Catherine of Aragon's marriage to Henry VIII. He became a warm friend and supporter of the Society, right up to his death (1548). See *Rem.* 93 for a passing reference.

7 Ignatius himself, Francis Xavier, Diego Laínez, Nicolás Bobadilla, Jean Codure and Simão Rodrigues were ordained priests; Alfonso Salmerón, who was too young for the priesthood, was ordained deacon.

8 These technical Latin phrases express the Canon Law requirement that a new priest should have some sort of economic support, usually from his local bishop

or from a personal benefice; 'voluntary poverty' or 'adequate learning' or 'both of these' can be accepted by the officiating bishop as a replacement.

9 The solution found was to ask Bishop Vincenzo Nigusanti to perform the ordination, and the Papal Legate, Bishop Girolamo Veralli, to receive their vow of poverty, to which was added, although not mentioned here, one of chastity.

10 Cf. Mt. 25:18.

11 Cf. Luke 12:48.

9 Thanks for support (Mgr Contarini 1538)

1 Then in charge of the Hospital of the Incurables in Venice, this noble and kindly cleric was related to the Cardinal Contarini mentioned in the letter. The latter had been made a Cardinal only in 1535 and is generally regarded as one of the most progressive of the humanist group that rose under Paul III to key positions and headed the reform movement. His admiration for Ignatius (under whose guidance in Rome he made the full Exercises) led him to present the initial draft of the new order's Institute to the Pope, even if he failed to win outright the approval he wanted.

2 Diego Hurtado de Mendoza was then Charles V's ambassador in Venice; he was later transferred to Rome, also as ambassador.

10 Roman trials and tribulations (1538)

1 New edition, *Fontes Narrativi*, I (MHSI 66), Rome 1943, pp. 6–14, used here. The incidents related here are alluded to very briefly in *Rem*. 98.

2 See Letter 3.

3 Paul III travelled to Nice on 23 March 1538 to arrange a peace agreement between Charles V and Francis I; he did not return to Rome until 24 July. In his absence Cardinal Vincent Carafa was appointed Papal Legate, and Bishop Benedict Conversini continued as City Governor.

4 Towards the end of November 1537.

5 Ignatius himself and two companions, Pierre Favre and Diego Laínez.

6 One month-long retreat was given in Monte Cassino.

7 Shortly after Easter, which fell on 21 April 1538.

8 Miguel Landívar gave testimony in Rome, found himself playing the role of accused instead of accuser, and was then banished. His previous relations with Ignatius were tempestuous: he had been a servant of Francis Xavier and at one time attempted to murder Ignatius, later joined him in Venice and went with the first companions to Rome but soon left them. The other, Lorenzo García, was questioned outside Rome; he subsequently became a Jesuit.

9 Other sources indicate that the Pope went to Frascati and that the interview was conducted in Latin.

10 Juan Rodríguez de Figueroa had been the Archbishop of Toledo's Vicar

General in Alcalá (cf. *Rem.* 58); later he became Charles V's Regent for the Kingdom of Naples and afterwards (in 1563) President of the Council of Castile.

11 Gasparo de Dotti was later put in charge of the Sanctuary of Loreto and in 1556, shortly before Ignatius died, given permission to make simple vows in the Society while retaining his post at Loreto until his death in 1563.

12 Matthieu Ory (spelt 'Ori' by Ignatius), the Dominican who had taught Ignatius in Paris and held the post of Inquisitor there (see *Rem.* 81, with note 123).

13 Probably Bishop Francesco Varchioni, who was standing in as suffragan for the absent Cardinal Rodolfo.

14 Hercules II d'Este, 1508–59.

15 Jaime Cazador, at this time an archdeacon in Barcelona, son of a wealthy German family (the Jaegers, they translated their surname into Castilian) and a generous benefactor of Ignatius; in 1546 he became Bishop of Barcelona.

11 Benighted obedience (Fr Viola 1542)

1 A young Italian priest from Parma, Viola did the Exercises with Favre or Laínez (1540) and joined Ignatius in Rome (1541), being sent shortly afterwards with some eight other students to Paris (Collège des Lombards). He later became Superior of the Paris house (1552) but made a hash of the negotiations with the *Parlement*, so that the Society was banned. In 1556 he was Rector of the College at Billon. Despite his poor health and rather gauche ways he was an exceptional retreat giver.

2 Probably the initial logic course, based on the text of Peter Hispanus, *Summulae logicales.*

12 Vocation doubts of a young man (1544)

1 Cf. Mt. 16:26 and parallels.

2 An application of a rule for the discernment of spirits (Exx. 318).

13 Borgia's early steps (1545)

1 Eldest son of the Duke of Gandía (b. 1510), at the court of Charles V since 1528, married 1529 and father of eight children by 1539 when he was profoundly affected by the sudden death of the Empress; appointed Viceroy of Cataluña the same year, inherited the Ducal title in 1543, when he moved to his palace in Gandía and ceased to be Viceroy. His spiritual interests had developed since 1539, partly under the guidance of a Franciscan, Fray Tejeda, but in 1542 he established contacts with the Jesuits (Pierre Favre, who saw him again in 1544 with Antonio Araoz). He is known to have consulted Ignatius by letter about the use

of frequent communion, and then about the foundation of a college (later a university) in Gandía.

2 Cf. Rom. 8:28.

3 Antonio Araoz, a nephew of Ignatius's sister-in-law, and thus 'one of the family'; born in 1516, he studied in Salamanca and went to Rome when he was 23, joining the nascent Society in 1539. He was sent to Spain and developed an intense programme of preaching and foundation work, so that he was appointed the first Provincial (1547–54) for the Spanish area, and later for Castile. He died in 1573.

4 Psalm 18 (Vulgate):13.

5 1 Cor. 4:4.

6 John 14:6.

7 Ignatius gives this spelling; she is usually known as Juana de Meneses.

8 The first community (set up on 18 November 1545) consisted of five members: Andrés de Oviedo and François Onfroy (see Letters 22 and 23), Ambrose de Lyra, Pierre Canal and Alberto Cavallino. Later they were joined by Jacobo Marín and Jean de la Goutte.

9 A Portuguese nobleman, Antonio Munís (or Moniz), who joined the Society in 1544 and accompanied Fr Mirón to Valencia to start the college there. A little later he abandoned the order for a series of long pilgrimages, then repented and by 1546 was in Rome seeking re-admission and practising dramatic public penances. Ignatius treated him kindly, but at a certain distance. He died shortly afterwards.

14 Conduct at Trent (1546)

1 In May Laínez and Salmerón arrived in Trent as theologians appointed by Pope Paul III. Claude Le Jay was already there representing a German bishop.

15 Refusing episcopal dignities (1546)

1 Ferdinand I (1503–64), a staunchly Catholic prince, brother of Charles V and Holy Roman Emperor 1556–64; within the federation of the Empire he was elected King of the Romans, ruling over parts of modern Germany.

2 Claude Le Jay (1504–52), a Savoyard and friend of Pierre Favre, one of the first companions, active in Germany (since 1542) and at the Council of Trent, known to King Ferdinand since the Diet of Worms, 1545. He had already refused the King's invitation to become Bishop of Trieste, but Ferdinand appealed to the Pope in the winter of 1546, and Ignatius then intervened.

3 In the prologue to the 1540 Bull, *Regimini militantis ecclesiae*, approving the Society, the first companions are described in this way.

4 St Francis Xavier (1506–52), another of the first companions, despatched to India as early as 1540 and very active throughout the Far East; see Letter 32; full information in G. Schurhammer's biography (see Bibliography).

5 Simão Rodrigues, see Letter 16. On the College of Coimbra, see Letters 16, 20, 31.

6 Ignatius seems to avoid calling them 'members of the Society', perhaps because at this stage he was still not clear in his own mind about the status of the non-professed; it is only in 1548 that the first 'spiritual coadjutors' will be formally acknowledged, and even then only for India.

7 Of the original ten (six together in Rome and two more in 1541, the others later), one (Jean Codure) had died.

8 Apart from Le Jay, attempts were made to make bishops of Bobadilla, Broët, Laínez, and Rodrigues, and moves had already started to appoint a Jesuit Patriarch (with coadjutor bishops) for Ethiopia.

16 Ideals for newcomers (Coimbra 1547)

1 Inspired by the 'folly of the cross', and a misinterpretation of certain passages in the Exercises (e.g. Exx. 98, 146), some of the students had been parading through the streets of Coimbra carrying skulls and dressed in ridiculous fashion.

2 In 1547 a city with a recently founded university; the first Jesuit house there was set up in 1542.

3 Fr Simão Rodrigues (1510–79), a Portuguese nobleman, joined Ignatius while a teen-age university student in Paris and was one of the founding group. A man of outstanding social gifts, and later a favourite at the Portuguese court, he was always treated by Ignatius with great affection, despite their radical differences of view and the major disturbances he caused. He was made a superior as early as 1540, and appointed Provincial of Portugal from 1546 to 1553 when his idiosyncratic form of government had brought the Province to the brink of disaster. He was moved to Italy, trying once more to go on pilgrimage to Jerusalem, and stayed there (causing considerable tremors in the handover of power on Ignatius's death) until 1564, when he moved to Spain and (1573) Portugal.

4 Letters from this young priest scholastic (a member of the Society only since 1540), sent by Ignatius to help start the new house in Coimbra, still exist; Ignatius had great difficulty in persuading Rodrigues to write letters.

5 Mt. 5:48.

6 1 Peter 2:9.

7 Col. 1:13.

8 See Luke 16:8.

9 Source not identified.

10 See Proverbs 13:4 (Vulgate).

11 Rev. 2:17.

12 Rom. 8:18.

13 2 Cor. 4:17.

14 See Dan. 12:3.

15 Jer. 48:10.

16 1 Cor. 9:24.

17 2 Tim. 2:5.

18 For all this paragraph, see the 'Contemplation for attaining love' (Exx. 230–37). Later paragraphs in this letter recall other meditations from the *Spiritual Exercises*, especially that on the Incarnation (Exx. 101–09).

19 Ignatius plays here on the double meaning of the word *compañía*, both a 'society' (hence the normal English name for the Society of Jesus), which does not have a military connotation, and a military detachment, a 'company' of soldiers.

20 See Heb. 1:14.

21 See Phil. 2:21.

22 Rom. 12:1.

23 Psalm 98:4 (Vulgate).

24 See Lev. 2:13. Salt symbolizes here for Ignatius the virtue of obedience (one should not be misled by associations with 'a pinch of salt'), see Letter 20.6.

25 St Bernard, *In Canticum* 19, 7, PL 183, 866D.

26 See Eccles. 7:17 (where the Latin Vulgate seems to mean, 'Do not play the wise man to excess' [tr. R. Knox]).

27 Prov. 13:11.

28 Prov. 19:2.

29 Rom. 6:6.

30 The work *De vita solitaria ad FF. de Monte Dei* I 11 (PL 184, 328C), attributed in Ignatius's day to St Bernard, is now recognized as the work of William of St Thierry.

31 St Bernard, *Epist.* 82, PL 182, 203C.

32 1 Kings (Samuel) 17:38–40.

33 Really William of St Thierry, *loc. cit.* I 1, 9, PL 184, 324A.

34 Ecclus. 14:5.

35 Perhaps a reminiscence of St Bernard, *In circumcisione* 3, PL 183, 142B.

36 St Bernard, *In Canticum* 19, 7, PL 183, 866B.

37 See 1 Kings 15:23, and Letter 20.6 for a fuller quotation of the passage.

38 John 15:12.

39 Ecclus. 30:24.

40 Aristotle, *Physics* 2, 11, 194b 12, quoted by Aquinas, *Summa Theologiae* I, 76, 1 ad 1.

17 Need for structures of government (Gandía 1547)

1 The Spanish word here ('*prepósito*') would be used in the *Constitutions* to mean 'Superior'; the word 'general' is not a military term, but simply means 'overall' as opposed to 'local'.

2 See Letter 19.

3 Luke 2:51.

4 Mt. 2:13.

5 John 21:17.

6 Heb. 13:17.

7 1 Kings 15:22.

8 Perhaps a reminiscence of Gregory the Great, *Moralia*, 35, 14:28, PL 76, 765B, quoted below, Letter 31 (see note 4). But a more exact verbal parallel is to be found in Augustine, *Contra adversarium legis et prophetarum*, I 14, PL 42, 613.

9 This quotation, formerly attributed to Gregory, is to be found in Augustine, *Sermones ad Fratres in eremo*, 61, PL 40, 1344.

10 Josh. 10:12.

11 Josh. 10:14.

12 Source not identified.

13 Prov. 21:28 (Vulgate).

14 St Bernard, *In Canticum*, 19, 7, PL 183, 866B.

15 Gal. 2:20.

16 The title 'Minister' is given to the official in a Jesuit house subordinate to the Superior and responsible for material well-being.

17 The model used here is that employed in the election of the first 'superior' in the Society, that of Ignatius in 1541.

18 Experience of poverty (Padua 1547)

1 Compare Letter 30.

2 Andrea Lippomani, Prior of the Holy Trinity in Venice.

3 Cf. Ecclus. 11:14.

4 Cf. Wisd. 18:15.

5 Cf. Exx. 116.

6 Mt. 8:20.

7 Bernard, *Sermon 1 on the Eve of the Nativity*, 1, 5, PL 183, 89C.

8 Mt. 5:3, 6.

9 Psalm 12:5 (Vulgate 11:6).

10 Luke 4:18.

11 Mt. 11:5.

12 Mt. 19:28.

13 Mt. 5:3.

14 These last words, also in Latin, may not be a quotation, but simply a comment by Polanco, to whom Latin came easily.

15 Luke 16:9.

16 Augustine, *Sermo* 245, 4, PL 39, 1520.

17 Mt. 25:40.

18 Mt. 13:44.

19 'Poverty has no resources to sustain its amours', a quotation from Ovid, *Remedia amoris*, V 749, and a curious example of what was considered polite learning at the time. One suspects that it came more naturally to Polanco's mind than to that of Ignatius.

20 Psalm 10:17 (the Vulgate version 9:38, adapted by Polanco, differs from the Hebrew).

21 Eccles. 10:19.

22 See Mt. 19:29.

23 'Poverty, fertile in men of valour', Lucan, *Pharsalia*, I 165–66.

24 Prov. 27:21.

25 Mt. 19:21.

26 Psalm 18:27 (17:28 Vulgate, where Polanco has added the words in brackets).

27 Cf. Mt. 5:3.

28 'Saepius pauper et fidelius ridet; nulla sollicitudo in alto est,' Seneca, *Letter* 80, 6, ed. R. M. Gummere, *Seneca ad Lucilium Epistulae Morales* (Loeb Classical Library), II, London and New York 1920, pp. 214–16.

19 En route to the *Constitutions* (Louvain 1547)

1 This metaphor of the 'glue' of love may derive from St Augustine, *De Trinitate* X, v, 7.

2 Mt. 5:16.

3 James 1:17.

4 1 Peter 4:10.

5 James 1:17.

6 Mt. 18:19.

7 Cf. Is. 9:3.

8 On Christmas Day 1545 Ignatius, under strong pressure from Paul III, had accepted the vows of Isabel Roser, then a widow without children, and two other women, but it soon became clear that this female branch of the Society of Jesus could not continue and a Brief of Paul III (May 1547) abolished it – clearly to Ignatius's great relief. As an exception to prove the rule, one woman was accepted as a member of the Society of Jesus (27 October 1554), but only under conditions of strict secrecy and as an exceptional case: this was the formidable Juana of Austria, daughter of Charles V and Regent of Spain.

9 2 Cor. 10:8 and 13:10.

10 The privileges in question (e.g. allowing all fathers of the Society, and not only the professed, to grant absolution in certain reserved cases) did not appear in a Papal bull until 1549 (*Licet debitum* of Paul III).

11 This date is mistaken.

20 Defining obedience as an ideal (Coimbra 1548)

1 See Letter 16, note 3. The letter mentioned proposes that the King of Portugal be approached concerning a possible foundation in Sicily using Portuguese Jesuits.

2 Early in 1544 Ignatius was confined to bed for four months, the most acute crisis since his attacks of fever in Venice (1537), but he suffered on and off

continually while in Rome from stones in the liver (several were extracted in the autopsy of 1556). In 1548 he had to keep indoors for much of April.

3 Prov. 4:18 (tr. R. Knox).
4 Song of Songs 1:6 (Vulgate).
5 Is. 9:6.
6 Fr Rodrigues.
7 St Bernard, *De oboedientia et eius gradibus, Sermo de diversis* 41, 4, PL 183, 656A.
8 Luke 10:16.
9 1 Kings 15:15, 19, 22–23. The last verse, in a less literal form, occurs in Letter 16.23.
10 See Gen. 4:1–7, especially v. 4.
11 Gen. 8:21.
12 Lev. 2:13, and see Letter 16.17, for this and the following text.
13 Rom. 12:1.
14 St Bernard, *In Canticum* 19, 7, PL 183, 866C.
15 See Rom. 15:4.

21 Developments in the spiritual life (Borgia 1548)

1 See Letter 13, note 1.
2 The archive copy of this letter kept in Rome is unusual in that it has Ignatius's corrections and additions written in his own hand; they are printed here in italics.
3 '*Mens sana in corpore sano*', the well-known Latin tag (Juvenal, *Satires*, 10, 356).

22 Dealing with a radical crisis (Borgia 1549)

1 Ignatius's original hand-written note was still extant, with the signature picked out in gold, in a convent in Spain when the first edition was published.
2 See Letter 13 for the previous history of the Duke and Letter 21 for his spiritual development. By the time of the present letter he was a fully professed member of the Society.
3 The use of initials (both here and in the following letter) occurs in other letters, and is clearly a security measure. The two persons are François Onfroy (B) and Andrés de Oviedo (C): see Letter 23.
4 Exx. 332.

23 On prophecies and revelations (Gandía 1549)

1 Andrés de Oviedo (1517–80), mentioned frequently in these Letters, entered the Society as a priest (1541) and was sent to help found the College in Gandía,

being elected Superior (Letter 17); his lack of balance was soon noted, but he weathered the crisis of 1549 (Letters 22 and 23), moving to Tivoli in 1551. He was later ordained bishop (1555) as coadjutor to the Patriarch of Ethiopia, becoming Patriarch himself and living in Abyssinia in great hardship until his death.

2 Exx. 314–36.

3 Further detailed information available in the article by M. Ruiz Jurado, 'Un caso de profetismo reformista en la Compañía de Jesús: Gandía 1547–1549', AHSI 43, 1974, pp. 217–66.

4 See Letter 22. In this case, as with Letter 21, the archive copy has Ignatius's corrections and additions written in his own hand. Once again they are printed in italics.

5 Rev. 1:3.

6 Acts 11:28.

7 Acts 21:9.

8 1 Thess. 5:20 (Vulgate).

9 1 John 4:1.

10 Ecclus. 19:4.

11 In other words, a charism given as a 'bonus', which cannot be 'earned' in any sense.

12 1 Cor. 12:10 (Vulgate).

13 Jonah 3:4.

14 See 1 Chron. 22:8.

15 This young Frenchman (at this point aged about 28) had joined the Society and then studied in Coimbra (1542); he had been teaching philosophy at Gandía since the foundation of the house (1545), was ordained a priest in Valencia (1547), but soon gave signs of suffering from tuberculosis and had been transferred to Valencia when this letter arrived, dying there in 1550. The use of initials (see Letter 22) is a security measure.

16 Here is the clearest indication that a group had been deputed to consider the case, although the members are not known. There are several instances indicating that it was Ignatius's standard procedure to set up small consultative committees to consider important questions.

17 This tell-tale phrase seems to point back, at least remotely, to the influence of the twelfth-century Joachim of Fiore (see Marjorie Reeves, *Joachim of Fiore and the Prophetic Future*, SPCK, London 1976), and may have reached Fr Onfroy through the Franciscan, Fray Tejeda, mentioned below.

18 The Portuguese founder of the 'Amadeites', and confessor to Sixtus V, João da Silva e Menezes (1431–82), is said to have written a *'New Apocalypse'* largely about the angelic pope of the future. His congregation was later incorporated into the Observantine Franciscans and his writings were largely discredited.

19 Part of the campaign that led to his execution (1498) originated because of his impassioned preaching in favour of the reform of the Church. The relatively favourable account of him here is surprising.

20 Cardinal Pietro Columna or Colonna, called Galatino after his place of birth

(Galatina de la Apulia), author of works on the Joachite prophecy in the 1520s.

21 A cryptic phrase, but probably a sarcastic reference to Ambrogio Recalcati, secretary to Paul III and chief of the Apostolic Chancery, arrested in December 1537 and accused of extortion and high treason, who was rumoured to have sold Papal secrets to Charles V.

22 The Minims were members of a religious order founded by St Francis of Paola in 1435.

23 This brilliant scholar and linguist from the Low Countries joined the Roman novitiate under Ignatius in 1543. Although ordained a priest in 1544 he was not allowed to enter the Society and left in 1545, subsequently writing violent criticisms of Ignatius.

24 Deut. 3:23–28.

25 A nephew of Pope Paul III.

26 Provincial of all Spain (see Letter 13, note 3). In a letter to Rome (10 March 1549) Araoz reported on the long hours of prayer (three in the morning) and Friday use of the discipline in Gandía, but seems to suggest that he is not prepared to stand up to Borgia and Oviedo to restrain them. There is no record of his direct intervention in this case.

27 John 7:17 (quoted in the Latin).

28 See 1 Cor. 12, for example.

29 See note 11 above.

30 From here the general headings are those given in the document.

31 In letters to Rome (3 November 1547 and 8 February 1548) Fr Oviedo had described Onfroy as 'of a speculative bent, but confused', and as 'learned . . . but I doubt if he will make a good teacher as order is needed for the latter . . .'

32 A first reference to a lost document containing statements by Frs Onfroy and Oviedo considered by the committee set up by Ignatius.

33 Is. 24:16 (Vulgate).

34 See §4 above.

35 The contention seems to have been that the Society should take part in an uprising to replace the Pope, and that those who died in the undertaking would be martyrs.

36 Mt. 7:16.

37 John 15:26.

38 Wisd. 1:7.

39 The term seems to refer to the overall Superior (later to be called in the *Constitutions* the Superior General), rather than to the local or provincial superior.

40 John 3:20; and see Exx. 326.

41 See note 11 on a similar scholastic term, part of the developed medieval teaching on grace.

42 The exact topic discussed here is not clear.

43 Fray Tejeda had visited Rome and stayed at the Jesuit house in 1547 while seeking permission to be ordained a priest; he did so independently of his superiors, but under the patronage of none other than Borgia.

44 Unfortunately the reaction of Borgia himself to this notion is now lost. In a conversation reported by Nadal the key word used by Borgia to describe Tejeda's visions is illegible.

45 The initial 'R' is due to the code name 'Raphael' used by and of Borgia in the letters.

46 See 2 Cor. 12:2 and Gal. 2:1.

47 See Cassian, *Collationes* 24, 21, PL 49, 1313A–14A.

48 See note 26 above.

49 See Mt. 13:25.

50 See John 8:44.

51 Probably a reference to a measure taken by Polanco on Ignatius's instructions (29 March 1548), when Borgia was given carte-blanche (quite literally in the form of two blank sheets of paper with Ignatius's signature at the foot) to settle the troubles at Gandía, if necessary sending away Oviedo, Onfroy and Tejeda. It is not known what use he made of these powers, which overrode those of the local elected Superior (Fr Oviedo).

52 See John 14:17.

53 A fifteenth-century Franciscan mystic; his works had been edited in 1536 and became very influential (the third edition by the Carthusians in Cologne, 1556, was dedicated to Ignatius), but by the end of the century they were on the Index apparently because of his bold language about the sensible effects of grace, the vision of God, and the annihilation of the self in union with God (cf. *Dict. Sp.*, 7, cc. 346–66).

54 Cassian, *De coenobiorum institutis*, II, 4, 10, PL 49, 78B–C, 83A, 99A. Cassian mentions that thirty or twenty Psalms at one session are too many; twelve were more normal in Egypt.

55 The classical definitions to be found in Aquinas and in John Damascene (*De fide orthodoxa*, III, 24) quoted in Aquinas.

56 Augustine, *Ad Probam, Ep.* 130, 10:20, PL 33, 1075.

57 Luke 18:1.

58 See §40 on Nos 20, 21 above.

59 Psalm 33:6.

60 At this point the office copy of the letter (11 folios long) breaks off, but editors and commentators agree that not much has been lost.

24 Spreading God's word in a German university (1549)

1 William IV of Bavaria died in 1550 before the projected college was under way; his son and successor, Albert V, started new negotiations and eventually a Jesuit college was founded in Ingolstadt in 1556.

2 Phil. 2:21.

3 1 Cor. 9:22.

4 The future St Peter Canisius (1521–97).

5 Mt. 9:17 and parallels.

6 Cf. 2 Cor. 10:8 and 13:10.

7 Leonard Eck, one of the Duke's counsellors, had been sent to Rome to negotiate the sending of Jesuit theologians to Ingolstadt.

8 The College of Coimbra.

9 The organization and study methods that Ignatius had experienced in Paris remained his educational model: cf. G. Codina Mir, *Aux sources de la pédagogie des Jésuites: le 'modus Parisiensis'*, Bibl. Inst. Hist. SI, Rome 1968.

25 Placating a parent over a son's vocation (1549)

1 This priest, a great benefactor and friend, had donated a house in Tivoli to the Society.

2 He had died at about this time, although his brother, Lucio, was to learn of this in Sicily only a couple of months later.

27 Consoling a sister on her brother's death (1551)

1 The de Vega family were all very close to Ignatius, especially the father, Don Juan, one of Charles V's outstanding generals, a former ambassador in Rome, later Viceroy in Sicily. In March 1550 the wife of Don Juan died, and then in September the eldest son, Hernando, died unexpectedly after a short illness. Hernando's sister, Isabel, the only daughter and the youngest in the family, was particularly affected, and wrote to Ignatius fearful for her brother's eternal salvation. There is a full account of the very close friendship that developed between Ignatius and Isabel in Hugo Rahner, *Saint Ignatius Loyola: Letters to Women*, pp. 452–78.

2 Wax candles figure among these Lenten gifts.

3 He had accompanied Don Juan on his recent North African campaign and assisted the mother of Isabel on her deathbed.

4 Francis Borgia, who had come to Rome in October 1550, set out for Spain, where he was to be ordained priest, in February 1551. He first appeared as a Jesuit a few days after his ordination.

28 Refusing a Cardinal's hat (Borgia 1552)

1 Both Ignatius and Borgia feared that when Paul III learned of Borgia's decision to enter the religious life he would insist on making him a Cardinal, but the Pope's death in 1549 removed the immediate threat and Borgia ventured to visit Rome and call on Julius III in 1550. Two years later it was his friend, Charles V, who proposed to the Pope that Borgia be made a Cardinal. With some difficulty Ignatius was able to persuade Julius III that the hat should be offered but not imposed.

2 Borgia had left Oñate shortly after his ordination in May 1551 and was preaching in various places in Spain; in 1553 he entered Portugal.

3 One revealing remark contained in this letter of Polanco (who describes Ignatius's visit to the Pope) is that of Julius III, that the Emperor seriously doubted if Borgia would accept, and had taken the precaution of sending three other names so that the Spanish contingent of Cardinals would be adequate, cf. *Epist.*, No. 2620, IV 257.

30 Agreeing to be royal confessors (1553)

1 A Spanish Jesuit, born in Valencia, he was appointed Provincial of Portugal, where he became well known for his piety and well-meaning meticulousness, but less admired for his administration (he preferred to spend his time preaching among the needy).

2 On his role in requesting the *Reminiscences*, see the introduction to *Reminiscences* earlier in this volume.

3 The project for a mission to Ethiopia was first mooted in 1546, and although Ignatius at first resisted any member of the Society being given a dignity, he was convinced by the special mission conditions to accept this drawback and flung himself whole-heartedly into the plan. The Portuguese Jesuit João Nunes Barreto, who had worked in North Africa for the liberation of captives and was familiar with Islam and the Arab world, was chosen as first Patriarch. He sailed for Abyssinia in 1555 but was refused permission to enter, landing in Goa and working there till his death (1562). He was succeeded as Patriarch by his coadjutor, Andrés de Oviedo (see Letter 23, note 1), who had been allowed entry, and had survived the death of the Emperor Claudius and the transfer of power to a Negus much more hostile to the Roman Church. The subsequent history of the mission, ending in débâcle in 1633, has been admirably recounted by Philip Caraman, *The Lost Empire: The Story of the Jesuits in Ethiopia 1555–1634*, London 1985.

4 See 1 Cor. 9:22.

5 See Phil. 2:21.

31 The final word on obedience (1553)

1 Many paragraphs are expanded from (i) Letter 16 (7 May 1547); (ii) Letter 17 (29 July 1547); (iii) Letter 20 (14 January 1548); (iv) a letter from Polanco (27 March 1548, No. 295) to the local superior of Gandía; (v) a letter (1 June 1551, No. 1854) to a Portuguese scholastic. The paragraph numbering was introduced by the MHSI editors.

2 See *Rem.*, Introduction.

3 E.g. Letter 16.

4 Gregory the Great, *Moralia*, 35, 14:28, PL 76, 765B. The same quotation may be that referred to in the earlier letter to the Jesuit community at Gandía (Letter 17.9).

5 Phil. 2:8.

6 Luke 10:16.

7 Mt. 23:2–3.

8 Eph. 6:5.

9 1 Sam. 15:22.

10 Gregory the Great, *Moralia*, 35, 14:28, PL 76, 765B.

11 Cassian, *Collationes* 4, 20, PL 49, 608C–09A.

12 See Luke 10:38–42; Ignatius presumes that Mary the sister of Martha and Mary Magdalene are the same person.

13 See John 11:2 and 12:3, with Mt. 26:7.

14 St Bernard, *Sermo ad milites templi*, 13, PL 182, 939B.

15 St Bernard, *Sermo de diversis*, 35, 4, PL 183, 636A–B.

16 Prov. 3:5.

17 Cassian, *Collationes*, 2, 11, PL 49, 541B.

18 St Bernard, *Sermo 3 de circumcisione*, 8, PL 183, 140C.

19 Rom. 15:5.

20 Cf. Rom. 12:1.

21 St Leo, *Sermo 5 de epiphania*, 3, PL 54, 252A.

22 Col. 3:23–24.

23 St Bernard, *De praecepto et dispensatione*, 9, 19, PL 182, 871D.

24 St Leo, *Sermo 4 de jejunio septimi mensis*, 1, PL 54, 444B.

25 Gen. 22:2–3.

26 Cassian, *De institutis*, 4, 24, PL 49, 183D–84B.

27 Cassian, *De institutis*, 4, 26, PL 49, 185B–86A.

28 St Gregory, *Dialogues*, 2, 7, PL 66, 146A–B.

29 *De vitis Patrum*, 3, 27, PL 73, 755D–56B.

30 Normally Ignatius went to great pains to avoid confrontations, and a favourite ploy was to appoint Vice-Rectors (to act as buffers between subjects and superiors), or Visitors (with powers over Provincials), or to give special powers (Borgia, Nadal). This introduced some confusion into the linear model sketched here. Cf. A. Ravier, *Ignatius of Loyola and the Founding of the Society of Jesus*, p. 369.

31 Wisd. 8:1.

32 The last call to Francis Xavier (Japan 1553)

1 The true date was 29 January, when Xavier happened to be in Cochin (South India); he then wrote three letters, one to Ignatius, one to Simão Rodrigues in Portugal, and one long 'open letter' to the companions in Europe.

2 This plan had to be altered, and Fr Gaspar Barzaeus (a convert soldier from Flanders) was brought from Ormuz and appointed Vice-Provincial in Goa while Xavier was away in Japan (1552). For more information on him, see Schurhammer, *Francis Xavier*, III, pp. 496f.

3 Two letters were dispatched by Polanco (Nos 3521 and 3604), 5 and 30 July,

the latter referring explicitly to Ignatius's affectionate desire to see Xavier ('this affection alone has the value for us of many, very strong reasons').

33 Criteria in the choice of parish work (1554)

1 Nothing is known about this correspondent, who may have been a cleric, apart from his name and residence.
2 Situated in the Valtellina, north of Bergamo.
3 Posted for a five–six months' period to Morbegno, Fr Galvanello became so dear to the local community that the municipal authorities wrote to Ignatius and to some of the Roman Cardinals requesting that he be left there permanently. It took several letters (one threatening Fr Galvanello with dismissal) to extract him.
4 The Latin version of Romans 14:5 ('*in sensu suo abundare*') had become a cliché in the sense, 'Let each be allowed to have his own opinion.'

34 Financial worries (1555)

1 See Letter 40.
2 About five months earlier Princess Juana of Austria, a widow at the age of nineteen, had been secretly admitted to be a member of the Society of Jesus (see Letter 19, note 8). Early in January Ignatius had written to her confirming that the difficult legal process was under way (*Epist.* VIII 235, No. 5066).

35 Norms for dealing with superiors (1555)

1 After his appointment as Secretary in 1547 Polanco began to keep records of the correspondence despatched from Rome, at first with summaries of letters, later with full copies, entered in the *Regestes*, still extant in five volumes. In addition there was a special volume, entitled *Instructiones*, where the present document has been entered.

36 The Society and the Inquisition (1555)

1 See Letter 30 for another example of this Provincial's ingenuousness.
2 The key 'arrangement', as becomes clear in the next sentence, is that if the King is not willing to write to the Pope, the latter is to be approached directly for an explicit order.

37 Catechizing the sign of the cross

1 In Spain one still sees people making the sign of the cross, then kissing the crossed thumb and first finger, which are then raised to the mouth to complete the gesture.

38 Consoling the mother of a student (1556)

1 Both are contained in Hugo Rahner, *St Ignatius Loyola: Letters to Women*, pp. 391–95.
2 Once ordained Fr Fadrique was put in charge of the main Jesuit house in Rome; he died 'after a virtuous life' in 1588. According to Fr Rahner he never returned to Spain.

39 Norms for food in Louvain (1556)

1 Exx. 210–17.
2 1 Cor. 8:13, and Rom. 14:21.

THE SPIRITUAL EXERCISES

1 These introductory notes are referred to as the 'Preface' in one of Ignatius's letters (No. 5150).
2 Cf. 'affections' in the Glossary.
3 For convenience sake the person giving the Exercises is sometimes designated in this translation as the 'director', but it should be noted that this term does not occur in the vocabulary of Ignatius, who consistently refers to 'the one who gives'. Similarly 'exercitant' is not found in the original text, but rather 'the one who makes' or 'the one who receives'.
4 The standard expression is 'the illuminative *way*' (in contrast to the purgative and the unitive ways).
5 Reading '*abrasándola*' instead of '*abrazándola*': cf. *Diary*, 18 Feb.
6 The Latin version adds in brackets, 'and it is advisable to write down a summary of the things so that they do not slip one's memory'.
7 Ignatius wrote the letter 'g' at the head of each line, 'which seems to stand for "gluttony"' (Dalmases, ed., Exx. pp. 60–61). It is not clear if he envisaged the pairs of lines growing shorter (as in the Latin edition) or thinner (as in the Spanish Autograph).
8 See Mt. 12:36.
9 The classical translation of this word is 'Prelude', which reflects the Latin version of the Exercises more than the original Spanish. The detailed explana-

tions given by Ignatius for this First Exercise are intended to introduce a complete beginner to the sort of methods that can be used throughout the Exx. He would not want to apply this elaborate structure in a mechanical way (see Exx. 162), but unfortunately his text can easily give the impression of inhibiting prayer by an excessive stress on system and procedure; hence his insistence on the 'giver' of the Exx.

10 See Glossary.

11 See Glossary.

12 See Glossary.

13 The last two words are added from the Latin version.

14 The text of this and the other prayers mentioned is given in the Appendix to Additional Material.

15 The Latin translation adds here: 'In the opinion of the one giving the Exercises it might be of benefit to the exercitant to add other meditations, e.g. on death and other punishments of sin, on judgement, etc. It should not be thought that such meditations are not allowed, even though they are not given here.'

16 Although marked as part of the Second Week, this contemplation takes place on a transition day (see Exx. 99) before the full first day of that week (Exx. 101).

17 The phrase 'in Their eternity' was a later addition by Ignatius in place of 'among themselves', and similarly the phrase 'when the fullness of time came' was also added later.

18 Gal. 4:4.

19 A marginal note added by Ignatius to the Autograph.

20 Cf. Glossary, 'application of the senses'.

21 The 'and' translates the comma after 'divinity' found in the MHSI edition, but some editors omit the comma and would translate 'the divinity of the soul [of Christ]'.

22 Ignatius uses the curious term '*binario*', explained as a late Latin synonym for a 'person' (i.e. one made up of two parts, the body and the soul), used in moral teaching at the time when various 'cases' were being presented.

23 This contemplation includes the events that happened in the desert, events which are, in fact, the main subject of contemplation on this day.

24 'Point 1' appears here in the Autograph, but seems to have been misplaced from below.

25 On 'spirits' see Glossary; the rules for the discernment of spirits are given later.

26 The Spanish text reads: 'the divinity goes into hiding ... but allows ... the sacred humanity to suffer'. It is clear however, despite the concision here, that Ignatius is referring to one person, Jesus Christ, whom he does not name as such; he would not want to imply an independent pair of agents (the divine and human natures).

27 The word for 'delicacies' (*manjares*) can mean simply 'dishes' or 'foods' in general (cf. Exx. 215); however, as dishes that are especially attractive are being mentioned, the more general sense is less appropriate here.

28 The words 'of a fire' are added (appropriately) in the Latin version.

29 The Spanish here is ambiguous ('your love and grace' or 'love of you and grace'), but the Latin translation approved by Ignatius reads '*amorem tui solum cum gratia tua*' ('love of you alone with your grace'), which reveals better the true meaning.

30 This phrase is in Latin, '*habet se ad modum laborantis*', in the original text.

31 Ignatius, translating from the Latin Vulgate, gives the Gospel words, which are translated here into English.

32 The term used for 'rational moral judgement' is *sindéresis*, a technical Thomistic term, deriving from the Greek philosophers.

33 In Latin in the text; cf. 2 Cor. 11:14.

34 Cf. Letter 4.

35 The bracketed words are in Latin in the text: '*iuxta illud Gregorii: Bonarum mentium est ibi culpam cognoscere ubi culpa nulla est*', cf. Gregorius Magnus, *Epistolarum Libri*, XI, 64 (PL 77, 1195).

36 Once again a Latin text: '*iuxta Bernardum eidem respondentem: Nec propter te incepi, nec propter te finiam*', but this time taken from the *Golden Legend* that Ignatius knew in Loyola; see *Rem*. 5 with note 6.

Index

READ MORE IN PENGUIN

In every corner of the world, on every subject under the sun, Penguin represents quality and variety – the very best in publishing today.

For complete information about books available from Penguin – including Puffins, Penguin Classics and Arkana – and how to order them, write to us at the appropriate address below. Please note that for copyright reasons the selection of books varies from country to country.

In the United Kingdom: Please write to *Dept. EP, Penguin Books Ltd, Bath Road, Harmondsworth, West Drayton, Middlesex UB7 0DA*

In the United States: Please write to *Consumer Services, Penguin Putnam Inc., 405 Murray Hill Parkway, East Rutherford, New Jersey 07073-2136.* VISA and MasterCard holders call 1-800-631-8571 to order Penguin titles

In Canada: Please write to *Penguin Books Canada Ltd, 10 Alcorn Avenue, Suite 300, Toronto, Ontario M4V 3B2*

In Australia: Please write to *Penguin Books Australia Ltd, 487 Maroondah Highway, Ringwood, Victoria 3134*

In New Zealand: Please write to *Penguin Books (NZ) Ltd, Private Bag 102902, North Shore Mail Centre, Auckland 10*

In India: Please write to *Penguin Books India Pvt Ltd, 11 Community Centre, Panchsheel Park, New Delhi 110017*

In the Netherlands: Please write to *Penguin Books Netherlands bv, Postbus 3507, NL-1001 AH Amsterdam*

In Germany: Please write to *Penguin Books Deutschland GmbH, Metzlerstrasse 26, 60594 Frankfurt am Main*

In Spain: Please write to *Penguin Books S. A., Bravo Murillo 19, 1°B, 28015 Madrid*

In Italy: Please write to *Penguin Italia s.r.l., Via Vittorio Emanuele 45/a, 20094 Corsico, Milano*

In France: Please write to *Penguin France, 12, Rue Prosper Ferradou, 31700 Blagnac*

In Japan: Please write to *Penguin Books Japan Ltd, Iidabashi KM-Bldg, 2-23-9 Koraku, Bunkyo-Ku, Tokyo 112-0004*

In South Africa: Please write to *Penguin Books South Africa (Pty) Ltd, P.O. Box 751093, Gardenview, 2047 Johannesburg*